ON ANY GIVEN SUNDAY

A Life of Bert Bell

ON ANY GIVEN SUNDAY

A Life of Bert Bell

Best Wishes, Robert S. Lyons

Robert S. Lyons

FOREWORD BY DON SHULA

TEMPLE UNIVERSITY PRESS   🇹   PHILADELPHIA

For more than 35 years, **Robert S. Lyons** has covered professional and college sports for the Associated Press and has contributed articles to numerous national publications. He is the author of *Palestra Pandemonium: A History of the Big Five* and co-author (with Ray Didinger) of *The Eagles Encyclopedia* (both Temple). He is the former director of the La Salle University News Bureau, editor of the university's alumni magazine, and an instructor in the school's Communications Department.

Temple University Press
1601 North Broad Street
Philadelphia PA 19122
www.temple.edu/tempress

Library of Congress Cataloging-in-Publication Data

Lyons, Robert S., 1939–
    On any given Sunday : a life of Bert Bell / Robert S. Lyons.
        p. cm.
    Includes bibliographical references and index.
    ISBN 978-1-59213-731-2 (cloth : alk. paper)
    1. Bell, Bert, 1894–1959. 2. Football coaches—Pennsylvania—Philadelphia—Biography.
    3. Football commissioners—United States—Biography. 4. Philadelphia Eagles (Football
    team)—History. 5. Football coaches. I. Title.
    GV939.B455L96 2009
    796.332092—dc22
    [B]   2009020966

2 4 6 8 9 7 5 3 1

To My Grandchildren,
who are very dear to my heart.
You have enriched my life with warmth and love.

Contents

Foreword

Don Shula

It's hard to believe that it's been fifty years since Bert Bell's death and that no one has ever chronicled the life of this remarkable man. Fortunately, Bob Lyons has finally filled the void with a fascinating, thoroughly researched biography that not only details the accomplishments of one of the finest commissioners in the history of professional sports but also offers a unique glimpse into a long-forgotten era of the National Football League.

I didn't know Bert Bell that well, but I certainly admired and respected him when I was a player in the NFL from 1951 to 1957 and later as a young coach. Every year we played a preseason game in Hershey, Pennsylvania, and my first memory of him was when he came up and talked to our squad. I was all eyes and ears at that time and he certainly made quite an impression. It was mostly about the integrity of the game. He always stressed playing within the rules and doing it the right way—lessons that I followed later when I spent many years on the Competition Committee.

Ever since my coaching days, I've had a great association with the Bell family. His sons, Bert Jr. and Upton, worked for me, and when I got the job in Baltimore, Bert picked me up at the airport and took me into the Colts' offices for the first time. Later, I got to spend a lot of time with both boys. I put Upton into the Colts' scouting department and made him director of pro scouting.

We don't realize how much Bert Bell did for professional football. He saved the league from bankruptcy by conceiving the concept for a player draft—a great idea that paved the way for colleges preparing athletes to play in the NFL at no cost to the league. In addition to describing for the first time how Bert sold this idea to the reluctant club owners, Bob Lyons recounts in colorful detail the background behind some of his other exciting innovations like sudden-death overtime. He also tells how Bell carefully developed the use of television, masterfully cultivated members of Congress when the federal government was trying desperately to nail the league for antitrust violations, and aggressively protected the sport against unsavory characters.

I never knew that it was Bert Bell who coined the phrase *On Any Given Sunday*. Nor did I know that this privileged descendant of one of Pennsylvania's most influential families quarterbacked the University of Pennsylvania to the Rose Bowl, then became a hero in World War I. I never knew that he played professional football against Jim Thorpe or once talked a young man by the name of Pete Rozelle out of quitting his job as general manager of the Los Angeles Rams.

As Bob Lyons points out, Bert Bell wasn't perfect. Art Rooney, the late owner of the Pittsburgh Steelers, probably said it best when he quipped that his good friend "touched all the bases" in his younger years. But all that changed when Frances Upton, one of the biggest names in show business and a delightful woman, came into his life, reformed him, and helped to bring out a tender, kindhearted personality that was often masked by a rough, tough exterior.

I know from personal experience that there were occasions when Bert was unfairly criticized. On the first play of the opening game of the 1954 season when the Los Angeles Rams beat us, 48–0, their halfback Skeets Quinlan lined up next to his bench virtually obscured in a sea of yellow Rams jerseys. I was playing at the right corner calling the defensive signals and none of us noticed Quinlan streaking down the sidelines when the ball was snapped. Norman Van Brocklin hit him with an easy touchdown pass. Bell immediately labeled the sleeper pass play *unsportsmanlike* and instructed all referees and coaches that any similar incident in the future should be penalized. Los Angeles officials were livid. One Los Angeles writer even demanded a public apology from Bell after claiming that the Rams frequently used such a play to compensate for players who couldn't block effectively. But the commissioner was vindicated when the NFL Rules Committee changed the rule the following year and outlawed such a play.

Bert Bell ruled the NFL with an iron hand. He was criticized in some quarters for sometimes overstepping his authority, like the time that he arranged the trade of Van Brocklin to bolster the struggling Philadelphia Eagles and when he helped the financially strapped Green Bay Packers obtain Vince Lombardi as their coach. A number of club owners didn't like it when he pushed for a players' union and pension plan. But this was precisely the type of courageous, strong-willed guidance that the league needed. That's been the secret of the NFL's success—it's always had great leadership at the right time. After Bert Bell, it passed on down to Pete Rozelle, who did a tremendous job with Monday Night Football and promoting the league. Then it was Paul Tagliabue when legislation and litigation became more important. Now they have Roger Goodell to lead them through the early part of the twenty-first century.

The NFL is an amazing story and much of it started with Bert Bell, an incredible man whose life is captured vividly in *On Any Given Sunday*.

April 2009

Acknowledgments

Writing *On Any Given Sunday* was truly a gratifying experience. The idea was triggered by a chapter on Bert Bell's life that I wrote for *The Eagles Encyclopedia*. Much of the encouragement and valuable assistance for this project was provided by my co-author of that book, the talented Pro Football Hall of Fame writer Ray Didinger, as well as Bert Bell's sons, Bert, Jr., and Upton, who welcomed me with open arms and offered complete access and cooperation.

I am particularly honored to have Don Shula, a member of the Pro Football Hall of Fame and the winningest coach in the history of the NFL, write the Foreword. Mr. Shula's accomplishments during his 33-year career are legendary. They include four Super Bowl championships (twice each with the Miami Dolphins and the Baltimore Colts) in six appearances. He is the coach of the only undefeated team in NFL history (the 1972 Dolphins) and four-time Coach of the Year. He served the game of professional football with dignity and class, and has continued to demonstrate these characteristics with a distinguished lifestyle that has included numerous contributions to charitable and civic endeavors.

Providing essential background information, context, and support were my friends Ernie Accorsi, the longtime NFL general manager who is now a league consultant; Gordon Forbes, the Pro Football Hall of Fame writer for *USA Today*; and Jim Gallagher, who spent many years in various executive capacities with the Philadelphia Eagles.

Others who helped in various ways were Pete Fierle, the information services manager of the Pro Football Hall of Fame, in Canton, Ohio, who responded, along with his staff, to my numerous requests with the highest degree of enthusiasm and professionalism, and a number of National Football League public relations officials. They include Greg Aiello, the league's senior vice president of public relations; Jeff Blumb, of the Green Bay Packers; Derek Boyko, of the Philadelphia Eagles; Jack Brennan, of the Cincinnati Bengals; Rich Dalrymple, of the Dallas Cowboys; Mark Dalton, of the Arizona Cardinals; Harvey Greene, of the Miami Dolphins; Bob Hagan, of the Minnesota Vikings; Bill Johnston, of the San Diego Chargers; Dave Lockett, of the Pittsburgh Steelers; Bob Moore, of the Kansas City Chiefs, and Rick Smith, of the St. Louis Rams.

A special word of appreciation goes to the late Ralph Bernstein, the long-time sports editor of the Philadelphia Bureau of the Association Press. I had the pleasure of working with Ralph for more than 30 years during which time he spent countless hours regaling me with anecdotes about Bert Bell, one of his favorite people whom he truly respected and admired. Unfortunately, I had no idea at the time that I would be writing this book and, naturally, didn't take notes. By the time that I formally interviewed Mr. Bernstein shortly before his death, many of the specific details of their delightful professional relationship had disappeared with age and time. However, I was able to recall anecdotally his descriptions and characterizations of some of Bert Bell's memories, personal concerns, and insights that he shared with Ralph many years ago. Much of this priceless information came from Mr. Bernstein's own recollections, but a good bit was vividly described to him over the years by Bert Bell's good friends like Joe Donoghue and Joe Labrum.

I am indebted to Dawn Blake, the assistant director of communications at the Haverford (PA) School; Rev. Robert J. Chapman, pastor, Saint Margaret's Roman Catholic Church, Narberth, PA; Mark Lloyd and Nancy Miller, of the University of Pennsylvania Archives and Records Center; Mike Mahoney, director of athletic communications at the University of Pennsylvania; Phyllis Martin, assistant director of communications at Episcopal (PA) Academy; Michael Panzer, library supervisor of the *Philadelphia Inquirer* and *Daily News;* Lawrence D. Rubin, president of Rubin Public Relations, Narberth, PA; Rich Westcott, the highly-respected Philadelphia author and sports historian, and Brenda Galloway-Wright, interim head, Urban Archives, Temple University Libraries, for assisting with my research.

I can't say enough about the support provided by the dedicated professional staffers at Temple University Press, headed by its director, Alex Holzman, and my editor, Micah Kleit, who guided me through this project enthusiastically, smoothly, and efficiently. I am also appreciative of the superb production and copyediting provided by Michael Haggett and Ellen Lohman, of Westchester Book Services, Danbury, CT.

Finally, I am most grateful to my dear wife, Joan, for her encouragement, patience, and helpful advice. I never would have met my deadline without her careful proofreading.

Southampton, PA
2009

Prologue

"A Football Man!"

John C. Bell, the esteemed attorney general of Pennsylvania, couldn't understand what young de Benneville saw in this crazy professional gridiron game. Occasionally, he would come to watch the Philadelphia Eagles practice. It might be 90 degrees outside, but he'd sit in his chauffeur-driven Stutz Bearcat with a bowler hat on, looking down and just shaking his head. In ten minutes he'd be gone. John C. considered professional football on the same general level as burlesque.

Bert Bell was christened de Benneville, a name he detested but one befitting the scion of one of the wealthiest, most influential families in the Philadelphia area—a family of blue bloods with distinguished ancestors dating back to the Revolutionary War.

But de Benneville Bert Bell wanted nothing to do with high society even though he had a nanny, a Marmon roadster, and all the trappings of a privileged lifestyle.

This is the story of Bert Bell, a college football star, hell-raiser, war hero, club owner, coach, and NFL commissioner—a man who was once called the most powerful executive figure in the history of professional football and the greatest commissioner in the history of professional sports.

Above all, it is the story of Bert Bell, "A Football Man."

1. The Early Years

Bert Bell was born in his family's center city Philadelphia home on February 25, 1893, with a silver spoon in his mouth and a soon-to-be hatred for his given baptismal name, de Benneville.

The younger of two sons of John C. Bell and Fleurette de Benneville Myers, Bell once said that 90 percent of his friends never knew him by the name that he detested—a name bestowed on him in honor of his mother's ancestors, who were members of one of the wealthiest, most influential families in the Philadelphia area.

Bert Bell grew up "amid such turn of the century wealth and power that it took John O'Hara more than a dozen books to completely describe it," wrote Phil Musick in *PRO!* magazine. "He had a nanny when he was 2, a pony when he was 6, a tux when he was 12, and a Marmon roadster when he was 17."

"If I can lick the name of de Benneville, I can handle anything," Bell's son Bert Jr. recalls his father frequently saying. Bert Bell wanted nothing to do with high society even though he enjoyed all the frills of such a privileged lifestyle. He was known to engage in fisticuffs with anyone who taunted him about his name.

"If you don't think I had to fight many times to get people to call me 'Bert,' then I must have dreamed of all those schoolyard battles," Bell often said.

"Although he came from a proper conservative Republican family, Bert walked with a swagger as a kid and found a way in high school to talk out of the side of his mouth," his son Upton remembers. "He didn't want to talk like all those proper jut-jawed, society people. He decided that everything he was going to do was in some ways completely different from the way they acted."

Bert Bell's maternal grandfather, Leonard Myers, was a Civil War veteran and a member of Congress who participated in one of the "Great Debates in American History," during which he strongly endorsed Secretary of State

William Seward's purchase of Alaska in 1867. Myers argued successfully that "if we did not acquire Alaska, it would be transferred to Great Britain." A prominent Philadelphia-area attorney, he was an intimate friend of U.S. presidents Abraham Lincoln and James A. Garfield. He lived in Attleboro, Pennsylvania, a town north of Philadelphia now known as Langhorne, where he died in 1905.

Bell's mother, Fleurette de Benneville Keim Myers, was the daughter of Leonard Myers and Hetty de Benneville Keim. A lineal descendant of Nicholas Keim (who migrated to the present city of Reading, Pennsylvania, in 1698) and a descendant of the de Bennevilles of Colonial times, Fleurette grew up in the old Myers mansion in a section called Branchtown on York Road near La Salle University's campus in northwest Philadelphia. She and John C. Bell were married there in 1890. Fleurette became a noted bridge player. She died in 1916, about two years after the mansion was razed.

Adjacent to the mansion, at the corner of Green Lane, was the de Benneville Cemetery, where some 135 descendants of Dr. George de Benneville—including Leonard Myers—were buried. Dr. de Benneville, who died in 1793, was a distinguished physician and preacher who ministered to soldiers during the Revolutionary War. He acquired the 20-acre plantation and cemetery for his family in 1758, about 12 years after it was built on land owned by Thomas Nedro, a bitter Tory, who fled to England before the Revolution—never to return. According to legend, the remains of two British officers who were killed in the Battle of Germantown, Brigadier General Agnew and Lieutenant Colonel Bird, were also buried there.

Bert Bell's father, John C. Bell, was the first great end on the University of Pennsylvania's football team. He played from 1882 to 1884 and starred in the Quakers' first win over Harvard when he was a senior. A well-respected lawyer, he was district attorney of Philadelphia from 1903 to 1907 and Pennsylvania attorney general from 1911 until 1915. In the latter capacity, John C. Bell served under Governor John K. Tener, a former pitcher for Cap Anson's Chicago White Stockings who later became president of the National Baseball League.

During this time, John C. Bell became a Penn trustee for life, chairman of its powerful Athletic Association, and a member of the Intercollegiate Football Rules Committee, where he was next in seniority to Walter Camp. It was as a member of this committee that John C. Bell helped in the effort to rescue college football by forming the National Collegiate Athletic Association (NCAA) in 1906 for the specific purpose of establishing safe football rules. President Theodore Roosevelt had warned the colleges that unless they accomplished this, he would have the sport abolished by an act of Congress. John C. Bell, who had been featured on the cover of the 1898 *Spalding Guide*, a popular national football publication, died in 1935.

"Probably no two men in America contributed to the constructive science of the game than Messrs. Bell and Camp," wrote Philadelphia sportswriter D. L. Reeves in 1919. "For years they were the leading figures in the annual conventions of the football rules committee. Both possessed and still retain a sound fundamental knowledge of the balance requisites of the sport and each was a forceful, fearless fighter for his convictions and each was fortified by a dominating personality. The rules ever will carry the imprint, knowledge, originality and resource of these two men."

John C. Bell was once asked where his young son, de Benneville, would attend college. "He'll go to Penn or he'll go to Hell!" he bellowed.

Bert's brother, John C. Jr., who was born in 1892, enjoyed outstanding careers in the worlds of tennis and politics. He reached the national doubles finals as one of the top-ten-ranked players in the nation five times between 1926 and 1936. He was elected Pennsylvania's lieutenant governor in 1942. Five years later, he served as the commonwealth's governor for 19 days—the shortest term in history—when Governor Edward Martin was elected to the U.S. Senate. In 1950, John C. Bell Jr. was appointed Pennsylvania Supreme Court justice and was elected to that position for a 21-year term in 1951. In 1961, he became chief justice of the court. John C. Bell Jr., who frequently assisted his brother as legal counsel during Bert's tenure as NFL commissioner, died in 1975, three years after he retired.

Bert Bell's earliest recollection of football was being taken to Penn games in 1899, when he was six years old, and learning to kick a football while serving unofficially as a little mascot on the sidelines. He was "arrayed in gridiron togs, head gear, trousers, cleated shoes, red sweater on which was a blue varsity 'P' as large as the sweater itself, with football tucked under his arm in charging position or trying to drop kick in which skill he is so expert today," wrote Reeves in 1916.

Bell grew up in posh surroundings at a home where he was born at 334 South 24th Street, just below Delancey Street, in Center City Philadelphia and about a mile east of Penn's campus located on the other side of the Schuylkill River. He first started playing football with boyhood friends in a nearby city square at 24th and Pine Streets. For practice, he would tackle the family butlers. "Watch out for little de Benneville," his mother would warn the servants. "He'll throw you for a loss if you're not careful."

Later, the Bell family moved to another spectacular three-story residence a few blocks away at 229 South 22nd Street, above Locust Street, near Rittenhouse Square.

Former Columbia football coach Lou Little, who was one of Bell's teammates and his closest friend at Penn, once shared his memories of Bell's boyhood homes, which also included a summer residence at Radnor on Philadelphia's Main Line that had 11 acres and a beautiful lake.

"For a fellow like me," Little told W. C. Heinz of *The Saturday Evening Post*, "that beautiful city home with the servants and everything was like walking into a hotel. And that summer home was like walking into a country club."

As a youngster, Bert Bell attended the most prestigious of schools— Episcopal Academy, the Delancey School, and The Haverford School, where he had the unique distinction of being captain of the football, basketball, and baseball teams in his senior year. He attended Episcopal Academy from September 1904 until he transferred to the Delancey School, in Center City Philadelphia, in June 1909.

Bell entered The Haverford School in 1911 as a 5-foot-6½-inch 139 pounder. He was far from being a model student, studying just hard enough to get by, retain his athletic eligibility, and get elected president of the executive committee of the Athletic Association in his senior year. But he also participated in a number of nonathletic extracurricular activities at Haverford, including the Dramatic Club, where he served as head usher, and recording secretary of the YMCA, which organized Bible study. He was elected class secretary for a year before graduating in 1914.

Under "Class Landmarks" in the school yearbook, Bell was listed as the "Best Kidder" and "Most Sarcastic" and was the subject of this profile:

Bert Bell is another famous athlete. Who has not seen or heard of Bert? Hero of countless football, baseball and basketball battles. Bert has the rather unique honor of being captain of three teams—football, baseball, and basketball. Seldom is any one man honored to this extent. Bert, besides being one of the best athletes in the history of the School, is very popular, and a fellow anyone might be proud to name as a classmate.

DeWitt Clinton, who graduated from The Haverford School two years ahead of Bell, once told Heinz, "I remember he was very much looked up to, even then. He had the qualities of leadership. He seemed so much more mature than the rest of us, and he used to swagger a little and talk out of the side of his mouth and try to shock us with the stories he told. I remember one day at breakfast he told us his father would give him $50 if he'd have his nose that had been broken in a game, re-broken and reset. To the rest of us, that seemed like a lot of money then."

"The nose got straightened out in the next game," Bell told Heinz. "Besides, I didn't have to do that for 50 bucks. My father and mother gave me anything I ever asked for, and I was a pretty good asker."

Years later, when Upton Bell was a student at Malvern Prep, he ran into a guy who knew his dad at Episcopal and Haverford. "Your father was so much older than the rest of the kids," he told me. "He would swagger around school—we thought he was a college student—and athletically he seemed so much more mature than the other kids. We never knew what to believe."

During his days at The Haverford School, Bell began dating a longtime childhood friend, Theodora Lillie, a young lady three years his junior who lived near the intersection of Buck Lane and Panmure Road in Haverford— not far from the Bell family's summer home. The two teenagers shared an interest in sports—both were excellent golfers—and Bert took her to her first football game, featuring the Quakers, of course, at Franklin Field. Each youngster also owned an automobile, a rarity in those days.

"They were great buddies," recalls Theodora's daughter, Jean Wheeler Parsons, who lives in Cambridge, Massachusetts. "He was her first boyfriend. She thought he was sweet and a lovely fellow. They probably dated for quite a few years. I don't think they were sweethearts the way people are now. It's a different world. They were boyfriend and girlfriend, but in those days it was not a passionate situation like it might be today. I think they were certainly very close."

Although a number of his buddies at The Haverford School expressed the opinion that Bert Bell could have made the major leagues as a baseball player—he led the team with a .510 batting average as a senior—his true love was on the gridiron.

In the fall of 1914, a headline in the *Philadelphia North American* proclaimed, "BERT BELL ENTERS U. OF P." For the Quakers, football would never be the same, especially since he would somehow end up playing *five* seasons for the Red and Blue, four of them on the varsity.

2. The Quarterback of the Quakers

A few weeks after enrolling at the University of Pennsylvania, Bert Bell surprisingly won the starting quarterback job on the first day of freshman team practice even though he was a scrawny 5-foot-8-inch, 155-pound lightweight. He also won over his new teammates. As Jack McKinney recounted years later in the *Philadelphia Daily News*, they "were mesmerized by the peppery little guy with the devil-may-care attitude and the huge heart. If anyone was in short pockets, Bert could always be counted on for a touch."

Early in the season, however, Bert ended up in the university hospital with a badly infected eye, an injury he suffered in a game against Exeter Academy. According to the *Philadelphia Bulletin*, the eye was swollen black and blue. "He paid the bruise no heed," the newspaper reported, but a couple of days later, "it was giving him so much pain that he was prevailed upon to go to the hospital." After missing two games, Bert returned to the lineup and played well enough to show the coaches that he would bypass the traditional route to the varsity. There would be no action for him on the scrub team as a sophomore.

Not only did Bell make the varsity in 1915; his coach, George Brooke, also praised him as a "brainy quarterback." Then Bert surprised everyone by starting the opening game. It was a 7–0 win over West Virginia, "the strongest first-game team that has ever visited Franklin Field," according to the *Bulletin*. Calling him a "sagacious" quarterback, the newspaper added, "Bert Bell played a heady game, and once when West Virginia was offside, he reached through the limbs of [teammate Lud] Wray, tugged the ball loose, and started a play so that he would get a penalty from the official for the offside."

Bell started the following week and "played well" in a 63–0 victory over Albright. Following a 10–6 win over Franklin & Marshall, Bert shared signal-calling duties with Howard Berry, the future All-America fullback, for the next four games. But the Quakers went winless in their final seven contests.

Particularly galling, according to Philadelphia sportswriters, was a 17–0 loss to Lafayette, a decided underdog. Although most of their wrath was directed at Berry, "Bell was way off, too, but he did drive the team with better skill," wrote one writer. "Little Bert Bell is hindered by the fact that he lacks speed and he cannot reach punts," wrote another. "This makes him fumble where a faster player would be able to set and make his catch perfectly."

Two days before Penn's next game against Dartmouth in Boston, Brooke suddenly resigned as coach and Bell got the starting quarterback job back, replacing Berry, who surprisingly quit the team after that Wednesday's practice. It was Bell's first start in a big game and he received rave reviews despite the fact that Penn dropped a 7–3, last-minute heartbreaker in what the *Bulletin* called "one of the hardest-fought football games ever seen in New England."

Bert Bell, the newspaper continued, "clung to his task like a bull terrier, and though a shower of punts were shot at him by Dartmouth, he fumbled but once. Dartmouth tried every type of kicker it had to detect a weakness in Bell's work, but the youth refused to be either trapped or baffled. Bell not only filled a gap, but he used rare judgment in picking his plays. His running of the team was heady, and he showed lots of grit and dash."

Penn played its best game of the season the following week, tying powerful Michigan, 0–0, at Franklin Field. "Bert Bell played another star game," reported the *Bulletin*. "He did not fumble a punt. He used excellent judgment. He missed two field goals; but as a matter of fact, no one expected him to score with the 42-yard-kick, for the wind was against him and he was way off at an angle when he made the drive. Bell's punting was really a treat."

On the evening of September 24, 1916, Bell's mother, Fleurette de Benneville, passed away at her Center City Philadelphia residence following a stroke and complications from previous surgery. Bert had been notified at Penn's football training camp and hurried to the family's residence on 22nd Street but failed to arrive before her death.

Six days later, Bell was in the starting lineup as the Quakers opened the 1916 season by nipping West Virginia, 3–0. The most spectacular play of the game was a crisscross forward pass that went from Bell to Hobby Light to Heinie Miller, a maneuver that netted the longest gain of the day—20 yards. But it wasn't enough for Penn's new coach Bob Folwell. Unhappy with Penn's lack of offense, Folwell replaced Bell with Light

at quarterback the following week as the Quakers beat Franklin &
Marshall, 27–0.

Bell saw some action at fullback, returned punts, and played well enough
to regain his starting signal-calling position for the next game against Swarthmore "because of his greater experience and his generalship," according to
the coach. It turned out to be a disastrous move. Bert played the worst game
of his collegiate career and Penn lost, 6–0. It was bad enough that the Quakers turned the ball over *eight times* within Swarthmore's *five-yard line*. But
Bell completed only two of 20 passes, kicked one punt straight up in the air,
and fumbled another.

After the game, Folwell told his bedraggled quarterback to go down to
Atlantic City and relax for a couple of days.

"On the train, a guy sat down next to me and said, 'Did you see the
game today?'" Bert recalled. "I told him I had and he went on from there.
He said, 'Isn't that Bell the lousiest thing you ever saw? He's a safety man
who can't catch punts and who kicks the ball straight up in the air.' I agreed
with him. Then he said, 'You know he wouldn't be playing if his old man
wasn't a trustee. If it wasn't for pull, that crummy little bum couldn't buy
his way into the park!' He went on like that, chewing my ear until we got
to the station. Then he got up to get off and he said, 'My name's so-and-so.
What's yours?' I said, 'Bert Bell.' He took off down the aisle like the cops
were after him."

Bell sat out the next game, a 15–0 triumph over Penn State, and came
off the bench to see limited duty in a 20–0 loss to Pittsburgh, a 19–0 win
over Lafayette, and a 7–7 tie with Dartmouth. When Bell was told that he
would be starting again against Michigan, his mood improved considerably and he kept his teammates laughing throughout the long, tedious train
ride to Detroit.

As the *Bulletin* reported, "Had it not been for Bell, the trip would have
been as silent as the Texas Panhandle desert. During the trip, Bert took a peep
into the black grip that Dr. Frank B. Hancock lugs around with him. Bell
blinked his eyes as he saw the many rolls of tape, plaster, witch hazel, and al-
cohol, and said, 'What's Michigan going to do, Doc, use blackjacks on us?'"

Penn won, 7–0. "Bell piloted his team in masterful fashion," said one
sportswriter. The Quakers were greeted by 5,000 fans when they returned
to campus. All classes were canceled for the day. But Bert suffered a se-
verely bruised right leg in the game and missed the following contest, a
16–0 win over West Virginia Wesleyan.

On Thanksgiving Day, the young quarterback came back to lead the
Quakers to their first win over archrival Cornell in four years, 23–3, at
Franklin Field.

"One month ago, the hecklers were after Bert Bell," reported the *Bulletin*. "Penn's quarterback played a game of football yesterday that was faultless from a tactical standpoint, and not a punt slipped through his fingers. Jimmy Bryant, his rival, sat on the bench, and a flow of praise of his substitute quarterback was continually turned by Bryant's tongue.

"With five minutes to play, toward the end of the game, Bell edged toward the side lines and shouted to Folwell, 'Send Jimmy in, Bob.' Bryant's teeth clicked and he said, 'How can a fellow ever repay Bert for a sportsman's stunt like that?' And into the game Bryant went galloping but he did not allow Bell to leave the field before he gave him a hug. Then some wonder why the players swear by Bell as a field master."

Lou Little, Bell's teammate who later became the great football coach at Columbia, recalls that one reason why the players respected Bell so highly was because the Quakers didn't use a huddle. "Bert would stand there and study the defenses as he barked out the signals," Little once explained to sportswriter Jack McKinney. "You could hear him all over the stadium. I've seen quarterbacks who could run harder, kick further, and pass more accurately, but I've never known one who could yell louder than Bert Bell."

Three days before Christmas, the Quakers left snowy Philadelphia for the biggest game in their fabled history, a much-awaited intersectional clash with heavily favored Oregon in the 1917 Rose Bowl. Penn's team, comprised of 28 players, was joined by some 100 undergrads in the special train, which chugged out of Reading Terminal pulling a diner car, club smoker, baggage car, and five Pullmans.

The *Bulletin* reported that the team spent much of its time on the train developing a string quartet. "Graves Williams can tickle the ukulele, Ben Derr thumbs the banjo, Neil Mathews evokes noises out of a guitar, and, according to his own admission, Bert Bell is an artist on the linoleum. A porter with a musical foot watched the string quartet try to get together while the train was scooting to Buffalo, N.Y. The musicians struggled through the verse, but when they hit the chorus they played as if they heard the piece before."

Then the team took part in a couple of good-natured snowball fights with local residents. The *Philadelphia Inquirer,* calling it a "torturous trans-continental trip," said that heavy snow delayed the team's arrival in Chicago by twelve hours. The players ate Christmas dinner in Albuquerque, New Mexico, and finally arrived in Pasadena on December 28.

Although most observers were touting the game as the best ever contested between eastern and western collegiate powerhouses, Oregon fans argued that Penn was not a true eastern champion because the Quakers dropped regular-season games to Swarthmore and Pittsburgh. Oregon closed its pregame practices to the public, but Folwell conducted the Quakers' workouts openly. He even invited Oregon's coach, Hugo Bezdek, to attend one of the drills.

All of the trash talking didn't matter, because Oregon won the game with a pair of second-half touchdowns, 14–0. One of the scores came on a reverse-pass, a play that Bezdek had requested to see during Penn's pregame workout. "Folwell told me to run it for him," Bell recalled. "Reluctantly I complied. Imagine what we thought when Oregon scored its first TD on our own play!" After Oregon picked off Bell's pass and turned it into its second touchdown, Bryant replaced him as Penn's starting quarterback late in the fourth quarter.

"Bell took a terrible hammering from the big Oregon men and that is why Bob Folwell pulled Bert from the battle," reported Penn's captain-elect Heinie Miller in an *Inquirer* article. The Ducks outweighed the Quakers 15 pounds to a man. Bell did have the distinction of rushing for Penn's longest gain of the game, a 20-yard pickup.

War clouds hung heavily over Franklin Field as the Quakers prepared for the 1917 season. Bell was one of only four experienced players returning to the team. Freshmen comprised the rest of the squad because the draft and other military obligations had stripped the club of the other veteran players. And, at the end of the season, seven of the 11 starters, including Bell, were on the way to serve in the war. It was a great season on the field with the Quakers losing only twice in 11 games.

Bell had his brilliant moments although he missed three games (including a loss to Pittsburgh) after suffering a shoulder injury during a 41–0 trouncing by Georgia Tech. He scored three touchdowns and passed for another in a 73–10 opening-game win over Albright. It was Penn's highest point total in 20 years. Later, he guided the Quakers to a late-fourth-quarter touchdown in a 7–0 win over previously unbeaten Dartmouth in a game described by the *Inquirer* as "a rip-tearing battle from start to finish." The *Bulletin* said that Bell played the best game of his career.

"Bell is a great field general, a man who is never bluffed and never at a loss to know what to do. He can also throw a forward pass accurately and quickly. To this line of accomplishment on Saturday he added some beautiful open field dodging and even some desperate line plunging from the quick-opener formation. His running back of kicks was the best he has ever done. He dodged Dartmouth tacklers like a Stevenson [automobile], seemingly stepping out of the way while they missed and sprawled on the ground."

Bell turned in another spectacular performance to trigger a 16–0 upset win over one of Michigan's strongest teams in years although he was forced to leave the game with an injured elbow late in the fourth quarter. It was the first time an eastern team ever knocked off two unbeaten squads in a period of eight days.

Calling it "the greatest surprise of the 1917 foot ball season," the *Bulletin* said, "Bert Bell proved himself one of the best quarterbacks who has ever worn the Red and Blue. His generalship was first class and he used such a varied selection of plays that at times he had the Michigan defense completely bewildered." Afterward, Bell admitted that he hurt his right arm during the game. "It's cracked below the elbow, but it will be all right," he added. Bert started the following week and played a little more than a quarter in an easy 26–0 triumph over the Carlisle Indians.

A few days before the game with Carlisle, however, the *Inquirer* reported two ominous pieces of information. Bell and some of his teammates had earlier joined the University Base Hospital Unit No. 20 and expected to be activated after the football season for duty overseas in World War I. The newspaper said that it had learned that the hospital unit would be mobilized the day before the Cornell game on Thanksgiving Day. But Dr. John B. Carnett, the commanding officer of the hospital and an 1899 graduate of Penn, replied later that the mobilization orders had not been received.

The *Inquirer* also reported that Bell would be held out of the Carlisle game because he had failed a French examination. Both Coach Folwell and Bell denied the latter report. Bell added that it was possible that even if he did fail, he would still be eligible for the game against the Indians. He was.

At 3:00 A.M. on the day after Penn's methodical, 37–0, thrashing of Cornell in the first Thanksgiving Day wartime game at Franklin Field since the Spanish-American War, Bell was sworn into University Base Hospital Unit No. 20 in the First Pennsylvania Calvary Armory adjacent to the campus at 32nd Street and Lancaster Avenue. With a patch on his nose, which had been lacerated in the Cornell game, Bert was joined by a number of his teammates and other prominent Philadelphia-area athletes like future Olympic singles rowing champion John B. Kelly.

That night, at the team banquet, Bell was unanimously elected captain of the 1918 squad, an honor that would have to wait.

3. A War Hero Tastes the French Nightlife

After training for five months at the armory at 32nd Street and Lancaster Avenue, as well as in Philadelphia-area hospitals, Bert Bell and fellow members of Base Hospital Unit No. 20 arrived in France on May 2, 1918.

Their unit was located in several hotels in Châtel Guyon, one of the nation's famous health resorts. ("I think that place was named after that Indian at Georgia Tech," Bert quipped.) Bell's unit consisted of 22 medical officers, two dentists, a chaplain, 65 nurses, and 153 enlisted men. It included a number of his Penn football teammates, like Lou Little, Lud Wray, and Heinie Miller.

No sooner had the Pennsylvanians arrived in the war zone than they discovered that they were terribly shorthanded. Equipped to handle a hospital of 250 patients, they watched U.S. Army authorities deliver trainloads filled with 450 soldiers. By the time their tour was over, seven months later, their facilities had been expanded to 33 buildings with a capacity of 2,500 beds. They eventually cared for some 9,000 patients, of which only 65 were lost. Most of their patients were American soldiers, but they also handled a substantial number of wounded French soldiers and German prisoners. The unit achieved a remarkable record in the prevention of the influenza epidemic and did not lose a single patient to the disease.

Bell's unit, which was commanded by Lieutenant Colonel John B. Carnett, another former Penn football standout, was one of the first to come under fire at the battlefront. It endured four days of heavy shelling from the Germans. Its duties were mainly at field and evacuation hospitals close to the battle lines. Within months, Bert was cited for bravery for aiding numerous wounded soldiers under fire.

"We were operating for seven hours while the Germans were shelling the hospital," wrote Bell in a letter to his father. "Finally they got our range and dropped two high explosives in the sick ward and killed some of the patients. We stopped operating and carried the sick and wounded to the dugouts and as I was going over with the stretcher, a shell dropped and killed one of my buddies not over seven yards away. This continued until our airplanes found the Boche guns and put them out of order long enough to get the patients out."

Lt. Col. Carnett later explained that Bell volunteered for this dangerous work, although the former Penn captain was too modest to tell anyone. In a letter to a friend, Carnett wrote, "I wonder if Bert wrote that at the hospital where we were located on July 11 (the one from which the Huns shelled us) he had volunteered to remain behind with the patients and did so until all were removed. The military commander asked for an officer, a Sergeant, and five men as volunteers, and Bert was one of the first to step forward."

The *Philadelphia Bulletin* described the scene: "At 12:59 A.M. on July 14, Bell was playing poker with some bunk-mates in a hurriedly erected hospital building near the front when a gas alarm broke up the game. Soon the Boche began dropping shells loaded with mustard and phosgene gas on the hospital. The place was ordered evacuated, but some of the wounded were too sick to move. Volunteers were called for to remain behind and face almost certain capture or death. Bert was the first to step out of [the] line."

"I guess I got ahead of my interference," Bert recalled. "But I was so darned anxious."

Even though American intelligence forces learned that the Germans planned to extend their position 30 kilometers to the west the following day, Bell remained at his post. Fortunately, the enemy's expected advance never materialized. Exactly 24 hours to the minute after the bombardment started, it stopped. The next morning, the work of carrying back the wounded began. Bert and another fellow were bearing a stretcher when a stray shell dropped near them. Bert's companion was killed instantly, but Bert and the wounded man escaped unscratched. "I played poker with him the night before," Bell said, referring to his fatally wounded comrade. "Never know the name of men we play poker with."

When General John J. Pershing learned of the heroic action of Bell and the other volunteers, he had his chief of staff send the following message of commendation for "extraordinary bravery and untiring attention to the wounded under fire":

The Commander-in-Chief was proud to learn from a report from the Office of the Inspector General, A.E.F. [American Expeditionary Forces], of the fine courage shown by your personnel under shell fire when stationed with the Division in France. He congratulates Mobile Hospital No. 20 and requests you to inform its members that he is proud to have them in his command.

Lt. Col. Carnett described another successful exploit of Sergeant Bell's, when he was put in charge of a detail to make a 400-mile trip to the seacoast and fetch a truck and three ambulances to the hospital base. Carnett was outspoken in his praise of the unit. "I doubt if any base hospital in France was blessed with a better group of officers, nurses, and enlisted men than we had," he told the *Pennsylvania Gazette*. "They did everything that was expected of them and more. Whether at the front or in the hospital, they were always faithful and efficient. Whatever record we have made is due to them."

Later, Bell served in the town of Château-Thierry, then near the Veuilly Woods, and finally at St. Mihiel, where he was stricken with dysentery. Lt. Col. Carnett ordered him to the rear of the battle zone, but Bert refused to go. Finally he said as a friend and not as a commanding officer, "Bert, if you don't go, you'll be dead in a week. I won't be responsible for your life." Bell finally agreed to return to the hospital base at Châtel Guyon, where he was promoted to the rank of top sergeant.

Despite the horrors of war, Bert found ample time to get away from the battlefield. Two of his favorite running mates from Base Hospital Unit No. 20 were Joe Donoghue, who later became an executive with the Philadelphia Eagles and the National Football League, and John B. (Jack) Kelly, a young Philadelphia oarsman who would later go on to win three Olympic gold medals. Both became Bert's lifelong friends.

Donoghue had been rejected for military service because of his 5-foot-4-inch height, but he convinced the army to let him enlist as an entertainer. He was in Europe entertaining troops as an actor and, as he said later, "living it up" with Bell.

Kelly, who would later become a prominent Philadelphia contractor and the father of Hollywood legend Grace Kelly, was an excellent boxer, with or without gloves. He knocked out 12 straight opponents in the American Expeditionary Forces Boxing Tournament before a broken ankle prevented him from squaring off against a promising young fighter named Gene Tunney, who would go on to become heavyweight champion of the world. One of Kelly's victims, whom he polished off in one round, was a Frenchman who took Tunney three rounds before losing the AEF title.

Never one to miss any action, Bert decided to make some money with Jack Kelly's pugilistic ability as they sampled French nightlife.

"As you know, my dad was a big bettor," Bert Bell Jr. explained. "In every little town there'd be a local tough guy who supposedly beat everyone. Usually it was the biggest guy in the bar."

"Bert would pick a fight with him," added his other son, Upton. "And just when the guy was about to tee off on my dad, Bert would announce that he was willing to bet anyone in the joint that his buddy Jack, right here, could punch the big guy's lights out."

After Jack cold cocked and usually kayoed the hometown boy, Bell and Kelly would collect their cash winnings and hastily move on. But in one town, Jack lost. He got beaten badly. "My dad paid them off in United Cigar coupons, which the French thought was American money," said Bert Jr. "And they took off! Very quickly! It was probably the first army scandal."

Because of his medical condition, Bell returned to the United States on March 26, 1919, about two weeks ahead of other members of his unit. He landed in New York on the transport *George Washington* and was sent to Camp Merritt at Tenafly, New Jersey, to await his discharge from the service. He landed with 5,015 other officers and men of the AEF and a group of distinguished civilians. Among the former was Captain Kermit Roosevelt, his wife, and his two sons, Kermit Jr. and Willard.

According to published reports, Sergeant Bell became quite chummy on the trip with Captain Roosevelt, the second son of President Theodore Roosevelt. Bert's father, former Attorney General John C. Bell, received preferential treatment and was permitted to board the *George Washington* as it docked, a privilege that congressmen, like James W. Cox of Ohio, and governors, like Al Smith of New York, were not afforded.

"That's a Philadelphia trick," said John C. Bell when urged to tell how he managed to get on board. "Nobody knows but me and the ship. The ship can't tell and I won't."

4. Back to Penn as Captain of the Quakers

Relaxing on the ship steaming its way back from France, Top Sergeant Bert Bell was asked if he would still accept the captaincy of the 1919 Quakers. This was the position that he had been elected to serve before the war intervened.

"Will I?" Bert exclaimed. "Well, you just bet your life I will. I'm going to get there as quick as I can. And let me tell you something: I'd rather have that honor than anything I know. Why, if General Pershing came up and said, 'Here, boy, you can have my job and I'll take yours at Old Penn,' I'd say, 'Thank you kindly, General, but there's nothing doing.'"

Bell had been slated for an officer's commission if the Armistice hadn't been signed. Now all he could think of was getting home and leading the Red and Blue once again.

As the respected captain of one of the nation's top football teams, Bert was consulted by the coaches on all personnel matters. He helped with play selection and even devised some new plays. Once, in fact, he shocked teammates and coaches alike by having the gall to suggest to Bob Folwell that the team throw a pass on its first play from scrimmage. The coach was not amused but he continued to let Bell supervise the training routines and give postgame interviews to the press.

Bell was, undoubtedly, the primary reason why expectations were so high going into the 1919 season—especially when he was connecting with long, precision passes and nailing 40-plus-yard field goals with regularity in preseason practices.

"Bert Bell is a natural leader endowed with physical requisites to class him as a brilliant player," wrote sportswriter D. L. Reeves. "He has qualified as a skilled general in field techniques and is fortunate at having at his command the best material seen on Franklin Field for more than a decade. Pennsylvania seems destined to take the leading position in the intercollegiate football world in the East this fall."

Unfortunately, things did not go as well as fans had expected. The Quakers started off exceptionally strong, blowing away their first five opponents by a combined 237–7 margin. But they finished with a 6–2–1 record which included disappointing, back-to-back losses to Penn State and Dartmouth and a frustrating 3–3 tie with Pittsburgh.

Bell required three stitches over his right eye after suffering a cut during a brawl in the 16–0 opening game win over Bucknell. At one point, a small riot broke out in the stands between Bell detractors and Bell supporters. This occurred after a group of fans in the south stands began chanting, "Take Bell out!" Some fans thought that Bert had kicked Bison star Johnny Hendren in the teeth, but Hendren himself said later that it never happened. Others recalled watching Bell's father, John C., the distinguished attorney general, stoically sitting on the Quakers' bench while fans on one side cheered his son and fans on the other side screamed, "Get your kid out of there. He stinks!"

Even with their starters playing less than a half, the Quakers blanked their next two opponents, PMC College, 54–0, and Delaware, in the rain, 89–0. It was the most points for a Penn team in a single game since a 93–0 win over South Jersey College in 1893.

"Penn has the greatest team I have ever seen," said Delaware coach Bert Shipley. "My team was made to look bad but they were up against one of the best elevens of all time."

The Quakers then rolled over Swarthmore, 55–7. "The game cannot be allowed to pass without a mention of Bert Bell's gallant leadership," the *Philadelphia Bulletin* reported. "Bert ran the team flawlessly, choosing just the right play at the right moment in almost every case. Bert also did his share of carrying the ball and making interference, but the latter goes without saying."

By now, interest in the Quakers reached a fever pitch. Work began immediately after the Swarthmore game on adding 5,000 seats in the west stands to accommodate the crowds expected for the Penn State, Pittsburgh, and Cornell games. This would increase Franklin Field's capacity to more than 28,000.

After the unbeaten Quakers methodically took care of Lafayette, 23–0, they went into the Penn State game full of confidence—justifiably so because they had been scored upon only once in their first five games. But Bert had a terrible day, maybe because he had missed a few days of practice during the week after banging up his arm in the Lafayette game. He shanked three field goals on the soggy field, had a pass intercepted on Penn State's 10-yard line, and punted terribly as the Lions won, 10–0, in perhaps college football's biggest shocker of the season. One of his punts sailed sideways into the temporary stands only five yards beyond the line of scrimmage. Another one went out of bounds from a short distance.

"We didn't think much of Penn State," Lou Little later recalled to the *New York Times*. "We hadn't lost a game. We were conquering heroes," he said, adding that Penn fans and alumni had given the team a big dinner the Monday before the game. "We ate as though the season was already over. I think we were still stuffed with food when we met Penn State and they kicked the stuffing out of us. We thought all we had to do was blow up the football and go out and run over those birds. As a matter of fact, they had a whale of a team. So there we were, all swelled up like poisoned pups, fit to be killed—and they killed us."

Nevertheless, with all classes dismissed, 5,000 students came out to cheer for the Quakers as they prepared to board a train for New York City and the game against Dartmouth.

"Loyal sons of Old Penn snake-danced their eleven through West Philadelphia to Broad Street Station in one of the greatest ovations ever given a team on the eve of a big game," reported the *Bulletin*. "Off came trolley poles, policemen were laughingly pushed aside when they remonstrated, motorists were compelled to stop and hold their cars at the curbs until the long line of students passed, a line that stretched for more than eight squares."

With Bots Brunner replacing Bell as the punter, the Quakers dropped a heartbreaker to Dartmouth in New York's Polo Grounds, 20–19. The *Times* labeled the contest "one of the most spectacular and exciting games ever played by college teams." Calling the game "one of the most thrilling ever played on a gridiron," the *Bulletin* added that "fatal mistakes in judgment" cost Penn the game even though "the Red and Blue outplayed the Big Green team in almost every department of the game."

One of those mistakes—by Bell—turned the game around and gave Dartmouth the go-ahead touchdown late in the third quarter. It happened after Dartmouth was forced to punt from its own 10-yard line. Bert not only failed to catch the ball; he let the spiral drop and roll.

"Everybody has seen a third baseman on a baseball field watch a bunt roll down the third base line, hoping for it to roll foul and the ball refused," explained the *Bulletin*. "That was what happened to Bert Bell. He trotted along beside the ball which bounded along within inches of the sideline all the way to Penn's ten-yard-line."

Bell later badly missed a short field goal that could have regained the lead. He was lambasted by the *Times*, which commented that the Quakers could put the blame for the loss "squarely upon [his] shoulders. Playing as the last man in the defense, he twice allowed touchdowns to score when a comparatively simple open-field tackle was offered him. In each case his effort was half-hearted and the runner easily slipped past him."

Three days later, the *Philadelphia Inquirer* reported that Bell lost more than just the game against Dartmouth:

"All sorts of reports are flooding over the Penn campus as to just what caused the defeat by Dartmouth when Penn played a generally better brand of football, and as to who is responsible for the unfortunate result," the newspaper said. "But probably the most spectacular report of them all, although it could not be verified, is that Captain Bert Bell is today no longer in possession of a $1,000 touring car, but instead this machine is now burning the roads of New England, as goes the report. For it is whispered that Bert staked her on the game, and when victory faded, so did the bus."

"My father had just given me a new automobile," Bert told sportswriter Marshall Bainbridge many years later. "After I bet all the money I had and could borrow, I still felt certain we would beat Dartmouth. That's how I lost my automobile."

While rumors were swirling around Bert's missing automobile as well as his problems on the gridiron, Coach Folwell suddenly whisked his team away from campus to the Pine Valley Country Club in the wilds of New Jersey for three days of secret workouts. The move was suggested by Penn's captain himself, who was very familiar with the exclusive country club that counted among its prominent members his father and Philadelphia Athletics manager Connie Mack.

Folwell said that the main reason for the trip to the secluded practice site was to rebuild the morale of the team, whose confidence had been shattered by the unexpected setbacks. In addition to predicting a "sure" victory over Pittsburgh the following Saturday, Bert described Pine Valley to reporters as "the best place in the country," and added, "We all think it is great here."

"This trip proved a masterstroke," said the *Bulletin*. "The fresh air and freedom from campus worries proved a tonic. Today the men dashed over the links of the Pine Valley Club like colts in a pasture." Penn's coaches admitted that the trip would not have been successful if there had been the least dissension on the team and said that Bert Bell's popularity had been a major factor in bringing the players back to form.

With more than 30,000 fans looking on—the largest crowd ever to see Penn play at Franklin Field—the Quakers battled the mighty University of Pittsburgh to a 3–3 tie. Bell drop-kicked a 36-yard field goal on his first attempt of the day early in the first quarter. But he later missed four other chances from 37, 43, 39, and 18-yards out, with the final attempt coming in the closing seconds of the game.

Legendary Pitt coach Glenn (Pop) Warner praised Bell after the game, saying that Penn's captain "used excellent judgment in executing his plays. His leadership was flawless. To him should be given the credit for preventing Pitt from winning."

"That Pitt team can play football," Bell said. "The game was clean. Our trip to Pine Valley this week helped the boys a lot."

"Barring the Army-Navy battles waged on Franklin Field in the past, yesterday undoubtedly furnished the greatest football spectacle in the history of the sport in Philadelphia," the *Inquirer* gushed. "More spectacular games have been played in Franklin Field, but never did two great teams, evenly matched, fight with greater courage or more dogged determination than did Penn and Pitt yesterday."

Bell closed out his collegiate career by masterminding Penn to a brilliant 24–0 win over Cornell on Thanksgiving Day.

"Bert Bell's Generalship Proves Too Much for Ithacans' Stubborn Defence," said a headline in the *Bulletin.* "On several occasions," the newspaper reported, "Bell completely fooled the Ithacans by calling for unexpected plays, displaying excellent generalship throughout, but especially within the 20-yard line." Praising Penn's captain for his best work since the Swarthmore game, the newspaper added, "He used his head in selecting plays. He shot his forward passes with accuracy and caught punts fearlessly, usually getting away for from five to 15 yards after catch."

Although Coach Folwell called Bell "the most brilliant field general I've ever known," most football observers considered the skinny, cocky field leader a good, but not a great, quarterback. But they did have tremendous respect for the incredible toughness of the peppery signal-caller, who never backed down from protecting his teammates on the field. During his collegiate career, he would suffer a broken collarbone and cracked ribs and have three front teeth knocked out. Still, he had his detractors, even in his senior year. Some of them criticized his football ability; others simply resented his family's wealth and the fact that Bert loved tooling around campus dressed in his raccoon coat and sitting pompously in his maroon Marmon—until losing the car after the Dartmouth game.

Bell's performance in the classroom was a different matter. According to some of his teammates, he never came to class if the weather was bad outside. Joe Labrum, a lifelong friend who later became the NFL's public relations director, enjoyed telling how he covered up for Bell's absence in class that final year:

"We were in the same English Literature class and (I think) Bert showed up for the first day of class. But after that, when the roll was called, I sat in the back of the room and I'd answer to Bert's name in the most powerful voice I could muster, like a quarterback barking signals, and then answer to my own name in my natural voice, a softer voice. I thought I was fooling our professor, Dr. Cornelius Weygandt, until one day in November—the week before the Cornell game—he ordered me to stand up after he finished the roll. 'Gentlemen,' he said, 'I want you to meet Mr. Bell and Mr. Labrum, the new Dr. Jekyll and Mr. Hyde.' Then he said to me, 'You tell Mr. Bell he'd better get to class or be dropped.' I told Bert, but I don't think he ever came."

Bell withdrew from school in February 1920 without graduating. It was time to get on with the rest of his life.

5. Bert Bell's Coaching Career Begins

In 1920, Bert Bell finally realized that he was not good enough to play professional football. He decided to return to Penn as the backfield coach under John Heisman, who had succeeded Bob Folwell as head coach after the 1919 season. Heisman later became one of the greatest coaches in college football history. The award presented annually to the nation's outstanding collegiate gridiron player carries his name.

Bert would remain as an assistant at Penn for nine years, the final six campaigns under Louis Young. It didn't take him long to make an impact. He eventually coached players like future NFL colleagues Carroll Rosenbloom, the owner of the Baltimore Colts, and Don Kellett, the Colts' general manager.

By the 1922 season, Bell's reputation as a coach was well established. As Wyncie King wrote in the *Philadelphia Public Ledger*: "There are many men who can teach the fundamentals of the gridiron and who can even go beyond that and instruct in the advanced method and theory of the game; but those who are real strategists are rare. Such a one is Bert Bell, captain of that mighty 1919 team at Penn and now assisting in the process of the Red and Blue by the lore and cunning in the fray that made him a great field general."

One day in September 1923, Bell was having lunch during a break in Penn's football practice in New Jersey when he overheard one of the players talking about a horrible day he had on the golf course. "Good night," Bert shrieked. "You don't mean that you took a 12 on that 311-yard first hole, do you?" Bell was known to occasionally score in the 70s on Merion's classic East Course. "That's terrible," he exclaimed. "Why I could make that hole in 12 blindfolded!"

Within minutes, players were making wagers and Bell quickly agreed to go out and prove his point. He explained his stipulations: he wanted to be permitted to take his stance and then have his eyes bandaged. Then he would make his shot and proceed to the spot where he had hit the ball—if he hit it—and repeat the entire process. Although some players supported Bert, most of them thought that he would need between 50 and 100 strokes to complete the hole.

Soon, carloads of players and others were headed toward Cape May Golf Club. Dr. Arthur Light, the team physician, was appointed by both factions to put the blindfold—a heavy towel—around Bell's eyes before he attempted each shot. Bert took his stance on the first tee, unleashed a mighty swing, and sliced his drive 200 yards out of bounds into a nearby road. His next shot went into the rough about 50 yards from the tee. Six shots later, however, he was on the green. His approach shot rolled 30 feet and stopped within a foot of the cup. He took his stance, was blindfolded, and sank the perfect putt.

He was down in ten!

Midway through the season, Bell created a stir at football practice when he climbed into the front row of the second deck at Franklin Field carrying a machine that he called a *Telautograph*. Soon, he was sketching football plays and writing coaching observations on the device. Then he watched as the material was reproduced on a pad next to Penn's new coach Louis Young, who was sitting down below on the players' bench. Bell had become familiar with the machine in his early days as assistant manager of the St. James Hotel, one of the Center City Philadelphia properties owned by his father. Penn's coaches were impressed but decided to use the device only on game days.

Surprisingly, no other colleges were believed to be using Bell's new-fangled device even five years later, according to Art Morrow of the *Philadelphia Record*. "Wonderful is the mechanical genius of man," he wrote.

In 1924, the Quakers were declared national champions after finishing with a 9–1–1 record, marred only by a 14–0 loss to California in the last game of the season. Bell and line coach Lud Wray received a number of unspecified offers to coach at other colleges, but both assistants decided to remain at their alma mater.

Sportswriters covering the 1925 team, like Ross E. Kauffman, of the *Philadelphia Bulletin*, and Ned Irish, of the *Record*, hinted that a coaching shakeup was in the works after the Quakers suffered unexpected losses to Illinois and Pittsburgh and finished with a 7–2 record. But the chairman of the university's Football Committee, Sydney E. Hutchinson, said emphatically, "There will be no important changes in the Penn coaching system."

In August 1926, Bell helped to bring one of the greatest sporting events of all time, the Dempsey-Tunney heavyweight championship fight, to Philadelphia. Bert was relaxing at Saratoga, one of his favorite haunts in upstate New York, when he learned from a friend, Herbert Bayard Swope, the former chairman of the American Turf Committee, that New York had just turned down the chance to host the much-coveted bout.

Bell was told that Jim Farley, the state's biggest politician, refused to approve the fight because he wanted Harry Wills to get the shot at Dempsey's title. Tex Rickard, one of the greatest promoters of his era, wanted Tunney. Farley, who would later become President Franklin D. Roosevelt's campaign manager, had tremendous clout. Virtually nothing happened in New York State without his approval. Even though it was the middle of the night, Bert swung into action and placed a telephone call to the chairman of the Pennsylvania Athletic Commission.

"It was about 3 o'clock in the morning when I got a call from Bert," Frank Weiner later told Art Morrow. "He was in Saratoga and had just learned that New York would not okay a Dempsey-Tunney match. I went to New York first thing in the morning, saw Tex Rickard and, Bert's dope proving right, he eventually brought the fight here."

But not without a few anxious moments.

After seeing Philadelphia's brand new Municipal Stadium with its huge seating capacity, Rickard assured Weiner that he would bring the bout to the Quaker City. "But I didn't know him except by reputation and I was worried," Weiner later told Ed Pollock, the sports editor of the *Philadelphia Bulletin*. "I didn't want him to use Philadelphia and me to get what he wanted in New York. That's been done, you know. What Bert told me was true. The New York Commission was split."

Weiner said that Rickard "never blinked an eye" when he demanded a $100,000 guarantee to stage the fight in Philadelphia. "His financial backer was John Ringling, the circus man. Rickard and I went to see Ringling at his home in New York. It was in the evening. There was no place where he could pick up a bond and he didn't happen to have 100 grand in cash around the house. But he got the cash at a night bank and I had a bundle of money in my hotel room all night. I didn't sleep well, but the next morning I gave the cash back to Mr. Ringling and got a bond."

Gene Tunney took the heavyweight title away from Jack Dempsey on September 23, 1926, before upward of 125,000 fans in Municipal Stadium. The fight was part of Philadelphia's Sesqui-Centennial celebration. It temporarily put the Quaker City at the center of world's stage. The *New York Times* trumpeted the event with an eight-column, three-line headline spread across the top of the front page in a space usually reserved for presidential elections and catastrophic events. The fight attracted more celebrities than any sporting event held up to that time.

Journalistic giants like William Randolph Hearst, arguably the world's most powerful publisher, and Joseph Pulitzer were there. So were the

Rockefellers, the Harrimans, and the Biddles; countless congressmen, governors and mayors, and actors like Charlie Chaplin and Tom Mix, Hollywood's biggest star who brought 500 of his closest friends to Philadelphia in his private train. Financiers Andrew W. Mellon and Charles M. Schwab sat near gangsters like Al Capone and Arnold Rothstein, the man behind the famous Black Sox scandal of 1919.

"As you know, it was a great fight, a great crowd, and a great thing for Philadelphia," Weiner told Pollock. "I doubt if we could have brought it here without that early tip from Bert Bell."

During the 1926 season, Bell unveiled his most notorious coaching innovation—the devious hidden-ball play in which all 11 Penn players lined up with patches designed as footballs sewed onto the elbows of their uniform jerseys. This created a confusing optical illusion that befuddled opposing defenses. It featured "a bit of passing hocus-pocus," wrote sportswriter Stan Baumgartner. Bert talked the coaches into implementing the gimmick extensively during a game at Franklin Field against Williams College on October 23.

The Quakers won easily, 26–0. But scouts from their next opponent, the University of Illinois, became suspicious after visiting Penn's locker room and inspecting Bell's crafty, lightweight brown leather elbow pads. Legendary Illinois coach Bob Zuppke arranged to have a sample sent to his office, then lodged a protest, only to have it overruled by the Eastern Football Rules Committee. It really didn't matter because the Illini thwarted the hidden-ball offense, held the Quakers to only three first downs, and won the game, 3–0.

Bell's hidden-ball play was soon adopted in various forms by a number of coaches including Zuppke and Bell's ex-teammate Lou Little, who was now running the program at Georgetown. But before the 1930 season, the Football Rules Committee ruled that uniform attachments similar to Bell's "gave the wearer an unfair and unsportsmanlike advantage over their opponents."

The rule-makers suggested that colors for such protective devices be broken up by two stripes of markedly contrasting color at least two inches in width and that the solid color of such jerseys or attachments be definitely broken up by stripes or numbers of markedly contrasting color.

Bert was undeterred. He insisted that the success of his system was always due to the speed and cleverness of the players handling the ball in the backfield.

The Quakers went 6–4 in 1927, then lost only one game the following year, a stunning 6–0 upset by Navy. It was a loss that never should have happened, said Bell. Bert privately blamed Lud Wray, his former Penn teammate, who endorsed Louis Young's harsh training methods that emphasized too many scrimmages. As a result, Bell charged, the Quakers left their game on the practice field.

Bell gave university officials his letter of resignation after Penn's 49–0 triumph over Cornell on Thanksgiving Day 1928, but it was not accepted in hopes that the coaches would get together and settle their differences. His decision did not become public until the following January, when he returned his contract for the following season unsigned. Bert then declared that he "was not wanted" by Young as an assistant for the 1929 season, and his feud with Wray exploded into the open.

Young denied Bell's allegation. He emphasized to friends that he wanted both Bell and Wray to stay. "I have a tough nut to crack," he said. "But I want both Bert and Lud on my staff and I have sent them contracts."

Hosting a dinner for friends in January, Bell said that he would not return to Penn until "existing conditions are changed." He added that he wanted to continue somewhere in a coaching capacity but ruled out accepting a head coaching position. "I consider a head coach must give at least ten months in a year to study of the game, and business connections preclude the possibility of that for me," he told the *Public Ledger,* which called him "the professor emeritus of the hidden-ball attack."

Bell also released copies of his letter of resignation, which was written immediately after the Penn-Cornell game. It said, in part:

> I am sorry to say that one, sometimes more, of our coaching staff have of late, and without any deliberate study on their part, persistently and almost invariably opposed the adoption of any style or system of play or plays recommended by me, as a result of my years of experience as a coach and after diligent study and observation.

Bulletin sportswriter Earl Eby said that the feud actually dated back to 1925 when Lawson Robertson was Penn's track coach and served as trainer for the football team. Robertson, who later became head coach of the U.S. Olympic team, sided with Bell.

"Robby's method was to save the players," Eby reported. "He did not believe in heavy scrimmage after the season started. Bert, it is said, rode along with Robby, but Lud opposed Robby and called for exercises he deemed would toughen the players. He preached that constant scrimmage put the fight into men and enabled them to play 60 minutes of football. Bell, on the other hand, chose to follow the methods of Bill Ropers, Knute Rockne, Glenn Warner, and Bob Zuppke. That is scrimmage the men a bit at the start of the season and then after they had reached their physical peak hold them there, which, he says, could not be accomplished by incessant scrimmage."

Bell said that the Navy defeat in 1928 was precipitated the previous week by two long scrimmages that sapped the players of their strength. Many Penn players admitted being tired after the game and said that their heavy workload that week "made them a prey" for the Middies. Bell and Wray disagreed on other issues including the size of the defensive line. Bell wanted six men up front on certain occasions; Wray wanted seven men at all times. The two coaches couldn't even agree on the starting lineup for the Cornell game.

Penn's Council on Athletics tried to sugarcoat the resignation by issuing a statement blaming Bell's action on "the pressure of business" that he was facing. "If existing conditions change," continued the statement, "it is hoped to retain the services of Mr. Bell."

Eby said that "existing conditions refers to a fight between two rival schools of football coaching," with Bell representing the modern system and Wray, the old fashioned school. Bell told Eby that he confronted Wray at a recent Athletic Department event and said, "Lud, one of us must go. If you stay, I'm out. If I stay, you're out." Lud Wray stayed.

Bell told the *Philadelphia Inquirer* that "business pressure" had nothing to do with his decision.

"If I can get a position, I will coach next year," he explained. "I love football. I have given a lot of time studying the game and I do not intend to give it up. I may not coach at Pennsylvania, but I will no doubt take a position at some other place. I can say, however, that Pennsylvania is my home. There is nothing that I would rather do than be a member of the coaching staff of an undefeated Pennsylvania football team. I hope to do this before I am forced out of football."

In November 1929, the Carnegie Foundation for the Achievement of Teaching issued a scathing indictment of college athletics, entitled *Bulletin 23*. The report pointed out that 81 of 112 colleges surveyed, including the University of Pennsylvania, were guilty of subsidizing their athletes. Only 28 institutions were free from any such taint of professionalism. Most college administrators were reluctant to comment on the 283-page document. Others issued strong (but unpersuasive) denials. Dr. Josiah H. Penniman, Penn's provost, announced that he had not read the report but would probably have nothing to say after he waded through it.

But Bell had plenty to say, even though he was no longer associated with the team in an official capacity.

"Pennsylvania is as clean as any college in the world," Bert said. "There is no reason why a boy who happens to be an athlete should not be helped as much as the student who receives a scholarship for high scholastic standing. It is a significant and potent fact that in the perpetual scholarships founded and endowed by Cecil Rhodes, the great empire builder, in Oxford University—two of these scholarships for periodical award from every state in our Union—be provided and required that the appointees must, in every instance, have shown an excellence in athletics as well as scholastically."

Bell spent his weekends during the 1929 season watching many of the best offensive college teams in the East. He also scouted Notre Dame when the Irish played Army and Navy. On December 3, as rumors swirled that he was going to be named to replace the recently resigned Young as Penn's head coach, Bell announced that he had agreed to become backfield coach at Temple University under head coach Heinie Miller, his old teammate at The Haverford School and Penn.

"The athletic authorities at Temple made a ten-strike when they succeeded in signing Bert Bell," said Charles C. Erny, a member of the university's Athletic Council who had recently provided the $450,000 financing needed to build Temple Stadium. "Without a doubt he is one of the most brilliant coaches in the land."

Penn's followers were shocked and disappointed. They had hoped that somehow Bell would return to the Quakers, but it wasn't to be. Bert stayed with the Owls for three seasons, from 1931 until 1933 when Miller was surprisingly replaced as head coach by Pop Warner, who had gone from Pittsburgh to take over the program at Stanford in 1924. Even though Miller had compiled a respectable 50–15–8 record, Temple authorities decided that Warner could take the Owls to another level.

Miller, who is Bert Bell Jr.'s Godfather, had done an excellent job with Bell at his side—especially in 1931 when the Owls lost only to Carnegie Tech. In 1933, Temple's only defeat came at the hands of Villanova in a 7–6 heartbreaker. The Owls were also tied that year by Carnegie Tech and the Haskell Indians.

Warner immediately announced that he would be picking his own assistants. Bell certainly didn't endear himself to the new coach when he wrote a scathing column in a Philadelphia newspaper entitled "Pop Goes the Warner."

For the second time in less than four years, Bert Bell was out of football. It wouldn't be for long.

6. The Roaring Twenties—
Off the Field

Although he was nearing his thirties when he coached at Penn and Temple, Bert Bell spent most of his nights and weekends partying and gambling.

"Before he was married, Bert touched all the bases," said longtime Pittsburgh Steelers owner Art Rooney, who later became one of his best friends. As a result of his playboy lifestyle, Bert found himself having problems *off* the playing field.

In 1923, a jury in Philadelphia's Common Pleas Court awarded $1,000 in damages to a local taxi driver, Waldo E. Ghilon, who suffered a broken kneecap and spent 22 days in the hospital after Bell's car crashed into his cab in the wee hours of the morning in Fairmount Park. Bert denied charges that he was speeding and driving recklessly but was still ordered to pay after the jurors deliberated for three hours.

Every August, Bert would join friends like the Vanderbilts, the Whitneys, Henry Sinclair, and Bernard Baruch and travel up to New York State for an extended vacation. There they spent days at the Saratoga Racetrack—where Bert would wager up to $500 on a horse—and evenings gambling and enjoying the nightlife at the Brook and Piping Rock clubs. Future New York Giants owner Jack Mara, then the bookmaker on Saratoga's plush lawn, was a frequent companion.

"I know my father went into a casino there one time and he wanted to play, but they wouldn't take his check," Bert Jr. remembered. "So later he got even. One night he won a quarter of a million or something and they wanted to give him a check. He said, 'You wouldn't take my check. I won't take yours.'"

Bert Bell Jr. also recalls that his dad played a lot of poker and bridge. "I remember him telling me one time, 'Don't worry about losing streaks. Sometimes they could last three weeks; sometimes a month.'"

Charles Goren, the famed international bridge champion, wrote about his frequent games with Bell in *Sports Illustrated* shortly after Bert's death in 1959. They often played at the Racquet Club and Penn Athletic Club in Philadelphia. Sometimes they were joined by Swede Youngstrom, the great Dartmouth guard who played across the line from Bell when the Indians upset the Quakers, 20–19, in 1919.

Goren explained that because women were never present at these contests, "some of the social amenities were not always observed. Bert Bell did not impress me as a man of many superstitions, but on one point he was adamant: he refused to play bridge with his head uncovered. He also preferred to play with a minimum of convention in his bidding, and he did not always conform even to that minimum. If this made him a somewhat difficult partner, it also made him a difficult opponent."

Although the total amount has never been verified, Bell lost tons of money, especially during the Depression. He also took some financial hits while working for a while at Carstairs and Company, a brokerage house located in Philadelphia's Ritz Carlton Hotel. He dropped $50,000 during the stock market crash of 1929. Some accounts have estimated his total losses at $1 million by today's monetary standards. But most of his losses came from wagering at bridge, golf, poker, and the racetrack.

Bert's father, John C. Bell, insisted on certain rules of social decorum, even though the younger Bell's behavior on the outside was quite the opposite.

"I don't care how late you stay out or what you do," his father would say. "I insist that you get up and come down and have breakfast with me. And you must be dressed in a shirt and a tie."

Bert complied faithfully, but after a while his father grew impatient and finally exploded. "Dammit," he said, "you're thirty-something and still drinking, gambling, and running around. I'm tired of bailing you out. It's time you settled down!"

John C. offered a solution. He and some friends arranged to have the young man marry a friend of the family, someone who was a Main Line debutante, and, of course, a wealthy member of high society. Bert resisted strongly, so his dad sweetened the offer. "If you agree to marry this young woman, I'll give you $100,000," he promised. Bert reluctantly agreed and the engagement was set.

The next day, Bert headed back up to Saratoga with some of his cronies. By nightfall, the wedding gift—all $100,000 of it—was gone.

Very early the next morning, he pulled up to the family mansion, washed, and changed from his jogging outfit into a three-piece suit and tie. He wasted no time in facing the music. As breakfast began, he admitted that he had lost the entire wedding gift, which would be worth approximately $1 million by today's standards. Then he blurted out, "I ain't marrying that broad!" To which John C. responded, "Well, Bert. If that's the way you want it, no more money. You can go run my hotels and do your coaching, or do whatever you want, but that's the last penny you're ever getting from me. You're not going to see another red cent."

Although it's entirely possible that Bert's dad might have helped him financially at some later point, there is no record of him ever doing so, according to Bert's son Upton.

"Despite their philosophical differences, Bert was his favorite child," Upton explained. "My uncle Jack was the prized one, but my grandfather absolutely *loved* Bert because Bert was all the things that he wasn't. Bert was a chance-taker, he was a gambler, he was all these things. Even when he lost all the money, he would come in, have breakfast with his father, and I think that got him off the hook.

"Jack was the prized guy because Jack became the lawyer and the governor and all the other things. That's the irony of the story: One of the most brilliant jurists in American history at that time never ever got the credit or any of the things that the Black Sheep of the family got."

The senior Bell was also quite successful as a real estate entrepreneur. He had recently acquired the Ritz Carlton and St. James hotels, two valuable Center City Philadelphia properties, as default payments from clients who had purchased the hotels on huge margins, then lost tremendous sums in the stock market crash and couldn't afford to keep up with the payments.

"My grandfather went and paid off all the debts," recalls Bert Jr. "But he saw so many people suffering financially like this that he later said in his will that no Bell money will ever go into second mortgages."

By 1928, at the height of Prohibition, Bert was managing the Ritz Carlton and, later, the St. James hotels in an effort to work off his considerable debt. He was quite successful. He built the occupancy rates significantly at both hotels by calling on his many friends and contacts from the sports world. They came not only from football circles; many were track-and-field competitors and officials who traveled to Philadelphia from throughout the world to compete in the Penn Relays at Franklin Field. Famous writers like Grantland Rice, Jim Bishop, and Walter Winchell were regulars. One of his bouncers was Toots Shor, a lifelong friend who would later become one of the most famous nightclub owners in America.

"The Ritz Carlton was frequented by the classic people at that time," recalls Bert Jr. "One of them was Cesar Romero, the film star who would call my father on the phone weeks ahead of time and say he was coming to town. He would be playing in some nearby theater and would tell my father to call this particular girl because he wanted to have her to dance with while he was staying at the hotel."

Bell frequently threw lavish parties at the Ritz, especially the night before the annual Army-Navy football game. Bert Jr. was told that Bob Hope met his wife, Dolores, at one of these soirees, always the gridiron social event of the year, according to sportswriter Stan Baumgartner. "Bert threw the party and before it was over, four or five of the football coaches invariably threw punches at each other. But it was all in good pigskin fun and the next day everything was forgotten."

Bert just couldn't get away from football and never stopped studying the game while he was managing these hotels. "He had huge filing cases at the Ritz loaded with all the great plays," Bell's buddy Joe Labrum told Jack McKinney of the *Philadelphia Daily News*. "He particularly admired Bob Zuppke's theories."

Although he never dreamed it at the time, Bert Bell's return to the gridiron would come about in one of the most astonishing ways imaginable. An amazing turn of events would soon end his wild lifestyle and pave the way for a distinguished career in the NFL.

7. Frances Upton: One of America's Brightest Stars

They first met at a party in New York—a gathering similar to so many get-togethers in the Big Apple where celebrities from the worlds of sports, entertainment, and politics mingled with underworld figures in lavish surroundings befitting the Prohibition Era as the Roaring Twenties moved into the Thirties.

It was a brief introduction, but to the brash, financially strapped football man, she was the most beautiful woman he had ever met. *She* was Frances Upton, one of the nation's top musical comedy stars who had recently appeared opposite Eddie Cantor in the Broadway hit musical comedy *Whoopee!*

A few weeks later, in the spring of 1932, Frances came to Philadelphia to sing as the featured performer at the Rooftop Club on top of the Ritz Carlton Hotel. As one of the most popular members of the Ziegfeld Follies, Upton frequently played the major hotel roof-garden clubs between shows. Bert was managing the hotel and quickly offered to show the stage idol around. He knew right away how much he was attracted to this fabulous woman. But Frances didn't have the same feelings for Bert. At least not right away.

Just like her future husband, Frances Upton had some distinguished ancestors. Her grandfather, William Cleary Upton, was a noted member of Ireland's Fenian movement of the 1860s and 1870s and author of the highly controversial 1882 novel *Uncle Pat's Cabin,* a popular book at the time that vividly described life as tenant farmers under English rule in his homeland.

Frances herself also enjoyed some success as a novelist. On August 1, 1933, just before she opened in *Hold Your Horses,* the *New York Post* reported that her novel *Back Stage Shadow,* a mystery story with a theatrical background, was about to be published.

Miss Upton's father, Francis, was a decorated New York City police sergeant who enlisted in the army at the beginning of World War I after serving for 17 years as a plainclothes detective. He was slightly wounded when he was one of the first seven Americans to be captured by the Germans in France early in the war. For several months, he was declared missing in action and presumed dead. Fortunately for him, he proved to be a very valuable prisoner to the enemy because he spoke German, Italian, and French fluently. As a result, he spent his time in captivity as the concentration camp's interpreter until the armistice was signed. In a letter to NYPD colleagues from prison, he described his captors as "friendly enemies" and "good-natured people."

Frances started taking ballet lessons at a young age and first danced on the stage before she was 12 years old. She appeared in Red Cross benefits as well as in shows at New York's Majestic Theatre. Years later, she often told her children how her father, the detective, would be waiting for her at the stage door to escort her home after performances.

The young dancer was working behind the perfume counter at Macy's when she was "discovered" at the age of 16 by a talent scout for the Shubert brothers. The timing of her "discovery" couldn't have been better, because shortly afterward she was fired from her job for dancing in an office at the store, where she also worked as a secretary.

"The scout took one look at her deep-set brown eyes, pouty lips, and alabaster Irish complexion and told her she was the most beautiful thing this side of County Cork," her son Upton recalls being told by family members.

Frances soon landed a spot as a chorus girl in *Little Jesse James,* an original musical comedy on Broadway. In 1923, she replaced the show's ailing leading lady with such success that she was signed to a three-year contract by the Ziegfeld Follies, a series of lavish reviews and vaudeville shows that featured some of the biggest names in the world of entertainment.

Quickly Miss Upton became one of America's biggest female stars and one of the nation's most popular comediennes. One year, she was voted America's most beautiful woman. She appeared with some of the most brilliant names in show business including "America's Sweetheart of Song" Ruth Etting, Gracie Allen, Fanny Bryce, Bing Crosby, W. C. Fields, Will Rogers, Peggy Wood, Paul Whitman, and Ed Wynn.

Miss Upton starred for the Shuberts and Flo Ziegfeld and George White's "Scandals Reviews" and played the Palace Theatre in New York, the most prestigious vaudeville house in America. She made guest appearances with celebrities like Gertrude Lawrence and Damon Runyan, the famous writer who would later interview her husband on occasion.

In 1929, she appeared with a host of personalities on an historic National Broadcasting Company (NBC) radio show beamed to Commander

Richard E. Byrd and his expedition at Little America in Antarctica. Two years later, she joined other prominent sports and entertainment luminaries in the first "Radio Talkie," a blend of sound and television images transmitted to various locations in New York City.

After a number of critically acclaimed appearances in various Broadway musical comedies, Miss Upton received rave reviews for her feature role with Eddie Cantor in the 1927 Ziegfeld Follies musical review written by Irving Berlin, at the New Amsterdam Theatre.

Writing in *Billboard*, Gordon M. Leland praised her as one of "the outstanding personalities that make the production so delightfully fresh." Leland called the production "a sumptuous offering," adding: "In about as perfect a state of readiness as any big extravaganza has been for a Broadway opening, the performance is remarkably well-balanced and goes off without a hitch."

One of the best scenes in the Follies, according to Herbert G. Goldman, the author of *Banjo Eyes: Eddie Cantor and the Birth of Modern Stardom*, was "The Taxi Cab," in which Eddie portrayed a modest boy-man being taken home by an aggressive young woman (played by Miss Upton).

"Upton as a bold bad lady, flirted with the shy resistant Cantor until she exclaimed in disgust, 'You're the coldest proposition,'" Goldman recounted. "'I'm sorry,' he indignantly retorted. 'I'm sorry we're not the same temperature.' He was finally invited to walk the remaining ten miles—*or else*—agree to be mauled with affection. 'I guess, I'll else,' he wailed, crawling back into his seat. Frances, of course, played what amounted to a 1920s version of Fania, Eddie's 'older woman' girlfriend of the early 1900s."

In December 1928, Miss Upton opened as "Sally Morgan in Ziegfeld's much-awaited production of *Whoopee,* a musical comedy featuring Eddie Cantor, at the New Amsterdam Theatre. Brooks Atkinson, the highly respected theater critic of the *New York Times,* praised her singing—her rendition of "Making Whoopee" helped make that song the nation's number-one hit—and lauded the show as "another gorgeous spectacle . . . enlivened with splendid dancing [and] long stretches of excellent comedy."

Two months after the show opened, Paul Whitman's orchestra replaced George Olsen's group. Whitman's contingent included Bing Crosby and the Rhythm Boys, the first and only time Crosby ever did a Broadway show. *Whoopee!* ran on Broadway for almost a year before closing on November 23, 1929, four weeks and two days after "Black Thursday."

In 1930, Miss Upton joined a host of musical comedy stars and headed to Hollywood. As nationally syndicated gossip columnist Elizabeth Yeaman reported in her *Studio Roundup* on May 23: "Less than one week after she landed in Hollywood, Frances Upton, Broadway musical comedy favorite, had signed a contract which ultimately will make her a star of Pathe Pictures." She costarred with Eddie Quillan as Aggie, a nurse, in *Night Work*, a heartwarming drama about a department store worker who falls for her charms and ends up supporting her and her adopted orphan boy.

A year or so after returning from Hollywood, her friendship with Bert Bell slowly, gradually started to blossom. Frances later told her children that she was engaged at the time to Bernard Mannes Baruch Jr., the son of the famed financier-philosopher. The younger Baruch, a 1923 graduate of Harvard, was a member of the New York Stock Exchange who made a fortune in rubber and steel interests. Both families objected to the relationship for religious reasons—he was Jewish and she was a Roman Catholic.

After Frances stepped off the stage the first night that she appeared at the Ritz Carlton's Roof Garden in the spring of 1932, Bert invited her to come over to his table and have some champagne. There was a lot of small talk, laughing, and joking around, but later in the evening she told him in no uncertain terms that she was not interested in accompanying him downstairs to his private apartment.

"He probably thought: 'This is the end of this relationship forever,'" recalled Upton, who heard the details of that encounter from his mother. "But as soon as he heard her reply, he was challenged. He was going to follow her everywhere because she was the only one who ever said 'No' to him. And then he started chasing her all over the country, trying to get her to break her engagement with Baruch and marry him."

As Bert Bell would quickly learn, Frances Upton knew her way around. On one hand, she was a devoutly religious woman who attended Mass at St. Patrick's Cathedral, in New York City, with friends like Danny Thomas. "All the entertainers would go to church and pray when they were out of work," Upton explained. "It was always a struggle for people in show business. Many times after she got another job, she'd go back to church and light a candle."

But, like other entertainment celebrities, Frances also knew how to have a good time after the stage lights went down. At one party, she found herself having a conversation with Charles A. Lindbergh, whom she recalled as "quite handsome, but a very shy person."

Once while in Chicago, Frances went to a party with her roommate Ruth Etting, who was dating her future husband, Mo (the Gimp) Snyder, an underworld figure who was later portrayed by James Cagney in the film *Love Me or Leave Me* with Doris Day. Here Upton picks up the story as recounted by his mother:

"She said that when they got into a private room, all the women were seated facing the men with their backs against the wall, with the women with their backs to the door. My mom thought it was quite odd. As she explained it, she was sitting across from this guy smoking a big cigar. It was Al Capone. I'm not sure she knew who he was at first. I mean she was only 22, 23-years old. She told me that she had a wonderful conversation with Mr. Capone. I don't know if it was Ruth Etting, but she turned to one of the women at the table and said, 'It's really funny. Why aren't we just sitting with the men?' She explained that the women didn't know that they were sitting ducks. The whole idea was, if somebody came in with a machine gun and wanted to mow anyone down, they would be the ones to be shot first."

A few months later, Bert and Frances went to dinner at a restaurant in Margate, New Jersey. They were joined by two of his former Penn teammates, Heinie Miller and Lou Little, and their wives.

"On that occasion," said W. C. Heintz in The *Saturday Evening Post,* "Miss Upton made it plain that she and Bell could never be more than friends if he did not give up drinking." Bert replied, according to Little: 'All right. I've had my last drink.'

"We thought it was idle talk at the time,' " Little told Heintz. 'But he meant it and he's a man of strong will power.' "

Meanwhile, Frances was helping to usher in a new era for New York's famed Winter Garden Theatre. In September 1933, she opened as Dolly Montague in Shubert's frothy musical comedy *Hold Your Horses.* Appearing opposite the star of the show, the popular comic and juggler Joe Cook, Miss Upton generated a lion's share of the publicity.

It would be her final appearance on Broadway. Shortly after the show closed on the Great White Way in December 1933, the entire company moved to Chicago. She still wasn't convinced about Bert Bell's sincerity.

A few days after Frances left for the Windy City, Bert visited Atlantic City with his buddies and spent the night beating their ears about how much he loved her. Finally, they had had enough. "Bert," one of them blurted out. "Can't you see that she doesn't want you?" "Like hell she doesn't," he replied, picking up a nearby telephone and dialing her number in Chicago. "Frances," he said. "I'm here with all my friends and I have something to tell you. I want them to be my witnesses. If you marry me, I'll never take another drink as long as I live!"

"And he never did have another drink—nothing—for the rest of his life," Upton recalled. When his father died and I said, 'Dad, you ought to have a drink. Have a shot,' he wouldn't do it. And when his mother died, the same thing. He never had a drink again."

Upton said that his dad even had his friends continue to call Miss Upton: "Hey, Harry, call Frances. Tell her I'm really a good guy. Tell her I'm an upstanding guy!"

"I didn't believe him for a moment," Frances later told her son. "But I gave him a chance to prove it. I told him he had six months to show me he could do it."

Actually, Frances didn't make Bert wait for that long. They were secretly married on January 4, 1934, in Chicago because Ziegfeld prohibited his performers from marrying without his permission. At the time, Frances was living at the Ambassador Hotel in Chicago while appearing in *Hold Your Horses*. Later, she became seriously ill with kidney problems and was confined to St. Luke's Hospital in the Windy City for several weeks.

After getting tipped off that Bell had snuck into town to visit her, a Chicago newspaper plastered the top of one of its pages with this headline: MILLIONAIRE PLAYBOY VISITS STRICKEN ACTRESS GIRL FRIEND IN CHICAGO.

"That was supposed to be me," Bert later told sportswriter Ed Prell. "What this journalist didn't know was that I was practically broke and, more important, already was wedded to Miss Upton."

Bell's visits to his new bride in Chicago, though, were few and far between. Obviously missing her dearly while he struggled to get his newly acquired Philadelphia Eagles franchise up and running, the outwardly gruff football man showed an entirely different, warm, sentimental persona in his correspondence with her. The following letters indicate how much he was capable of speaking from his heart. The first one was postmarked February 12, 1934.

Miss Frances Upton
Hotel Ambassador
Chicago, Illinois

The Racquet Club
Philadelphia

Dearest Darling Sweetheart,

Gee but it was wonderful to talk to you last night as I was scared & worried to death when I did not speak to you the both other times I called. I certainly hope you are a lot better and not suffering so, I really am heart sick and wish I could do something to help you my sweetheart as I love you so & am just crying my heart out to help in some way. Please darling let me know of anything I can do to help you it would make me feel so much better if I could do something at least for my little gal. You are so kind and thoughtful to me and here I am helpless to do anything to help you, so please darling tell me. I love you with all my heart and soul and pray our little prayer all the time no matter where I am for the good Lord to help you.

You know I went to St. John's [Roman Catholic Church in Center City Philadelphia] yesterday afternoon and just prayed for my darling girl and it was so sweet and quiet in there I could just picture you and it helped so, I was scared and I did not know where to go or how to act but as soon as I got inside it was all so nice and wonderful. I cried a little and prayed for you and I got more confidence and felt much better. Please darling you are the only person in the wide world who really matters and I love you with all my heart and soul and I'm your one and only husband and simply adore the ground you walk on so if you are not a lot better tell me the truth and I will be on my way to old Chi to see you and help you with all your troubles, now please Sweetheart tell me the truth.

I am going over to St. John's this afternoon and will say our prayer for you. I know it by heart now & it gives me so much comfort to say it as it is so beautiful and you picked it out & anything you like, I love with everything in me. You are the most wonderful girl in all the world and I idolize you from the top of your head to the tip of your toes, we will just be sweethearts for ever and ever and I will do everything in my power to make you happy and sweetheart you have made me so happy I did not think a fellow could be so lucky as to have a person so kind sweet thoughtful & good as you are my darling sweetheart. I only hope I can in some way repay that wonderful love & confidence you have had in me.

Please darling do what the doctor tells you & don't hurry back to the Theatre until he says it is OK & please tell me the truth if you are not much better so I can come out and be with you & take care of you. I love you sweetheart with everything that is in me and pray the good Lord to help my sweetheart.

Please good Lord help my dearest Frances, I love her so.

With all my love for you alone

Bert

Meanwhile, Bert and Frances were still denying reports that they had been married. In an interview with a reporter from the *New York American* on March 25, she said: "The real reason we haven't married before this is that Mr. Bell wants me to give up the stage after our marriage and

I don't know what agreement we'll come to on it. I don't know what started the rumor that I am to marry Mr. Bell in West Palm Beach in April. We plan to be married in Philadelphia sometime in September."

On March 27, 1934, Bert even refused to confirm or deny reports of his *engagement* to Frances. "Some ingenious mind devised the report that Miss Upton talked of an engagement between us," he said to a Philadelphia reporter. "I happen to know that Miss Upton has been and is so ill in Chicago that her own mother has not been permitted to see her. She is too ill to talk even over the telephone."

Frances had been quoted the previous day as saying that she and Bert were planning to be married in September and that the reason they had not been married before this was because he wanted her to give up the stage after their marriage. When asked again if he were engaged to Miss Upton, Bert laughed and said: "I have nothing more to say on the matter. When my engagement is ever announced, it will be done formally and properly."

In a letter dated April 4, 1934, as Frances was preparing to move to Florida for a few months of convalescing, Bert urged his wife not to take any showers, promised to call her only once every night, and added: "Now my darling please always tell me the truth whether it depresses me or not as it will be much better for all of us."

Later, alluding to his activity in the brokerage business, Bert wrote:

> It looks like we will have inflation of some kind and that should stimulate the market anyway. Be sure my darling sweetheart to have the Drs. send me their bills and I will take care of them. Now don't hesitate or think anything about this as I am your husband and it is my duty and pleasure. I mean this very sincerely. By the time you get this letter my darling, we will be married three months.
>
> Again I want to tell you darling every day I love you more and it has made me the happiest person in the whole world and you have been wonderful to me in every way and I certainly do love you and appreciate your wonderful spirit and your love.
>
> You are my everything and I love you till it hurts (and oh boy, how I like it). Just wait my darling. It won't be long now till we are together once and for all and will I be happy.
>
> God bless you and oh how I love you.
>
> With all your husband's love for you alone.
>
> Bert

On April 14, Bell told the *Philadelphia Bulletin* that he had no comment to make regarding a report about their secret marriage by Walter Winchell, who added in his nationally syndicated column: "Frances Upton, who married Bert Bell months ago, is ill again and her condition is not so good. She was last in St. Luke's Hospital in Chicago."

Winchell's account was quite accurate. According to Bert Bell Jr., Winchell called Frank Upton and asked whether it was true that his daughter had married Bert Bell. "Yes, Walter, it's true, but don't tell anybody," Frank replied. Naturally, Winchell ran the item in his column the very next day.

Finally at 8:00 A.M. on May 6, 1934, after she returned from Florida, Frances and Bert were officially married. The ceremony took place in the rectory of St. Madeleine Sophie Roman Catholic Church, at 6440 Greene Street, in the Germantown section of Philadelphia. Only one or two intimate friends attended the wedding officiated by the Rev. J. Joseph Ullman, an assistant rector at the church and a close friend of Bell's.

Most of Bell's other friends were unaware of the marriage until he sent them telegrams from Ventnor, outside Atlantic City, a few hours after the couple arrived there on their honeymoon. Reclining on a chair on the sun porch of their rented mansion at 6803 Atlantic Avenue—a beautiful structure that took up almost an entire city block—Frances chose that moment to announce that she was giving up her show business career.

"I shall not return to the stage unless there is another Depression and I am called upon to aid in replenishing the family treasury," she declared in the midst of a sunbath, according to Philadelphia newspaper reports. Dressed becomingly in a black velvet skirt and a white jersey blouse, Frances added: "I have never been so thrilled in my life during the ceremony. Getting married is so exciting. Bert and I are very much in love with each other. That's why I am giving up my career."

Bert, who was 39 years old, appeared "already domesticated," according to a published report. He was in shirt sleeves on the lawn, cutting the grass outside the house that was filled with large bouquets of flowers and congratulatory telegrams from friends in the theatrical and sports worlds.

"I'm training for the football season," he announced. "Already I have a couple of college fellows in mind who promised to sign up with me for the new season when they finish school."

Bert described to reporters how he met his wife, whom he called "Uptown," at a party in New York. "I don't remember who introduced us. It doesn't matter now, anyhow. We have been engaged for about a year. She's feeling pretty good now although she was sick several months ago."

Even though he was on his honeymoon, Bert found it difficult to keep his mind off the gridiron. He even invited his players from the Eagles to stay in the mansion while the team practiced on the beach nearby.

One time while they were taking a stroll, hand-in-hand along the Jersey shore, Frances said, "Look at that moon, Bert. Isn't it romantic?"

"Yeah," he replied. "If only I had a punter who could kick that high!"

8. The Yellow Jackets Become the Eagles

During their long-distance courtship, Bert Bell was pleasantly surprised to learn that Frances Upton not only loved the game of football but, in some ways, knew more about the sport than he did. They frequently attended University of Pennsylvania football games together. As a celebrity showgirl, her social circle included some of the nation's top professional football players.

"She had seen the Decatur Staleys play out in Chicago, and the Canton Bulldogs in Ohio, and the New York Giants at the Polo Grounds," Upton Bell recalled in a *Philadelphia* magazine article written with David Chanoff. "She'd go with Bert to those Penn games and she'd say, 'This can't compare to the pros. They've got people like Jim Thorpe and Red Grange and Bronko Nagurski. You think this is good? You ought to see *them* play! Please get with it, Bert: The pros *throw* the football. The running game? Forget about it!'

"Bert was in heaven. How many other girls had ever *heard* of the Decatur Staleys or the Canton Bulldogs? How many foresaw the impact of the forward pass (which Bert himself had tried during his quarterbacking days)? All Frances's talk was getting him heated up, and suddenly he saw a way to lift himself out of his funk: He'd buy a professional football team, one of which just happened to be for sale at that very moment in Philadelphia—the Frankford Yellow Jackets," a colorful team that actually had a better overall record than the Green Bay Packers during the 1920s.

The Yellow Jackets, who were revered by residents of the Frankford neighborhood of northeast Philadelphia, had been granted a franchise in the two-year-old NFL in 1924. Five new clubs were admitted the following season. One of them, the Pottsville Maroons, had been the most successful independent semi-professional team in the Anthracite League, which was composed of teams from eastern Pennsylvania mining towns. Covering the Maroons for the Pottsville *Republican* was John O'Hara, who would later become a world-famous novelist.

Late in the 1925 season, the NFL gained instant national recognition. Shortly after the University of Illinois' season ended, All-America halfback Harold (Red) Grange, the first true football superstar, signed to play for the Chicago Bears. In December, the Bears began two barnstorming tours, the first of which saw them play eight games in 12 days in the Midwest and East. The second tour—nine games in six weeks—took the "Galloping Ghost" through the southern and western states.

"It was like a coast-to-coast ticker-tape parade," Dan Daly and Bob O'Donnell wrote in *The Pro Football Chronicle*. "Bands blaring, crowds cheering, cash registers ringing."

Grange was under contract to play a minimum of 25 minutes each game and rarely played more. In Philadelphia, the second stop on the first tour, 25,000 fans braved the rain and mud at Shibe Park to watch him lead the Bears to a 14–7 triumph over the Frankford Yellow Jackets. Grange scored both Chicago touchdowns.

Pottsville and the Chicago Cardinals were the top contenders for the NFL title that year, with Pottsville believing it had clinched the championship by winning a late-season showdown, 21–7, at Comiskey Park. Pottsville then scheduled a game against a team of former Notre Dame stars—including the legendary Four Horsemen—at Shibe Park. The Frankford Yellow Jackets immediately lodged a protest.

Not only was the game being played in Frankford's protected territory, but it was also scheduled at the same time as a Yellow Jackets home game. NFL Commissioner Joe Carr gave the Maroons three specific warnings not to play the game. But they played anyway, beating the Fighting Irish, 9–7, on a last-minute 30-yard field goal by Charlie Berry, who would later become umpire-in-chief of the American (Baseball) League.

Pottsville's team was immediately suspended, had the final game of its season against the Providence Steam Roller canceled, and had its franchise returned to the league. Not only that but Carr took Pottsville's league title away, even though the Maroons finished with a 10–2 record, recorded seven shutouts, and outscored their opponents, 270–45. In 1926, Pottsville was reinstated in the NFL. But after suffering through losing seasons for the next two years, the franchise was moved to Boston before the 1929 campaign.

Also in 1926, Red Grange's manager C. C. Pyle formed a new league, the American Football League because the Chicago Bears refused to meet his contract demands. The nine-team league—including Grange's New York Yankees and a team from Philadelphia called the Quakers—lasted one season. It folded after the Quakers won the AFL title and then lost to the New York Giants, the NFL's seventh best team, 31–0. It was the first professional interleague game on record and preceded the modern Super Bowl by four decades.

Bert Bell served as an informal coaching advisor for the Quakers. The team featured some of his former Penn teammates like Heinie Miller, Lou Little, and Lud Wray, who later played for the Yellow Jackets.

Bell also suited up to play in at least one game for the Quakers in his only known professional appearance. It came against Jim Thorpe and the Canton Bulldogs, according to Fats Henry, Thorpe's teammate, who was one of the legendary linemen of the early days of pro football.

"Philadelphia was pretty rugged," Henry told Arthur Daley of the *New York Times* years later. "But when our Indians got going for one supreme push, it was like cattle stampeding through the canebrake."

Meanwhile, late in the 1926 season, the Yellow Jackets scored in the last two minutes to beat the Chicago Bears, 7–6, at Shibe Park and move into first place in the NFL.

"The Bears were the Dallas Cowboys–type team of that period," recalled Matt Goukas many years later in a *Philadelphia Bulletin* interview with Michael D. Schaffer. "Beating them was a major feat." Goukas, who was the Yellow Jackets' 11-year-old water boy at the time, later starred for the Philadelphia Warriors of the National Basketball Association and served as the longtime public address announcer for the Philadelphia Eagles.

Playing to capacity crowds in a 9,000-seat stadium built on a converted horse track at Frankford Avenue and Devereaux Street, the Yellow Jackets outlasted 20 other teams and clinched the 1926 NFL title by battling third-place Pottsville to a scoreless tie in the final game of the season. A loss would have dropped Frankford into second place behind the Bears. Their 14–1–1 record was the best mark in the club's eight years of existence. It took 46 years before another NFL team—the Miami Dolphins—equaled that win total en route to an unbeaten season and a Super Bowl title.

Coached by Guy Chamberlin, the Yellow Jackets shut out 11 opponents in 1926. They blanked the Canton Bulldogs, with Jim Thorpe, 17–0. They beat Duluth, with Ernie Nevers, 10–0. They handed George Halas's Chicago Bears their only defeat of the season, 7–6. The Yellow Jackets "tackle like demons," said Halas afterward. Frankford's only loss, 7–6 to Providence, was avenged when they bounced back to shut out the Steam Roller twice, 6–0 and 24–0. Chamberlin was elected to the Pro Football Hall of Fame in 1965, the only member of the Yellow Jackets to be so honored.

The NFL in those days was a barnstorming circuit with haphazard schedules and rosters that were constantly changing. Some players wore baseball caps instead of helmets and used newspapers for hip pads. Teams frequently sprung up and disappeared in a matter of weeks. One team called the Los Angeles Buccaneers never played a game west of Kansas City. Joe Carr, the NFL commissioner, just liked the idea of having a team with a Los Angeles label because he thought it added a touch of glamour.

Because the Pennsylvania blue laws prohibited professional sports on Sundays, the Yellow Jackets were forced to play their home games on Saturdays. Other NFL teams preferred to play their home games on Sundays, so Frankford was frequently forced to hop on a train after Saturday's game, ride all night to Duluth or Milwaukee, and play back-to-back games.

Once, according to football historian Hugh Wyatt, the Yellow Jackets rode a train 12 hours to Buffalo only to learn upon arrival that the game had been canceled because of "wet grounds." Philadelphia sportswriters accompanying the team noted that the streets were dry and speculated that an earlier whipping given to the New York team by Frankford really prompted the cancellation. The writers also heard that the Buffalo players weren't even in town—they had all gone to see the World Series.

In 1930, the Yellow Jackets started running out of money and lost most of their key players. The Great Depression of October 1929 had taken its toll on many people in the area, especially those who lost their jobs in the textile mills in Frankford and Kensington. Their original stadium was damaged by a fire in 1929, and it would suffer the same fate again in 1931. It was vandalized several times afterward, leaving it in total disrepair. Frankford dropped all the way to ninth with a 4–13–1 record.

In 1931, Herb Joesting, the former Minnesota All-America considered by many to be the best player in Yellow Jacket history, was named head coach. The team moved most of its home games to the Phillies ballpark at Broad Street and Lehigh Avenue. But most of their supporters from Frankford stopped attending the games because of the economic situation as well as the distance to their new home field. Fans started calling them the *Philadelphia* Yellow Jackets.

Early in the 1931 season, the Yellow Jackets hosted the first professional night game in NFL history. Some 2,000 fans watched Brooklyn blank Frankford, 20–0, at Municipal Stadium. But midway through the season, with only one victory in eight games, the Yellow Jackets folded their franchise. Their final game was a 13–0 loss to the New York Giants at the Polo Grounds.

Although he wasn't officially active in football, Bell continued to circulate as one of the more familiar faces in the Quaker City. He was still going to the best parties, hanging with the right people, and for the most part, enjoying the good life. Hence it was no surprise that he would become involved in the search for Charles Augustus Lindbergh Jr. after the 20-month-old son of the world famous aviator was kidnapped on the night of March 1, 1932.

"A dozen people have told me this story," Bell's son Upton explained. "My father had an unbelievable number of contacts. Some people came to him and said, 'Bert, you know everybody. Can you find out if this is an underworld job?'" At the time, Al Capone was sitting in Cook County Jail in Chicago, appealing an 11-year sentence for tax evasion. "My father had someone get to Capone in prison and within 24 hours the word came back that the kidnapping was not an underworld job. They had no clue who could have committed the crime."

In 1933, with Frances Upton lending him the cash, Bell and Lud Wray called a truce to their stormy relationship and teamed up with four other prominent Philadelphians to purchase the Yellow Jackets. Two of the minority partners were Jack Potter, the son of former Phillies co-owner James Potter, and Fitz Eugene Dixon Sr. The partners paid $2,500 to the league as a guarantee in case the club folded. They also assumed $11,000 in debts owed by the Frankford franchise to the Chicago Bears, New York Giants, and Green Bay Packers.

On the day the sale became official, Bell was walking along Chestnut Street in Center City Philadelphia. As he reached the intersection of Broad Street, he looked up and saw a billboard promoting President Franklin D. Roosevelt's National Recovery Act The sign was emblazoned with the NRA's new symbol, a majestic bald eagle. Bert was suddenly inspired. He would call his new team the *Philadelphia Eagles*.

9. The Eagles Struggle
under Bell and Wray

Bert Bell's first move as co-owner of the Eagles was to convince his old friend Lud Wray to become the team's head coach. The two men had just recently patched up their personal and philosophical differences dating back to their coaching days at Penn. Wray had been fired after lasting only one season as the Quakers' head football coach in 1930 and Bell suddenly felt some compassion for his old gridiron comrade.

"Bell and Wray probably have fought more with and for each other than any two men in sports," *Philadelphia Bulletin* sports editor Ed Pollock wrote. "Like brothers, they have argued and belted each other around, but each with temper has turned on anyone else who dared voice an adverse opinion of the other. It was a case of 'I can say what I please about him, but you can't.' Seldom did a season pass without bitter argument or at least a wrestling bout or two or a series of them in fraternity houses or elsewhere."

In 1932, Bell had recommended Wray for the coaching job with the new NFL Boston Braves franchise. It was owned by a group of investors headed by one of Bell's Saratoga Racetrack cronies, George Preston Marshall, a flamboyant laundry operator from Washington, D.C. Wray guided the Braves to a 4–4–2 record that first season, but the team lost $46,000 and Marshall suddenly found himself not only as the club's sole owner but also as an owner without a coach when Wray jumped to the Eagles.

The NFL was only 13 years old when Bell and Wray came into the league. Just as the Depression had ruined the Frankford Yellow Jackets, the economic downturn created havoc throughout professional football. In 1926, there were 26 teams in the NFL. By 1929, the number had been whittled down to 12, and when the Eagles joined, there were only nine other franchises with the ninth being Pittsburgh, thanks to a little arm-twisting by Bell.

The new Eagles owner convinced one of his racetrack buddies from Saratoga, a 32-year-old former semipro football player from Pittsburgh named Art Rooney, to buy into the league for $2,500 as a personal favor.

"But if I'd resisted Bell's suggestion just a little," Rooney later told Phil Elderkin of the *Christian Science Monitor,* "I think I could have gotten it for nothing." The Eagles and Pirates were admitted into the NFL on the same day—July 8, 1933. Bell and Rooney would go on to become the closest of lifelong friends.

Marshall chuckled when he heard how Bell persuaded Rooney to join the NFL, because he had done exactly the same thing. "I remember visiting Bert Bell in Atlantic City after we reorganized the league," Marshall later explained to the *Bulletin*'s Hugh Brown. "I asked him to join up with us. He said to me, 'You're wasting your time. This league will never amount to anything. You can't make a go of it.' The next year he was in the league himself."

Philadelphia's application for a franchise was filed by Wray, "heading a group of prominent Philadelphia citizens," according to the minutes of the league's annual meeting that day at the Blackstone Hotel in Chicago. Wray was accompanied by a fellow member of the syndicate organized by Bell, Jack Potter.

Even though he was officially the club's president, Bert, surprisingly, did not attend this meeting or the following one in December. He made his first appearance on June 30, 1934, at the Commodore Hotel in New York City, at which time he was recognized by league president Joseph F. Carr, who called on him for a few remarks which were "well received," according to the minutes.

The motion to admit the Eagles was made by New York Giants owner Jack Mara and seconded by L. H. Joannes, president of the Green Bay Packers. The new franchise was ordered to settle liens against the Frankford Athletic Association on the basis of 25 percent of the amount due, held in the sums of $5,000 by the New York Giants and $3,000 by the Chicago Bears and Packers, with these clubs reserving the right to press for collection of the entire amount.

The entire face of the league was changing dramatically. George Halas had taken over the Decatur Staleys and moved them 100 miles up the road to Chicago as the Bears in 1922. The Portsmouth (Ohio) Spartans were moved to Detroit and renamed the Lions in 1934. Marshall changed the name of his Braves to the Redskins in 1933 and moved the team to Washington four years later. The Pittsburgh Pirates became the Steelers in 1940.

Marshall, who "set new NFL standards for flamboyance and irascibility," according to *Total Football: The Official Encyclopedia of the National Football League*, "was a giant in the NFL meetings, though his fellow owners often paid a fearful price when his arrogant independence disrupted meetings and caused great bouts of consternation."

In 1933, with the backing of his longtime fierce rival George Halas, Marshall convinced league owners to split their teams into two divisions with the two winners meeting annually in the NFL Championship Game. The Eagles were put into the Eastern Division along with the Brooklyn Dodgers, New York Giants, Boston, and Pittsburgh. The Western Division was comprised of the Chicago Bears and Chicago Cardinals, Green Bay Packers, Cincinnati Reds, and Portsmouth.

Bell hoped to play Eagles home games during the 1933 season at Shibe Park, the home field of the Philadelphia Athletics, the American League baseball team, located at 21st Street and Lehigh Avenue. But when Bert sent Wray to discuss a deal with John D. Shibe, the A's owner said that the Eagles would have to negotiate with Lou Schwartz, a member of the State Legislature from Philadelphia who had no official connection with the Athletics. Schwartz, at the time, was one of the sponsors of a statewide referendum to liberalize the tough blue laws and permit professional baseball and football on Sundays—a measure that would be approved by the voters later that season, in November.

Bell grew impatient over the runaround. Instead of prolonging negotiations with Schwartz, he worked out a deal with Gerry Nugent, the owner of the city's National League baseball team, the Phillies, to use the Baker Bowl, a run-down stadium located a few blocks away from Shibe Park at Broad Street and Lehigh Avenue. Nicknamed "the Hump" because it was on a hill that had a Reading Railroad tunnel running underneath the outfield, the Baker Bowl had a capacity of only 18,500. This was considerably fewer than Shibe Park could hold, which was more than 33,000 fans.

As part of the deal, Nugent agreed to Bell's request to erect about 5,000 temporary bleachers along the right field wall, parallel to 20th Street, to increase the stadium's capacity for football. According to Bruce Kuklick, author of *To Every Thing A Season*, these uncovered east stands were 20 feet high and had 22 rows of seats. "The goalposts stood along the first base line and in left field." There was no official agreement signed, just an understanding that the Eagles would pay a percentage of the gate and have use of the park for football as needed.

Bell and Wray welcomed 40 candidates to their first training camp in Atlantic City. They unveiled their new team at the Baker Bowl on October 4, 1933, in a preseason game played under rented portable floodlights before a crowd estimated at 3,000. The Eagles defeated a U.S. Marine team—coached by their former Penn mentor Louis Young—40–0, but the conditions were less than satisfactory. The portable lights were powered by a generator and strung up on poles. Players had no trouble keeping track of plays at ground level, but punts and forward passes broke through the lights into darkness overhead. Receivers had to guess where the ball would return into light. It was almost impossible to make a diving or running catch.

After finishing the exhibition season with a perfect 5–0 record, the Eagles were demolished by the New York Giants, 56–0, in their official NFL debut. The first regular-season home game was played three days later under the lights at the Baker Bowl on October 18. But only 1,750 people turned out to watch the Portsmouth Spartans walk away with a 25–0 victory.

By the time the Eagles embarked on their first road trip to Green Bay and Cincinnati, Bell was broke. "It was way before my time," recalled Art Daley, who covered the NFL for more than 30 years for the *Green Bay Press Gazette*. "I was told that the Packers put him and the team up in a hotel for a whole week. They took care of meals, everything. It didn't cost him a cent."

Later that season Bell obtained what he considered "one of his proudest possessions," the first license ever issued in the Commonwealth of Pennsylvania granting permission to play a game on Sunday. It happened on November 12, 1933, five days after Governor Gifford Pinchot signed the bill granting professional sports teams (with the exception of basketball and ice hockey) permission to play on Sundays, thus repealing some of the blue laws that dated back to 1794 and restricted "any worldly employment or business" on the Sabbath.

Bell and his colleagues had lobbied extensively for the right to play home games on Sundays. Finally the matter was put to a referendum on November 7, 1933. Philadelphia voters overwhelmingly approved abolishing that part of the blue laws by almost 371,000 votes out of approximately 428,500 cast. Philadelphia Mayor J. Hampton Moore quickly put his signature on the city council ordinance granting permission for games to be played on Sundays for license fees ranging from $1 (for crowds of fewer than 1,000) to $50 (where capacity was 5,000 or more).

A short time after the mayor signed the ordinance, Bell arrived at City Hall with Cornelius Haggerty, the Eagles' attorney. Haggerty produced the required affidavit, setting forth that the game was to be played at the Phillies' Ball Park, giving the seating capacity, the hour, and other information to accompany the formal application.

Acting superintendent of police Joseph A. LeStrange then dictated the following permit, which was written on the stationery of the Department of Public Safety. It was signed by LeStrange and approved by acting director of public safety Theodore F. Wood:

Permit No. 1—Permission is hereby granted to Mr. DeBenneville [*sic*] Bell to conduct a foot ball game at the Philadelphia National League Base Ball Park, Broad and Huntingdon sts., between the Chicago Bears, Inc., and the Philadelphia Foot Ball Club, otherwise known as the Philadelphia Eagles, on Sunday November 12, between 2:00 and 6:00 P.M.

The Eagles, who had dropped three of their first four games by a combined 116–9 margin, held the mighty Chicago Bears, the defending NFL champions, to a 3–3 tie before 17,850 fans.

The Bears, led by Red Grange and Bronko Nagurski, took a 3–0 lead midway through the second quarter when Jack Manders converted from the 20-yard line "from an oblique angle with a host of Eagles charging in on him like angry bees," according to Stan Baumgartner of the *Philadelphia Inquirer*. Philadelphia's Guy Turnbow connected from the 18-yard line to tie the game in the opening seconds of the final quarter, setting off a wild celebration led by Philadelphia A's catcher Mickey Cochrane, the future Baseball Hall of Famer. "Mickey forgot all his dignity as he tossed his hat in the air, jumped from seat to seat, and cheered," Baumgartner reported.

The Eagles defeated the Pittsburgh Pirates, 25–6, the following Sunday for their first victory ever at the Baker Bowl, before an estimated crowd of 7,500. The Birds won again at home on November 26, this time over the Cincinnati Reds, 20–3. Swede Hanson, "the lantern-jawed, lank-limbed will o' the wisp of the professional gridiron," according to Baumgartner, set up two Eagles touchdowns with his brilliant running. The victory climaxed a four-game unbeaten stretch in what would turn out to be the most successful month in the club's first decade of existence.

The Eagles finished the 1933 season with a 3–5–1 record, good for fourth place in the Eastern Division. Actually, they should have played one more game, but Bell told his players not to suit up for a scheduled contest against the Boston Redskins because it was raining heavily and only a few fans were in the stands. Lone Star Dietz, Boston's coach, wouldn't take no for an answer, however, and ordered his team to take the field. "The Redskins are ready for the kickoff," he told Bell. "Well, then, kick off to them," Bert snapped. "I'm going home!"

"It took a long time, but Bell finally came up with the money to pay the Redskins' salaries for a game they didn't play," Boston owner George Preston Marshall later told Francis Stann of the *Washington Post*.

In 1934, the Eagles tied for third place with a 4–7 mark. The season was highlighted by the most explosive performance in the club's history.

On November 6, Bell arranged for the Birds to play the first of two home games at Temple Stadium, a 20,443-capacity facility located in northwest Philadelphia near the Montgomery County border. Only 2,000 fans turned out to watch the Eagles demolish the winless Cincinnati Reds, 64–0, in a game that still stands as the worst regular-season defeat by any team in NFL history and the highest single game point total ever for the Eagles. The Reds were disbanded after the game, leaving the league with nine teams.

Philadelphia's last win at the Baker Bowl occurred on December 3 when they blanked the New York Giants, 6–0, before 12,471 fans.

With their team struggling at the gate and losing money fast, Bell and Wray needed some kind of a gimmick to get the fans excited. Then they discovered Edwin (Alabama) Pitts in, of all places, Sing Sing Prison in upstate New York. Pitts, a navy veteran, had been convicted with three accomplices of robbing a grocery store in New York. Their haul was only $78.25, but they were sentenced to serve from eight to 15 years. Even though he had never played organized sports, Pitts turned out to be the best athlete on Sing Sing's baseball and football teams. After five years, he was eligible for parole. He signed a professional baseball contract with the Triple-A Albany Senators only to wash out by hitting .233 and committing eight errors in 43 games.

The Eagles quickly jumped in and outbid two other NFL franchises, Brooklyn and Pittsburgh, for his services. When they signed him to a four-game, $1,500 contract as a running back in September 1935, his photograph in his Eagles number 50 jersey appeared in every newspaper in the country. Pitts also had a ready excuse for his poor performance in the minor leagues—the frequent night games. "You see, where I was, we didn't get out much at nights," Alabama explained. "If any did, it wasn't to play ball."

On September 13, some 20,000 fans jammed Temple Stadium. Most of them weren't there for opening-day festivities. They came to see the debut of Alabama Pitts. Not only were they disappointed by Pittsburgh's 17–7 upset victory; Wray never put Pitts in the game, even though the largest crowd in the Eagles' three-year history constantly chanted, "We want Pitts!" He did play briefly in the next two games and finally got to handle the ball during a 39–0 loss to the Chicago Bears when he caught two passes for 21 yards with one of his receptions—an 18-yarder—being the longest Eagles advance of the day.

Wray was so upset by the Eagles' lackadaisical play early in that game, he stormed into the locker room at halftime, gazed at his players, and screamed "Dogmeat!" before stalking out. "The second half started and Alabama Pitts did not appear on the field," sportswriter Red Smith recalled. "Bell rushed into the locker room, found Sing Sing's most famous alumnus glowering at the floor. 'Edwin,' the president said, 'what was the trouble?' 'He called me "Dogmeat,"'" the ex-con said. 'I don't take that from nobody.'"

Pitts's original contract caused resentment among some of his teammates, who were being paid only between $100 and $150 a game. "Pitts has a bright future," Bell said. "And we appreciate that he tries all the time and eventually should be a top-flight player. But he lacks experience and needs a lot of work."

When time came for a new contract, Bell offered Alabama a deal for considerably less money—$50 a game. Pitts rejected the offer. He knocked around minor league baseball for the next five years and went to work for a knitting mill in North Carolina. He was stabbed to death in a fight in a dance hall there in 1941 at the age of 33.

Bell suffered another indignity during that 39–0 loss to Chicago when a Bears end named Luke Johnsos tricked Edgar (Eggs) Manske, one of his former teammates who had been traded to the Eagles, into lateraling the ball to him.

"Manske caught a long forward pass and was in the clear except for the safety man who had a clear shot at him," recalled Arthur Daley of the *New York Times*. "Leading the vain pursuit was Johnsos and he never got better than a step behind his ex-teammate. But as the safety-man braced himself for the tackle, Johnsos yelled, 'Lateral to me, Eggs!' Obediently, Manske, of the Eagles, threw a perfect lateral pass to Johnsos, of the Bears, who gleefully collared the ball, wheeled and headed for the other goal line, 60 yards away. No one was near him in his downfield touchdown journey except for Bell. Racing down the sidelines right alongside Johnsos, the irate Eagles coach berated and showered him with abuse until his wind and legs gave out."

Bell and Wray learned quickly how difficult it was to sell professional football in the early days, especially because the Eagles would go on to win only three of 15 games they played in the Baker Bowl between 1933 and 1935. As inducements, fans were given a free car wash if they purchased a ticket to a game. Children were admitted for one cent when accompanied by an adult.

Aside from the game introducing Alabama Pitts at Temple Stadium, the Eagles' largest crowds were 18,000 for the final contest of the 1933 campaign, a 20–14 defeat by the New York Giants, and 17,850 who watched the fabled tie with the Chicago Bears that season. Attendance, when it was made public, was usually announced at between 4,000 and 9,000. Gate receipts were embarrassingly low. The game against Cincinnati at the Baker Bowl in 1933, in fact, generated only $150 in revenue.

"Bert was so desperate to win a game, he even tried divine intervention, his son Upton recalled in *Philadelphia* magazine. "He announced that each Sunday, a different clergyman would be sitting on the Eagles' bench: one week a priest, a Presbyterian the next, then a rabbi, then a black Baptist. All the denominations would be represented in turn, so the Eagles would have an across-the-board shot to win favor from the Almighty. When that didn't help, one Sunday he put all four of them on the bench at the same time."

The Eagles were playing the Chicago Bears that day in 1935 and getting slaughtered, 39–0. After the game, George Halas, the Bears' owner, shook his head and said, "Bert, the only thing you haven't done is hire a good football team. Have you thought about trying that?"

One Sunday the Eagles were playing a game at the Baker Bowl at the same time Connie Mack's Philadelphia Athletics were playing a doubleheader against the New York Yankees virtually up the street at Shibe Park.

"Everybody was going to the ball game and I was getting desperate," Bell later told sportswriter Harold Weissman of the *New York Mirror*. "Then I noticed the sky beginning to cloud up. So I gave a guy five bucks, handed him a megaphone, and sent him over to the ball park and had him yell into the traffic lines, 'No game today. Rain!' It might have helped get a few customers into the football game."

After going 0–5 at the Baker Bowl and winning only two of 11 games in 1935, Bell decided that a change in scenery was necessary. He immediately began looking for a new home field for the following season—a year that would have lasting impact not only on Bell and his Eagles, but on the entire NFL.

It had less to do with the Eagles' new home and everything to do with Bert's historic suggestion.

10. The Player Draft Comes in 1936

The idea for a player draft was actually triggered by an incident that occurred in 1933. That's when Bert Bell telephoned Stanley Kostka, an outstanding Minnesota fullback and linebacker, at his home in Minneapolis.

"I asked him point blank if he would sign with the Eagles if I came out there and offered him a contract for more money than anyone else in the league would give him," Bell told the Associated Press years later. "He said yes. So in the situation, I went to Minneapolis. We met in a hotel. I asked him how much he had been offered by other clubs. He told me the top was $3,500. I'll give you $4,000, I told him. But Kostka hemmed and hawed, said he had to think it over, give my offer more serious consideration. I told him to take an hour to make up his mind. Actually in the situation, I knew what was in his mind. He wanted to get to a telephone and call the club (Brooklyn) which had offered him $3,500 to see if they'd top my offer. Apparently, he couldn't make the connection because when he came back, he still hadn't made up his mind. I told him, look, I'll give you $6,000 if you'll sign now and let me go home. He hedged. So I left."

Bell said that he thought about the Kostka situation all the way home. (Kostka eventually played one season for Brooklyn.) "I made up my mind that this league would never survive unless we had some system whereby each team had an even chance to bid for talent against the other," Bell explained to the AP.

In the years before the draft and for almost a decade afterward, four teams—the Bears, Giants, Packers, and Redskins—dominated the NFL. They were the only teams drawing respectable crowds and making money. Every other franchise was awash in red ink and some were on the verge of going out of business. Between 1933 and 1946, the Giants, Bears, and Packers won the title nine times among them. Between 1932 and 1943, George Halas guided the Bears to four league championships and seven appearances in the title game.

Meanwhile, Bell's Eagles were getting killed. After finishing 2–9 in 1935 and taking over as head coach to cut expenses, Bell set out to convince his fellow owners that only an equitable player draft could save the league from going out of business.

Finally after some vigorous politicking and arm-twisting, Bell introduced his unique proposal at the league meetings at the Fort Pitt Hotel in Pittsburgh on May 18, 1935. He was, wrote columnist Arthur Daley in the *New York Times,* "probably the only man who then had sublime faith in the draft as the salvation of pro football."

At the meeting, Bell addressed the other eight club owners. "Gentlemen," he said, "I've always had the theory that pro football is like a chain. The league is no stronger than its weakest link and I've been a weak link for so long that I should know. Every year, the rich get richer and the poor get poorer. Four teams control the championships, the Giants and Redskins in the East, the Bears and Packers in the West. Because they are successful, they keep attracting the best college players in the open market—which makes them more successful.

"Here's what I propose. At the end of every college football season, I suggest that we pool the names of all eligible seniors. Then we make our selections in inverse order of the standings, with the lowest team picking first until we reach the top-ranking team, which picks last. We do this for round after round until we've exhausted the supply."

Some club owners, especially Halas, still weren't convinced.

"At a distance," wrote Bob Carroll of the Professional Football Researchers Association, the Chicago Bears owner "seems to have been almost schizophrenic about the draft. While having only one team bid for the services of a player was a good way to keep salaries under control, an idea that Halas could embrace wholeheartedly, the ultimate result—if all went according to the script—would eventually be to cycle chronic losers like Bell's Eagles to the top of the standings and push annual winners like Halas's Bears to the bottom. Asking Papa Bear to willingly put his team at a disadvantage was like asking Patton to give up his tanks. And nothing was likely to get done in the NFL in those days unless Halas agreed to it."

But Halas finally did agree because, as Carroll said, "No one was more a booster of the league, and few more farsighted than Halas. Bell came up with the idea, but Halas let it happen. Possibly, he simply knew that the draft idea was good for the league and any idea good for the NFL would be good for the Bears in the long run."

Later, in his memoir, Halas wrote: "I thought the proposal sound. It made sense."

Bell's suggestion elicited a long, contentious debate. But when Halas finally convinced Tim Mara, the New York Giants' owner, that the league would benefit, Bert's revolutionary proposal was adopted unanimously to become effective for the 1936 season.

Here are the official minutes of that historic NFL meeting pertaining to the draft:

SUNDAY, MAY 18, 1935 at the Fort Pitt Hotel, in Pittsburgh: Motion by Bell, seconded by Marshall, that the following rule relative to the selection of players entering the National League for the first time become operative beginning with the season of 1936:

(1) At the annual meeting in February and each succeeding year thereafter, a list of first year eligible players to be presented by each club and their names placed upon a board in the meeting room for selection by the various clubs. The priority of selection by each club shall follow the reverse order of the championship standings of the clubs at the close of the preceding season; for instance, the club which finished last in either division to be determined by percentage rating shall have first choice; the club which finished next to last, second choice, and this inverse order shall be followed until each club has had one selection or has declined to select a player; after which the selection shall continue as indicated above until all players whose names appear on the board have been selected or rejected.

(2) Any first year player who was not so chosen or whose name does not appear on the list referred to above is eligible to sign with any club in the league.

(3) If for any valid reason it would be impossible for a player to play in the city by which he has been selected, or the player can show reasonable cause why he should be permitted to play in a city other than that designated for him than through such arrangements as can be made by sale or trade with another club, he shall be permitted to play in the city he prefers if the president of the league approves his reasons as valid. (The fact that a job is to be secured for a player in any city as an added incentive to sign a contract shall not be considered sufficient reason for his transfer from the club by which he has originally been selected.)

(4) In the event of controversy between a selected player and a club, the matter shall be referred to the president and his decision shall be accepted by all parties as final.

(5) In the event a player is selected by a club and fails to sign a contract or report, he shall be placed on a Reserve List of the club by which he was selected.

(ALL CARRIED UNANIMOUSLY)

"League meetings in those days weren't exactly the formal affairs they've become in more recent times," Upton Bell recalled. "They were usually held in some hotel room, where the owners sat and argued with each other all night long. Whoever could drink most, shout loudest, and stay up longest usually got his way. Those rules of order gave Bert a big advantage. He was a natural night person, and he hadn't touched a drop since that night in Atlantic City. By early morning, when only a couple of others were still fully conscious, he could almost always get his motions passed. That's how the draft idea got through."

Joe Carr, the president of the NFL, praised the decision of the owners. "As a result of this rotation of negotiation rights," he explained, "every city in the league will be sure of seeing some of the college stars of the preceding season, and will prevent *promiscuous scrambling* for one or two players which disrupted the players so sought." Carr added that a club would be permitted to trade its negotiation rights to another team if it was unable to come to an agreement with a draft choice.

The first NFL draft was held on Saturday and Sunday, February 8 and 9, 1936, at the Ritz Carlton, the Philadelphia hotel on South Broad Street owned by Bert Bell's dad.

"Franchise owners crowded into Bert Bell's hotel room, shucked their jackets, and cleared sitting room on beds and bureaus," wrote Robert Lipsyte in the *New York Times.* "Bottles circulated, solemn oaths of league solidarity were taken, and the college stars were distributed."

Surprisingly, not a word about the draft appeared in the three major Philadelphia newspapers—the *Bulletin, Inquirer,* and *Record*—on Saturday or Sunday. The *Bulletin* ran five paragraphs about the topic on Monday without mentioning any details about the players selected.

The *Inquirer* ran a piece by Stan Baumgartner on Saturday detailing a proposal to be submitted to league owners by Bell and Wray requesting permission for the Eagles and one other NFL team to make a world tour at the end of the 1936 season. The jaunt, lasting from three to six months, would extend from Hawaii to Australia, Italy, France, Germany, and Great Britain. Baumgartner predicted that the proposal "is expected to be the highlight of what will be a quiet love fest among the magnates." However, there is no indication from the official minutes that the proposal was ever introduced or discussed, and the trip never happened.

According to the official minutes of the meeting that was convened at 1:30 P.M. on Saturday, the names of approximately 90 players were placed on a blackboard and the selection of players by each club proceeded with the inverse order of the standings of the close of the season of 1935. At the conclusion of the selection of five players by each club, a motion by Bell, seconded by Marshall, that the selection be extended to permit each club to select nine players was carried unanimously. Each club in their respective turn selected an additional four players. The complete list of selections was mailed to each club on February 14, 1936.

Five days later, on February 19, Bert Bell and Frances Upton welcomed their first child into the world when John Bert was born at Presbyterian Hospital in Philadelphia.

The player-evaluation process was quite primitive in those days. Teams just didn't have the time, money, or manpower to prepare for the first draft. "We used to go down to the train station on Saturday night and buy the out-of-town newspapers to read about the college games," Pittsburgh Pirates owner Art Rooney explained to Bob Barnett of the Professional Football Researchers Association. "We also looked in the press books of various schools, read magazines and All American lists. I spent a lot of time going out to local colleges and looking at players, and I had some very good friends in the coaching ranks who would talk to me about players they knew about or played against. It wasn't as complicated as it is today."

The Eagles, who finished in last place in 1935 with a 2–9 won-lost record, barely nosed out the Boston Redskins (2–8–1) for the first pick. Bell quickly selected the first Downtown Athletic Trophy–winner (later changed to the Heisman Trophy in 1936), Jay Berwanger, the nation's outstanding college player from the University of Chicago.

"That move came as a surprise to everyone because Berwanger was reportedly asking for an exorbitant contract of $1,000 a game and everyone knew Bell didn't have that kind of money," recalled Barnett. Bell never thought to even ask Berwanger if he were interested in a career in pro football. Before the end of the day, after his offer of $150 a game was declined, Bell traded the rights to the All-America halfback to his hometown Bears for Michigan tackle Art Buss, a two-year veteran who played the next two seasons for the Eagles.

Francis J. Powers and Ed Prell claimed in a 1948 *Sport* magazine article that the deal for Berwanger's draft rights had actually been arranged earlier because Halas knew that Bell needed players badly. He also knew that the last-place Eagles would have the number-one draft pick. "So George slipped him a couple of athletes with the stipulation that Bell draft Chicago's Jay Berwanger for the 1936 season, then transfer him to the Bears."

The nine NFL teams each selected nine players including Alabama end Paul "Bear" Bryant, who went to the Brooklyn Dodgers in the fourth round. But the future coaching great never signed. In fact, a vast majority of the 81 players drafted decided against signing pro contracts, primarily because of the low salaries. Wally Fromhart, Green Bay's seventh-round pick from Notre Dame, was offered $125 a game but didn't even try out because Mt. Carmel High School in Chicago offered him much more money to coach. When the 1936 regular season started, only 24 of the 81 players selected were on NFL rosters.

Berwanger didn't sign with the Bears, either, but he wasn't the only talented collegian to forgo the pros. Gerald R. Ford, a promising Michigan center, had declined offers from the Green Bay Packers and Detroit Lions in 1934 and decided to attend Yale Law School instead.

According to Barnett, the Boston-Washington Redskins got the most immediate help from the first draft, going from next-to-last place in the league in 1935 to the Eastern Division championship the following season. Marshall signed four draft picks including his number-one choice, blocking back/linebacker Riley Smith of Alabama, and seven free-agent rookies. The new players enabled the Redskins to win five more games in 1936 than in the previous season—quite a feat over a short 12-game season.

Barnett said that the "booby prize" in the 1936 draft went to the Eagles. Unable to sign any of his other eight picks, Bell brought in 12 free-agent rookies including five local Philadelphia college standouts. It didn't work. The Eagles beat the New York Giants, 10–7, in their home opener, then lost 11 straight games.

In 1937 when each team was permitted to select one additional player, Bell was again unable to sign his number-one draft choice. To make matters worse, he was forced to trade that pick, Sam Francis, a multipurpose offensive and defensive back and Olympic shot-putter from Nebraska, to the dreaded Bears in a move that turned out to be a blessing in disguise. To obtain Francis's rights, Halas gave up his star end, Bill Hewitt, and $4,000 in cash. Although Bell didn't sign any of his number-one draft choices until 1939 when he hit the jackpot with Texas Christian University quarterback Davey O'Brien, he did have his first future Pro Football Hall-of-Famer.

There was no doubt that the new, unique player selection process was going to have a life-saving effect on pro football—and eventually be adopted by every other major professional sport.

"The draft was the greatest thing that ever happened to the NFL," Bell said in 1957. "Over the years, it has brought balance to the league," he added, emphasizing that it took ten years for the concept of selecting players this way to equalize the talent.

One of its top proponents turned out to be Halas himself, who was still singing its praises 30 years later. "The National Football League college draft has been the backbone of the sport and is the primary reason it has developed to the game it is today," he testified at an antitrust suit hearing in Washington, D.C., in 1976.

A few months before Bell's death, Arthur Daley called Bert "a brilliant commissioner" and observed: "The draft is Bert's monument and this is the proper time to cast a bow in the direction of this extraordinary man with such unusual credentials." The draft "is the key to the continuous success of the NFL. That's why none should ever forget the far-seeing man responsible for it."

Mark Yost said in his 2006 book *Tailgating, Sacks and Salary Caps: How the NFL Became the Most Successful Sports League in History* that Bell's idea for the draft "in fact, has turned out to be the single greatest contributor to the NFL's prosperity over the past 84 years."

11. Additional Shock Waves
from 1936

Early in the spring of 1936, after the Eagles had absorbed losses of more than $90,000, the club was offered for sale at a public auction held at the Samuel T. Freeman and Company on Chestnut Street in Center City Philadelphia. Bert Bell made the only bid—$4,500. Suddenly he was the sole owner.

A few days later, on April 28, Bell and Lud Wray went their separate ways—again. After a noontime meeting of stockholders, the club announced in a statement that Wray refused to accept the 66 percent reduction in salary offered to him to continue the next campaign in the role of coach and business manager. The stockholders then voted to turn the dual role over to Bell, who had previously been reelected president of the corporation. Bert immediately appointed John "Ox" Da Grosa, the former line coach at Georgetown and Temple, as his assistant coach.

"The spring house cleaning proved a popular move with all football enthusiasts and gridiron fans in this vicinity," wrote Stan Baumgartner in the *Philadelphia Inquirer.* "Bell as backfield coach at Temple and Pennsylvania proved himself one of the most capable strategists in the country. He also was very popular with his men—a trait that should carry him a long way in the professional end of the game."

Wray was visibly angry at Bell for not fighting harder to save his job. "It is with regret that I am forced to sever my connections with the Eagles," he said. "I had great hopes for the future of professional football in Philadelphia, even though the first few years were rocky. Recently, I had raised $20,000 to aid the club treasury. It is a wonderful game, and I may associate myself with another club in the National Football League or take a coaching job with a college."

For many months Wray and Bell were separated with a frigid silence between them, *Philadelphia Bulletin* sports editor Ed Pollock recalled. Then Wray was involved in a near-fatal automobile accident and remained in a coma for days. Worried about his friend's condition, Bell stayed in touch with Wray's physician, Dr. John McCloskey, another former football star at the University of Pennsylvania.

"How is Lud? Is there anything I can do?" Bert would ask anxiously. Shortly afterward, McCloskey called Bell. "Bert," he said, "I think Lud needs something to stir him out of this. He shows no interest. He opens his eyes, sees who's in the room and either doesn't recognize anyone or isn't interested. I have a hunch he wants to see you. Come up."

Bell immediately went to the hospital. He was determined to snap Wray out of it, but he was frightened speechless when he saw his friend in such a stupor. "After a while, Lud opened his eyes, stared, and for the first time registered interest," Pollock wrote. "Then his lips moved and his voice wasn't too weak. He said: 'Where the hell have you been?' Dr. John laughed. Lud had started to recover."

On June 3, Bell announced that the Eagles would play all of their six home games at a new home field, the cavernous 102,000-capacity Municipal Stadium in South Philadelphia. Two of the games would be against the Chicago Bears, a perennial fan-favorite, and all of the home contests would be played in the afternoon.

"Only in the event of inclement weather will the Eagles play any of their home games as nocturnal affairs," announced the *Bulletin*. "Municipal Stadium has a lighting system recognized as one of the best in the country so that any necessary postponements will hold no fears for the local club officials."

Now the club's sole owner and also its coach, trainer, scout, business manager, janitor, publicist, and ticket seller, Bell would have one brief moment of glory. It happened on September 13, 1936, at the Eagles' opener on their new home field.

"Electrifying 20,000 hysterical fans with one of the greatest upsets ever achieved in professional football, Bert Bell's Eagles defeated the famed New York Giants at the Municipal Stadium by the score of 10–7," Baumgartner proclaimed.

Hank Reese won the game with a field goal late in the fourth quarter, but the big play occurred early in the game when Joe Carter scored the Eagles' only touchdown on a 20-yard lateral from Eggs Manske, a second-year end from Northwestern. The winning play actually began when Dave Smukler, standing on his own 48-yard line, hit Manske with a 34-yard-pass.

"As the Giants closed in about him like giant claws, there did not seem an avenue of escape," Baumgartner reported. "But quick as a flash, Manske made a complete pivot, left his foes riveted to the ground, and shot toward the sidelines. By this time, other Giant tacklers thundered in upon him. Again, he seemed at the end of the trail. But with a lightning-like stroke of genius, the blond spiraled a lateral pass to Joe Carter, captain and end 20 yards away. Carter snuggled the pigskin to his jersey on the dead run and raced over the goal line unmolested.

"In conquering the New Yorkers," Baumgartner continued, "the Bellmen showed power, versatility, and defensive strength that opened the eyes of the many football critics who were in the throng. Even Pop Warner glowed with pride as he watched Dave Smukler play one of the finest games of his career, and when the former Owl ace left the game late in the fourth period, Pop was delighted to join in the applause that cannonaded through the stadium."

After that, it was all downhill for the rookie head coach and his Birds. The October 25 rematch with the Giants at the Polo Grounds was particularly ugly. Field judge George Vergara needed a police escort to escape an angry group of Eagles players after the Birds dropped a 21–17 heartbreaker to the New Yorkers. Vergara's controversial pass interference call late in the game led to the winning touchdown.

"By this time the Eagles were frothing at the mouth," reported Arthur J. Daley in the *New York Times*. "As soon as the game was over, they descended in a body on the one-time Notre Dame end. Vince Zizak took a preliminary swing and he was soon joined by Eagles and spectators (estimated by the *Inquirer* as 1,000 fans). Vergara had his tie pulled, his shirt torn, and his hair mussed before finally escaping to the safety of the clubhouse, a policeman escorting him there."

Late in that disastrous 1–11 season, the worst in franchise history, Bell had seen enough. It wasn't only the ugly losses—at one point his Eagles were shut out by a combined score of 75–0 in four consecutive defeats by the Chicago Bears, Brooklyn, Detroit, and Pittsburgh—but crowds were slim, money was short, and the franchise appeared to be falling apart at the seams.

Not even Bronko Nagurski's encouraging words could mollify the Eagles' owner. When Bert went out on the field to tend to an injured player during a 17–0 loss to Chicago, the Bears' future Hall-of-Famer walked over to him and said, "Bert, your club is coming along in great shape. I hope they don't get any tougher than they are now."

Worst of all, though, Bell felt personally betrayed by the very forces that had carried him to modest success so far on the gridiron. As the *Bulletin*'s Cy Peterman put it on November 3, 1936, "Bert just got a bellyful of trying to make a team out of the highly-publicized hotshots from well-known eastern colleges."

"The eastern football player, compared to the hungry type from the west or south, is an overfed, easy-going, conceited individual who can't play as well as his provincial rival, and won't even try to learn," Bell complained to Peterman. "I know this because I have several on my payroll and have for ten weeks been trying to pound some ideas of the game in their domes. I have come to this conclusion further after watching a good many of the better eastern college teams in action, and seeing none that measured up to what I'd call a great team. There are only two squads worth a second thought along the Atlantic seaboard. Fordham is a good team, Pittsburgh the other."

Much of the problem, Bell explained, concerned just too much publicity.

"The excessive headlines and praise heaped upon mediocre football players of the east was one of the main causes of their ineptitude," he added. "For these breed conceit, foster a spirit of 'I'm good enough and don't have to work.' The average eastern grid hero plays on Saturday, spends Sunday reading how good he was, takes Monday off to watch himself in the movies, loafs Tuesday or takes a ride in his car before attending a squad meeting, spends Wednesday wondering what they'll say about him Saturday night, gets another blackboard session, and on Thursday grudgingly goes out to practice a little for Saturday's game. Friday he rests up for the ordeal of additional applause."

Bell wasn't finished.

"This sort of thing not only makes him a *softie* who would have to collapse if he had to play 60 full minutes in midwestern or coast competition, but ruins the boy's attitude for the future. For this heroic figure is often drawing down a pretty fair return for his footballing. He is on a scholarship, getting an education for one thing. That is, he has the opportunity to get the education if he's not too lazy. Secondly, he more than likely is getting his board and room and possibly a little besides. At any rate, he goes through four years of college that costs less fortunate fellows a hard struggle and their parents a goodly sum. The result is that he comes out without any appreciation of the value of cold cash.

"How do I know this? It's easy. I run a professional football club. Let me cite you an example of what I consider a lack of good sense. We have on our squad a young man who got about as much praise for his college football deeds as anybody could and be anything less than deified. He had, to all appearances, what it took to be a star in the pro game. All but sense and appreciation, as I discovered. This individual was not only hired by the Eagles and given every opportunity to improve his earnings, but was also placed in a local brokerage office where as an employee near the chief, he could have learned the game from the inside, gained a start toward a splendid future. Although the pay was nominal, he really had an opportunity few young men are offered.

"So what? So he has played far from what I'd call satisfactory football for us, and he also quit his job after a couple of weeks because it didn't carry his idea of the proper reward for such work. Do you wonder why I am sick and tired of what eastern football ranks are sending forth? We want players like Art Buss, of Michigan State [who was traded to the Eagles for the rights to Jay Berwanger] or Joe Carter, the end from Texas [who played well for the Eagles from 1933 to 1940]. There are boys who can play. Give me more from those wide-open spaces. No more of the boys who keep watching the water bucket in practice. No more fellows who get sore feet or sore knees or sore necks instead of trying to learn how a play really goes. Why half these birds don't know what the average high school boys should have mastered about football.

"I sent one of our supposedly bright stars to the board the other day and he couldn't diagram a simple pass play. Believe me or not, Cy, but I had them run one play 37 times one day last week before they got it right, and we're in the tenth week of practice now."

Peterman explained that Bert's theory is that the Northwestern, Minnesota, or Michigan State type of player, the boy that goes to Nebraska or even some of the smaller schools beyond the east, has a rugged background to begin with. He is so glad to get to college that his capacity for hard work increases, and he thrives on rough going the whole way. He looks upon a dollar with respect, and has no automobile to give him the *cowi knees.*

"I asked one of our players how much he made last summer and he said $15 a week," Bell continued. "He drove a bus. That's why at $125 a week which I pay him, he's out there playing real football today. Those are the ones who get in at 10 P.M., who study their plays, who take practice seriously. They are *hungry* lads, and they play real football. The rest—well, we'll see no more of them if they don't change their ways."

Then came the shocker: Bell told Peterman that he was "taking steps" to purchase the Boston Redskins and combine George Preston Marshall's franchise with his own Eagles. "Out of that combination of the present cast—or those who are left after he swings the axe—and new acquisitions will attempt to give Philadelphia a winner," Peterman analyzed.

Bert's outburst had apparently been triggered by the action he had been forced to take earlier that day—the indefinite suspension of Dave Smukler, perhaps his favorite player. Smukler, who played for Temple in the first Sugar Bowl in 1934, had quit school and joined the Eagles following a falling out with Owls coach Pop Warner before the 1936 season. His

outstanding play in the big upset over the Giants endeared him to Bell—
for a while.

Bell made the announcement as the Eagles team train chugged into
Harrisburg in the midst of a three-week road trip that would carry the
team as far west as Chicago. When it was discovered that Smukler was not
aboard the team's private car, Bell confirmed that Dave "had been left at
home because of infractions of training rules."

"Bell did not elaborate this statement," the *Bulletin* reported, "but it was
inferred that the suspension was for the remainder of the season and possibly might mean the end of Smukler's short career as a professional player."

Smukler's suspension actually lasted two games—the team's fifth and
sixth shutout losses of the season to Pittsburgh (6–0) in a game played at
Johnstown, Pennsylvania, and the Chicago Cardinals (13–0). He returned
for the final games, a 28–7 loss to the Chicago Bears and a 13–7 defeat at
the hands of the Brooklyn Dodgers.

On November 10, 1936, exactly one week's after Bell's tirade to Cy
Peterman, the estate of John C. Bell was settled in Philadelphia's Orphan's
Court. The holdings of the former Pennsylvania attorney general were
valued at $504,828, including a balance of $487,604 for distribution. Each
of Bell's sons—de Benneville (Bert) and John C. Bell Jr., the principal
beneficiaries—received $41,287 and $46,824, respectively, on account. Each
was bequeathed the income from one-fourth of the estate, and the remainder would be shared outright, the *Bulletin* reported.

In the division of their father's oil paintings, Bert Bell received "Boat-
man in the Marshes" by Corot, at an appraised value of $1,750, and his
brother obtained "Evening at Lake Albans," also by Corot, at $2,500. Other
paintings were purchased by the sons at an auction sale of Mr. Bell's effects. Bert Bell bid $3,695 for eight paintings by artists including Diaz La
Pena, J. F. Murphy, J. Dupre, George Innes, and Blakelock.

St. David's Church and St. Martin's Church, Radnor, and Washington
Memorial Chapel, Valley Forge, each received $5,000, and the University
of Pennsylvania, $10,000, to maintain statues of C. C. Harrison and Edgar
Fahs Smith, former provosts, and for the decoration of Irvine Auditorium.

The *Bulletin* revealed after the last game of the 1936 season that there
was a movement afoot to cut the NFL down to eight teams. "Boston was
on the auction block and Bert Bell was supposed to have purchased the
club from Marshall," the newspaper reported.

There is nothing on record to confirm that Bell succeeded or even attempted to convince George Preston Marshall to sell his team even though
they had developed a civil working relationship and their wives—Frances
Upton and Corrine Griffith—had appeared together in the Ziegfeld Follies.

At any rate, Marshall was determined to get out of New England. He had lost approximately $90,000 in five years in Boston, so he moved his franchise to Washington for the 1937 season. According to *The Pro Football Chronicle*, the team drew more people for its first three games in the nation's capital than it did for the entire 1936 season. With new quarterback Sammy Baugh leading the charge, the Redskins won their first NFL title that year and were well on their way to becoming a successful franchise.

That wasn't the case for the Eagles, whose financial fortunes continued to nosedive. At the next league meeting, held at Chicago's Sherman Hotel on February 12, 1937, Marshall made the following motion that was carried unanimously on a roll call vote:

> Due to the emergency existing at this time relative to completing the schedule in order to give an equal alignment to all clubs, that the president be instructed to authorize the treasurer to issue a check to the Philadelphia club in the sum of $1,000 in consideration of the Philadelphia club surrendering its rights to a game with the Bears in 1937, and that in further consideration the Philadelphia club shall not be required to play in excess of five games at home during the 1938 season providing a schedule of 11 games is played again in 1938. In the event the league decides to play a 12 game schedule in 1938, the Philadelphia club is not required to play more than six home games.

The NFL was making its first of many efforts to salvage the Philadelphia Eagles' beleaguered franchise.

12. The Struggle to Survive: 1937 to 1939

On February 15, 1937, George Halas agreed to trade his prized possession, the outstanding veteran end Bill Hewitt, to the Eagles in exchange for the draft rights to Sam Francis, the great University of Nebraska football and Olympic star.

More important to Bert Bell, Halas threw in a much-needed infusion of $4,000 in cash as part of the deal. The Eagles' owner immediately doubled Hewitt's salary to $200 a game and arranged for a $24-a-week, off-season job as a repairman in an auto service station—a position listed in the team's game program as "lubrication and fuel oil salesman."

Hewitt, who would become the last NFL player not to wear a helmet, played significant roles in the Birds' only two victories that year—both upsets on the road. Using only 15 players—with seven of the 11 starters going the entire 60 minutes—the Eagles knocked Washington out of first place in the East, 14–0. Hewitt set up the first touchdown with a sensational one-handed catch of a pass from Emmett Mortell. Hewitt lateraled to Johnny Kusko for a 47-yard gain and scored the touchdown on the next play after catching a nine-yard pass from Dave Smukler. Then, in a 14–0 win over the Brooklyn Dodgers, Hewitt scored the first TD on another nine-yard pass from Smukler.

Unfortunately, the Eagles continued to suffer at the gate. Although they drew 20,000 fans to watch them defeat the Eastern College All-Stars, 14–6, at Temple Stadium in August, their home crowds ranged from a high of 6,580 against the Redskins to a low of 3,107 against the Cleveland Rams.

Bert and Frances did have another reason to celebrate, though, when their second child, another son, George Upton was born on October 13, 1937, at Presbyterian Hospital in Philadelphia.

At one point, after another pitifully small crowd attended one of the Eagles' games, Smukler stopped into Bell's office after the final whistle. "If you're going to have a hard time making out this week, Bert, just forget my check. I looked awful out there today, anyway."

"I thought he looked like the greatest football player of all time, particularly at that moment," Bell said.

Art Rooney was having his own financial problems. "The biggest thrill wasn't winning on Sunday, but meeting the payroll on Monday," he once told sportswriter Vito Stellino. But the Pittsburgh owner knew that things were much worse on the other side of the state, especially since Bell was being plagued by a string of rainy Sundays.

According to Arthur Daley of the *New York Times,* Rooney started phoning Bell regularly. "Need any money, Bert?" he would ask. "No," answered Bert. "I can struggle through." Daley said that this continued for five weeks. Then one Monday morning, a special delivery letter arrived for Bell. It contained no message, only a check for $5,000.

Bell wasn't having much success as a coach, either. His two-year won–lost record now stood at 3–19–1, dead last in fifth place in the Eastern Division both times. Moreover, Bert's father—the esteemed attorney general of Pennsylvania John C. Bell—still couldn't understand what young de Benneville saw in this crazy *professional* gridiron game.

"My mother would tell me that my grandfather would come in a chauffeur-driven Stutz Bearcat to practices," Upton Bell recalled. "It might be 90 degrees, but he'd be sitting in a car with a bowler hat on, looking down and just shaking his head. In ten minutes he'd be gone. John C. considered professional football on the same general level as burlesque."

Shortly after Christmas, 1937, Bell received an unsolicited endorsement to return to his beloved University of Pennsylvania to succeed Harvey Harman, who had served as head football coach for the previous seven seasons. It came from Fred Byrod of the *Philadelphia Inquirer.*

"Pennsylvania men are said to be divided in their choice for Harvey Harman's successor," Byrod wrote. "Some seek a return to the graduate coaching system followed by the Quakers from 1888 to 1931. Others loudly declare Penn needs a 'big name' coach to restore the Red and Blue football fortunes to their once proud position. Close by the West Philadelphia campus is a man who fills both bills—de Benneville (Bert) Bell."

Byrod's recommendation went no further. George Munger was hired soon thereafter and went on to coach for 16 seasons, twice guiding the Quakers to national rankings and becoming president of the American Football Coaches Association.

Before the 1938 season, Bell moved the Eagles' preseason camp to West Chester State Teachers College. It would be the first time the team would train on an actual college campus.

The preparation appeared to pay off as the Eagles won two of their first three games and prevailed in their final two contests to finish with the best single-season coaching record of Bell's career (5–6). For the first time, the Birds finished out of the basement, in fourth place, in the Eastern Division, beating out Rooney's Steelers, who dropped nine of their 11 games.

Also for the first time, the Eagles had two players selected for All-Pro honors. Ends Joe Carter and Bill Hewitt were both named to the Pro Football Writers of America All-Pro team.

Better still, home crowds were beginning to pick up. Not counting "home" games against Pittsburgh in Buffalo, New York, and the Chicago Cardinals in Erie, Pennsylvania, the Eagles averaged 17,333 fans for three home games against Washington, the New York Giants, and Brooklyn. (Attendance was not announced for the 6–28 loss to the Chicago Bears at Municipal Stadium.)

Unfortunately, Bell—who was still carrying gate receipts around in a cigar box—was again having trouble making his payroll of $35,817 during another Depression year. He was forced to borrow $2,500, this time from George Halas.

According to the *Philadelphia Bulletin*'s Hugh Brown, who caught a glimpse of the Eagles' dusty 1938 financial records some 25 years later, Bert had estimated quite accurately that his game-day payroll expenses would total $36,300, or $3,300 per game. Through various economies, including player fines as low as ten cents, Bell actually operated $482 below his estimate.

"A flock of checks drawn on the Tradesmens National Bank and Trust Company and in a remarkable state of preservation, found de Benneville Bell paying Bert Bell a salary of $200 weekly," Brown reported. "And also taking care of such creditors as:

—Towel Company . . . $19.13 (paid in full, including 45 missing towels).
—Cash . . . $9.60 . . . In payment for laundry at the Ritz.
—Bell Telephone Company of Pennsylvania . . . $7.66.
—National Football League . . . $50 . . . For dues due November 1 (the check was dated December 28)."

Some of the typical player checks per game included to Dave Smukler, $196.82; Joe Carter, $271.18; Emmett Mortell, $200.28; Ted Schmitt, $149; Bill Hewitt, two checks for $198 and $194; Hank Reese, $150.07; Ray Keeling, $74.25, and Richard Riffle, $64.77.

Brown also noted that some of the players drew advances before payday with Smukler demanding "piddling sums" of $7 and $11. One check drawn to Bert Bell for $80 explained the disbursement thus: "$70 for executives' trip to draft meeting and Jim McMurdo, $10 advance. [McMurdo had succeeded John Da Grosa as assistant coach at the beginning of the 1938 season.] Five trips by railroad, one of them as far as Detroit, cost only $1,506.50. The players traveled by day coach. The hotel charge for the five trips was $1,050, and the total spent on meals $180. When Bell took the Eagles to New York and gave each man a punch-ticket in a cafeteria, the limit was one buck."

The Eagles' owner had to travel on a tight budget because of such items as $200.35 for the team's 25 percent share of stadium concessions and $559.15 for the Internal Revenue Department tax on the Brooklyn game of November 6, 1938, that drew 12,000 fans.

"The largest check drawn by Bell in 1938 was one for $2,500, and the recipient was George Halas," Brown added. "The notation was: 'Repayment in full for loan made to Eagles in 1938.'"

At the end of the year, Bell had made his first profit—$7,000—which he promptly used to finally sign a number-one draft pick, Texas Christian University quarterback Davey O'Brien. The contract was for $12,000 a season and a percentage of the gate receipts from 1939. Bert then took out a $1 million insurance policy with Lloyds of London whereby the Eagles would receive $1,500 for each game the 5-foot-7-inch, 150-pound Heisman Trophy–winner missed. Fortunately, Bell never collected a cent, although he did take tons of criticism for signing arguably the nation's smallest player.

"When I drafted him, I wasn't thinking about buying a name," Bell told Ray Hill of the *Inquirer*. "I'm interested in building the Eagles into a championship team. I think he's the quarterback who can spark us ahead. Otherwise, I wouldn't be interested, no matter what his college reputation might be."

O'Brien was outplayed by Washington's Sammy Baugh, 7–0, in the Eagles' 1939 home opener witnessed by 33,258 fans, the largest crowd in the franchise's history. Davey, who also played defense, went on to set a new single-season NFL passing record with 1,324 yards. But he was only able to guide the Eagles to one win that season, 17–14 over Pittsburgh at home on Thanksgiving Day. The Birds were coming off a 27–14 loss to the mighty Chicago Bears and snapped an eight-game winless streak that day. But they were in the midst of perhaps the zaniest schedule in NFL history—three games in eight days.

Much of the blame for that debacle fell on Bell's shoulders. It all began when he postponed the Eagles' opening day game with Pittsburgh, scheduled for September 10, because of "threatening" weather.

"It is our policy not to play football games in the rain because we think spectators do not enjoy themselves," Bell told the *Inquirer* the following day. "We called off the game two hours before the scheduled 2:45 o'clock starting time after being in communication with the Weather Bureau most of the morning. We were informed that thunder showers were expected during the afternoon. At the time it was drizzling in some sections of the city and suburbs and threatening in others."

"A dark cloud passed over the sky somewhere north of Manayunk," the *Bulletin* reported sarcastically. Meanwhile, at the same time, the Athletics hosted a double-header against the Boston Red Sox and old-timers game in-between. Some 23,235 fans watched 21 innings of precipitation-free action.

"Our advance sale for the game was 14% better than for any game played by the Eagles last season," said Bell, who offered fans the opportunity to swap their unused tickets for the following Sunday's home game against Washington. "It actually cost our club money to postpone the game, but we called it off because we deemed it best for the interest of the fans. The Pittsburgh club agreed to the postponement. In fact, a league ruling says both clubs must agree before a game can be postponed."

Bell's decision threw the NFL schedule into chaos. The Pirates' game was re-scheduled for November 23. Afterward, the two teams hopped a train to Pittsburgh, where they faced each other again three days later with only 8,788 fans watching the Pirates rebound with a 24–12 victory.

Three weeks after the Pittsburgh game was postponed, the Eagles were scheduled to meet Dan Topping's Brooklyn Dodgers at Municipal Stadium. The night before the game, Bell took the Dodgers' owner to dinner at one of his favorite haunts, Lew Tendler's Restaurant in Center City Philadelphia.

Arthur Daley of the *Times* recalled their get-together: "'Dan,' said Bert Bell, his raspy voice freighted with anxiety, 'we've got to postpone tomorrow's game. It's been raining all week and the forecast is for more rain tomorrow. We haven't sold a ticket and there will be no one at the game. How about calling it off?'"

"'I'm sorry, Bert,' said Topping. 'Pro football never will catch on if we offer it on a hit-or-miss basis. The game is scheduled and it must be played.'"

"Topping had driven from New York with his lady [and future wife, Sonja Henie, the two-time Olympic figure-skating gold-medalist] and a carful of well-heeled cronies," Upton Bell remembers being told. "When the advance ticket sale turned out to be zilch, my father said, 'Dan, there's no point in playing. We haven't sold a ticket.' 'Yeah,' said Topping. 'But I can't disappoint my girlfriend. We've driven all the way down here from New York.'"

The rain came lashing down in torrents as the two teams battled to a scoreless tie. It was a horrible storm. Every one of the 50 spectators rattling around in the 102,000-seat stadium was invited to take refuge in the press box.

"And they weren't crowded in there, either," Bert Bell recalled. "Not only that, but the smart young man I had hired to dole out the coffee and sandwiches to the press took every last one of the press-box occupants for newspapermen and served 'em all lunch. It's days like that when it takes a very good sense of humor and an utter lack of regard for your bank balance to stay in professional football. I'm glad I had both."

Meanwhile, on the same day in Washington, it also rained heavily. But no thought was given to sending 26,342 spectators home until they saw the Redskins battle the New York Giants to another scoreless tie in the mud.

Years later, Bell reiterated to John Kieran of the *Times* that the game never should have been played: "It was senseless," he explained. "Brooklyn coach Potsy Clark was willing to postpone it, but Dan Topping wouldn't hear of it. We could have played to ten times the crowd if we put the game off. But no! Dan Topping said that he was abiding by the rules. Then he offered to toss a coin with me to see whether we postponed it or not. That topped it! I told him that maybe money meant nothing to a rich bird like him, but I was a poor workingman and I couldn't afford to flip a coin with that much money at stake. If we were going to lose it, I wasn't going to lose it by chance."

According to *The Pro Football Chronicle*, "Bell's and Topping's difference of opinion engendered one of the strongest owner feuds that the National League has ever known. The next time the teams played, Bell was rumored to have threatened his players with fines or suspensions if they didn't beat Brooklyn." They lost, anyway, 23–14, two weeks later.

The inclement weather continued to haunt Bell and his team. On November 5, the Eagles were upset, 7–6, in Washington when Franny Murray missed the tying point-after-touchdown.

"Nobody could have kicked that ball across the bar," Bell told attendees at the Robert W. Maxwell Memorial Football Club luncheon the following day. "The mud was ankle deep when we scored. But I'm not as much concerned about the score as about the fact there were two broken legs and five dislocations. Colleges have to play rain or shine, for they have no other dates they can postpone to, but in our league we could arrange for the change."

Meanwhile, the naysayers were still criticizing Bell for paying so much money to his talented quarterback. "The trouble is that O'Brien was so built up by his play at TCU, the public expected a magician who would complete 99 of 100 passes," Bert explained to Harry Robert of the *Bulletin*. "No rookie can come out of college and burn this league up. O'Brien is playing as well as any first-year man could possibly be expected."

Throughout the season, Bell had trouble blending the talents of his rookie quarterback with the veteran players, according to John Hogrogian of the Professional Football Researchers Association. "Last year's Eagles used a ball-control offense, featuring fullback Dave Smukler and a surprising tenacious defense," Hogrogian wrote. "This year's Eagles would pass frequently and lose frequently." Bell started making O'Brien the focus of the passing game during a 23–14 loss to Brooklyn in Game 5 when he connected on only 11 of 25 attempts for a season-high 140 yards.

Constantly strapped for cash, Bell bundled his team into a creaky old bus and told each player to bring along a box lunch during road trips. After stopping overnight in rooming houses on the longer excursions, Bert would sit in front of the bus beside the driver. "Pull up here," he would bellow as he spotted a plot of farmland. "That looks like a nice level field. Everybody out! Time for practice!"

The Eagles closed out their season by dropping a 35–13 decision to the Cleveland Rams in Colorado Springs. Bell didn't even make the trip. He decided instead to take in the New York Giants' 9–7 win over the Washington Redskins at the Polo Grounds in a game that decided the Eastern Division title. McMurdo handled the team against the Rams at Will Rogers Memorial Stadium.

Although the Eagles finished with a 1–9–1 record, their average home attendance improved to 26,580 (not counting that horrendous crowd announced at 1,880 for the infamous Brooklyn Dodgers game). The total of more than 80,000 fans included 10,000 children who were admitted for ten cents each. The Eagles and Cleveland enjoyed the biggest percentage jump in the league and the entire NFL drew a record 1,100,000 spectators in 1938, a figure that Bell estimated would increase by 300,000 when the 1939 figures were tallied.

The city of Philadelphia responded by increasing the Eagles' rent from $600 to $1,000 a game for the 1940 season. Bell immediately threatened to move the franchise out of town. "I don't know where we'll play next year, but it won't be at Municipal Stadium unless the city changes its attitude," the Eagles owner fumed to Ray Hill of the *Bulletin* on December 5. "Perhaps we'll try to make arrangements at Shibe Park, or maybe we'll go out of the city altogether. I already have started to look into possible sites at Hershey and Camden. This 1940 contract they want me to sign is all out of order. It calls for a minimum increase of 66 per cent in the rent and also gives the city a percentage privilege if our attendance exceeds a certain figure. It just doesn't make sense to me."

Army-Navy, which just recently played before 101,600, fans, paid $10,500 for the stadium. The city also waived the amusement tax charge for the service game, but not for other football tickets. Bell estimated that Philadelphia realized $4,000 amusement tax revenue on Eagles tickets for the 1939 season.

"Here they are yelling about business conditions in the city and then they try to drive people out by unfair practices such as this," Bell said. "I guess it was that 30,000 crowd which saw Davey O'Brien in debut here against the Washington Redskins that put this idea into the city fathers' bonnets. Somebody should tell them about the Brooklyn game. We played it here in the rain and it cost us $11,600."

Bell conceded that the Eagles "made a little money" the previous two seasons after operating at a "large deficit" for several years before that when they paid the city rent on property that was otherwise lying idle. "It will be a long, long while before we're out of the red," he explained. "Philadelphia needs education as far as professional football is concerned. We can't afford to take chances that might bankrupt us. You can always lose your shirt on a rainy day in this business. Still and all, perhaps we'll be willing to pay the rent—if the city is willing to guarantee the crowds and the weather conditions."

Meanwhile, Bell was conducting negotiations with his old friend Heinie Miller to join the Eagles as co-coach for the 1940 season. Bell had previously tried to lure the former Quaker All-America away from St. Joseph's College where he had been the head coach for six years. Miller finally agreed to make the switch on December 6, 1939.

"Possibly it's the way Bell has presented the professional picture to me by making it look very attractive, both financially and from a working standpoint," Miller explained to sportswriter Ross Kauffman. "I am familiar with the National League set-up and know many of the players personally, especially the Eagles."

Formally introducing Miller at a dinner at the Racquet Club on December 14—and dispelling rumors that he would be stepping down as coach—Bell disclosed that he had recently refused an offer of $100,000 to sell the Eagles and another offer of $75,000 for a half interest in the team. He also emphasized that he had so much confidence in the Eagles' money-making potential that "in no event" would he sell the franchise.

"I never sold a player for cash," Bell added. "The year the club lost $26,000 I could have recouped $17,000 by selling one of my players, but I wouldn't make any such move. No player who I think can help the club will ever be sold for cash while I'm at the head of it. In the years I've had the Eagles, I've never sold a player who was really of value. I've released more than 200, and not one of them is playing in the league.

"My payroll has averaged $55,000. I doubt if there's another team in pro football—even including the New York Giants—who pay that much. I have paid high prices for great college players but not for my own use. They are for trade to teams that can afford to carry them as reserves and give me players who can measure up to the rest of the professional league.

"I am firmly convinced that the only way the young clubs in the National League can catch up with the older teams, such as the champion Green Bay Packers, the New York Giants, and the Chicago Bears, is by trading new college stars for the experienced pro players. With very few exceptions, it takes three years for a college football player to develop to a point where he really helps a pro team. I am determined to give Philadelphia a winning team. I don't know how much longer it will take, but I'll stick with the club until that ambition is realized."

Bell also gave a vote of confidence to Miller, his new co-coach. "I have the highest regard for his ability," the Eagles owner said. "If there is ever a disagreement between us as to football tactics, I can assure you that Miller's judgment will prevail."

The Eagles finished with the NFL's worst record for the decade of the 1930s (18–55–3), but Bell had plenty of changes in store for the decade of the 1940s.

13. Bert Bell and Art Rooney Get Together

Faced with a whopping $400-per-game increase in rent if his Eagles continued to play at Municipal Stadium, Bert Bell signed an agreement with Connie Mack, the owner of the Philadelphia Athletics, to play all six home games at Shibe Park in 1940. They agreed at a meeting on February 8 that the Eagles would play four of the games under the floodlights and the other two contests on Sunday afternoons.

"I'm delighted to have Bert Bell as a tenant and also think his Eagles will make Shibe Park more popular," Mack said after the papers were signed calling for the Eagles to pay 15 percent of their gate receipts for rent. "If our lights are good enough for American League teams to play baseball at its best, they certainly are going to be more satisfactory for football."

The Eagles drew a crowd estimated generously by the *Philadelphia Inquirer* at 40,000 fans—their largest ever—for a preseason 27–21 loss to the Chicago Bears at Temple Stadium. But the regular season was another disaster. The Birds lost their first nine games before defeating Pittsburgh, 7–0, before the smallest home crowd of the year, announced at 4,200.

A few days later, Davey O'Brien confirmed that he was retiring from pro football at the end of the season to join the FBI. His grand finale would be on December 1, at Washington. And what a finale it was as O'Brien broke NFL records with 33 pass completions in 60 attempts for 316 yards. But the Redskins still won, 13–6.

Although he was not the most sentimental guy around, Bell recognized the historic significance of the moment. Before the game, he presented O'Brien with a silver plaque. The inscription read: "Davey O'Brien, the greatest player of all time; retiring from pro football to serve his country. Small in stature with the heart of a lion. A living inspiration to the youth of America."

Then, as Arthur Daley of the *New York Times* remembered:

"I want you to call time out for Philadelphia when there are thirty seconds left to play," Bell demanded of the field judge as the Eagles and Redskins squared off for the last half of their NFL finale.

"I can't do that, Bert," said the official. "It might cost you a 5-yard penalty for extra time-out."

"I don't care if you penalize us the entire distance of the field," snapped the owner-coach of the Eagles. "This is special occasion and I want to take that kid out so that the crowd can give him the ovation he deserves."

As O'Brien left the Griffith Stadium playing field, 30,838 fans, as well as the Redskins players, stood and applauded.

"Long after the battle was over the cheers echoed and re-echoed in the most spontaneous sports outburst the capital has ever had," Daley wrote. "In the dressing room Slingshot Davey's uniform was ripped off his back and torn into souvenirs. Some one made off with his helmet, pads and shoes. About all the little fellow had left was a dazed smile. But it was not until a bit later that the nicest gesture of the day was made. Gridiron tradition has decreed that the winning team is entitled to possession of the football. Not this time, however. Every man on the Redskins squad autographed the ball and it was presented to O'Brien as a sincere token of esteem."

"O'Brien was one of the greatest football players of all time," Bell said later. "He played 299 minutes out of a possible 300 in his last five games for us, despite his 144 pounds. When I took him out of his final game in Washington with a minute to go, the entire Washington team escorted him to the sideline. He set three league records for passing that afternoon and the ovation those Washington fans gave him was something that Hitler and Mussolini always dreamed of."

Although all of the official NFL and Philadelphia Eagles records indicate that Bell was the club's head coach in 1940, one person associated with that team and a number of newspaper articles from that period indicate that Bert may not have actually served in that role.

Bill Mackrides, a wide-eyed 15-year-old water boy at the Birds' training camp at West Chester that year, remembers Heinie Miller handling the coaching duties.

"Bert would sit in the stands during practice and Heinie was the coach on the field," recalled Mackrides, who later played as a backup quarterback for the Eagles from 1947 to 1951. "Bell was a very commanding kind of person. He would yell over to Heinie, telling him what to do. It was kind of intimidating for the coach. When he said something, Heinie made sure it got done. Bert wasn't there all the time because he had other business to attend to, but he was out there a couple of times a week, watching what was going on, overseeing everything. He was the coach in name only."

In a story previewing a game at Brooklyn on October 4, the *Philadelphia Bulletin* referred to "Co-Coaches Heinie Miller and Jim MacMurdo (sic)." On October 20, the *Bulletin*'s Ray Kelly mentioned "co-coaches Bert Bell and Heinie Miller" in a pregame story before the Eagles hosted Washington. In a May 23, 1941, article in the *Bulletin,* Ross Kauffman wrote, "Miller officially was head coach of the Eagles last season with president Bell and Jim MacMurdo (sic) also assisting."

On December 10, 1940, the NFL experienced its most dramatic shakeup since Bell and Rooney joined the league in 1933. The totally unexpected developments that have never really been fully explained were, in fact, engineered by the longtime horse-racing buddies from the opposite ends of Pennsylvania.

Rooney had lost "between $100,000 and $150,000" in his eight years as owner, according to the *Pittsburgh Sun Telegraph,* and had recently changed the name of his team from the Pirates to the Steelers in an effort to relate more to the blue-collar fans of the Smoky City.

Rumors of the unprecedented league shakeup had begun swirling around Griffith Stadium during the Chicago Bears' 73–0 shellacking of the Washington Redskins in the NFL championship game on Sunday, December 8.

As he walked into the Willard Hotel for the start of the annual owners' meeting the following day, Bell confirmed reports that he might merge his Eagles with the Steelers and that he had been working on a deal with Rooney for several months.

"We both have agreed that a merger might be the solution to our mutual problems, financial and otherwise, but that's as far as the deal has progressed," Bell explained. "We intend to seek approval of the consolidation at this meeting. Whether we will accomplish anything is questionable. After all, we don't know whether the league will permit us to dispose of one franchise or whether that franchise must revert to the league."

Bell added that the two owners had not decided where the merged team would play its home games. "Perhaps we may move away from Philadelphia and Pittsburgh entirely and try some other city," he said.

Asked about reports that he had recently told friends that he might try to purchase the Cleveland franchise, Bell said, "I haven't gone into that lately. The deal is off, I guess."

Here's how Arthur Daley of the *Times* broke the story at the annual league meetings in the nation's capital:

Friendly rivals of former seasons, Art Rooney of Pittsburgh, and Bert Bell of Philadelphia, have consolidated forces in joint ownership of the Philadelphia Eagles franchise and the Steelers have been purchased by Alexis Thompson, who will keep the team in Pittsburgh.

Rumors of the deal were in circulation all day long but it was not until the executive committee of the league approved the transaction and the magnates followed suit in a night session that it was formally consummated.

It was an unusual transaction in one respect. Rooney and Bell pooled the 51 players on the two squads and divided them between Philadelphia and Pittsburgh in as even a distribution as was possible.

Thompson, 28-year-old heir to a steel fortune, will be at the draft meeting tomorrow and will make the Pittsburgh choices. His assistant in that endeavor will be Earl (Greasy) Neale, now of the Yale coaching staff. Thompson was graduated from Yale in 1936. Neale has not yet been signed as Pittsburgh coach, but there is no doubt that he will get the job. Neale's contract at New Haven runs until March 1. He has an option of renewing it for another year, but Neale considers the opportunity with the Steelers so good that he cannot turn it down.

The formal statement by League President Carl Storck on the deal declared that it was for "an undisclosed sum." The general estimate here was that Thompson and his syndicate paid $165,000. [Claire Burcky, of the *Pittsburgh Press*, said the price was $160,000.] The Bell-Rooney combination will give Philadelphia better financial backing that it had formerly. The Thompson syndicate will be known as the East-West Sporting Club, with offices in Radio City in New York, the building from which Thompson operates a drug manufacturing concern.

Rooney told the *Pittsburgh Post-Gazette* via telephone on December 8 that Bell had done all of the negotiating with Thompson before the deal was actually consummated a few days before it was approved by the league.

"I never talked to Thompson until today after all the details were practically ironed out," Rooney explained. "Bell did all the dickering."

At the same time, Cy Peterman of the *Inquirer* confirmed earlier reports that Bell "was dickering with Cleveland, hoping to make one team bloom where two went burst before." Instead, according to Claire Burcky, Rooney paid Bell $80,000 from the proceeds of the sale of the Steelers to Thompson for a 50 percent share of the Eagles.

Post Gazette sports editor Havey Boyle said that the deal between Rooney and Bell "throws together two friends who are temperamentally at opposite poles of the football axis. On the one hand, it is the Pittsburgher who was forever making up excuses for his coaches and players, and Bell who, at least, affects about the same amount of sentiment toward professional football players as a house detective toward the stranger who inquires at which desk you get the checks cashed.

"Bell's may be part of a pose, but he can harangue in picturesque languages on the frailties of the college boys turned into cash-and-carry players and his scorn for those who fail on or off the field is fabulous. Bell's nickname for Rooney is *Champ* or *Prez*, and while Rooney won two posts in the new cabinet—the coach Walter Kiesling, and the under-secretary of accounts Joe Carr—both of whom will move from Pittsburgh to Philadelphia, Rooney, almost by the laws of nature and certainly by the powers of Bell's eloquence, will be a silent partner—a traveling minister without portfolio."

Boyle offered the following sample of "Bellishness" with his players:

Oh, so you don't think the coach is treating you right. Well, now that's too bad. Well, now let me tell you something, and always remember it. You don't like the coach because he is doing exactly what is right and you're not and so you want me to change the coach to suit you. Well, understand, the coach is my man and if you don't like it—why there's nothing stopping you from going out and trying to make as much as we're paying you at whatever else you can do—which I guess is nothing minus.

Fred Byrod of the *Inquirer* reported that under terms of the deal, the Eagles and Steelers divided the 51 players they owned at the end of the 1940 season. Bell confirmed by telephone from Washington that the new Eagles would keep 16 of their players and take 10 of Rooney's former players.

Bell told Byrod that it was not yet decided who would coach the Eagles. However, Steelers coach Walter Kiesling was quoted in a Pittsburgh paper as saying that he and Heinie Miller, "Bell's present coaching associate," would share the task. Miller was with Bell in Washington when the franchise swap was announced.

"I feel that we have greatly strengthened our club," Bell said, adding that he had retained the nucleus of the 1940 Eagles squad, including nine players who started against the Steelers on Thanksgiving Day when the Birds recorded their only victory of the season.

Primarily because of World War II, only two of the players retained by Bell—guard Eberle Schultz and fullback/linebacker Elmer Hackney—would ever play another down in the NFL. Such Eagles favorites as end

Don Looney, center Maurice Harper, and backs Dick Riffle, Franny Murray, and Jay Arnold, among others, were finished in pro football after the 1940 season. Of the 10 players obtained from Pittsburgh, only tackle Ted Doyle and guard John Sanders ever played for the Birds.

Later that week, Arthur Daley reported how Halas "made a travesty" of the annual player draft. "The Chicago Bears apparently are just as dangerous in a meeting room as on a football field," he wrote. "The Monsters of the Midway, not at all satisfied with their 73–0 championship victory over the Redskins here Sunday, today added so much talent to their already talent-saturated squad that the closest competition the National Football League figures to get next year is when the first Bear team plays the second one. This was supposed to be the annual draft meeting whereby negotiation rights to college seniors are distributed evenly among the ten clubs in the league. George Halas made a travesty of it.

"Before the first round had been completed he not only had his initial choice but also the first selections of the Philadelphia Eagles and the Pittsburgh Steelers. As a result he came out of the meeting with three of the finest college backs in the land—peerless Tommy Harmon of Michigan, bruising Norman Standlee of Stanford, and clever Don Scott of Ohio State, all great triple-threat performers. As if that was not bad enough, he had the fifth Philadelphia selection (Dave Rankin of Purdue, the best end in the Western Conference), and the fifth Pittsburgh man (Fred Hartman, 250-pound Rice tackle)."

Daley explained that Philadelphia and Pittsburgh were "riddled" by player deals with the Bears, adding that Halas "took over Harmon from Philadelphia because he had traded Lester McDonald, an end, and Dick Bassi, a guard for John Schiechl of Santa Clara, a center who never reported. The agreement they reached at that time was that if the Pacific Coast ace did not come to terms, then Halas was to get the first Eagles draft choice in exchange." Halas then traded multipurpose back Billy Patterson to Pittsburgh for Standlee, the Steelers' initial selection.

A few months earlier, Bell had angrily denied reports coming out of New York that he had already made plans to draft Harmon and then sell him to the Bears for a stiff price. "That's not so," he shouted to Ray Hill of the *Bulletin*. "I've never sold a player in my life just for the money involved. I'm out to build up this team if I can. The records speak for themselves."

As 1940 drew to a close, the Philadelphia-Pittsburgh situation continued to raise more questions than answers. It would soon become even more confusing.

14. Bert Bell Ends Up
in Pittsburgh

On January 17, 1941, the NFL owners took the first step in establishing the new position of commissioner to govern their rapidly growing sport. Meeting in Chicago, they rewrote part of the league's constitution by inserting a clause legalizing the establishment of this new post in the event that the league members decided to authorize such a position at their regular April meeting.

Chicago Bears president George Halas told the Associated Press that should a commissioner be chosen, the office of president still would be continued. "We are paving the way for employment of a commissioner in case we want one," he explained. "In case we pick a commissioner, he would have more power than the president, but the latter office would be retained."

After considering such people as American Olympic Committee Chairman Avery Brundage, the club owners quickly narrowed the field of candidates. The finalists apparently were Notre Dame football coach and athletic director Elmer Layden and former Olympic gold medal–winning oarsman John B. Kelly, a lifelong friend of Bert Bell dating back to their hell-raising days in France during World War I.

Halas and Bell were sent to interview the two men—Layden first, then Kelly—and neither candidate knew that the other was being interviewed. On Tuesday, February 4, the Associated Press reported that the committee told league owners the previous Saturday (February 1) that they had reached an agreement with Layden but the announcement would be delayed to give him time to inform Notre Dame officials.

Not so, said Bell. He and two other club owners charged that Layden was "railroaded" into office, not only over Kelly, a Philadelphia contractor who had become a nationally prominent Democratic Party leader, but also over another newly identified candidate, Frank McCormick, the athletic director at the University of Minnesota.

"Dissension broke out in the National Football League today," said the Associated Press in a story from Chicago on February 6 as Bell and his colleagues—Alexis Thompson, of Pittsburgh, and Dan Topping, of Brooklyn—traded charges with Halas, Washington's George Preston Marshall, and the other five owners.

Declaring that the entire league was entitled to vote on Layden's selection, Bell, Thompson, and Topping asserted that the appointment was illegal and could not be official until action could be taken to amend the constitution at the annual league meetings in April.

"Every voting member knew in advance of publication that Layden was to be appointed," Halas retorted. "Every step we took was legal. A majority is sufficient to elect a new officer and we have a substantial majority in favor of Layden. Bell knows that his partner Art Rooney cast his half-vote for Layden. It is true that we were unable to inform Bell of the official vote, but that was because he was traveling en-route to Florida."

According to *The Pro Football Chronicle*, Halas pulled a power play while Bell was traveling to Florida, with Bert thinking that a decision wouldn't be made until they had talked to McCormick. Halas "hastily conferred in Chicago with Detroit's Fred Mandel and the Cardinals' Charles Bidwell. At the same time, Eagles' co-owner Art Rooney lobbied New York's Tim Mara, Washington's George Preston Marshall, Green Bay's Curly Lambeau, and Cleveland's Edward P. Bruch over the telephone and got all of them to agree to hire Layden."

Speaking in Philadelphia, Bell insisted that he had been delegated with Halas to interview three candidates and that the first he knew of Layden's appointment was when he read it in the newspapers. "We interviewed two men without reaching a decision," Bell told the AP. "I was waiting to interview the third when I learned that Layden had accepted. I do not know who made the announcement but it came from Chicago and that's where Halas lives."

"Well, that's one thing Bell got right," replied Halas. "I do live in Chicago. He knew all about the progress of negotiations. We interviewed Layden together in Pittsburgh last week. Then we talked to Thompson and Topping by phone. Layden's appointment was strictly legal. No announcement was made until Layden had been handed an official binding agreement containing the signatures of a majority of our club owners."

From New York, Thompson told the Associated Press that Halas and Bell were appointed to interview Layden, Kelly, and McCormick but that McCormick never was approached. "They were given authority to make an unofficial offer to one of the three and report back to the league," Thompson said. "Bell wasn't even in on the signing of Layden."

Marshall termed Layden's appointment "the most constructive and finest move ever made by the National League." Rooney added that

"Layden had a new Notre Dame contract on hand and that further delay was unfair to the school or the coach."

Layden resigned from Notre Dame on February 3 to accept the new post of commissioner at an annual salary of $20,000 for five years. He had originally been recommended for the position by *Chicago Tribune* sports editor Arch Ward, who had himself recently turned down the presidency and commissionership of the league.

Will Furlong of the *Chicago Sun-Times* said that Halas and Marshall were so impressed by Ward's work as founder of the annual College All-Star game, pitting the cream of the college crop against the defending NFL champions, that they offered him a reported salary of $25,000 a year to assume both roles.

Carl Storck, who had served as the league's acting president since 1939, did not take the news of the new commissioner's post well. "He spent seven weeks in bed with nervous exhaustion and attended the league meetings against the advice of his doctor," *The Pro Football Chronicle* reported. "His right side was partially paralyzed. But he vowed to fight to keep his job—and created a scene doing so."

Storck, one of the league's founders who became secretary-treasurer in 1921, finally resigned on April 4, saying "it was for the best interest of the game." The following day, Layden was unanimously elected the NFL's first commissioner-president. Bell seconded the nomination.

Layden's appointment was overshadowed by a development three days earlier described by the Associated Press as "one of the most unusual swaps in sports history"—a *trade* engineered by the owners of the Philadelphia Eagles and Pittsburgh Steelers franchises whereby Alexis Thompson agreed to move his entire Pittsburgh team to Philadelphia and Bert Bell and Art Rooney transferred their complete Quaker City squad to Pittsburgh.

The bizarre move was prompted by Rooney, who had noticed that Thompson hadn't even opened up an office in Pittsburgh four months after purchasing the franchise. "I asked (Thompson) how he'd like to make a switch and let me stay in Pittsburgh and take over Philadelphia for himself," Rooney told the *Pittsburgh Sun Telegraph*. The young entrepreneur quickly agreed.

Bell made the announcement himself with a surprise telephone call to the *Philadelphia Bulletin*'s Ray Hill on April 3. "This has been pending for six weeks," he told the shocked sportswriter. "I kept holding out against the move, but finally Rooney made me an offer that could not be refused."

"All that's involved is a change of cities," Bell explained to Frank O'Gara of the *Philadelphia Inquirer*. "No cash or other considerations were involved." Bert said that he was sorry to leave Philadelphia but that the financial arrangement entailed in the change was too good to pass up.

"I have long appreciated the interest of the Philadelphia fans and the sportswriters," he added. "I believe Philadelphia is the finest city in the country and I'm mighty sorry that circumstances make it advisable for me to leave. However, my family will continue to live there."

Actually, Bell continued to spend as much time as possible living with his family in Philadelphia and commuting frequently to Pittsburgh. He almost never missed a weekly meeting of his beloved Maxwell Club on Mondays, often quipping to sportswriters about having "just time to count the money in Pittsburgh and get back here to quarterback the luncheon."

Bell insisted that the shift of franchises would not entail any change in the personnel, the direction or the tactics of the team. "He and Henry J. 'Heinie' Miller, the Eagles co-coaches last year, and Walt Kiesling, who came from Pittsburgh in the original deal, will continue to direct the team," O'Gara reported. "Bell said he was to be president of the club, with a separate salary for the position." A few days later, though, Miller decided not to move to Pittsburgh and serve as an assistant coach. That left Bell in charge of the Steelers' football operation with Kiesling his assistant.

"We have the pick of the Philadelphia and Pittsburgh clubs," Bell explained to the *Sun-Telegraph*. "For the first time, we'll have seasoned players backing up seasoned players at all positions, and we'll be able to put up a battle against the rich teams like the Giants and Redskins who have always had the bulge against us."

However, according to Andrew O'Toole, in his book *Smiling Irish Eyes: Art Rooney and the Pittsburgh Steelers*, "If the 'switch' of franchises wasn't confusing enough, the brain trust of the two teams decided to shuffle the rosters of each club almost beyond recognition. To the press, Rooney explained that he and Bell opted to keep their 'favorite' players from each team. The quality of players in question wasn't a major concern considering the dismal performance continually turned in by each squad. The rosters were actually set [the previous] December 10 when the coaches and owners of each team enjoined in a lengthy debate on every individual player before dividing up the clubs. Roughly half of each team switched to the other, creating a hodgepodge mess."

Thompson told O'Gara that he tried to purchase the Philadelphia franchise before he acquired the Steelers because he had long wished to transfer his football operations closer to his New York home. As it turned out Thompson and Rooney had met at least twice previously but failed to reach an agreement. Rooney had lost "between $100,000 and $150,000" in his eight years in Pittsburgh, according to the *Sun-Telegraph*, and was anxious to sell. But he refused to allow Thompson to relocate the franchise to Boston. Finally Thompson agreed to keep the club in Pittsburgh.

Thompson, who was named after his grandfather, the founder of the Republic Steel Corporation, inherited more than $3.5 million when he was 15 years old. After graduating from Yale University, he launched a profitable wholesale company that distributed an eye solution called Eye-Gene for hayfever victims. But sports were his first love.

Thompson was well known as a fierce competitor and almost earned the rare distinction of competing in the Olympics in *two* sports. He was a member of the 1936 U.S. Olympic field hockey team that lost all four of its games in Berlin and finished dead last in 11th place. Later, during the trials for the 1948 U.S. Olympic bobsled team at Lake Placid, his four-man sled went over the side of the chute. He ended up in the hospital with a fractured ankle and assorted cuts and bruises.

Shortly after graduating from college, Thompson went looking for a "sports hobby." He considered buying a National Hockey League franchise but quickly turned to football after seeing two amateur teams draw almost twice as many fans to Madison Square Garden as the New York Rangers had attracted the night before.

Thompson later told John Kieran of the *New York Times* how he came to purchase the Philadelphia Eagles the previous December.

"I went to Pittsburgh in November and asked Art Rooney how much he wanted for his club," Thompson explained. "He told me. I said it was too much. He asked me how much we would pay. I told him. He said it was too little. I said good-bye. It was all over in 15 minutes.

"My next play was around end. I went to Philadelphia and asked Bert Bell would he sell. He said he wouldn't. I asked him why. He said he didn't want to get out of the game. I suggested he and Rooney get together to own one club and I'd buy the other. They did. It was all over in four days. I owned the Pittsburgh franchise. Rooney had gone in with Bell in Philadelphia."

Later, Kieran asked Thompson to explain "the big puzzle," the subsequent switching of the franchises and the shuffling of the players. "That was Rooney," Thompson replied. "Maybe Philadelphia seemed too quiet for him. Or he may have been homesick for the smoke of Pittsburgh. Anyway, he persuaded Bert Bell and Bert put it up to us. As a matter of fact, we preferred Philadelphia all along. We were glad to swap franchises."

Thompson said that he and his new coach, Greasy Neale, met Bell and Rooney at the Racquet Club in Philadelphia to divide up the players from their respective franchises.

"We didn't pick them blind, either," Thompson added. "Greasy and I saw every game Pittsburgh played last fall. They played Philadelphia twice, so we knew a little about those players, too. Not only did we see all of the Pittsburgh games of last year, but we had movies of those games. And Greasy ran them over and over again in my apartment. He'd sit there for five hours, studying the way the different players worked."

If the 1941 NFL results are any indication, Neale's filmwork did pay a slight dividend. Thompson's Eagles finished with a 2–8–1 record, a game higher than the Bell-Rooney Steelers at 1–9–1. Philadelphia won its first head-to-head meeting, 10–7, and the two teams tied, 7–7, in the other game.

Before the season started Bell had been quite optimistic. "This is the finest squad I've ever worked with in the National Football League—as good as any I've seen in the loop," he told the *Pittsburgh Press*.

But as O'Toole recalled in his book, Bell's partner did not share Bert's enthusiasm:

"On a blistering August afternoon, Claire Burkey, the beat writer for the *Press*, spied Art in the bleachers inspecting his team going through their pre-season workout. Rooney had stopped off in Hershey while making his way to Saratoga expecting to see an upgrade in his team after the previous winter's overhaul. 'Well, Art, how does your team look to you?' the reporter inquired. Puffing on his ever-present cigar, Art gave a succinct response. 'Those new uniforms they're wearing threw me off a bit, but once I saw them practice a couple of minutes, I could see they were the same old Pirates.'

"Burkey quoted Rooney in the following day's *Press*. It would be a statement Arthur would long rue to ever have uttered. 'Same old Pirates' would amend to 'Same old Steelers,' or 'S.O.S.' In the coming years, patrons sitting through another blundering performance by the home team at Forbes Field would hear the murmur of the refrain throughout the stands, 'Same Old Steelers.'"

Bert lasted only two games as head coach, both losses to the Cleveland Rams (17–14) and the Eagles (10–7). On the way back to Pittsburgh after the first loss, Chicago sportswriter Ed Prell recalls that Bell told Rooney that he felt terrible.

"Let's make some deals," he suggested to his partner. "I told Bert that the people in Pittsburgh were tired of our deals because they always backfired," Rooney replied. "Then Bert asked me what I thought we should do. I had only one concrete proposal. 'Bert,' I said, 'did you ever think about changing coaches?'"

After the second defeat, according to *Chicago Sun-Times* sportswriter Dick Hackenberg, Bell called Rooney and said, "We gotta do something. Something drastic. Nobody'll come out to see us at this rate." Rooney replied, "I know what to do, but you won't go for it." Bell said, "Name it." Rooney said, "You gotta quit!"

Three days later, Bell announced his resignation.

"Next to my wife and children, coaching football has always been my greatest love," he said in a typewritten statement.

> However, resulting that I have had better material than either Cleveland or Philadelphia, and having lost both games, I believe it would be in the best interests of the Pittsburgh fans and the City of Pittsburgh that I resign as head football coach of the Pittsburgh Steelers and confine my duties to the business end of the corporation. My deepest regret is that I did not produce a winner for the many well-wishers of the press, radio, and loyal fans of the City of Pittsburgh. My partner, Arthur J. Rooney, and my assistant coach, Walter Kiesling, gave me every cooperation that was honestly possible. I further wish to state that our loss to Cleveland and Philadelphia was not the fault of anyone but myself. In my new capacity, I again will continue to give every ounce of energy that I have trying to bring a winner to Pittsburgh.

According to Hackenberg, Bell told Rooney that he would quit only if he could get Aldo "Buff" Donelli, the highly regarded Duquesne coach, to replace him.

"Bert didn't think I could pry him loose," Rooney recalled. "But I did, so Bert quit as promised and I had to give him back the presidency of the company. Every time I fired Coach Bell, I had to resign the presidency to make room for him."

Donelli's coaching career with Pittsburgh lasted five stormy weeks. He had already negotiated a three-year, $30,000 annual deal to take over the Steelers beginning in 1942, but Rooney asked him to come in immediately to replace Bell. So the morning that Bell resigned, Donelli was at St. Vincent's College directing Steelers workouts. That same afternoon, according to O'Toole, he was on Duquesne's campus putting the Dukes through their paces.

Layden was incensed even though he had close ties to Donelli. The new commissioner had coached at Duquesne from 1927 to 1934 and Donelli served as captain of his unbeaten 1928 team.

"None of which kept the commissioner from putting his foot down," reported *The Pro Football Chronicle*. "'It is impossible physically and mentally to direct two major football teams at the same time,' Layden said. 'If Donelli is not in a position to sever connections completely at Duquesne, or if he is unwilling to make such a change, the Steelers will have to secure another coach.'"

Donelli then "resigned" as Duquesne's head coach but remained as the school's athletic director. He also promised Layden that he would limit his role to that of a spectator, but there was little doubt who was still calling the shots when he appeared at Duquesne's practices in the afternoon and sat on the bench for their games. Although his Dukes went unbeaten in eight games and finished first in the East, the Steelers were terrible from Week 1 when they were humiliated by the New York Giants, 37–10.

"During the game, Donelli was shocked that players asked to come out when they were winded," said *The Pro Football Chronicle*. "He accused some of faking injuries when the Giants started to roll."

"He seethed and raged up and down the benches, turning loose a flood on every player," the Associated Press added. "It was the worst licking any Donelli-coached team ever took, and 'The Buffer' breathed fire as he emphasized the way in which it was taken."

The Steelers responded by improving slightly but still lost their next four games to Washington (twice), the Bears and Giants by a combined score of 109–37. In November, Donelli finally got caught in an impossible conflict. Duquesne was scheduled to play St. Mary's in San Francisco at the same time the Steelers were in Philadelphia to face the Eagles. Layden ordered Donelli to be in the Quaker City or resign. Donelli refused and boarded a train to California.

"The commissioner did not appreciate Buff's insolence and immediately severed the coach's relationship with the Steelers," O'Toole reported. "Donelli did not quit, nor did Rooney step forward and fire his friend. Instead he was banished from the professional game by Layden. It would be the first, and only, time a coach would be castigated from the league."

A few days later, Kiesling took over as coach and Bell found himself in hot water when he told a local sportswriter that Donelli "couldn't take it in the pros." Donelli was quite piqued and confronted Bell before a Steelers game at Forbes Field. Bert claimed that he was misquoted.

One week after the Steelers' season ended—with Bell and Rooney confirming that they lost $8,000 for the year—the Japanese attacked Pearl Harbor. The world and professional football would never be the same.

Bert and Frances did have another reason to celebrate early in 1942 when their third child and first daughter, Jane Upton, was born on February 1 at Presbyterian Hospital in Philadelphia.

15. Bracing for World War II

Financially, Bert Bell and Art Rooney continued to struggle in 1942 despite experiencing their first winning season with a 7–4 record. The owners were so heavily in debt, said Barney Nagler in the *New York Morning Telegraph,* that they were confronted with the task of feeding their players without spending money that they didn't even have.

"Out of desperation, by necessity, Rooney made a deal with a grocer: The Steelers could eat on credit. Finally the grocer lost patience. He was doing a rushing business with the hefty footballers, but there was no money coming in and prospects for payment seemed remote. He refused to shell out another peanut until Rooney and Bell shelled out."

"It was a tough situation," Bell told Nagler. "There we were with a team on our hands and no money to pay for groceries. We're in this hotel room, Rooney and I, and we get a call from Harry Thayer. He was Alexis Thompson's business manager with the Philadelphia Eagles, and we knew Alex had money so we're happy to hear from him. He says, 'Bert, you got a player named Steele?' I put my hand over the telephone and said, 'Art, we got a player named Steele?' He thought for a moment and said we had a halfback named Steele.

"I thought to myself that if we had a player named Steele he couldn't be very good because we didn't have any players, but I said to Thayer, 'Steele? Sure. He's a top player.' Thayer said Thompson wanted to buy Steele for the Eagles. I said, 'Okay, how much?' He said he'd pay $1,500. I said, 'Make it $2,000 and it's a deal.' Rooney shook his fist in my face. He said, 'If they turn us down, I'll kill you, Bert.' I said to Thayer, 'Let me know by five o'clock.' When I hung up, Rooney was fit to be tied.

"Here's the picture. We have no money for food, a guy wants to give us $1,500 for a player and I'm holding out for $2,000. Now it's five minutes before five o'clock and the phone rings. We both jump for it but I beat Rooney to it. It's Thayer, sure enough. He says, 'We'll pay you $1,500 for

Steele.' I said, 'Okay, Harry, but can you do us a favor? Can you send the $1,500 by Western Union?' "

Ernie Steele, a halfback/defensive back from the University of Washington, ended up playing seven productive seasons for the Eagles.

As if they didn't have enough to worry about with their embattled Steelers, Bell and Rooney were sent on an undercover mission by their sometimes friend, sometimes adversary George Halas, the wily owner of the Chicago Bears.

Halas had sent his 18-year-old daughter, Ginny, to attend Drexel Institute in Philadelphia, where his older brother, Walter, was football coach. Soon she was dating Ed McCaskey, a senior at the University of Pennsylvania, who asked her to marry him during the summer. Even though a wedding date was set for December, Halas still had not given his permission. Instead, McCaskey found a couple of visitors wearing camel hair overcoats and fedoras standing at his door.

"One was smoking a cigar," Ed said years later in Jeff Davis's book *Papa Bear: The Life and Legacy of George Halas*. "The other took out his upper plate and introduced himself as Bert Bell and his cigar-smoking friend as Art Rooney. Both, they said, were with the Pittsburgh Steelers. 'Halas sent us here to investigate you,' Bell said."

Later that night, according to Steve Halvonik of the *Pittsburgh Post Gazette*, Bell and Rooney caught up with McCaskey at a smoky Philadelphia saloon where McCaskey was a singer. They had been to see Bill Lennox, the ticket manager at Bell's alma mater, Penn.

"Bill Lennox says you're OK," Bell told McCaskey. "If Lennox says you're OK, you're OK with me." "If you're OK with Bert, you're OK with me," Rooney said, taking the cigar out of his face. "And whoever said Halas was an angel?"

A couple of months later, the young couple eloped and were married by a priest in Baltimore. But not before Halas asked Rooney to hire a private detective to check McCaskey out.

"What the detective found infuriated Halas the rest of his life," Davis wrote. "The detective reported that not only was Ed a saloon singer, but worse, he was also a gambler, a plunger at the racetrack. One of the reasons the Old Man brought him into the club a quarter-century later was to keep an eye on him. And he put Gin on an allowance so Ed couldn't blow it all on the ponies."

Ginny eventually became principal owner of the Bears and McCaskey served for a while as the team's chairman and treasurer.

Throughout the year, the NFL owners constantly bickered and argued among themselves. They ignored pleas for proper decorum from Commissioner Layden at the league meeting on March 26 at the Commodore Hotel in New York City.

"In our discussions, let us stick to the subject," Layden said. "Personalities are exempt. Whispering and walking around the room are against the rules of order. The speaker is entitled to all courtesies. Argument is fine and, I believe, healthy. The air should be cleared of any season hangovers at the annual meeting so that we can go forward with the business of the coming season and not be distracted from important business at hand with no *bias* against anybody. All actions taken and all words spoken are business of the meetings and no publicity is to be given outside of this room to any actions or any words. All publicity should clear through the director of public relations in order that we may have united action."

In August, Bell, who handled most of the player's contracts, pulled off the most significant signing in the Steelers' young history. He inked the club's top draft choice, (Bullet) Bill Dudley, an outstanding offensive and defensive star from Virginia.

"I met Bert at his office in Philadelphia," recalled the future Pro Football Hall-of Famer, who would become a lifelong friend. "He could be a lot tougher with the dollar than Mr. Rooney could. That's why he handled most of the player's contracts. He went into this long spiel about the ballplayers and the league.

"After he finished talking, my father looked at him and said, 'Mr. Bell, I think my son ought to have at least $5,000.' I'll never forget. The commissioner couldn't get the contract in front of him fast enough. He said, 'Mr. Dudley, I certainly do agree with you! All he has to do is sign right here.' My father was a $400-a-month traveling salesman. It was more money than he ever made."

On the field, Bullet Bill was everything as promised. The triple-threat running back, passer, and punter led the league in rushing as the Steelers rebounded from a 0–2 start to win seven of their last nine games. Dudley, who fought in World War II for two years, would go on to play with Pittsburgh, Detroit, and Washington until 1953. Rooney called him "the finest player I ever had."

At the end of the 1942 season, the NFL voted by a slim margin to continue operations during the war. Bell echoed the sentiments of most league owners after the annual player draft when he told sportswriters, according to author Andrew O'Toole:

We drafted thirty kids from college and we'll be lucky to get four. Like all other clubs, most of the men we drafted are now in the armed forces, and those not yet enrolled cannot be pinned down.

In fact at least a dozen have not even answered my letters, and I know they received them. Our league player limit is twenty-five. That will be plenty, but where can one team hope to get that many first class players under the present conditions?

Conditions would soon worsen for Bell and the rest of the NFL.

16. The Steagles

More than 600 players, coaches, and team administrators from the NFL would eventually go into military service during World War II. When Cleveland Rams owner Dan Reeves joined the Navy early in 1943, his club was permitted to suspend operations, leaving the league with nine teams and an awkward scheduling problem. Moreover, the Office of Defense Transportation ordered the league to cut travel by 37 percent and reduce the size of rosters to 28 players.

"Most significant," wrote author Andrew O'Toole, "was a rule change that received little notice in 1943—free substitution. Football had long been played by men who 'went both ways,' performing for both their offensive and defensive teams. The wartime rosters, however, were too exhausted to take full advantage of the new tenet. Nonetheless, free substitution smoothed the way for separate offensive and defensive units, and led to specialists such as field-goal kickers and punters. Until this rule change came into effect a player could enter a game once in each quarter, except in the fourth quarter when two players on each team could be substituted twice. Free substitution not only initiated the birth of 'skilled' players, but also drastically reduced the number of injuries incurred."

In March, Rooney told Jack Sell of the *Pittsburgh Post Gazette* that the Steelers would be "going through the motions" of preparing for the annual player draft in April, "although, personally, I am not very optimistic about the National League operating next autumn.

"My partner, Bert Bell, is handling the personnel problem along with coaches Walter Kiesling and Jim Leonard. They did a pretty good job last year. Of course, many of the names chosen this time will be of players who may be scattered all over the world in the armed forces by mid-September when the league race usually starts."

Chester L. Smith, the sports editor of the *Pittsburgh Press,* wrote that NFL commissioner Elmer Layden would use "every legitimate means in his command to force the circuit to function" because of a war clause in

Layden's annual $25,000 contract stipulating that in the event of a league breakdown, he doesn't get paid.

One NFL official predicted to Smith that the league would be able to field only five teams in the fall. "If it weren't for George Preston Marshall, of the Redskins," he added, "the el-foldo would be certain." Marshall fought vigorously to keep pro football alive during the war because he had sold more than $60,000 worth of season tickets for 1943 in an amusement-starved city.

Before the NFL owners convened in Chicago on April 6, Bell and four other club owners met as an executive committee and recommended to Layden that the league proceed with plans to operate in 1943. The commissioner then announced that the upcoming sessions would be conducted on the "We can and we will play football" theme.

On May 27, with his roster down to five players, Rooney told the *Pittsburgh Press* that he had conferred by telephone with Bert Bell in Philadelphia and that there was a good possibility that the Steelers would merge with the Eagles only for the duration of the war.

"As we maintained at the last league meeting, we are doing everything in our power to continue operation," Rooney explained. "But, the prospects of continuing on our own look very bad. As I see it, about the only way we could continue to field a representative team will be to merge with Philadelphia."

Bell and Rooney approached Eagles owner Alexis Thompson early in June and suggested merging their two teams, at least for the 1943 season. Thompson, however, was not immediately enthralled with the idea because he thought that it would hurt the team's image and wasn't really sure that such a move was necessary. Eagles general manager Harry Thayer told Thompson he was "reasonably sure" that the Eagles could field a team by themselves.

"In addition to the 16 players the Eagles still had under contract, Thayer said they had 'strings attached' to about a dozen more," wrote Matthew Algeo in his book *Last Team Standing*. Thompson said that he would have to think about the merger for a while.

On June 15, 1943, Thayer, speaking for Thompson, told reporters that "on the whole" his team preferred to operate alone but would consider a merger only if they were able to retain the name "Philadelphia Eagles" and play all their home games in the Quaker City.

Confident that more favorable details could be worked out later, Bell and Thayer submitted a formal application for permission to merge the two franchises. When the league owners convened four days later at Chicago's Blackstone Hotel, they expected to discuss only one potential merger—the

Eagles and Steelers. They quickly learned, however, that the two Chicago teams—the Bears and Cardinals—were requesting to do the same thing.

For five hours, the owners bitterly debated the two requests. George Preston Marshall, leading a group attempting to block the mergers, made a motion saying that if the teams merged, one of the teams would have to disperse its players among all of the league's remaining clubs just as Cleveland had done. That motion passed 5–2 with Philadelphia and Pittsburgh voting no and the two Chicago teams abstaining.

When the meeting was adjourned midway through the afternoon, Bell and Rooney began lobbying their colleagues, begging the Chicago owners to abandon their merger request and asking Giants owner Jack Mara, who supported Marshall, to change his mind. Even Commissioner Elmer Layden jumped onto the side of the Pennsylvanians.

After the meeting resumed, the Chicago teams withdrew their merger request and Bell made a motion

> to allow Pittsburgh and Philadelphia to merge from the end of the meeting to the close of the National Football League season, that is, the week before the playoff game, retaining their players from both teams and the right to play in both cities.
>
> And it is understood that we are not suspending and will retain all our rights under the Constitution and Bylaws except that Philadelphia and Pittsburgh will only have one vote during the period of the merger, namely from the end of this meeting until the Sunday before the playoff game, and automatically then the merger will be over and both teams will return to their former status under the Constitution and Bylaws as of June 19, 1943 and that during this period Philadelphia will cast one vote.

Ralph B. Brizzolara, of the Bears, seconded the motion that eventually carried by the narrowest of margins, 5–4, following "a long and bitter debate," according to Algeo.

The Pittsburgh and Philadelphia owners eventually came to an agreement on such issues as pooling expenses, sharing profits equally, and keeping team headquarters in Philadelphia, Bell's hometown. Not as easy to resolve, however, was the scheduling situation—Rooney and Bell insisted on splitting the home games evenly—and the selection of head coach.

Trying to determine a complete NFL schedule resulted in one of the "longest and most bitter" battles in the 22-year history of the league, wrote Tommy Devine of the United Press. The owners were hopelessly deadlocked after 16 hours and were forced to continue deliberations the following day. Finally on June 21, a 10-game schedule was adopted with the Steelers and Eagles reluctantly agreeing that four "home" games would be held in Philadelphia and only two in Pittsburgh.

Bell later told the *Pittsburgh Press* that attempts were being made to move a pair of home games of the Green Bay Packers and Brooklyn Dodgers to Forbes Field. But negotiations proved to be futile. The Steelers' president insisted that it was imperative that the NFL resolve its scheduling difficulties.

Before the league could be an unqualified success, each team must play all the others every season, Bell explained to Chester Smith. "Washington didn't play the Chicago Bears or Green Bay Packers last year in the regular campaign—and won. In 1941, the Giants finished first—without meeting the Bears or Packers. I'm not saying both elevens wouldn't have landed where they did with a full round-robin schedule, but it would have been fairer if they had."

It was also decided at the league meeting, after lengthy, sometimes heated, discussions, that the Steelers' Walt Kiesling and the Eagles' Greasy Neale would become "co-head coaches" and that the teams would wear Eagles Kelly green and white uniforms for all games.

"Bell and Rooney wanted the team to wear the Steelers' black and gold jerseys, at least when they played in Pittsburgh," said Algeo, but they "probably gave in because it would have been too costly to clean and maintain two sets of uniforms all season anyway. Bell and Rooney practically gave up the farm, but considering the circumstances, the principals were satisfied with the merger."

"Without it," Bell told the *Pittsburgh Press*," we would have been pathetic and so would the Eagles. We had no backfield men left and Philadelphia had no linemen. Now, however, we have a fairly strong squad in the making."

The reaction in Pittsburgh was not as favorable. "So far as anyone in Pittsburgh needs to be concerned, there will be no National League football here in the fall," wrote Smith in the *Press*. "The temporary merger of the Steelers and Philadelphia Eagles was worked out on anything but an equitable basis."

Smith is credited with coining the term *Steagles* in a column published four days after the merger was approved.

During the preseason, Arthur Daley of the *New York Times* recalled Bell putting in a telephone call to Steve Owen, the coach of the New York Giants. "Help me out, Steve," pleaded Bell with a note of desperation in his voice. "We're so shorthanded that we can barely field a full team. I'll take anyone you cut from your squad." "Don't bother, Bert," said Steve good-humoredly. "I have nothing but dogmeat myself."

"It sounds like we had a big advantage putting two teams together as one," former Eagles tackle Al Wistert told Ray Didinger in *The Eagles Encyclopedia.* "But all it meant was we had twice as many lousy players." The Steagles were so desperate during the preseason that they gave a try-out to Don MacGregor, a 27-year-old former punting and passing star at Iowa State Prison, who was released after serving part of a 10-year sentence for car theft. He didn't make the team.

Bell did convince future Hall-of-Famer Bill Hewitt to reluctantly come out of his three-year retirement with an extremely generous offer and some persistent persuasion. As Hewitt described the negotiations to Algeo: "I said 'No thank you,' and he said 'Aw, c'mon,' and I said 'Sorry,' and he said, 'Four hundred per game.' I said 'Are you going to hand me that pen or do we sit here and stall all night.'"

But Hewitt, the great end from Michigan who was classified 4-F (ineligible for military service) because of a perforated eardrum, was forced to make one concession: because of a new league rule, he had to wear a helmet for the first time in his career. Hewitt's comeback attempt was a failure, however. He caught only two passes in six games and re-tired for good after the Steagles and Washington battled to a 14–14 tie on November 7.

"I presume he felt he could not do justice to his war job and still play with us," Bell told the *Post Gazette.*

The Pittsburgh players stuck to themselves at the start of preseason practice because they were in the minority and forced to practice away from home. But eventually players from both sides got along reasonably well. It was a different story with the coaches, however. They bickered constantly and almost came to blows on more than one occasion. They fought about everything from coaching philosophy to game strategy and personnel, even though Bell suggested that they split their responsibilities with Neale handling the offense and Kiesling coaching the defense.

Early in 1942, right after Pearl Harbor, Bell had convinced Rooney and Thompson to require all of the players to contribute to the war effort by working at least 40 hours a week in defense plants. "It isn't going to be enough to play, pay taxes, buy Defense Bonds, and continue as before," he explained to *Philadelphia Inquirer* sportswriter Cy Peterman.

Only the Eagles and then the Steagles adopted Bell's idea. Their players worked long hours at such places as the Philadelphia and Camden ship-yards along the Delaware River, Bendix Aviation, and the Kellett Aircraft

Corporation. Veteran Steelers tackle Ted Doyle kept his job as a fitter and group leader at the Westinghouse plant in Pittsburgh.

Bell unsuccessfully tried to convince other club owners to have their players join in the work effort during the day.

"If all the clubs were playing under the same conditions, we'd have a better chance," he explained to *Philadelphia Bulletin* sports editor Ed Pollock. "But we are the only club with 100 per cent of our personnel in war work. As a result, some of our inexperienced players may look greener and may make more mistakes than they would if they had plenty of time to practice. The players are tired, too, and the coaches can't bear down on them as they would otherwise. Why couldn't our professional squads be employed in defense work, cut down on the weekly practice, play on Sundays and thus combine the two and do double duty for the good of all?"

Most of the players welcomed the extra income and some, like defensive back/end Larry Cabrelli, worked 60 to 70 hours a week. "He was late for practice every night," Bell told Bill Dooly of the *Philadelphia Record*. "It made it a little hard on coach Neale when the players were late in reporting but we knew they were doing the right thing and so didn't mind it at all."

The players practiced for three hours beginning at 6:00 P.M. every night from Monday through Saturday. "You worked all day and you practiced all night," halfback Jack Hinkle explained. "By the end of the day you were tired as hell."

Hinkle finished the year by gaining 571 yards on 116 carries but lost the NFL rushing title by a yard to Bill Paschal of the New York Giants because a statistician erroneously credited teammate John Butler with a 37-yard-run that Hinkle made on the first play from scrimmage in Week 2, against the Giants.

The team's facilities were deplorable. Most of the time they practiced at River Field located on the edge of the University of Pennsylvania campus between railroad tracks and the Schuylkill River.

"Passing locomotives belched clouds of smoke that hung over the field," Algeo wrote in his book. "There were no lights; practice ended when dusk surrendered to the night. There was no locker room, either. Players had to change underneath a set of bleachers. Most of them took the trolley or walked to practice, since nonessential driving was banned at the time, and professional football practices were, as far as the government was concerned, not essential."

At other times, the team practiced at a playground in West Philadelphia or at 54th Street and City Line Avenue, on the campus of St. Joseph's College, on a weed-infested field littered with broken glass, tin cans, and oil from a nearby gas station that had used the field as a dumping ground. Some lights had been installed but they were not really satisfactory and the twilight practices were often conducted in half shadows.

"It was a junkyard," Wistert recalled. "And I came from the University of Michigan where everything was first class, A-Number 1. We played and practiced on *grassy fields*, not in back of a gas station. It was quite a comedown."

Most of the players lived at the old Hotel Philadelphia at 39th and Chestnut Streets near the University of Pennsylvania campus during the season. "Lex Thompson had a lot of Hollywood friends like Lana Turner and Clark Gable," Hinkle told William Ecenbarger of the *Philadelphia Inquirer*. "They would come to socialize with the players on Sunday nights after home games."

In an effort to ingratiate themselves to fans in both cities, the teams played two preseason games against a pair of NFL powerhouses within a span of five days.

Although Green Bay won the first one, 28–10, before 18,369 fans at Forbes Field, Packers coach Curly Lambeau called the Steagles "the best-looking National Football League entry ever seen from Philadelphia or Pittsburgh." The veteran coach added that with a little more experience, they had a good chance to win the eastern half title. More than 30,000 fans then watched the exhausted Steagles lose to the Chicago Bears, 20–7, at Shibe Park.

The Steagles opened the season by setting a franchise record that still stands, holding Brooklyn to *minus* 33 yards rushing in their home opening win, 17–0, over the Dodgers. The following week, they upset the mighty New York Giants, 28–14, despite fumbling an NFL-record ten times. Asked if the Eagles had ever started the season with two wins, Bell quipped: "Hell, I don't even remember them ever winning two games in a row before."

The other two Steagles "home" games were played at Forbes Field, the home of the National League baseball team in Pittsburgh. The Steagles erupted for three touchdowns in less than four minutes in the first quarter and went on to beat the winless Chicago Cardinals, 34–13, in the first game on October 31 before 16,351 fans. Later, on November 21, they rallied in the fourth quarter to edge the Detroit Lions, 35–34, as 23,338 fans watched.

Before the Lions' game, according to *Post-Gazette* sports editor Havey J. Boyle, Bell ribbed Rooney incessantly about the record-breaking crowd of 28,893 that the Steagles had attracted two weeks earlier for the game against the Redskins in Philadelphia. Ever since the two men had become partners, Bell had bragged about Philadelphia's superiority as a football city.

When he saw the large crowd and long lines waiting to get into Shibe Park before the Redskins game, Rooney moaned, "This is going to be terrible. Just think how I'll have to put up with Bell as he rubs it in. I was hoping for a nice little rain, but look how the sun is shining. I can hear Bell poppin' off already." Rooney even joked that he was considering canvassing fans by going door to door to ensure an impressive turnout for the Lions game.

The Steagles actually stayed in contention for the Eastern Division title until the final game of the season. They finished with the first winning record (5–4–1) in the Philadelphia Eagles' franchise history. They went unbeaten in Philadelphia until that last game, a 38–28 loss to Green Bay on December 5 before their largest home crowd of the year, 34,294.

The week before, even though they were 14-point underdogs, the Steagles had prevented the Washington Redskins from clinching the Eastern Division title with a 27–14 upset victory before a sellout crowd of 35,826 at Griffith Stadium. It was their only road win of the year.

"What a ball game," exclaimed Bell, fantasizing that the Steagles could still tie for the Eastern Division crown if they beat the Packers in the season finale and the Redskins lost both of their games to the New York Giants. "It would be a very funny thing. That George Marshall would be fit to be tied. I would love to see that. I sure would!"

Bell's dream did not come true. The Redskins and Giants tied for the regular-season Eastern Division title with 6–3–1 records. Washington blanked New York, 28–0, in the playoff, then lost to the Chicago Bears, 41–21, in the showdown for the NFL crown.

The era of the Steagles ended after that one season. In addition to the bitterness between the coaches, Rooney was unhappy over the unbalanced scheduling of "home" games and insisted that the team's base of operation be moved to Pittsburgh if the merger was to continue. Thompson announced at the league meeting in Chicago on January 13, 1944, that he refused to submit to Rooney's demands and the two franchises would go their separate ways.

Meanwhile, league officials spent 20 hours deliberating about possible expansion while seekers of franchises from Buffalo, Los Angeles, and San Francisco "paced the outer vestibule like expectant fathers," according to the Associated Press. Commissioner Layden announced that Buffalo's application would be discussed at the April 1944 meeting while the two West Coast teams would probably be considered after the war.

Bell told the AP that "this is no time to be talking about" adding other teams.

"It's not good judgment in my mind to even consider an expansion and it won't be good judgment until the war is over," he explained. "Los Angeles may be a very good city, but say you'd go there and play on a Sunday and had a game in Philadelphia the following Sunday. Know what would happen? You'd lose in Philadelphia. The players would be bruised up and on a train for three days where they couldn't work out the stiffness and get those whirlpool baths. You'd get in Philadelphia Wednesday night and you'd have only three days to limber up.

"That's supposing you could get a squad aboard a transcontinental train. Why, do you know that to get transportation for our game in Chicago I had to start working on it six days in advance? And then I couldn't get return tickets. I had to ask the Bears to work on 'em for me in Chicago."

After the meetings were adjourned, and with only six players left on their roster, Bell and Rooney immediately began working the lobby of the Blackstone Hotel, searching—unsuccessfully—for a new partner.

17. The Card-Pitts

After considering the possibility of merging with the Cleveland Rams, who were returning to the league after a one-year absence, Bert Bell and Art Rooney finally reached an agreement with Charles Bidwell, the owner of the Chicago Cardinals, to combine forces for the 1944 season.

The owners got together at the NFL's spring meeting on April 23 and decided that Walt Kiesling would share the coaching duties with Chicago's Phil Handler and that the club's headquarters would be located in Pittsburgh. The Card-Pitts were placed in the Western Division so that the Eastern Division could accommodate the addition of the new Boston Yanks franchise that was slated to begin play in 1944 under the ownership of singer Kate Smith and her business manager, Ted Collins.

In July, Bell invited all of the holdovers from Pittsburgh's contingent of the 1943 Steagles to a meeting at the Steelers' office at the Fort Pitt Hotel. Only five players showed up. The owners were so desperate to find players that they invited Warren Heller, who had played halfback for the club from 1934 to 1936, to try out. He didn't make the team.

Following preseason practice at the Cardinals' training facility in Waukesha, Wisconsin, the Card-Pitts opened the exhibition season at Philadelphia's Shibe Park with 28 players on their roster. It would be the first time that players from the previous year's Steagles would be facing each other. With Babe Ruth and other members of the New York Yankees in attendance, the visitors allowed three touchdowns in the first quarter and suffered a lackluster, 22–0, loss to the Eagles. Afterward, Bell told reporters the Card-Pitts were the worst team he had ever seen.

When the regular season began, the Card-Pitts got off to a fairly promising start by hanging tough against the Cleveland Rams in their opening game. But they dropped a 30–28 heartbreaker before the largest crowd of their three home games, 20,968 fans. Despite a 17–16 win over the New York Giants in a hastily scheduled exhibition game after Week 1, the rest of the season turned out to be a disaster on the field as the owners bickered and blamed each other's players for the dismal record, according to author Andrew O'Toole.

In addition to losing all 10 games, they earned a new nickname after *Pittsburgh Post-Gazette* sports editor Al Abrams quoted a letter written by a disgusted fan in his column, saying, "Why don't they call themselves the Car-Pits? I think it's very appropriate as every team in the league walks over them." They drew a crowd of 17,743 for a 27–6 loss to the Detroit Lions, but only 9,069 fans came out for their season finale at Forbes Field, a 49–7 humiliation by the Chicago Bears. Fullback John Grigas, the Card-Pitts' leading rusher with 610 yards, took one look at the muddy, partially frozen Forbes Field playing surface and refused to play against the Bears, possibly passing up the league's rushing title, and went home to Massachusetts.

Card-Pitts crowds in Chicago were worse: 14,732 attended a 33–6 loss to Cleveland and only 7,158 were on hand for their other home game in the Windy City, a 35–20 defeat at the hands of Green Bay.

The low point came at midseason. After watching their team being blown out in Chicago by the Bears, 34–7, Bell and Rooney had seen enough. Four starters were fined $200 for indifferent play and for missing practice. One of them, Johnny Butler, the league's seventh leading rusher the previous season, was suspended and put on the trading block. Infuriated, the players decided to go on strike immediately, according to Joe Ziemba in *When Football Was Football: The Chicago Cardinals and the Birth of the NFL.*

"Instead of showing up for practice, we'd go to a bar instead," recalled veteran tackle Chet Bulger. "We did that Monday, then Tuesday, then Wednesday. . . . We did this all week and finally Art Rooney called us all in to a meeting and told us that Johnny would get his check. He told us to be ready to practice on Friday. So what do we do? We all get to practice early and hide like a bunch of kids from the coaches so they'd think we wouldn't be there. We played terrible on Sunday." (And lost to the New York Giants 23–0.)

Despite the team's horrible performance on the gridiron—"The season couldn't have turned out any worse than this one," Bell said—both owners were satisfied with the off-field results generated by the Cardinals and Steelers. "We had a good season financially, a very good one, I'd say, and want to stand on our own next fall," Bert told sportswriter Bill Dooly while relaxing between one of his daily bridge hands at the Racquet Club in Philadelphia. But Chicago's management had nothing to look forward to. The Cardinals' losing streak now stood at 26 games over a three-year period.

Throughout the year, almost all of the Card-Pitts players continued to work in defense plants. "Our league has been operating to a great extent with 4-F men and medical discharges," Bell explained to Dooly.

"Outside of some of the medical discharges, practically every man has been putting in at least 40 hours in some defense plant or other. We installed lights in Pittsburgh just for that very reason. One thing we'd like is to get the boys on the day shift, say the 8-to-4 shift, but even there we can make arrangements for them to practice, no matter what time they get off. With our club, the players were working in half a dozen plants around Pittsburgh last season. We had several men who couldn't go to training camp because of their jobs. The ones that did go had saved up their vacation."

Bell, who originated the unwritten "work-and-play" rule in 1942, told Dooly that he wanted *all* the club owners at the time to pass a rule prohibiting players from participating in the league unless he had a job in essential industry. "The rule wasn't passed because it was pointed out that it might work a hardship on some player who was a medical discharge," Bert explained. "For that reason it was dropped, but every club in the league is observing it anyhow."

When the club owners convened for their annual meeting at the Hotel Commodore in New York City on December 18, 1944, Commissioner Elmer Layden warned all players under NFL contracts to "watch their steps and not get too *flirty*" with any of the teams in any of the three proposed professional leagues that were rumored to be in the process of getting organized. Layden announced that any player who joined any such club would be suspended from playing in the NFL for a period of five years.

Meanwhile, Bell made the other major news announcement, telling William D. Richardson of the *New York Times* that he had just signed "Bullet Bill" Dudley, "who according to rumor was being *rushed* by some of the clubs in the All American Football Conference," perhaps the strongest threat of the new proposed leagues. Dudley, the Steelers' number-one draft pick in 1942, led the NFL with 696 rushing yards in 1942 before going off to the war for two years with the Army Air Corps. The future Pro Football Hall-of-Famer's contract was up for renegotiation and Bell said that he wanted to make sure that the deal was "ironclad" when he returned.

Before the 1945 season, Bell renewed his on-again, off-again relationship with Lud Wray by hiring his former teammate and Eagles co-owner as the Steelers' line coach. "Now middle-age mellowness has settled over them and this reunion may not end as the others have," *Philadelphia Bulletin* sports editor Ed Pollock predicted. "For all their disputes, they've had a barrel of fun with each other, not only laugh-provoking fun, but the keen enjoyment of watching their strategy win football games."

After leaving the Eagles, Wray coached the linemen at Manhattan and Holy Cross, where he became friendly with Jim Leonard, who was serving as the Crusaders' backfield coach. When Leonard was named to succeed Kiesling as head coach of the Steelers during the 1944–45 off season, Bell told him, "I believe that every head coach should name his own assistants, so that's up to you, Jim." Leonard, who was familiar with the stormy relationship between Bell and Wray, expected some resistance when he told Bert whom he wanted to hire as line coach. "You don't have to tell me," said Bell. "You want Ludlow. You couldn't pick a more sincere guy nor anyone who knows more football."

With Dudley rejoining the team for the last four games of the season, the Steelers improved slightly by winning two of 10 games in 1945. They defeated the Giants, 21–7, before 43,000 fans in New York, and the Chicago Cardinals, 13–0, before their smallest home crowd of the season, 13,000. Even though they still finished in last place in the Eastern Division for the second straight year, Bell and Rooney again considered the season a success.

"Leonard and Wray did a great job for us this year, a great job," Bell told Dooly. "Last August 15 we had 58 players they had to coach and at the end of the season only 15 of them were left. Returning servicemen came back and we had to take care of them, but the result was the squad was always changing. In spite of that, Leonard and Wray kept plugging away. They worked night and day and, considering the handicaps, I think they did a marvelous job."

Two weeks after the season ended, Leonard unexpectedly resigned as head coach. Bell immediately made it known that the man he coveted to succeed him was Dr. John B. "Jock" Sutherland, the former legendary coach at the University of Pittsburgh and the Brooklyn Dodgers, who had recently returned after serving in the U.S. Navy as a lieutenant commander.

"Only one man can save us," Bell told Rooney. "I think I can get Jock Sutherland to coach our club."

"Sutherland's the one fellow we've had in mind for a long time," Bell admitted to Dooly. "We told Jim Leonard and Lud Wray that when we signed them. Sutherland happens to be the man for the town. He made his reputation there with those great teams he turned out for Pitt. Pittsburgh liked him and liked his ball clubs. He's a natural."

Bell and Rooney soon convinced Sutherland to take the job. Even though the terms of the contract remained unsettled, the co-owners called a press conference at the Pittsburgh Athletic Club on December 29 to announce the signing. Here's what happened next, according to Ray Didinger in his book *Pittsburgh Steelers:*

"Bert," Sutherland said to Bell as he was led into the room where the reporters and photographers were waiting, "we really haven't agreed to terms, you know. Isn't this whole thing a bit premature?" "Nonsense," Rooney said, smacking Sutherland on the back. "We just called this press conference to avoid another of those 'scoops' we had the last time we talked. This way, we release the story ourselves and things usually work out better that way."

Sutherland shrugged his shoulders and sat behind the big walnut desk as the photographers closed in with cameras loaded and poised. "Doctor," Bert Bell said, shoving a fountain pen into Jock's hand, "the *Gazette* needs a picture for its early edition. Here, just sign this paper, and the photographer will be on his way."

"But Bert," Sutherland protested, "I can't sign a contract yet. We still have some matters to resolve. I don't think this is such a good idea."

"Just sign the paper," Bell said, pointing at a line near the bottom of the sheet. "C'mon, it's just for the press."

Sutherland scribbled his name on the paper and the flashbulbs exploded. Bert Bell and Art Rooney beamed in the background. As Sutherland finished signing, Bell took the paper and held it aloft. "Boys," Bell announced, "we're finally going to have a winning team in Pittsburgh. Jock Sutherland has just signed his contract to coach the Steelers." The men jammed in the room burst into applause. Sutherland looked startled.

"What do you mean, Bert?" Sutherland said, standing up to get a closer look at the paper he had just signed. Sure enough, it was a legal contract binding Dr. John B. Sutherland—party of the first part—to coach the Steelers—party of the second part or fifth place, depending on your point of view. Old Jock had been flimflammed in front of everybody. It was the first time Art Rooney ever signed a head coach; all the others had worked under a verbal agreement. But with a quality man like Sutherland, Rooney wanted to make sure he had legal proof of ownership. Now he did.

"Don't worry, Doctor," Rooney said, offering Sutherland a fresh new cigar, "you'll be happy with the Steelers. We'll see to that."

Sutherland, who was also named a vice president of the club, signed an unheard-of deal—a five-year contract for $15,000 a year with an option to buy any or all of Bell's stock in the franchise should Bert ever decide to leave. In addition, the tall, bespectacled dentist was to receive 25 percent of any profits the team would make during his coaching tenure.

Sutherland guided the Steelers to a 5–5–1 record in 1946. The following year, they tied Philadelphia for first place in the East with an 8–4 record but lost to the Eagles, 21–0, in the divisional championship playoff. Sutherland died tragically of a brain tumor in the spring of 1948.

Bert Bell wasn't around to see Sutherland turn the Steelers' fortunes around—at least not in Pittsburgh.

18. The New Commissioner

On January 11, 1946, the first day of a special NFL meeting at the Hotel Commodore in New York City was winding down. It was late in the afternoon, the club owners were tired, and the sportswriters waiting outside fully expected that Elmer Layden's five-year contract as commissioner would be renewed. Just a formality, they thought, even though there had been persistent reports of behind-the-scenes sniping at the former Notre Dame football star.

At one meeting, in fact, the owners had asked Layden to step out of the room. While he was gone, several people spoke in favor of his dismissal, but no action was taken. Washington Redskins owner George Preston Marshall, one of Layden's chief critics, had promoted Emery (Swede) Larson for the job on a number of occasions, but the former Navy coach and World War II hero died suddenly of a massive heart attack in 1945 while serving in the Marines.

The writers surmised that the owners on this moderately warm winter day appeared to be more preoccupied with two drastic changes to the league's constitution that had been approved that afternoon—so much so that they never got to discuss the top agenda item of the day, the annual player draft. Instead, meeting as a constitutional committee, the owners voted to limit the league's membership to 10 teams. Moreover, they decided that never again would two franchises be allowed in any one city. Since this move applied only to the future, it did not affect the status of the Bears and Cardinals in Chicago.

The new rules were specifically aimed at the new All-America Football Conference (AAFC) and specifically the New York Yankees. "This action slams the door right in their faces," said NFL publicity director George Strickler. "Should the new league fold up in a few years, some of its stronger clubs might want to join the NFL, but the new amendments would eliminate that possibility," he explained.

After being organized under the leadership of Arch Ward of the *Chicago Tribune,* the most influential sports editor in the nation, the AAFC had planned to begin play in 1945 in eight or ten large cities. However, the war delayed inaugural operations for a year, and now they were preparing to go head-to-head with the NFL. With most of the AAFC owners considerably more affluent than their more established counterparts—only four NFL teams showed a profit in 1945—the upstart league had already signed up three dozen players from the older league and aimed its sights at bucking the NFL in several cities, notably New York, Chicago, and Cleveland.

The AAFC also placed franchises in Brooklyn, Miami, Buffalo, Los Angeles, and San Francisco. Most of the teams were owned by wealthy businessmen who had been rebuffed by the NFL. Tony Morabito, a lumber tycoon, owned the San Francisco 49ers. Ben Lindheimer, a Chicago racetrack owner, headed a group of Hollywood stars, including Don Ameche, Bing Crosby, and Bob Hope, that formed the Los Angeles Dons. Arthur (Mickey) McBride, who owned the Yellow Cab Company in Cleveland, had been unsuccessful in his earlier effort to purchase the Rams from Dan Reeves. Jim Crowley, one of Layden's fellow "Four Horsemen" at Notre Dame, was the loop's first commissioner.

Late in the afternoon, "It appeared to be a foregone conclusion to outsiders that Layden would be chosen for another five-year term," wrote *Philadelphia Bulletin* sports editor Ed Pollock. In a closed-door session, however, the tall, mild-mannered commissioner was able to muster only three of the required seven votes to extend his contract, which was scheduled to terminate on March 31.

The writers covering the meeting were unaware at the time of the intrigue that had surrounded Layden's ouster. Some of the owners had agreed among themselves the night before not to renew the commissioner's contract.

"Layden will be reelected over my dead body," vowed Marshall as he arrived in New York, according to Michael MacCambridge in *America's Game: The Epic Story of How Pro Football Captured a Nation.* "The next day, when Layden banged the gavel to begin the meetings, he did so to an empty conference room. Returning to his hotel room, he received official word later that the owners had voted on his ouster."

During the afternoon session, Bert Bell was asked to leave the room while the other owners discussed Layden's successor. When Bert returned, Chicago Bears owner George Halas and Marshall gave him the news—later characterized by sportswriters as a "sensational development, a bombshell, and as breathtaking as chloroform"—that he had been made a unanimous choice on the first ballot. Bell reportedly received the vote of seven of the 10 club owners before Halas persuaded the others to make it unanimous.

Bell was elected for a three-year term at a starting salary of $20,000 annually. He agreed to sell his "less than 50%" share in the ownership of the Pittsburgh Steelers to Rooney, his partner, and added that 25 of the shares he owned would be held in escrow for Jock Sutherland, the Steelers' coach.

"I'm delighted with the job," an exuberant Bell told the *Pittsburgh Sun Telegraph*. "I expected it and I will be a strong-arm guy."

The last straw for Halas, according to author Jeff Davis, had come a few weeks earlier when Dan Topping merged his Brooklyn Dodgers with the Boston Yanks and announced that he was joining the AAFC. As a wealthy co-owner of major league baseball's New York Yankees, he then moved the team from Ebbets Field to Yankee Stadium and declared war on the New York Giants and its owner Tim Mara, with whom he had been feuding over Sunday home dates.

"Fed up with the bumbling Layden," Halas put the word out that Bert Bell was the right man for the job. "Some owners thought Bell was a clown, a football version of baseball's Casey Stengel before he donned the Yankees pinstripes. Halas knew Bell as the man who dreamed up the draft and as a smart, honorable, and an able negotiator. With Rooney's endorsement and Marshall's help, Halas and his supporters stood fast for Bell and persuaded everyone else to step into line. It was a move the National Football League never regretted."

"Bell still bore vestiges of his old self," recalled MacCambridge, "the playboy raconteur of the '20s with slicked-back hair, by now silver, and an estimable paunch, neatly draped in blue serge suits during the fall and winter, and tan gabardine in the summer. His voice was a thing of wonder; a deep growling baritone that projected through office walls and over static-filled phone lines. He was a voluble man of motion, generally heard before seen. And he was what pro football needed most at the time: a true believer. His hiring came at a critical moment, and not only because of the challenge of the AAFC. The league was in danger of imploding, beset by factional rivalries and legislative paralysis, a result of ten strong-willed men, each with definite ideas about why their beloved sport was losing so much money."

After listening to Strickler's announcement that the league offices would be moved from Chicago to New York City, Bell set out to place a telephone call to Frances at their home in Narberth. This was no easy feat. Long-distance operators working in the New York office of the American Telephone and Telegraph Company (AT&T) were out on strike and supervisors were frantically trying to handle urgent calls. While sportswriters were scurrying, unsuccessfully, as far away as Newark, New Jersey, trying to find a place to make a long-distance call, Bert calmly picked up a phone in a pay booth and said with a big smile on his face, "This is an emergency call." He got through immediately.

The league then released a statement from Layden asserting that he had resigned. Later, Bell flatly denied a report that Elmer had been ousted. "That is not true, not true at all, Elmer resigned," the new commissioner told Roscoe McGowen of the *New York Times* after being tracked down at a late-night dinner at Toots Shor's Restaurant. "I never sought the job but I am honored. I will proceed with the job much along the same lines favored by Layden, fairly conservative and not too aggressive. I won't seek any fights, but I won't dodge any that come my way."

"Don't look for any radical changes in policy under my administration," Bell told Art Morrow of the *Philadelphia Inquirer,* who had just arrived at Shor's. "The All-America Conference? Sure, I recognize that there is a rival professional football league in operation, trying to take our players and planning to buck us at the gate. But so far as my own attitude is concerned, it's simply this: I expect to be so busy with the affairs of the National League for the next three years that I will have absolutely no time to think about the All-America."

One of the first people to congratulate Bell, who was responding to toasts with his favorite beverage, Pepsi Cola, was Eagles coach Earl (Greasy) Neale. "Gosh all mighty," he grinned, "you're going to give us some better officiating in our games with Washington, aren't you?" "We Philadelphians are doing all right for ourselves," quipped Bell's former bouncer Toots Shor between handshakes.

Layden had left the Commodore Hotel and made himself unavailable some time before his "resignation" was announced. But he dropped into the press room the next afternoon "just to say hello and thank all you fellows for being so nice to me while I was in." Asked if he was "pushed or 'did you fall?' Layden merely grinned broadly and said nothing," reported Roscoe McGowen. Even though he was urged to do so by Bell, Layden never accepted an offer by club owners to remain in an advisory capacity at $20,000 annually.

Many club owners had strongly objected to Layden's cavalier attitude toward the new league, especially his cryptic advice to the club owners. "Go out and get a football first," he remarked when representatives of the AAFC sought a meeting with NFL officials late in 1945. They also felt uneasy about Layden's apparent reluctance to confront his close friend, Arch Ward. But now, most of Bell's colleagues were ecstatic in praising the selection of the new 52-year-old mogul.

"Now we have a pro running our league and they [the AAFC] have an amateur," said Marshall. "Bert will give us the kind of aggressive leadership [former NFL president] Joe Carr gave us in the early days of our league. He is one of us, knows our problems. He was a great player, himself, a former college coach but more important he has been a pro player, coach, and owner and knows the answers to our problems."

"The new commissioner is a gentleman from a long line of Rittenhouse Square toffs," said Arthur Daley of the *Times*. "But—and this is important—he speaks the pro football language. Bell is aware of the problems of each and every owner as well as of the league itself. He seems admirably equipped for the job, even though he takes over in time of crisis. It's almost as if the NFL said to the AAFC, 'Okay, you asked for a fight and we'll give it to you because Bert Bell is the best scrapper we have.'"

"The selection of Bert Bell as the new boss is a ten-strike," said Robert Gray of the *Bulletin*. "The National League will definitely go forward under his leadership, for he talks the same language as the owners, coaches, and players."

"Aggressiveness, courage, and honesty are only a few of his qualifications," said Gray's boss, Ed Pollock. "He's a good business man. In fact, he had to be to survive the years he has spent in professional football. Bell saw lean years with the Philadelphia Eagles. He had some money, but not so much that he couldn't have lost it all in a few seasons. It took smart and shrewd management to see him through. So the National League will have real business management in the turbulent years ahead, and real direction, too. The only mistake the National owners make in the election of Bell as commissioner was their failure to put him in the position five years ago."

Before the owners reconvened for Bell's first session as commissioner the following morning, Saturday, January 12, Bert was asked by sportswriters what his policy would be toward the new All-America Conference.

"When anyone else goes into business in competition with you, my policy is to pay attention to my own business and try to improve it," he replied as he walked into the conference room. Bell then announced that one of his first objectives would be to revise the schedule. Hopefully, the season would start earlier, he said. More games would be played at night, and the championship game would be held no later than December 8.

Never again, he told William Tucker of United Press, would the championship game be played in zero weather like it had been a month or so before when quarterback Bob Waterfield led the Rams to the 1945 crown with a 15–14 win over Washington before a disappointing crowd of 32,178 in Cleveland.

As Marshall made his appointment official with a motion that was carried unanimously, a thousand thoughts must have raced through the new commissioner's mind. He probably marveled at how far the league had come since that meeting in 1934 when he was a young owner of the newest franchise, the Philadelphia Eagles. He remembered standing up and boldly making a motion that the league adopt a new official football. He recalled smiling when his motion carried, and how thrilled he was when two of the icons of the NFL, John Mara and Curly Lambeau, moved that the league adopt a Spalding J5 Unlined ball with the valve—precisely the football he favored.

There were other successful motions that Bert made along the way, including one in 1937 that for the first time permitted newspapermen to be admitted to all team practices. And just last year, he recommended that the home club be required to furnish a blackboard and chalk in the dressing room of the visiting team.

Bell also remembered the meeting in 1941 at the Willard Hotel in Washington, D.C., when he provoked a stimulating discussion by calling attention to the fact that NFL players were sometimes seen in public not properly attired and suggested that club owners see to it that players were as properly dressed off the field as they were on the field. The owners authorized the league president to send out such instructions.

At the same meeting, Bell suggested that all radio announcers be called to a meeting before the season and taught how to broadcast for the best interest of the league. They should be warned never to criticize items in any way no matter how little time there is left in the game. They should always give the impression that anything can happen in "pro" football, and should all know the rules, always make the game spectacular, and never call attention to its being slow or defensive.

Bell was probably still thinking about the past as he pounded the gavel to get his first meeting under way. After authorizing the new commissioner to draw up a formal player's contract that would be standard for all clubs, the owners approved a historic franchise switch—a move that forever changed the landscape of the NFL and set the tone of Bert Bell's commissionership.

It happened in a special session when Rams owner Dan Reeves was granted permission to move his Cleveland franchise to Los Angeles, making the NFL the first major professional sports team to play on the Pacific Coast—and leaving the Cleveland market to the Browns of the AAFC.

The league had rejected an application for a franchise by Los Angeles exactly a decade earlier—primarily because of the long distance between team cities—even though the California group had guaranteed each team coming to the coast $7,500. Since then, rapid advances made in the airline industry made traveling much quicker.

The decision was made, according to author MacCambridge, after Chile Walsh, the Rams' general manager, "made a passionate case" for the franchise switch as Reeves sat quietly at the conference table. "Eight votes were needed to approve a transfer, but as in years past, consensus could not be reached. Six teams supported the move, three were opposed, and the Green Bay Packers abstained." Halas, speaking for those opposed, explained that the owners didn't want to face the exorbitant costs of traveling outside the league's geographic area.

"Gentlemen," Reeves said, turning to leave, according to Art Morrow of the *Philadelphia Inquirer*, "you who know me know that I never bluff. I am not trying to force you into any action you might consider detrimental to the league. But when I return to this room after you have voted on my proposal, I am announcing that unless you go along with me, all my stock in the Cleveland club will be for sale. I am getting out. Not bolting, understand, for I do not expect to go with the All-America Conference. But I am leaving the National League."

Bell called a recess to the meeting and dispatched Halas, Marshall, and Chicago Cardinals owner Charles Bidwill to Reeves's hotel suite in an effort to negotiate a truce. Finally, an agreement was reached when Reeves promised to double the league's $5,000 road team guarantee for teams traveling to Los Angeles.

"It has been my long range plan to move to Los Angeles ever since I took over the Cleveland Franchise in 1941," Reeves told sportswriter William Tucker. "I have lost money every year—$40,000 even with a championship team last season—while I consider Los Angeles the greatest city for the future of football in the United States."

In Cleveland, the Rams played their home games in dilapidated League Park with a capacity of only 23,000. Reeves added that he didn't regard the greater distance to the West Coast as a handicap for visiting clubs, provided that he would be able to successfully negotiate a lease with the 103,000-capacity Los Angeles Coliseum. Although the newly established airline routes would be used if necessary, the Rams' owner emphasized that train transportation, especially from the Midwest, would also be adequate. A team could leave Chicago by train at noon on Monday and reach Los Angeles at 9:15 A.M. on Wednesday, he explained.

On January 13, the fourth day of the marathon meetings that recessed only for dinner, former NFL referee Tom Dowd, speaking as a representative of United Airlines, told the owners that a club of 40 men could be transported from New York to Los Angeles in 12 hours at a round-trip cost of $10,000—a fee less than the cost of train transportation, according to Tim Mara of the New York Giants.

At Bell's behest, the owner agreed to withhold any announcement of specific playing dates concerning the league's 1946 schedule, revealing only opponents to be played by each team. In another effort to keep the AAFC in the dark, they agreed to hold their draft meeting in secret, thus refraining from tipping off owners and coaches from the upstart league of their knowledge about potential professional talent.

Arch Wolfe, the general manager of the Chicago Cardinals, was assigned to stand watchdog outside the meeting room. Strickler said that the first two players selected "might be named" but that any announcement of the status of other players would be made at the discretion of individual teams.

According to *Total Football,* the AAFC didn't hold a draft in 1946 because its club owners had been urged to sign as many players as possible by offering more money than had ever been paid before. Their strategy worked. Of the 64 players on the College All-Star team that defeated the Rams later that year, 40 signed with the AAFC.

Before Sunday's meeting adjourned, Bell announced that he would be appointing a three-man committee to formulate plans with a group of Latrobe, Pennsylvania, business leaders to build "a suitable memorial" to professional football. Latrobe hosted a team from the nearby town of Jeanette on September 3, 1895, and one of the players from the home team, Dr. John K. Brallier, was paid $10 to play quarterback—making him the first football player on record to play for pay.

The *Philadelphia Inquirer* reported the next day that the NFL planned to establish its own Hall of Fame there, patterned after baseball's Hall of Fame in Cooperstown, New York. [However, Canton later won the right over Latrobe and Detroit to build the shrine after civic leaders in the Ohio city raised $378,026 in 1962. It opened on September 7, 1973. Bert Bell was the first of 17 charter inductees.]

On January 14, Day 5 of the meetings, Bell presided over his first player draft. It was a proud moment for the new commissioner. Just about a decade earlier, he had convinced his fellow owners that the draft was absolutely necessary to save the league. Now as the owners were about to wage another battle for survival, they spent much of the day wrangling over the 1946 schedule, then took a brief recess before moving into more spacious quarters to conduct their player selection process in secret.

Their first order of business was to vote against releasing the names of selected players, which they did, seven to three. The vote did not affect the owners' earlier agreement that each individual club could announce its selections at its own discretion, however, and two teams—Philadelphia and Washington—came out of the meeting later in the evening while the gathering was still in session to announce their early choices.

When the owners finally wearily emerged from behind closed doors early the following morning, they declined to identify their number-one selection—hinting only that he was a "sleeper back from the midwest," according to the Associated Press. They initially revealed the names of only six backs from the 300 players selected. Felix A. (Doc) Blanchard, the great Army fullback, was not the top choice, or even number two, because he was expected to remain at West Point for the following two years. Blanchard went number three to the Pittsburgh Steelers behind Notre Dame's T-formation quarterback Frank (Boley) Dancewicz, who was selected by the Boston Yanks.

The top pick was multipurpose back Dub Jones of Tulane, whose selection by the Chicago Cardinals was not announced until a few days later. Keeping his name secret was a waste of time. He was lured away by the new league and ended up playing four unspectacular seasons for Miami, Brooklyn, and Cleveland of the AAFC.

Later, the owners fired another broadside at the AAFC by reaffirming their imposition of a five-year ban from organized football on any and all players who run out on their contracts and play in the new league. The owners instructed Bell to check on every case of contract jumping to the new conference, emphasizing that the minute a player steps on the field to play in the AAFC, he's out of the NFL.

Finally, as the conclave was ending after seven days and seven nights of often-contentious deliberations, Bell was asked if the 1946 league schedule had been completed.

"No," he replied. "The schedule is not complete. We have agreed on an 11 game schedule for each club. The home-and-home competition for each division has been set, but the dates have not been arranged as yet. They probably will be arranged when we hold another meeting here in April."

Then, eyeing some New York sportswriters, including McGowan, Bell winked and reiterated that the league offices would be transferred to New York "as soon as we can find a place." Bell added that he hoped to "have our offices somewhere on 42nd Street," as some of the New York writers had suggested.

And with that, the new NFL commissioner headed home to Narberth, Pennsylvania.

John C. Bell, shown in his Penn football uniform in 1884 when he starred in the Quakers' first win over Harvard, and later sitting on the players' bench at Franklin Field watching his son Bert (right) in action as the captain of the Red and Blue in 1919.

Source: Image courtesy of Upton Bell.

University of Pennsylvania quarterback Bert Bell warms up before guiding the Quakers to an appearance in the 1917 Rose Bowl.

Source: Urban Archives, Temple University, Philadelphia Pennsylvania.

Bell and fellow members of Base Hospital No. 20 stand in formation before leaving for France in 1918. Bell was commended for extraordinary bravery by General John J. Pershing during World War I.

Source: Image courtesy of Bert Bell, Jr.

Bert Bell poses with his Penn teammates on his $1,000 touring car. He lost the automobile on a wager over Dartmouth's 20–19 victory over the Quakers in 1919. *Source: Image courtesy of Upton Bell.*

Frances Upton was one of the nation's top musical comedy stars before secretly marrying Bert Bell in Chicago on January 4, 1934. *Source: Image courtesy of Bert Bell, Jr.*

Bell, who coached the Philadelphia Eagles from 1936 until 1940, works with former Temple University star Dave Smukler, one of the Birds' early offensive leaders.

Source: Image courtesy of the Philadelphia Eagles.

Bert Bell meets with his team in 1937. They won only two games that year, both upsets on the road at Washington and Brooklyn.

Source: Image courtesy of the Philadelphia Eagles.

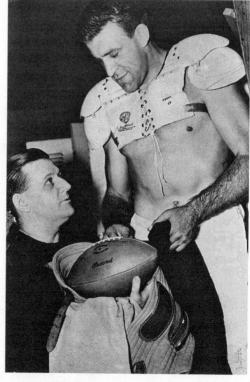

Bill Hewitt, the last NFL player not to wear a helmet, chats with his coach Bert Bell after joining the Eagles in 1937. Bell's son, Upton, served as Hewitt's presenter when he was inducted into the Pro Football Hall of Fame. *Source: Image courtesy of the Philadelphia Eagles.*

Texas Christian University All America quarterback Davey O'Brien receives the Maxwell Trophy as the Outstanding College Player of 1938 from Bert Bell on January 10, 1939.
Source: AP/Wide World Photos.

Bell stands outside his home in Narberth, Pennsylvania in 1943 when he was co-owner of the Pittsburgh Steelers.
Source: Urban Archives, Temple University, Philadelphia Pennsylvania.

Bert Bell's wife Frances Upton with their three children, Upton, Jane, and Bert, Jr. (right) in the 1940s. *Source: Image courtesy of Upton Bell.*

Bell's coaching career with the Pittsburgh Steelers lasted exactly two games in 1941—both losses.
Source: Image courtesy of Bert Bell, Jr.

Film actress Jane Russell receives a trophy emblematic of her husband Bob Waterfield being named the NFL's 1945 MVP from Commissioner Bert Bell during the Los Angeles Rams–College All Star game at Soldier Field in Chicago on August 23, 1946. *Source: AP/Wide World Photos.*

Bert Bell spent countless hours on the telephone while serving as National Football League Commissioner from 1946 until his death in 1959.

Source: Photo courtesy of the Pro Football Hall of Fame.

Commissioner Bert Bell and George Preston Marshall, owner of the Washington Redskins, present a gold lifetime NFL football pass to President Harry S. Truman on September 25, 1946.

Source: International News Photos.

Art Rooney (left), owner of the Pittsburgh Steelers, shows the club's player draft selection list to his good friend Bert Bell, on December 18, 1947. Rooney and Bell were granted NFL franchises on the same day in 1933. *Source: AP/Wide World Photos.*

Bert Bell and J. Arthur Friedlund, of the All-America Conference, chat after the two leagues agreed to merge on December 9, 1949. *Source: Urban Archives, Temple University, Philadelphia Pennsylvania.*

Commissioner Bert Bell demonstrates how he uses dominoes to arrange the 1951 NFL schedule during a league meeting at the Bellevue Stratford Hotel. Watching (from left) are: John Mara, of the New York Giants; Gene Ronzani, Green Bay Packers; Victor Morabito, San Francisco 49ers; John Michelosen, Pittsburgh Steelers, and Tex Schramm, Los Angeles Rams. *Source: Urban Archives, Temple University, Philadelphia Pennsylvania.*

Bert Bell (holding football) points to mural of Yankee Stadium shortly after the New York Giants announced that they were moving their home games there from the Polo Grounds on January 27, 1956. Also pictured are Wellington Mara (left rear) and his brother Jack (right rear), the sons of Giants' owner Tim Mara, and George Weiss, general manager of the Yankees. *Source: AP/Wide World Photos.*

Four of the twelve NFL owners who served as honorary pallbearers stand behind Bert Bell's casket outside of St. Margaret's Church after his funeral Mass on October 14, 1959. They are (from left): Dominic Olejniczak, of the Green Bay Packers; George Halas, Chicago Bears; Arthur Rooney, Pittsburgh Steelers, and David Jones, Cleveland Browns. *Source: Urban Archives, Temple University, Philadelphia Pennsylvania.*

19. Mysterious Negotiations
with the AAFC

As Bert Bell was working his way home from New York City, hopefully to get his first peaceful sleep in more than a week, storm clouds were quickly gathering over the new NFL czar.

They came in the form of a bombshell dropped by Jim Crowley, the All-America Football League commissioner, who told the Associated Press that he had talked to Bell "several weeks ago" over the telephone and in person regarding the establishment of an AAFC team in Philadelphia.

Crowley told the Associated Press that he was contacted by a group headed by Eugene Mori and Walter Donovan, the president and general manager, respectively, of the Garden State Park Race Track in Camden, New Jersey, regarding an AAFC team in the Quaker City. The initial conversation took place soon after Dan Topping, of the New York Football Yankees, had jumped to the new league.

"They said they would talk with Bell because he held an option for the use of Shibe Park in Philadelphia," Crowley explained. "At the time we were accepting bids for a tenth team. I talked with Mori and Donovan, then met Bell in Philadelphia. He seemed interested and asked a lot of questions. Later I talked with Bell again and he told me they weren't quite ready to go in at that time."

Then, Crowley added, "They blew from hot to cold, all of a sudden. I don't know why."

Reached by the AP as he arrived home later that evening, Bell said that he had "discussed the matter with Crowley, who sought to rent Shibe Park for the All-America Conference. I also talked to Mr. Mori and both understood that my interests were solely in the National League. I advised Mr. Mori that I felt it was to the best interests of both the National League and professional football as a whole that Shibe Park not be leased to the All-America Conference."

Bell told the *Philadelphia Bulletin* a few hours later that he hardly knew Mori. "I think I only met him once," the commissioner explained. "That was the time we discussed the lease."

Gene Ward, of the *New York News*, refused to let the matter die. In fact, he poured gasoline on the flaming controversy in the newspaper's January 17 edition under the headline BELL, NFL CHIEF, SOUGHT PHILLY AAC FRANCHISE.

"As a representative of a Quaker City syndicate—which included Walter Annenberg, Philadelphia newspaper owner, and Gene Mori, New Jersey racetrack operator—Bell came armed with a ten-year option on Shibe Park," Ward wrote.

"This significant, behind-the-scenes maneuver in the current pro-football war-of-nerves was revealed to this sports reporter yesterday as the old NFL met for the seventh straight day of a jitter-ridden confab which has been featured by frantic franchise switches, player 'bans' and an abrupt boot-in-the-pants for Elmer Layden."

Ward wrote that the negotiations between the Philadelphia syndicate and Crowley "cooled suddenly after George Halas, powerful owner of the NFL Chicago Bears, reportedly contacted Bell in Philadelphia. After that, Crowley heard no more of Bell until he popped up as the new NFC commissioner.

"When pressed for comment, Crowley said: 'We were accepting bids for a tenth team at that time. I talked with syndicate representatives here in my New York offices, then met Bell in Philadelphia. There were further conferences, but a few days later I talked with Bell again and he told me they weren't quite ready to go in at that time. I told Bell we had seven petitions and had to get this tenth team set, asking him if the plans were off. Bell told me the deal wasn't off but reiterated that they weren't quite ready to go in. Later, of course, we pared the conference down to eight teams. They blew from very hot to cool, all of a sudden, and I think I know why.' "

Although Crowley refused further comment at that point, Ward went on to quote other AAFC officials. "They hinted the cooling off came only after one of the NFL's Big Four, reported to be George Halas, had contacted Bell in Philadelphia. 'I think it is pretty plain that the new NFL commissioner got his $20,000 job by agreeing to stop negotiation with our conference,' was the way Bill Cox, co-owner of the Brooklyn AAFC team, put it."

Ward added that the "mysterious Shibe Park document was co-signed by Bell and Annenberg, still is in effect and, technically, leaves Alexis Thompson's Eagles without a park to play in. Thompson, youthful president of the Eagles, admits he didn't discover that Bell had an option on Shibe Park until he returned from Army service.

"'I was amazed when I called on Connie Mack and discovered the other option. But Bell assured me that it was signed for my protection, but I'll be gosh darned if I can see how. When Bell was put up as the new commissioner, I insisted he either tear up the Shibe Park lease or turn it over to me. He assured me he would, but so far nothing has been done, although I am anticipating no trouble.' Thompson also said there were several clauses, guarantees, etc., in the Bell option which he didn't like.

"Conclusion?" Ward snapped. "Draw your own!"

Thompson's comments to Ward were quite puzzling, inasmuch as Art Morrow, of the *Philadelphia Inquirer,* had gotten an entirely different viewpoint on the situation from the young Eagles owner four days earlier.

"Until the current confabulation, the Eagles had considered themselves at odds with the co-owner of the Pittsburgh Steelers as a result of playing rights to Shibe Park," Morrow wrote.

"Bert had formed a corporation and leased the Eagles' home grounds for football from Connie Mack and Alexis Thompson, the Eagles' owner, was fearful lest it meant ejection from the park. But at the current meeting Thompson and Bell got together. To his amazement, Thompson was told that sub-rental of Shibe Park from Bell would be exactly the same as rental from Connie Mack. Bell, who also had leased Forbes Field for professional football in Pittsburgh, was simply protecting the National League's rights to the park against the encroachment of the new All-America."

Donovan, the Garden State Park general manager, quickly issued a denial to Ward's story. "Bert Bell at no time represented us," he told the *Bulletin* on January 18. "We talked to Crowley and to Dan Topping, and then because Bell controlled Shibe Park and because he probably knows more about pro football than any other Philadelphian, we talked to him. But certainly he was not our representative."

Harry Thayer, the general manager of the Eagles, told the *Bulletin* that his office knew all the time what was going on.

"We knew Bell was talking to Crowley and Bert reported to us what went on," Thayer explained. "The day Crowley came over, Bell came to me and said, 'If you see me talking to Crowley, don't butt in. I'll tell you all about it later.' We thought it was smart to have Bell find out as much as possible about the new organization. Everyone in the National League has the highest respect for Bell."

Harry Robert attempted to clarify the matter in the *Philadelphia Record* on January 18 after Crowley again insisted that Bell "was very much interested" in negotiations for an AAFC franchise.

"They were very hot on it, Crowley told me over the telephone from New York, and then they suddenly cooled off," Robert wrote. "The 'cooling off' reputedly came after George Halas, owner of the powerful Chicago Bears and dominant figure in the National League, got in touch with Bell here."

"Halas seeing me had nothing to do with any decision on the matter," Bell told Robert. "I talked with Crowley and Mori. They came to me and naturally I was interested to hear their proposition. All they wanted to know about was leasing Shibe Park, because I hold the option. As I was part owner of the Pittsburgh Steelers, they knew my interests were with the National League.

"I told them that I thought it was best for the interest of pro football as a whole that Shibe Park not be leased to the All-America Conference. There was no secret about it. The whole National League knew it. The All-America Conference isn't the only party that has tried to lease Shibe Park since I held the option. Three or four others have approached me on it."

Thayer told Robert that NFL owners knew that Bell was talking to Crowley in order to learn what he could about the new league. "He was reporting regularly to us," the Eagles' general manager explained. "We thought it was a good thing to have Bell act as a sort of secret agent for us. Nobody in the league questions Bert's loyalty."

Thompson insisted to Robert that he still "can't see how" Bell signed the lease for his protection. "Thompson must mean that he hasn't seen the lease," Bert replied. "Harry Thayer knew I had it because I told him about it the day I got it."

Speculation about Bell's motives lingered for another week in the Philadelphia newspapers. Writing in the *Record* on January 22, Bill Dooly said he repeatedly questioned Thayer why Bell, as the owner of the Pittsburgh club, would want to lease fields in another city as he did when he signed ten- and five-year leases on Shibe Park and Municipal Stadium, respectively.

There's only one logical reason, the sportswriter wrote: "That was, bluntly, that he intended to simultaneously get out of Pittsburgh, make the Eagles the folk for whom the bell tolled and move into that city with a franchise in the rival league."

Thayer sidestepped the question when asked what he thought Bell was really up to, Dooly added. "The Eagles' general manager declined to theorize on the maneuver that could readily have put the Eagles out of business in Philadelphia."

In February, the NFL headquarters were moved from 310 South Michigan Avenue in Chicago to the campus of Bell's alma mater, the University of Pennsylvania, at 3657 Woodland Avenue. Sharing the cramped quarters on the second floor of a building directly over a men's shop was Dennis J. Shea, the league's treasurer, who traveled back and forth a few days a week between Philadelphia and the league's New York office on 11 West 42nd Street.

Bert enjoyed having Shea around the office. A colorful guy, Dennis had been a theatrical press agent from way back in 1890. He became affiliated with George Preston Marshall in 1932 when Marshall's team was located in Boston, then joined the Brooklyn (football) Dodgers five years later. In 1940, he was appointed NFL treasurer.

"Customers in the men's shop below can hear the voice of the commissioner dictating letters, telephoning, and discussing business," wrote Ed Pollock, who visited the commissioner on one of his first days in his new home.

Between phone calls, Bell tossed a document filled with legalese across the desk to the *Bulletin* sports editor. It was a copy of an agreement recently signed with the American Association, a minor pro football league that included the Wilmington Clippers, Bethlehem Bulldogs, and four other nearby teams.

Drawn up by the law firm in which Bell's brother, Lieutenant Governor John C. Bell, was a partner, the document was expected to be the basis for the NFL's agreements with the Pacific Coast, Dixie, and Texas leagues, all of which applied for membership in the growing organization of professional football to be known as the Association of Professional Football Leagues.

It was the most detailed and extensive agreement ever adopted in football, and it recognized the NFL as the only major league and the commissioner as the sole arbiter. It included a strong clause on territorial rights of association members and another chance that gave the association clubs the right to use players on the National League Reserve List as well as optioned players.

Bell told Pollock that he believed that the new professional football organization eventually would reach the proportions of organized baseball with the National as the only major league. "In times the leagues will be classified and players will move up through the chain as they do in baseball," Bert predicted.

The NFL owners gathered at the Hotel New Yorker on April 28, primarily to discuss the league's 1946 schedule. Before they got down to business, however, Philadelphia's general manager Harry Thayer moved that the owners immediately go into executive session because, as he explained, Eagles owner Alexis Thompson was not satisfied with his lease on Shibe Park and would not accept any schedule until he was.

"This matter pertains to the availability of Shibe Park to the Eagles," Thompson's attorney, Walter Thayer, explained when the session began. "Mr. Bell has given us a paper which allows Mr. Thompson to vote his 50 shares in Football Associates [the syndicate] which holds the lease on Shibe Park. We do not have the certificate, and furthermore Mr. Thompson sees no reason why he should not deal direct with Shibe Park, and will not accept a schedule until he is satisfied in full pertaining to this matter."

Bell slowly rose up from his chair and glanced around the room. Choosing his words carefully, he explained that he had obtained and signed the lease as president of Football Associates for the protection of the NFL, the Eagles, and himself.

Philadelphia Inquirer owner Walter Annenberg was included as a shareholder to protect the *Inquirer* Charities football game, Bell asserted, while emphasizing that although the Football Associates held the lease, they were morally obligated to get Connie Mack's approval on any lease. Football Associates had entered into this lease, which was drawn up by the Eagles, for five years with an option of five additional years. Since then, the Eagles had presented an amended agreement that Bell said he signed and would have Mr. Mack approve it as soon as possible.

"My certificate of 50 shares of Football Associates has only lately been issued to me as the corporation was not fully completed," Bell continued. "I am now turning over said certificate, signed in blank, to Mr. Thompson for the best interest of the National Football League and the Eagles.

"Mr. Walter Annenberg called me last night and told me in view of the fact that the National Football League and its member clubs have been his friends over a period of nine years, he was turning over his stock [50 shares)] in Football Associates to the National Football League. Gentlemen, under these conditions Mr. Thompson will have 50 per cent of Football Associates and the National Football League will have 50 per cent."

Harry Thayer then stood up, smiled at the owners, and said, "We are delighted to accept this as the solution for Mr. Thompson and the Eagles."

Before adjourning for the evening, three of the owners let it be known in no uncertain terms during the dinner break that they would never, at any time, vote for an agreement with the AAFC. John V. and Wellington Mara of the New York Giants, Ted Collins of the Boston Yanks, and Fred

Mandel of the Detroit Lions issued a statement that they would kill any motion that was ever made to bring about a harmonious relationship between the two leagues.

William D. Richardson of the *New York Times* reported that the owners were reacting to a report that AAFC commissioner James Crowley suggested to Bert Bell that the two leagues get together on such matters as a common draft (to bring salaries back into line), a postseason World Series between the winners in the two leagues, and an arrangement whereby original contracts between players and clubs would be binding.

The following day, the owners adopted a 55-game schedule. The New York Giants were awarded seven attractive home games to help offset the competition of the rival league's Dan Topping and his New York Yankees at the stadium. Then the moguls discussed ways of improving college relations and adopting a new player's contract, a pact that would basically abolish the reserve clause used by major league baseball that enables a team to control a player's services for as long as it chooses.

Concerning relations with college players, Bell said the league hoped to go back to the prewar standard of eligibility under which the player could not be signed or tampered with until his class had been graduated. But how far the league would go in this direction would depend upon policies adopted by the new league. "Our draft is the college player's best protection," Bell claimed.

The new contract, explained Bell to Allison Danzig of the *Times,* was a give-and-take proposition designed to bring about as much mutual consideration as possible. It specified obligations of the club and of the player and added to the protection of the player. The contract was for one year, with an option on the player's services for the succeeding season at a specified price.

"Heretofore," said Bell, "we have talked about the player. Now we talk about the player and the club about their responsibilities to one another. For example, if the player fails to report in condition to play, he can be suspended until he gets into condition, but if the player is hurt in the line of duty the club has the written responsibility of not only paying his full salary but of taking care of his hospitalization and medical bills. Also, instead of a game-to-game contract, the club now pays the player so much for the season. This contract eliminates servitude."

For that reason, the commissioner explained, the contract had a better chance of standing up in the courts. The contract specified that the club had the right to enjoin any player by injunction proceedings from skipping out. Thus, Bell and the lawyers who drew up the pact believed that it would serve to put a check on players jumping to another league, although they admitted that it depended a good deal upon the individual court's interpretation of the law.

When the meetings ended after three days and two nights of deliberations, Bell was "proud as punch," wrote Danzig.

"It was the best meeting the National League ever had," the commissioner exclaimed. "We have the best schedule we ever had. Every one had the chance to talk himself out and get what he had to say off his chest. There were no arguments, no fights. It was harmony all the way. Everybody pulled together.

"Only once did anyone so much as raise his voice. That was George Marshall. I told him, 'Keep your shirt on, George,' and George apologized. Say, there's a fellow that knows his schedules. That Marshall is a genius when it comes to schedules. If everyone in the league knew as much about them as he does, we'd never find ourselves with a poor one."

The next few months were uneventful for the new commissioner. On June 20, he joined a host of celebrities—ranging from New York Governor Thomas E. Dewey to United Nations Secretary-General Trygve Lie, entertainers like Clark Gable, Frank Sinatra, and George Raft, and such baseball luminaries as Leo Durocher and Mel Ott—at ringside at Yankee Stadium. They were among a disappointingly small crowd of 45,266 who watched Joe Lewis defend his world heavyweight championship for the 22nd time by knocking out Billy Conn with a thunderous left hook to the jaw at 2:19 of the eighth round.

A number of sportswriters noted the presence of two women in the press box for the first time in anyone's memory. "Neither pounded a typewriter, so their presence there was among the night's great mysteries," sniffed the *Times*.

Later, on a hot, sweltering day in July, Bert stopped into the NFL's other office in New York City to discuss some business matters with his publicist George Strickler. With their coats off and shirt sleeves rolled up, they delved through reports sent in by the ten teams. Soon they were joined by William Richardson.

"How does it look?" the sportswriter asked. "Great!" they answered in unison. "We're off to the greatest season ever," Bell exclaimed. "Everything's going fine and reports from all sectors are rosy, rosier than they've ever been. In some places, they're almost battering down the doors of club offices in order to get tickets for a season still some time off. The Steelers, for example, have their park half sold-out by now."

On September 23, Bell returned to the Big Apple for the first luncheon meeting of the New York Football Writers at Toots Shor's Restaurant. Sharing the dais with his AAFC counterpart Jim Crowley, Bell again painted a rosy picture for the NFL. He pointed to the recent Steelers–Chicago Cardinals game in Pittsburgh that was sold out two days in advance. "First time anything's ever happened like that out there," he quipped.

When league owners gathered for their meetings at the Hotel Commodore in New York City on December 16, their first order of business was to tear up Bell's original three-year contract and replace it with a five-year pact at an annual increase of $10,000 to $30,000 a year.

"It made me feel pretty good," Bell later told Pollock. "The meeting hadn't been on very long before I was asked to leave the room. The owners said they wanted to discuss something without me being there. So, as I was going out, one of them yelled, 'Don't forget what happened to (Elmer) Layden!'"

Later that day after the annual player draft was conducted, three teams—Philadelphia, Green Bay, and the Los Angeles Rams—refused to divulge their top picks. Again their strategy failed. Halfback Leo Riggs, the Eagles' choice from Southern Cal, never played pro football. Multipurpose back Johnny (Strike) Strzykalski, the Packers' selection from Marquette, played for four years with San Francisco of the AAFC. Halfback Emil (Red) Sitko, the Rams' top choice, didn't play until 1950 when he joined the San Francisco 49ers of the NFL.

Unfortunately, the NFL picture was not quite as rosy as Bell proclaimed. The AAFC survived its first season in much better fashion than its detractors had predicted, drawing more than 1.25 million (announced) fans and losing only one team, Miami.

Cleveland's attendance was an astonishing 437,017, but as Arthur Daley of the *Times* pointed out, if you eliminate Cleveland's numbers, the average crowd in the AAFC dropped to 18,744, considerably less than the 25,000 per-game average that league officials said was necessary to break even financially.

Despite astronomical payrolls that increased by 250 percent in one year, all of the NFL teams except Boston, Detroit, and Los Angeles finished in the black. But some teams like Philadelphia barely made a profit, and Eagles officials acknowledged that they had to sell out every home game to do so.

As Bell would quickly find out, however, the NFL's financial situation wasn't his biggest problem.

20. A Gambling Scandal
Nipped in the Bud

Bert Bell was relaxing at his home on Saturday, December 14, when the telephone rang. It was Jack Mara.

"The mayor wants to see you immediately," the anguished son of New York Giants owner Tim Mara blurted into the mouthpiece.

Two hours later, according to Alexander Feinberg of the *New York Times,* the commissioner joined New York City's Mayor William O'Dwyer at his City Hall office. The Maras were there. So were a number of law enforcement officials headed by the city's police commissioner Arthur W. Wallander and Captain Raymond Maguire of the NYPD's Safe and Loft Squad.

Everyone listened attentively as the investigators carefully described how Alvin Paris, a 28-year-old gambler and florist in Manhattan, had allegedly offered bribes to a pair of the Giants' players—Frank Filchock, a 29-year-old left halfback and star passer from Indiana, and Merle Hapes, a twenty-seven-year-old fullback from Mississippi—to fix the following day's NFL championship game between the Giants and Bears at the Polo Grounds. They heard how Captain Maguire, who had broken the basketball betting scandal involving Brooklyn College in 1945, supervised a team of detectives who lived with the New York players at their Bear Mountain practice facility and used wiretaps to gather evidence.

Mayor O'Dwyer, who was visibly upset according to eyewitnesses, took complete charge of the meeting. After dinner, the conferees returned to City Hall for a while, then traveled to Gracie Mansion, the mayor's residence.

Filchock, who was in the city to receive a "Most Valuable Player" award from a radio station, was summoned to the mansion. Hapes was brought down from Bear Mountain. For the next several hours, Bell listened as the mayor confronted the players with the allegations. He talked to each player separately, "like a father to a son," according to a firsthand description of the scene, with neither player knowing of the presence of the other in the house. Soon, both players were in tears. Hapes admitted having been offered the bribe, but Filchock denied it.

When O'Dwyer was notified that Paris had been arrested shortly after 2:00 A.M. on Sunday and brought to the West 54th Street Precinct, the mayor and his party, including Filchock, rushed to the police station. For some reason, Hapes was permitted to go home. By 5:15 A.M., police had obtained Paris's confession, painstakingly written down in longhand by detectives, that he had offered each player $2,500 to throw the game.

Bell immediately announced that Hapes was suspended "pending an investigation by authorities" but told Filchock that he could play in the championship game.

Confronted by reporters about his actions, Bell replied: "Apparently Filchock satisfied the police. He is absolutely in the clean. The only thing we have against Hapes is that he did not bring the story to [coach] Steve Owen or any of the Giants' officials." The commissioner added that the NFL would not conduct a private investigation until a full report was received from the police.

The following day, Filchock played "furiously" despite suffering a broken nose early in the game. He threw two touchdown passes and had six others intercepted (not surprising inasmuch as he had led the league in picks during the season), but the Bears won, 24–14. It was the exact winning margin that most bookmakers had predicted, although some had increased the spread to 14 points hours before kickoff.

Although Bell told *Philadelphia Bulletin* sports editor Ed Pollock a few days later that he was "convinced" when he left Gracie Mansion that Filchock had not been offered the bribe, the Giants quarterback soon would prove the commissioner wrong. Testifying at the first day of Paris's trial on January 7, 1947, in the General Sessions Courtroom, Filchock admitted that he had lied to Mayor O'Dwyer when he said that he had not been offered a bribe to throw the game.

Paris was convicted and later received a reduced one-year sentence. Despite Filchock's admission, Bell told the Associated Press that he would not take final action on the players until the New York District Attorney's office completed its investigation to determine if others were involved in the plot.

"If by a decision or other action I did something to hinder any further investigation, I'd never forgive myself," the commissioner explained. "Meantime, I am continuing my own investigation. However, there is nothing which points to anyone else in football in connection with the case."

Meanwhile, Bell started putting machinery in motion to press for as much state and federal legislation as possible against "fixers" and for strong antibribery laws in every state containing NFL teams. It would soon become a personal crusade—almost an obsession—that would consume much of his time for the rest of his life. Fans would continue to gamble, he acknowledged, but the big-time gamblers *had* to be kept under observation and control.

Bert's brother, Pennsylvania Governor John C. Bell, announced in Harrisburg that he would ask the General Assembly to enact a law making the fixing of athletic contests or bribing of athletes a misdemeanor punishable by imprisonment. Prior to this, only New York had such a law.

League owners wasted no time in unanimously adopting an antigambling amendment to their constitution. As soon as they sat down to begin their three-day meeting in Chicago on January 23, 1947, they gave Bell unprecedented final authority, authorizing him to bar for life "without appeal" any player or official withholding knowledge of any offer, directly or indirectly, to control or fix a game or for failing to report immediately the receipt of such an offer.

The commissioner was also empowered to bar anyone from NFL stadiums who, in his opinion, was detrimental to professional football. Bell said that the job of keeping gamblers and other undesirable characters out of ballparks would be the responsibility of the individual club owners. He intimated that such "policing" would be more effective than that done by baseball owners.

To make certain that the new rule did not escape the attention of "country boys," the commissioner ordered that the clause be inserted in all contracts, that adequate notices be placed in all clubhouses, and that club officials inform each player individually to protect them against the wiles of "city slickers."

This sweeping antigambling resolution made Commissioner Bert Bell "the most powerful figure in all of sports," said Luke P. Carroll of the *New York Herald Tribune*. "Never since the heyday of the late Judge K.M. Landis, the absolute ruler of the baseball world, has any person had such authority."

Bell wrote the amendment himself after he consulted with "several" club owners who told him that he would be supported regardless of what was written. Under the weak, indefinite language of the old rule, which affected Filchock and Hapes, players had to be caught betting on or fixing games before they could be suspended or expelled.

Although it went virtually unnoticed because of the Filchock-Mapes scandal, the owners tackled the issue of television for the first time at their meeting on January 24. They voted to allow each club to sell television rights for its home games for the 1947 season only, provided that the visiting team could televise the game back to its home area. The owners also stipulated that all TV announcers must be approved by the commissioner.

In mid-February, Bell watched as workers moved office equipment and files into the league's new office comprising three rooms above a bank on the sixth floor of a building at 1518 Walnut Street in Center City Philadelphia.

"These rooms were dance studios," the commissioner told Pollock. "Maybe that's why I feel so much at home. I can still trip the light fantastic and if I were 20 years younger, I'd show that Arthur Murray how to step. In my day, I was quite a *terpsichorean*. Say, that's a good word. I'll give it to [my former Penn classmate] Joe Labrum. That's how he got his great vocabulary. I've been giving him all my $10 words since I tutored him through English 90."

Bell showed Pollock two photographs that would soon be hanging on the wall. One was an autographed picture of his brother, by now the former Pennsylvania Governor John C. Bell. The handwriting at the bottom read: "To a great quarterback from a great grandstand quarterback." The commissioner chuckled and told Pollock that he used to rib Jack about calling plays from the stands.

The other photograph was a group shot of Bell, Lud Wray, Lou Little, and Heinie Miller in shorts and football shoes after a University of Pennsylvania football practice. "We were four of the greatest students the university ever had," Bell deadpanned. "Phi Beta Kappa's, but we never wore our keys on the football field."

Also helping with the move was Bill Mackrides's father, Mickey, a shoemaker who had a shop a few doors down from Bell's office on Woodland Avenue.

"My father knew everybody and arranged for everything to be moved out and for his office to be cleaned up," the future Eagles quarterback recalled. "Bert Bell offered to pay my father but he said no. Bert then said, 'I'm going to leave some things there. You just take whatever you want.' He left some pictures hanging on the wall. One was the original drawing of the NRA [National Recovery Act] symbol, the Eagle that he commissioned. I still have that."

On March 25, Bell appointed Joseph T. Labrum, his longtime friend, to be his assistant. Labrum replaced George Strickler, who resigned when the league office was moved from New York to Philadelphia. The first sports publicist ever hired by an eastern college back in 1924, Labrum spent 23 years at the University of Pennsylvania, where he also organized the annual Penn Relays.

After completing his investigation and consulting with his brother, Bell announced on April 3 that Filchock and Hapes were suspended indefinitely after the two were found "guilty of actions detrimental to the welfare of the National League and of professional football."

The commissioner's statement also said in part:

> Professional football cannot continue to exist unless it is based upon absolute honesty. The players must be not only absolutely honest, they must be above suspicion. In short, the game and its players must be kept free from corruption, from all bribes and offers of bribes, and from any possible "fixing" of games. I have given Merle Allison Hapes and Frank Filchock a hearing and an opportunity to tell me everything either of them desired to say in connection with the attempts of Alvin Paris to bribe them or either of them. I have carefully considered all of the statements each of these players has made as well as all the testimony of the court case.

While declining to comment further on his ruling except to say that he "never had a tougher decision to make than in this case," Bell emphasized that he was penalizing the two players to the limit—except for a possible monetary fine—under the rules in effect at the time of the bribe attempt. He added that had the amendment adopted at the league's January meeting been in force, he would have had the power to bar both players for life.

It was the most severe punishment ever handed down by an NFL commissioner. Ken Strong, a multipurpose back of the Giants, and Howie Weiss, a fullback for the Detroit Lions, had previously been suspended by Elmer Layden for five years for contract jumping. Later in the year, Bell meted out the same punishment for the first time to veteran Green Bay Packer guard Fred Vant Hull because he played for the Los Angeles Dons of the AAFC in 1946.

Hapes, who had recently accepted a high school coaching position outside Jackson, Mississippi, told the Associated Press that Bell's action "was a little bit stiff. It's a bunch of baloney about hurting the league. All they got against us is just not reporting the attempt. I don't think we did anything to hurt the league, but I'm through with professional football anyway."

On July 15, Bell traveled to the White House in Washington, where he joined Redskins owner George Preston Marshall in presenting President Harry S. Truman an 18-karat solid gold season pass to all NFL games. Later in the day he announced that in order to protect the integrity of the league, he was directing all of the teams' coaches and publicity directors to publish in advance of each game the names of injured players unable or unlikely to play.

Explaining that the new rule was aimed at protecting the public against professional gamblers, the commissioner pointed out that coaches often had withheld injury information in the past for strategic reasons. "But this information always had been available to professional gamblers," he added. "Therefore they often could manipulate betting points and odds to their advantage."

Bell said that he had in his possession the names of all big-time professional gamblers in each National League city—information that he received from a network of "counter-spies" that he hired to work part-time in each city trailing known gamblers and keeping alert for rumors and changes in the betting line.

"It's my business to know where these fellows are located —and who they are," Bell explained, adding that he was not targeting fans who bet $10 and $20 on games. "The only people I'm interested in watching are the out-and-out cheaters. I want to nail those rumor-mongers who are forever spreading the word that Baugh, Waterfield, Luckman and our other great stars are in the bag. They're my meat!"

Bell once told sportswriter Jack Orr, that he obtained the betting odds and point spreads early in the week and followed them carefully right up to game time. The heaviest betting, he explained, took place during the two hours prior to kickoff. If the numbers changed, he wanted to know the reason why.

"My dad used to get all his betting numbers every week from a guy named 'Footsie' Stein," Bert Jr. recalled. "The line would come out on Tuesday and he would talk to Footsie and write it down on a legal pad. He would always check again on Sunday because that's the day when the big-time gambling guys made their major bets."

"I remember one day my brother, Upton, and I were driving with my dad to a game at Shibe Park. We were maybe eight or nine-years old. We stopped somewhere near the Bellevue Stratford Hotel or Lew Tendler's Restaurant. My dad got out of the car and there was some kind of a confrontation. I couldn't quite get to see whom he was meeting, but later he came back disheveled. The report was that Cocky Sal or Lancaster Mac or one of the other bookies had started a rumor about Steve Van Buren to move the point spread. My father got into a fist fight with him, whoever it was."

Gathering for a special meeting in Pittsburgh on July 20, the owners made landmark decisions on the league's relationship with college football. At Bell's urging, the league adopted a rule prohibiting the signing of college stars who register for classes after an absence—such as war service—and thus retain eligibility beyond their normal graduation year. Previously the league could sign only players whose original classes had graduated or who had received a diploma in an accelerated course.

Bell said that the new ruling was part of the league's "avowed desire to cooperate with the colleges and prevent raiding." Asked whether the rival All-America Conference would be requested to draft a similar rule, Bell said: "We tend strictly to our own business."

A few days before the 1947 College All-Star game in Chicago in August, Bell visited with Admiral Jonas H. Ingram, the new AAFC commissioner, who was credited with driving the German U-boats from the Atlantic Ocean during World War II. Neither man would discuss the nature of their conversation with reporters. The admiral would say only that they chatted about old times and old friends.

Ingram later disclosed that he had sent a telegram to Bell, challenging the NFL to a championship game with the entire proceeds going either to the winner or to charity. Claiming that the postseason game could net $250,000, Ingram added, "We feel that we have four teams better than anything they've got," referring to Cleveland, the New York Yankees, the Los Angeles Dons, and San Francisco.

"Not interested, don't play post-season games," Bell responded. When prodded by the Associated Press to elaborate, Bert coolly repeated his words, emphasizing that he had no more to say. The NFL commissioner had the same response later for a Los Angeles city councilman who suggested a similar matchup for various charities.

Told that Ingram had accepted the LA invitation, Bell declined and added in his telegram: "So there can be no misunderstanding," it should be pointed out that the NFL has always been interested in worthy charities and member clubs raised over $1 million for various charities in 1946 and 1947.

A number of pundits immediately criticized Bell. Calling the NFL commissioner "a figurehead," Lawton Carver, the sports editor of the International News Service, wrote: "The All-America is up and coming at a time when the National is riding along on past glories under the domination of Tim Mara in New York, George Halas in Chicago, and George Preston Marshall in Washington. All three have worn-out ball clubs."

Cleveland Plain Dealer sports editor Gordon Cobbledick was even more vitriolic after watching the College All-Stars pummel the Chicago Bears, the defending NFL champs, 16–0 before 105,840 spectators in Soldier Field on August 22.

In an "Open Letter" to Bell, Cobbledick wrote: "You would be a sucker to go for a football 'world series' at this time because the Cleveland

Browns would chase your Chicago Bears clear out of the ball park and into the middle of the lake. They don't belong on the same football field with the Browns or, for that matter, one or two other All-America clubs."

United Press sportswriter Jack Cuddy interviewed Bell and wrote a colorful profile in August when the commissioner predicted that the league would set a new attendance record of at least 2.5 million people during the 1947 season:

> "I rarely go in for predictions of this sort," said the husky, middle-aged man in the tan gabardine suit, "but I believe my enthusiasm can be pardoned at this time because of the very favorable reports we have been receiving from the various clubs' front offices and from the training camps."
>
> Bell, a ruddy chap—who has a sharp, prominent nose like Bob Hope, and who parts his brown, gray-fringed hair in the middle, explained that his 2.5 million forecast verged on the conservative because last year the league's ten clubs hit a new high total of 2,288,378 spectators.
>
> He continued, "We certainly ought to do a couple hundred thousand better in '47 because the standard of play will be higher throughout the league and because a record number of 60 games will be played—five more than last season. Moreover, advance reports indicate that the Boston and Detroit clubs will be much improved this year. Boston was last in the Eastern Division in '46 and Detroit was the Western low club."
>
> A reporter, fanning with Bert in his office at league headquarters, asked why the standard of play would be higher in the next campaign. The robust commissioner nested this kickoff with ease and galloped conversationally down field. "Play will be better on all clubs," he said, "because the season actually will mark the beginning of the great post-war era of professional football. It will be the first season, he emphasized, in which all players who were in the service not only have had a chance to return to the gridiron, but have had the opportunity to condition themselves properly for a full season of play."
>
> Will there be any innovations in the game this season? "Yes, there was one in which the clubs were very much interested. There would be a fifth official on the field—a back judge. He would officiate in no man's land—on the opposite side of plays from the head linesman. His presence there would prevent any uncertainty about plays in his area, and would help to speed up the game.

"We are interested particularly in keeping the game moving at a fast pace, with as little delay as possible between plays," he pointed out. "Last season our games averaged 160 plays per game. And the games required an average of less than two hours and twenty minutes. That's what the fans want—a fast-moving game, and that's what we're giving them. I might add also that we're trying to keep the game as open and spectacular as possible for the sake of the spectators; but meanwhile keeping it as safe as possible for the players."

How much money did Bell figure was now invested in the 10 National League clubs? He made a rough estimate of slightly more than $6 million.

Are the clubs making money on their investments? "In 1946, only one club suffered a loss," he replied. "Two broke even and seven enjoyed a profit. This year, all should do better," he prophesied.

Are the players sharing in this prosperity? "Indeed they are," he declared. "Their salaries now average about $6,000 a season or about $400 a game. These are the highest-paid performers per game—on the average—in any sport," he concluded.

In September, Bell made his first visit to California since he quarterbacked Penn's football team in the 1917 Rose Bowl against Oregon.

"We couldn't exist without college football," he told writers before watching the Los Angeles Rams spank the Washington Redskins, 20–7, in a preseason charity exhibition game before 80,889 fans in the Memorial Coliseum. "We will do everything in our power to get along with the colleges. No boy can play in the National League until his class has graduated."

Privately, Bell was incensed over the attitude of college athletic administrators. As a group they all considered professional football beneath them and refused to provide any information about their athletes to the NFL teams. "There are a few coaches including [Michigan's] Fritz Crisler, who hate pro football," he later told Pollock.

"My father and my uncle Harry Standish decided to do something about it," Bert Bell Jr. recalled. "They developed a fake college football magazine and sent questionnaires on an official-looking letterhead to college publicity people. They asked for information about players' sizes, ages, what year they were academically in class. The information came right back to the league office. They didn't share it with any of the NFL teams. My father just wanted to make eligibility lists for the player draft. I'd say he did that for about five years."

After returning home from California, the commissioner told the *Bulletin* that he believed that the attempted bribe or fix in professional football had been licked. "We know the gambling situation in each of our league cities," he claimed, adding that there were now laws in every state in which the league teams played to deal with such illegal conduct.

A few days later, Admiral Ingram again challenged the NFL to a postseason game with the AAFC. "I'm going to needle the hell out of the National League until we get the recognition due us and they agree to meet us in a playoff," he said.

"No comment," Bell replied.

Early in December, the commissioner refused to be drawn into a controversy when Alexis Thompson of the Eagles became the first NFL owner to hint that his league was taking cognizance of the existence of the rival All-America League. That happened when Thompson told members of the New York Football Writers Association at Toots Shor's that he favored a common player draft with the AAFC.

The battle lines were quickly being drawn.

21. Blizzards, Gamblers, and a Rebellious Club Owner

Early in January 1948, Bert Bell sat down with one of his favorite sportswriters, Ralph Bernstein of the Philadelphia Bureau of the Associated Press. Starting his third year as commissioner, the "portly, graying former coach" told Bernstein that he was looking forward to bigger and better gridiron feats, even better than in the past year that he called the greatest season in the history of the NFL.

Although paid admission figures were not yet compiled, Bell estimated that 2.5 million people watched 60 regular season games and an additional dozen exhibition contests.

"It will take plenty of doing to top the '47 campaign, but watch us," Bell said as he leaned back in his swivel chair. "We play strictly for spectator appeal. Attendance should be even greater this season, possibly by a quarter of a million customers."

"Why the bigger gate?" Bernstein asked. "Competition will be closer than ever," the commissioner replied. "The real thing in spectator interest—the thing that means big crowds—is a close race. All ten clubs have championship hopes for 1948."

Bell described how the Chicago Cardinals had defeated Philadelphia for the 1947 NFL title after the Eagles had knocked off the Pittsburgh Steelers in a special playoff to reach the championship bracket. He pointed out that 11 records were broken during the season.

"I really believe the '48 season will be greater. It stands to reason that Washington, New York, and the Chicago Bears won't stay out of the championship race. And the drawing cards—Sammy Baugh, Steve Van Buren, Sid Luckman, Charlie Trippi, Paul Christman—will help pack them in."

Two weeks later, when they held their annual meetings at the Hotel Commodore in New York, the other club owners greeted with "utter disdain" Alexis Thompson's proposal for a common draft with the All-America Football Conference. Vocally, they unanimously rejected his insistence that it be placed on the agenda.

Thompson was not on hand when his idea was presented by Al Ennis, his general manager. He was in Switzerland for the Winter Olympics.

"It never had a chance," wrote Louis Effrat of the *New York Times.* "Ennis, with Commissioner Bert Bell waiving parliamentary procedure, was permitted to enlarge upon his proxy-motion. Ennis spoke for five minutes and when no second to his motion was heard, shrugged his shoulders and sat down, conclusively beaten, without even having reached the voting stage."

After two days and a night of wrangling, the owners were unable to agree on a 1948 schedule and dumped the entire issue in Bell's lap. This was nothing new. For years the owners had been bickering over opponents, game sites, and playing dates. On one hand, they wanted drawing cards like the Packers, Bears, and Giants on their schedules. They also desired a few cupcakes to enhance their won–lost record. Pittsburgh's Art Rooney enjoyed telling writers about the marathon stalemates.

The owners with the most staying power, who were willing to remain in the meeting rooms day and night arguing, were the ones who came away with the best schedules, he explained. The guys who got tired and snuck out to get some sleep or go nightclubbing wound up getting murdered the next season, because when they weren't there to defend themselves, we'd give them all the dates we didn't want.

One year, the owners debated for two or three days over the schedule. Just as it was about to be completed and most of it written on the blackboard, George Preston Marshall exploded because he hadn't been given some of the choice home days he coveted. The Washington Redskins owner stormed up to the blackboard and erased the entire slate as his colleagues screamed and yelled because no one had written any of it down. It took two more days to reformulate the schedule.

Finally, the owners reached the point where they were totally exhausted from arguing. They had enough confidence in Bell to let him come up with an equitable solution—not only for the upcoming season, but for the future. The commissioner was charged with arranging the complete schedule himself. His decision would be final. There would be no appealing, no complaining.

One of Bell's major problems revolved around the longer major league baseball season, which would affect three Sunday dates—September 26, October 3, and October 10—and eight of the ten NFL teams that played in baseball parks. No problem, Bert reasoned. He quickly tackled the issue and had a workable schedule completed within a few weeks.

One day during the summer, the commissioner left the office early to take his oldest son to a dentist in Ardmore, not far from their home.

"I remember riding down the elevator," Bert Jr. recalled. "The operator said to my dad, 'Listen, my brother just got back from the war. He played football at Radnor High and he's dying to get a tryout with the New York Giants. All he wants to do is play pro football.' My father took his name and called Jack Mara or someone at the Giants."

That's how Emlen Tunnell came to play for 14 years in the NFL as a safety with the Giants and Green Bay Packers. He later became the first African American and first purely defensive player to be inducted into the Pro Football Hall of Fame.

"Whenever people try to tell me that African Americans weren't allowed to play in the NFL, I tell them the story of Emlen Tunnell," Bert Bell Jr. explained. "That's how *prejudiced* my father was."

During the 1948 season, Bell took great pleasure in watching the Philadelphia Eagles defeat the Chicago Bears for the first time in history, 12–7, at Shibe Park on October 24. It wasn't just because his former team snapped a 15-year jinx against the Bears. More importantly, Bert beamed as his onetime waterboy Bill Mackrides, a quarterback making his first start because of an injury to Tommy Thompson, orchestrated a huge upset over the most famous team in professional football.

"For a rookie he gave one of the most remarkable exhibitions I have ever seen," Bell gushed. "He was ice water out there." Bell also remembered Mackrides's dad, Mickey, the shoemaker who helped him move into his new office in 1946 when he was named commissioner.

Still concerned about the effects of gambling and frustrated because Pennsylvania was the only state with an NFL franchise that still had not passed a law making bribery of athletes illegal (it finally did so three months later in February 1949), Bell collaborated with Pete Martin to write an extensive article for *The Saturday Evening Post*. It was entitled "Do the Gamblers Make a Sucker Out of You?"

Citing "chapter and verse" to demonstrate how the average fan can parlay inside information into sizable financial losses, Bell explained how rumors are the most effective weapon possessed by football gamblers.

"In addition to the gamblers and the sure-thingers, there is a growing number of cynical and disillusioned people who believe that there is something wrong with almost everything, not only with sports, but with business integrity and family life as well," the commissioner wrote.

Bell described the various measures that the league had enacted to prevent gamblers from obtaining "inside information" that could affect point spreads or betting odds. He explained why visitors were no longer permitted inside locker rooms and emphasized to players the importance of avoiding association with strangers whose antecedents were unknown to them.

He told how Steve Van Buren, the Eagles star, had been approached recently by a group of men who wanted to set him up in the restaurant-and-bar business.

"When I said 'no' to the project, Steve came to me about it," the commissioner wrote. "'Mr. Bell,' he said, 'they tell me you won't let me go into the restaurant-and-bar business. Why not?'

"Having been in the hotel business, I know a little about how restaurants and bars operate. I told him either you or a member of your family must be on duty 24 hours a day to check your food and liquor inventory constantly, and for you that's impossible. But the worst part is that you're the host. You've got to greet everybody who comes in, and the first thing you know, one of your customers will ask you to have dinner with him. You may refuse him the first time, but he's a good customer and you can't keep on refusing him forever.

"In the end, you have dinner with him. Let's say it's on a Thursday night. The following Sunday you go out to Shibe Park and make two or three fumbles. Maybe you aren't feeling right and your coordination is off. The result is that you'll begin to hear rumors like this: 'I told you he'd have a sour day, didn't I? I saw him having dinner with Luke McGook the big gambler, on Thursday night.'

"Steve saw the light. 'I guess I'll skip the restaurant-and-bar business, Mr. Bell,' he told me. He added kiddingly, 'That's for linemen who don't have to carry the ball.'"

Bell added that all teams must announce to newspapers at least 24 hours in advance of game time that a player is not going to play or that he is injured and may not play.

"Gambler's rumors spread with chain-reaction speed," he explained. "Last year, a few days before the Bears were going to play the Rams, the Bears were a 13½ point favorite. A photographer at a practice session asked permission to take a picture of Sid Luckman mounted on a horse. The flash bulb scared the horse. He bolted and Luckman fell off, cutting his wrist slightly. An hour later, through gambling channels, the rumor reached all corners of the country that Luckman had severed an artery and might not play. Sixty minutes after the horse tossed him, the odds on the Bears had shrunk from 13½ points to 10½ points."

Recalling the serious consequences faced by the two New York Giants' players who failed to report a bribe, the commissioner emphasized that he had "utmost confidence" in everyone in the league.

"I'd back the honesty of anyone in the National Football League against the honesty of any respectable citizen anywhere," Bell concluded. "I refuse to compare the honesty of those in the league with the rumor-mongers. I don't consider a rumor-monger a respectable citizen."

Two days before the NFL championship game, Alexis Thompson again stirred up trouble with his fellow owners. In addition to repeating his desire for a common player draft and a merger with the AAFC, the Eagles' owner, according to published reports circulating in New York, said he planned to transfer his team out of the NFL into the rival league and move his franchise to that city.

Claiming that his team was going to "lose close to $32,000" despite being on the verge of a championship, Thompson told the Associated Press, "I'd be a fool if I didn't try and resolve a situation for which most of us are losing money."

Bell reacted quickly. "I do not believe this story about Thompson and the Eagles," he told the *Philadelphia Bulletin*. He was correct. Thompson remained on board. Asked what action he would take if Thompson had made good on his threat, Bell referred reporters to the league's constitution and by-laws that dealt with acts detrimental to professional football for which owners may be forced to forfeit their franchises and lose their rights to players and park leases.

Denying Thompson's charge that most NFL teams are losing money, Bell told *Hearst* columnist Bob Considine: "Everybody's yapping about how much money is being blown in pro football. Despite all the belly-aching, our teams have made more money in the last five years than they made from 1933 to 1943."

Nevertheless, Boston Yanks co-owner Ted Collins had recently admitted to the Associated Press that he had lost $720,000 the past four years.

The commissioner then came under considerable criticism on December 19 when he permitted the NFL championship game to be played in a raging blizzard in Philadelphia's Shibe Park. The Eagles edged the Chicago Cardinals, 7–0, before 28,864 frozen fans.

Although Eagles coach Greasy Neale personally wanted the game postponed, according to *The Eagles Encyclopedia,* he felt that the decision should be left up to the two teams. While Neale was consulting with Chicago coach Jimmy Conzelman in the Cardinals' locker room, the Eagles players took a vote and overwhelmingly chose to play.

More than a foot of snow still accumulated on a ton of hay on top of the tarpaulin covering the field, and the grounds crew couldn't shovel it off. They finally called the two teams from the locker room and the players helped drag the tarp off the field. Also helping, recalls Upton Bell, was his dad.

"My brother and I went to the game with him," the younger Bell explained. "I had just turned 11 years old. We were up in the press box. Somebody said, 'Is that the commissioner down there?' We looked down and there was my father in his hat and brown overcoat helping to push the snow and tarp off the field. It was kind of a surrealistic thing. The tarp was frozen and the officials didn't think they could get it off the field. So I remember him making that long climb down the steps. I think that in some way signaled always to the players, this was a guy that was willing to be part of the whole thing. He never stood above them."

When the game started 30 minutes late, the yard lines were invisible, so referee Ronald Gibbs used his judgment to determine the downs and distance and the players agreed not to question his decisions. Ropes were used to mark off the sidelines.

"You look at the pictures and the field looks terrible," said Steve Van Buren, who rushed for 98 yards and scored the game's only touchdown. The only problem was seeing. It was snowing so hard that I couldn't see their safety."

"The game should never have been played," Marshall Goldberg, the Cardinals' safety, told David Cohen in his book *Rugged and Enduring: The Eagles, the Browns, and 5 Years of Football.* "The field was in no condition to play. There were no sidelines, no end lines; the goal lines were completely obliterated. And, it was such a miserable day that there was no possible way that a decent football game could be played, especially a championship game."

Syndicated columnist Jimmy Cannon described the field as "a big drift" and ripped Bell for his decision to play the game.

"Not even fight promoters, the greediest of them all, would try to get away with anything like that which was pulled off yesterday in Philadelphia," he wrote. "It is my opinion that nothing since the Alvin Paris [gambling] scandal harmed football more than yesterday's game. It proved that anyone who buys a ticket before the day of a football game played in December must be classed with guys who think they can beat the races."

"Television, radio, and newsreel companies had paid $33,000 for rights to the game and a postponement would have been costly," reported *Time* magazine.

Bell told Louis Effrat that he would have liked to have postponed it, but his hands were tied. "We must consider the many out-of-towners who made long trips to see the game," he explained. "There are 1,000 fans here from Chicago and many from Erie, Pittsburgh, New York, and other cities."

As it turned out the net gate receipts were $156,937, the second highest in NFL playoff history.

Alexis Thompson was not part of the windfall, however. Despite winning the NFL title, it was later revealed that the embattled Eagles owner had lost $88,000 during the 1948 season, not $32,000 that he had announced earlier. He was so strapped for cash that he could not meet his players' payroll the final week of the season. Bell and the NFL had to bail him out.

With rumors of a merger flying throughout the football world, the owners of teams in the National League and All-America Conference finally sat down to talk for the first time. It happened on the Monday following their championship games. The commissioner himself greeted the AAFC owners at North Philadelphia Station after they arrived from Cleveland following the Browns' 49–7 win over Buffalo. Cheerfully he escorted them to his favorite haunt, the Racquet Club in Center City Philadelphia.

The owners met for 10 hours behind locked doors without reaching an agreement. One of the major unresolved issues involved the fate of the American League's Baltimore franchise, located within an hour's drive of George Preston Marshall's lucrative Washington Redskins territory. "What do we want Baltimore for?" he told the Associated Press. "We have enough of our own headaches without adding more."

Sources told sportswriters that the NFL wanted to absorb only two AAFC teams, Cleveland and San Francisco, because the league's other cities had lost too much money. As a whole, the All-America Conference reportedly dropped $3 million during its three-year existence.

Another source said that the owners discussed a two-league setup that would take the Chicago Cardinals out of the NFL—a rumor that caused Chicago Bears owner George Halas to go ballistic. "If anybody thinks they can break up a rivalry which sells out twice a year, he's crazy," Halas roared. "I'll tear the league apart before that happens!"

Afterward, Bell and Benjamin F. Lindheimer, of the Los Angeles Dons, the chairman of the AAFC Executive Committee, jointly issued a statement that said in part: "Efforts by both sides to formulate a mutually satisfactory agreement were not consummated. The committees terminated the meeting with the expectation that future meetings might provide some formula for a common understanding between both leagues."

With both leagues admitting that their attendance had dropped in 1948, the owners did agree on one issue—the status quo could not continue.

22. A Bitter Dispute with Walter Annenberg and a Truce with the AAFC

On January 15, 1949, after weighing offers submitted by a number of groups anxious to buy out the beleaguered Alexis Thompson, Bert Bell announced his decision. The new owners of the Eagles would be a syndicate of 100 Philadelphia businessmen headed up by James P. Clark, who had built Highway Express Lines into one of the nation's largest trucking empires. Known as the "100 Brothers," each of the new owners invested $3,000 apiece to purchase the club for $250,000.

Asked by reporters why he favored the Clark group, Bell replied: "It is my duty as commissioner to recommend as purchaser to the league owners that group which in my opinion offers most for the best interests of the Philadelphia club and the league. I told all the applicants for purchase to whom I spoke that they were perfectly acceptable as individuals. But I also told them that I would make the final decision on what I thought was for the best interests of the club and the league. There was no question of turning anyone down. It was solely a matter of selecting."

Bell received another rousing vote of confidence at the league's annual meeting at Chicago's Blackstone Hotel on January 20, when the club owners tore up his five-year contract and replaced it with a 10-year pact at the same $30,000 annual salary. In addition to voting to increase the financial guarantee to visiting teams from $15,000 to $20,000,—with the visitors retaining the option of accepting 40 percent of the net gate, individual clubs were also given permission to televise their games in 1949.

Even though the rival All-America Football League's owners were meeting at the same time across the street at the Stevens Hotel, no attempts were made for further negotiations. However, both teams made news on the second day of their confabs.

The AAFC announced the consolidation of the New York Yankees and Brooklyn Dodgers and said that the new team would play in Yankee Stadium.

"Good luck to them," said Bell before announcing that the financially strapped Boston Yanks would move to New York, change their name to the Bulldogs, and share the Polo Grounds with the Giants who would have first choice of home dates.

The following week, Bell called a press conference to emphatically deny charges by Buffalo owner Jim Breuil that peace between the two leagues was blocked by owners Tim Mara of the New York Giants and George Preston Marshall of the Washington Redskins during recent negotiations.

Shedding some light on the developments behind closed doors at the Racquet Club in Philadelphia, Bell said, "Peace was not the subject of our meetings. Only once at the first meeting on December 20 was the suggestion made that the All-America Conference retain its identity. That suggestion was quickly dropped and thereafter the owners from both leagues discussed how many conference teams could join the National Football League."

Bell told the Associated Press that at no time did NFL owners leave their counterparts from the AAFC under any delusion that they were interested in two leagues. He said that he told Ben Lindheimer, of the Los Angeles Dons, prior to the December 20 meeting that NFL owners were interested in only two of their teams, San Francisco and Cleveland. Lindheimer replied that his owners would like to come to Philadelphia and discuss the situation, providing NFL owners would keep an open mind of adding four of their teams.

"I promised no such thing, but the AAC representatives came anyway," Bell explained. "We never wavered in our original demands and every action taken was by the ten owners of the NFL." Bell said that Tim Mara wasn't even at the meeting. The Giants were represented by his son, Jack.

"The stronger AAC teams wanted to come to an agreement with the NFL, but the other Conference teams would not permit this, claiming that they had a binding legal agreement which prohibited such a move without the consent of all members," Bell said as part of a prepared statement. "This closed the door on any merger since the NFL will not take in any new members except on a sound business basis, and for the best interests of football, and only where we feel it will add strength to the NFL, which has been in business for 30 years."

Bell admitted that several informal meetings took place in Chicago "between one or more owners from each league" and added: "Even these informal meetings demonstrated that the obstacles to a merger could not be overcome."

The commissioner also confirmed that a secret meeting had been held in Philadelphia early in December between him and three AAFC owners—Anthony Morabito of the San Francisco 49ers, Arthur McBride of the

Cleveland Browns, and Breuil of Buffalo. All parties agreed to keep the meeting secret, Bell said.

"Under present conditions, there will be no peace in the conflict between the National Football League and the All-America Conference, no pro football 'World Series,' and no common draft," the commissioner declared.

In June, new Philadelphia Eagles president James P. Clark announced that his defending NFL champions would not televise their home football games in 1949. "A great number of season ticket holders didn't renew their orders this year," Clark told the Associated Press. "We wrote them to find out why and they told us they'd rather stay home and watch the games on television. We can't afford that."

Informed that a college official predicted that in five years "television will wreck football," Bert Bell told the Associated Press that the NFL was not taking sides on the issue. "It's up to the individual clubs," he said.

It was a sweltering day in August. Upton and Bert Bell Jr. had just returned from the beach to their summer home in Margate, New Jersey, when they saw their dad slowly pulling his car into the driveway. The boys were familiar with his daily routine at the seashore. He hated the beach, so he would spend most mornings on the telephone, then either drive or walk (he was an extremely fast walker) to get a snack or takeout at Kramer's Delicatessen, a store that he affectionately called "The Stork Club." Sometimes he would stop to chat on the front porch of a neighbor like James P. McGranery, who would later be appointed U.S. attorney general by President Truman. Bert loved hearing tales about the latest behind-the-scenes happenings in Washington.

But this time, the boys knew that something was wrong—dreadfully wrong.

"I rarely saw him upset, but I could tell that he was really visibly shaken," Bert Jr. recalled. The commissioner then told the boys what had happened. He had been visiting his good friend Walter Annenberg, who lived a few blocks away, when the publisher of the *Philadelphia Inquirer* accused him of being anti-Semitic.

Bert Bell was devastated.

Annenberg had headed up Triangle Publications since 1942 when his father, Moses, died. The vast communications empire also included the *Morning Telegraph,* the nation's largest horseracing publication; *Seventeen* magazine; *TV Guide;* and Philadelphia's WFIL radio and television stations, among other interests.

Bert and Frances befriended Walter and his first wife, Veronica, after the two men began working together on various projects including promoting the annual summer exhibition game between the Eagles and another NFL team to benefit *Philadelphia Inquirer* charities.

"My mom and dad took them everywhere, introduced them around, and made them feel comfortable," Bert Jr. explained. "They quickly became good friends."

"It was a very complex relationship," Upton said. "I remember as a child, Annenberg and his wife were over at our house all the time. They would frequently come over in their tennis whites and have something to eat. I thought they were pretty close."

Annenberg told the commissioner in no uncertain terms why he was so upset. Before the 100 Brothers had won the bidding rights to purchase the Eagles, Annenberg and his close friend Harry Sylk, the millionaire owner of Sun Ray Drugs, expressed interest in buying the club.

Bell tried to explain that he didn't think it was a good idea for a newspaper publisher to own a football team. It would be too much a conflict of interest. Besides, he was looking for a football man and just didn't think that Sylk would be the right guy.

"My father really thought he was protecting the league in this case," Upton recalled. "Not that these guys weren't good businessmen, but it took a different type of person to run a team."

"My dad received tons of applications from prospective owners," Bert Jr. explained. "He would always tell them that they have to come in with clean hands, and an avid interest in the game, and not just be looking for a tax angle. It is most important that they love the game more than the love of money."

Although Sylk did obtain a piece of the team as one of the 100 Brothers, Walter Annenberg and Bert Bell never spoke again.

After secretly negotiating behind locked doors at the Racquet Club virtually around-the-clock for nearly three days, a haggard and tired Bert Bell and J. Arthur Friedlund, a Chicago attorney who represented the AAFC, jointly announced a peace agreement on Friday, December 9, at NFL headquarters in Philadelphia. Bell was given a 10-year contract to serve as commissioner of the new National-American Football League.

Three teams from the four-year-old AAFC were absorbed into the new loop, which was divided into two separate divisions. NFL franchises were awarded to the San Francisco 49ers, Cleveland Browns, and Baltimore.

The Colts were admitted after Washington's George Preston Marshall changed his mind when he realized that his Redskins could be the beneficiary of an attractive rivalry with Baltimore, which was located only 40 miles away. Marshall reportedly worked hard behind the scene to convince other NFL owners to accept the new teams. In addition he agreed to waive his territorial rights for three annual payments of $50,000, according to *The Pro Football Chronicle*.

The Redskins owner told the United Press that he was ecstatic about the merger. Puffing on an Indian peace pipe for the benefit of photographers interviewing him in Washington, Marshall picked up the telephone and called Bell in Philadelphia to clear up some points about the armistice.

"Hello, peace pipe," he greeted Bell. "What league am I supposed to be in?" After he finished talking, Marshall told newsmen that Bell would not announce the makeup until the first of the year. Bell said that the league would play the same 12-game schedule but that one club would have to play all the others at least once a year.

The merger that ended the financially devastating war between the two leagues forced two consolidations. Breuil agreed to fold the Buffalo Bills and buy into the Cleveland Browns. Lindheimer did likewise with the Los Angeles Dons and became part owner of the Rams. The Chicago Hornets of the AAFC were purchased by the new league and the franchise was disbanded. In the East, Ted Collins of the New York Bulldogs obtained a 10-year lease from Dan Topping to play in Yankee Stadium and changed the name of his team to the Yanks. The other players from the defunct Yankees of the AAFC were awarded to the New York Giants.

Bell, unshaven but beaming, appointed Emil R. Fisher of the Green Bay Packers president of the National Division and Daniel Sherby of the Cleveland Browns head of the American Division. The commissioner admitted that many details still needed to be resolved including the distribution of players from Buffalo, the Chicago Hornets, and Los Angeles Dons, as well as players not listed on the 32-man roster of each team.

What the commissioner didn't admit at the time were the tremendous concessions he made to get Cleveland's Paul Brown to go along with the merger. Years later, Tim Temerario, who was one of Brown's assistant coaches, described the deal to *Philadelphia Daily News* columnist Larry Merchant.

"Brown insisted on getting John Kissell, Rex Bumgardner, and Abe Gibron from Buffalo," Temerario explained. "Bell made the deal in private meetings with the Browns. When he told the owners they raised cane. They realized the three players Brown had gotten would make them a real power in the new league.

"Owners like Halas, McMillan, and Marshall blew their stacks, especially because Gibron was an All Pro offensive guard and Kissell, an All Pro defensive tackle. But they had to accept or Bell would lose face. The funny part was that none of the other teams asked for extra players. In truth, the agreement had to be made with the Browns and Bell knew it."

Bell credited a pair of New Yorkers who were more interested in their baseball clubs for bringing the warring factions together. Horace Stoneham, owner of the New York Baseball Giants and landlord of the Giants and Bulldogs' football teams at the Polo Grounds, had invited Bell to New York a few days earlier for a conference with George Weiss, vice president and general manager of the New York Yankees baseball team, the owners of Yankee Stadium.

At the meeting, Bell agreed to meet a single AAFC representative in Philadelphia. Weiss then prevailed on club owners from both leagues to empower Bell and Friedlund to hammer out a satisfactory agreement. Friedlund was general counsel for the Yankees in baseball and for the football enterprise that linked Topping and Branch Rickey, president of the baseball Brooklyn Dodgers.

Although some owners like Art Rooney of the Pittsburgh Steelers strongly endorsed the idea, Bell said that there was no chance for a championship playoff game between the two leagues in 1949.

"That would make a swell game, but a post-season game like that is barred by the NFL Constitution," he said. "The constitution can't be changed until the first meeting of the new league, January 19."

Afterward, Philadelphia Eagles president James P. Clark said that Bell "is to be congratulated for his patience and intelligence in working out this solution."

Dick Cresap of the *Philadelphia Bulletin* said that Bell accepted congratulations from all over the country hailing his work in solving the bitter struggle. "Although there was no gloating over the dissolution of the AAC—which actually is what happened despite the term 'merger'—there is no doubt the settlement was a triumph for the National League which repeatedly ignored earlier AAC attempts to operate two major leagues with a common player draft," Cresap wrote.

Some owners, including Mickey McBride of the Cleveland Browns, predicted that individual club operating costs would be cut in half by the merger.

"In 1941, George Halas won the National League title with a team that cost $140,000 for the season," McBride explained. "This year, salaries for my club will run between $260,000 and $280,000. That's what the war between the leagues meant in dollars and cents."

The AAFC champion Browns reportedly lost $150,000 that season. The New York Bulldogs dropped more than $200,000. The 49ers were the only AAFC team to show a profit, while five NFL teams—Philadelphia, Washington, the Los Angeles Rams, and both Chicago clubs—expected to make a profit.

Bell told Cresap that salaries for players would certainly drop. "They still won't play for peanuts," the commissioner added. "Economic conditions will take care of everything. Salaries will now be determined by owners in terms of the man's drawing and earning power. But the players won't be caught in any squeeze."

When a sportswriter mentioned that the merger plan was announced with "unexpected suddenness," Bell quipped, "We do things in a hurry when we do them." "Especially when there's money involved," someone replied. "You're right," Bell chortled.

With the NFL alone losing $3 million, the costliest war in the history of sports was over, according to *The Pro Football Chronicle,* but the battle to save Buffalo was just beginning.

Four days after the merger, a "Keep the Bills in Buffalo" drive was launched and more than $200,000 was pledged for stock in the proposed new team. Bell told its supporters that their application would be considered more favorably if they could sell enough season tickets to guarantee a gate of at least $60,000 a game. Within five days, their goal was reached—pledges were received for 10,000 season tickets.

"Only the iron-handed tactics of Bell saved the newly-merged league from dying at birth," Arthur Daley later reflected in the *New York Times.* "He couldn't please everyone, of course, but he was so eminently fair in every ruling that even the originally suspicious All-America Conference owners became his firmest supporters. He emerged with vastly increased stature and pro football reflected that gain."

"Bert Bell runs the show," wrote Associated Press sportswriter Ralph Bernstein. "Because of the farsightedness of Mr. Bell, pro football today faces the future—the last 50 years of the 20th century—with probably the brightest outlook of any major sport on the horizon. All the game needs is leadership. That it has in abundance with the ruddy-faced Bell, a man who was born to football."

Shortly after the merger, Bell visited Cleveland with his two sons. "We got into a cab and were riding along with Mickey McBride, who owned the Browns," Upton recalled. "He was telling my father about this wonderful extra group of players that they had. My father asked, 'Are they on the regular squad?' McBride said, 'Well no. They're on the Taxi Squad. That's something that coach Paul Brown invented where players who weren't quite ready to play yet would be on the Taxi Squad.'

We said, 'Mickey where did you get that name?' 'Well, I own all the taxis in Cleveland,' he replied. And that's how you got the name, Taxi Squad, which is still around in a different form today."

A few days before the 1949 NFL championship game between the Eagles and Rams, an exhausted Bert Bell reluctantly heeded his physician's orders and canceled reservations for Los Angeles.

"The endless work with only a few hours of sleep daily has left its mark on the commissioner in grayer hair and deeper facial lines," *Bulletin* sports editor Ed Pollock reported. "His physician had repeatedly ordered him to rest, but still he finds little time for sleep and none for recreation."

Although the four years he had spent as commissioner "have been the toughest of Bell's life," Pollock added, "It was a "great personal triumph" for him when the All-America, with hat in hand, agreed to come into the NFL under virtually the same terms dictated after the 1948 season. The little round man with the resonant voice, who can quip as well as the best master of ceremonies and yell a command like the toughest top sergeant, is Mr. Football now. Without doubt, he is the most important figure in the game."

One reason for Bell's deteriorating physical condition at the time was the stress he felt over the pending legal battle involving Bill Radovich, who had become the first NFL player to take the league to court, demanding the right to play for the team of his choice. Handling the case for Radovich was future San Francisco mayor Joseph Alioto, who would again, many years later, become an adversary of the NFL in antitrust court.

Radovich had been an All-Pro guard and linebacker for the Detroit Lions before serving in the U.S. Navy during World War II. When he returned in 1946, he told the Lions that he wanted to either be traded to the West Coast or be given a raise to pay for his travel expenses. After being turned down, he played for two years at twice his NFL salary for the Los Angeles Dons of the AAFC.

In 1948, the minor league San Francisco Seals, an NFL affiliate, offered him a contract as a player-coach but rescinded the deal when club officials learned that he had been notified by Bell that he had been suspended for jumping leagues, in effect "blacklisted" for five years.

Bell convened an executive session of league owners at the Racquet Club in Philadelphia on November 7 and called on his brother, John C., to discuss the ramifications of the case. Bert had recently appointed John C. to serve as attorney for the NFL. He had informally helped the commissioner sort out thorny legal issues occasionally in the past and this time his expertise was officially needed.

John C. told the owners that Radovich's lawyer had made an offer to settle for $13,000 and added that one of his legal associates in San

Francisco was of the opinion that the NFL would lose the case if they didn't accept the out-of-court settlement. John C. said that he disagreed with his West Coast colleague, however, and told the owners that he felt that the "league had a 50–50 chance" of winning, even though, in his opinion, the case would hinge on the thinking of the judge hearing it.

John C. also warned the owners that his counterpart in California said the case could cost the league up to $50,000 if it was lost. But if the owners settled, John C. continued, "there was a strong possibility" that a number of similar cases might be brought against the league.

Bert Bell listened patiently, tapping his pencil on the table, as the owners continued the discussion, sometime heatedly. He emphasized that, win or lose, all clubs would share equally in expenses and any damages. The owners questioned John C. about the league's old player contract as compared to the current pact with their respective reserve and option clauses.

The commissioner explained that he had lifted the suspensions of all players who had been suspended at any time for breaching their contract of their option clause. He said he had discussed the issue with his counterpart, A. B. (Happy) Chandler, adding that he got the impression that major league baseball would prefer that the NFL settle the suit.

"I believe that the National Football League should defend this suit," Bert Bell finally declared. "If the Supreme Court of the United States finally decides that the National Football League should come under Interstate Commerce, we better find out as soon as possible and comply with the law if it is so ruled by the Supreme Court."

The commissioner then requested a roll call vote. The owners responded by voting unanimously not to accept the offer made by Radovich's attorney to settle the case. The issue would languish in the courts for another eight years.

The rain started falling in Los Angeles the day before the NFC championship game on Sunday, December 18 and continued throughout the contest, won by the Eagles, 14–0. Despite the horrible conditions, Philadelphia's Steve Van Buren set playoff records by rushing for 196 yards on 31 carries.

"The field had about six inches of water standing on it," Eagles defensive back Dick Humbert told author David Cohen. "There was mud all over."

Bell was contacted 3,000 miles away in Narberth, Pennsylvania, to see if he would postpone the game, but the commissioner ruled that it must be played because of radio commitments. The players had hoped for a crowd of between 60,000 and 70,000—some observers had predicted 80,000— but the weather kept the attendance to an extremely disappointing 22,245.

Instead of getting a big paycheck, the winning Eagles received only about $1,094 apiece.

"Guys were saying, 'But I was going to buy a car with my share,'" halfback Bosh Pritchard told sportswriter Ray Didinger. "Our wives were even madder than we were."

Van Buren's roommate, center Alex Wojciechowicz, told Myron Cope, in his book *The Game That Was,* that the Eagles players expected a payoff of about $3,000. "We phoned Commissioner Bell—that is, we players phoned him—and we said, 'Postpone the game for one week. Play it next Sunday and we'll pay our own expenses to stay out here the extra week.' But Bell turned us down, as I recall, because of a commitment to radio."

Nevertheless, according to author David Cohen, Philadelphia tackle Al Wistert refused to blame the commissioner. "Bell did lobby the NFL owners to postpone the game, but only if they would guarantee the championship gate in case fewer than 27,000 people bought tickets for the rescheduled event. The owners, of course, got no money from the championship game, so, according to Wistert, they refused."

Los Angeles sportswriters lambasted Bell for his decision. "When Bertie sat back there in his Philadelphia apartment and told the Ram and Eagle owners and players that they couldn't postpone their title game, he pulled one of the biggest bloomers of his career," wrote Braven Dyer of the *Times.* "The players lost at least a grand, apiece."

"The game was the biggest event of the year for the league, yet 'Ding Dong' (Bell) was not among those present," said Ned Cronin in the *News.* "It would be comparable if Happy Chandler should decide to go fishing the week of the World Series. What Ding Dong didn't know or couldn't understand was that a 48-hour span in Los Angeles is enough to change the place from the world's biggest bath tub to a haven for sun worshipers."

"The Los Angeles Rams and Eagles were overruled by the arbitrary decision of Bert Bell," added George T. Davis in the *Herald Express.* "Bell's long distance ruling technically correct though it may have been—was a tough break for many fans. If he had been here, it is highly possible that he would have acceded to the request."

Dan Reeves, the president of the Rams, and Jim Clark of the Eagles actually had agreed to a postponement several hours before kickoff, providing that Bell assented. But a telephone call to the commissioner brought a ruling to "carry on."

Afterward, Bell explained why he insisted on playing the game. "I'm custodian of the players' pool and responsible for seeing they get the best break and the most money possible," he explained, adding that the nationwide broadcast was worth $14,000 to the players' pool and that money would have been lost if the game was postponed until Christmas Day.

Moreover, American Broadcasting Company (ABC) vice president Thomas Velotta told Bell that such a change was "impossible" because the schedule had already been filled for Christmas afternoon. Another ABC spokesman said that it would have been impossible to notify more than 200 stations carrying the game to switch out of the broadcast in the last minute.

ABC televised the game, but only on the West Coast—a policy that would soon change and bring considerable turmoil, not to mention windfall profits, for Bert Bell's restructured football league.

On December 20, the NFL and the Washington Redskins won a directed verdict in a bitter case testing the controversial reserve clause in federal district court, in Washington. But some of the testimony during the two-day trial proved embarrassing to the commissioner.

Ralph Ruthstrom, a former Redskins fullback, was seeking $4,100, which he claimed was owed to him by the Redskins after he was suspended by the club in 1947. Ruthstrom charged that the reserve clause kept him out of work because the Redskins did not issue him a written release until 1948. This kept him from joining the Buffalo Bills, of the rival AAFC, later in the 1947 season.

Bell told the court in a 54-page disposition that Ruthstrom never appealed to him for a hearing following his suspension (for "knowingly violating training rules," according to Washington owner George Preston Marshall) as the player had claimed. Bell emphasized that had a hearing in the case been held, he would have made a ruling ordering the Redskins to take him back or make him a free agent.

Ruthstrom had testified earlier that he telephoned Bell to enlist the commissioner's aid in getting back into football after his suspension. Ruthstrom claimed that he had been told by Bell that he would like to help the player but that he (Bell) had to look out for his own job and that Marshall was too powerful in the league.

Not only did Judge David A. Pine rule against Ruthstrom, he upheld a Redskins countersuit and ordered the player to repay $211.80 that the club contended was owed to them as an unpaid balance on an advance loaned to him prior to the 1947 season.

23. Buffalo, Dominoes, and Television

As the 1949 holiday season approached, Bert Bell began working feverishly on the league's upcoming schedule. Using sets of dominoes borrowed from Upton and Bert Jr., he spent most of Christmas, all of New Year's Day, and many full days afterward huddled over his dining room table—sipping coffee and grape juice, talking on the telephone, and shifting the game pieces around in an attempt to devise an equitable 12-game schedule for 14 teams.

Bell was well aware of the strong feelings held by most of the owners, especially the wealthy old-timers, about their scheduling preferences. He knew that they wanted to pad their records by playing the weaker teams early in the season to help ensure big home crowds later on. But he was determined to do the opposite and match the good teams against each other and do likewise with the weaker teams in order to keep the league standings as tight as possible. Nothing gave him greater satisfaction.

"I remember my father sitting home on Sunday afternoons," his son Upton explained. "'Guess what, mother,' he'd say. 'It's Week 4 and all the teams are still in the race.'"

Placing the dominoes face down, Bell taped a name of each National-American Football League team on the back. He shifted the pieces about on a huge cardboard outlined with two-inch squares. The left side of the master chart contained playing dates. Individual club names were printed at the top with subdivisions for home and away games. If Philadelphia was playing in Detroit, for example, the Eagles' domino was shifted to the away space under the Lions. A paper match was then inserted on the same date in the Eagles' column indicating an away game. At the end, if all the dominoes matched up evenly, Bell hand-printed a copy of the schedule on a smaller cardboard and filed it for future reference with other proposed drafts.

The 14th club on Bell's schedule board symbolized the proposed new Buffalo franchise. By the first week of January, he had lost count on the number of drafts; it was somewhere between 42 and 58. Conservatively he estimated that he had put in between 200 and 250 hours working on the frustrating exercise that had to be completed in time for the start of the annual league meeting on January 19.

Formulating a schedule was considerably more complicated than merely shifting dominoes. Philadelphia, Washington, Chicago, and Detroit were unable to use their stadiums until the major league baseball season ended. Games had to be arranged in a sequence that kept distance traveled to a minimum. The two West Coast teams, Los Angeles and San Francisco, had to be home at the same time because two other visiting teams had to remain in that area for a pair of games whenever they made that long trip. Moreover, the makeup of the divisions had not yet been decided. The proposed addition of Buffalo created additional problems.

"I can't get anywhere working with 14 clubs," Bell admitted to *Philadelphia Bulletin* sports editor Ed Pollock about two weeks before the NFL meetings. "Every time I try it, one club winds up with a schedule of seven or eight home games and that's out of the question." The commissioner added that he wasn't thoroughly satisfied with any one of his schedules although some proposed 13-game slates looked rather attractive.

On January 4, 1950, Bell telephoned the president of the proposed Buffalo club to inform him that he had finally worked out an "unsatisfactory" 14-team schedule that included the Bills. The news was greeted in the upstate New York city as evidence that the franchise had been accepted by the National-American Football League. This was not the case.

"Around 4:30 this morning, I called Mr. [Albert F.] O'Neill merely to tell him that I at least had something on paper," Bell explained to Frank O'Gara of the *Philadelphia Inquirer.* "I had told him 10 days ago and three days ago that unless I could work out a feasible schedule, I would not be able to recommend that the league admit Buffalo. I pointed out to him this morning that the schedule did not represent more than 10 per cent of what I thought necessary. For instance, it has Buffalo playing at home November 26 and December 10—both big risks due to the weather there.

"I also told Mr. O'Neill that I didn't think it was a schedule that Buffalo could accept from a financial standpoint, or one that the league would accept for the same reason. After all, a team with an unsatisfactory schedule can only lose its own money—and the money of the other league teams."

Bell reiterated that the other owners were impressed with Buffalo's enthusiasm and assured O'Neill that he would continue his efforts to devise a workable schedule.

When the club owners convened at the Bellevue Stratford Hotel in Philadelphia on January 19, 1950, they faced myriad issues. Besides Buffalo,

Houston and Oakland–San Francisco presented bids for franchises, raising the possibility of a 16-team league.

Houston's proposal included plans for a 110,000-seat indoor stadium and a claim that it would only cost $41 additionally for a man traveling from the west to stop off at Houston on the way back east. O'Neill announced that Buffalo had received pledges for more than 14,000 season tickets and predicted that the team would generate after-tax receipts of $522,018 for the season. The California proposal detailed an 80,000-seat stadium in Oakland, but its promoters assured the owners that the franchise could be successfully operated in either of the Bay Area cities.

Meeting behind locked doors all day and into the evening, the owners discussed a variety of motions, divisional alignments, and possible schedules covering 13 and 14 teams. After reconvening the following morning, Dan Reeves of the Los Angeles Rams asked that a vote to determine a thirteen- or fourteen-team league be delayed until Bell presented complete schedules covering both eventualities.

"It would take at least a month at 10 hours a day and many telephone calls to each club before I could present such a schedule," the commissioner responded before calling for a motion of some kind to resolve "so many long, drawn out discussions" pertaining to the three franchise applications.

After a motion was put on the floor to expand to 14 teams, Bell announced that unanimous consent would be needed, and if this motion was defeated, the applications of all three cities would be denied. The ensuing voice vote was not unanimous and, therefore, was not carried. Bell said that he would personally inform the Buffalo, Houston, and California interests that their applications had not been accepted.

Bell's close friend Art Rooney expressed disappointment in the decision. "I lobbied for a day-and-a-half for a losing cause," the Pittsburgh owner told Louis Effrat of the *New York Times*. "I thought Buffalo would be a very good football town."

The decision to continue operating with 13 teams did not make Bell's job any easier. "It may be May 1st before I am able to arrange a suitable schedule," he said.

Lost in the furor of the expansion question—and largely unreported in the press that day—was the decision by the Rules Committee, at Bell's urging, to follow the AAFC's earlier lead and allow unlimited substitution in games. This move significantly changed the character of professional football by making possible the evolution of separate offensive and defensive units.

"In the long-term," explained author Michael MacCambridge, "unlimited substitution would bring about the end of football's renaissance men, the two-way players, who would no longer play every down, but instead be used on one side of the ball or the other, depending on where a coach thought they'd be most helpful."

"Weary, confused, and disillusioned," according to Effrat, "the club owners continued on the road to nowhere until Commissioner Bert Bell, his patience and endurance exhausted, took matters into his own hands" for the rest of the meetings.

On Day 5, the owners agreed to a number of rule changes, including one vigorously endorsed by Bell that eliminated forfeiture of games by officials on the field. In the future, when teams refused to continue play because of an argument or from interference by fans, the situation would be referred directly to Bell for a resolution.

As part of his argument, the commissioner referred to a 1949 major league baseball game between the Philadelphia Phillies and New York Giants when a barrage of bottles from the stands led umpires to forfeit the game to the Giants.

"It's possible that a group of gamblers could start an affair like that in an effort to stop the game and get it forfeited," Bell explained. "The rule is only for protection for each club."

Then after hours of wrangling, the exhausted owners finally approved a divisional setup. Their agreement came after Bell said that he was fed up with the bickering. "I told them if they couldn't agree, I would make the decision for them," the commissioner explained. "I banged down the gavel and started for the doors. Someone stopped me. I cooled off for the minute and then they put the action across."

The vote was 12–1 with Bell casting the lone "no" vote, acting for Marshall, who left the meeting in a huff when he realized that he couldn't put through a motion to have any team other than Baltimore named the "swing" team.

The new setup looked like this:

DIVISION 1	DIVISION 2
Cleveland	Chicago Bears
New York Giants	Los Angeles
Philadelphia	San Francisco
Washington	Detroit
Chicago Cardinals	New York Bulldogs
Pittsburgh	Green Bay
Baltimore (swing team)	

"It was a most important decision in the new league," the Associated Press reported. "A decision that seemed impossible until Bell waved his gavel and threatened direct action. From all indications the owners would have been in conference, arguing until next week, if Bell hadn't called a halt."

One important item still remained on the owners' agenda, however— resolving the distribution of some 150 players on the reserve lists of the disbanded All-America Football Conference teams, Buffalo, Chicago Hornets, Los Angeles Dons, and remaining members of the New York Yankees.

Bell initially planned to prepare such a list himself, but he was strongly dissuaded from doing so by his brother and legal advisor, John C. When the owners reconvened, the commissioner carefully explained why he had changed his mind and answered the owners' questions "in keeping with the instructions given to him by the league's attorneys," according to the minutes of the meeting. A motion was then unanimously carried to authorize the commissioner to call a distribution meeting of the veteran pro players on June 3, in Philadelphia.

The following morning, Saturday, January 21, the owners went into another executive session to discuss the equitable distribution of all of the remaining players in the league including those college players eligible for the draft, active and reserve players belonging to 13 member clubs, and others. Some teams with valuable players on their reserve list or draft rights on 1949 college stars were unwilling to give them up by throwing all players eligible in the draft into a common pool. After arguing for four and a half hours, they again threw the problem in Bell's lap.

The commissioner said that he had no idea when he would have a plan to present. "How can I do in two hours what these fellows couldn't do in 72?" he asked. "It will take a lot of study. I don't want to rush through a decision that may later prove regrettable."

As Bell later explained to W. C. Heinz of *The Saturday Evening Post*, the 70 hours that he had just endured as the owners sat arguing, seconding, and then vetoing motions had taken its toll.

"I've listened to all I can listen to," Bell said finally at 1:30 in the afternoon that Saturday. "I'll have to take over. We'll adjourn until four o'clock."

On his way out of the room, the commissioner was confronted by a couple of owners. Arthur McBride of Cleveland announced that he was getting out of football. "Don't say you're getting out," Bell replied. "When I come down at four o'clock, if you're not satisfied it's honest, then get out."

Bell shut off the phone in his hotel room and went to work on drafting an equitable distribution plan. At 4:45 P.M. he rejoined the owners.

"You could hear a pin drop," Bell said. "I was so nervous I couldn't see straight. I read my distribution list and George Marshall, of Washington, made a motion it be accepted. Somebody seconded it, they voted and adjourned. Some of them, like Halas, got the worst of it, but they never kicked."

Bell's distribution plan included the following elements:

- Each team shall cut to 32 active players, including any player on its injured list from the 1949 season.
- Any player who has played professional football with a member club and was on its active list during the regular season and is now on its reserve list shall remain reserve-list property of that club.
- Each club shall retain on its reserve list three of the players currently claimed. Where there is a conflict between two clubs, the two conflicting teams shall arbitrate. If no decision is agreed upon by April 1, 1950, they shall toss a coin for choice of players involved.
- All other players on the existing reserve list and all college players selected, and those not drafted in prior All-America Conference or National Football League meetings, will go into a common pool. They will be selected under the constitution and by-laws, irrespective of contracts signed or not signed.

The commissioner then declared that the draft would start at 9:00 P.M. with each club drafting 30 players from a list of 390 men.

On March 3, Bell announced that he had finally completed the 1950 schedule. Its highlight would be the opening game in Philadelphia pitting the defending champions of both leagues—the Cleveland Browns, of the old AAFC, against the Eagles, of the NFL. Asked later by a United Press reporter his reasoning for scheduling this game, Bell replied: "A one-word reason—money!"

The commissioner also announced that professional football, on the advice of counsel and unanimous consent of the 13 owners, would continue to operate as the National Football League and not the National-American Football League, as indicated when the merger was announced.

The two divisions would become *conferences*, to be known as the National and American. The six teams in the American Conference and six in the National Conference would play 12 games. Each team would play home-and-home games with the other five clubs in its conference, one with a "traditional" rival, and one against Baltimore. The Colts were designated as the swing team, playing each of the other 12 clubs once during the season. The two conference winners would meet in the championship game at the end of the regular season.

Meeting at the Bellevue Stratford Hotel in Philadelphia for two days in June, the owners voted to hold a professional All-Star game beginning in January 1951 in the 100,000-seat Los Angeles Coliseum. The game, to be sponsored by the Los Angeles Publishers Association, would pit the best players in the American Conference against their counterparts in the National Conference.

Bell announced that each player participating in the game would receive not less than $500 plus traveling expenses. The league office would work out a satisfactory plan of selecting the players and the coach of each division champion would direct the teams.

Speaking to reporters between sessions, Bell dispelled rumors that the Green Bay Packers were in such dire financial straits that they might not start or finish the 1950 season. He said that Packers officials were confident of selling between 18,000 and 20,000 season tickets. Moreover, a recent nonprofit stock-selling drive in the Green Bay area produced $89,000 in cash.

Before adjourning, the club owners appointed committees from the east and west to study all television and radio operations and present proposals for adoption by the league the following October. Until then, Bell said that no games would be televised unless approved by the home team, visiting club, and Commissioner's Office. It was generally understood that the league would continue its informal policy prohibiting games to be televised in cities where NFL contests were being played.

Two weeks later, Bell announced that he had reached an agreement with ABC to televise 15 regular-season games—one contest each Sunday—as well as the championship playoff during the 1950 season. Bell said that the live broadcasts, which would be sponsored by Sun Oil Company, would only reach points at least 75 miles from the city in which the game was being played. The only exception would be the highly anticipated Cleveland-Philadelphia game that would be blacked out 150 miles from Philadelphia, as agreed by the club owners.

Although no official figures were ever released at the time (and, apparently, no records were kept by the league), a San Francisco official told the NFL Commissioner's Office years later that the 49ers received $8,000 for TV rights in 1950. It can be assumed that the other clubs received the same amount.

On July 18, the commissioner reinstated Frank Filchock, who had been suspended indefinitely along with his New York Giants teammate Merle Hapes for failing to report a bribe offer in 1946.

Filchock, who like Hapes was playing in Canada, failed to generate any interest in the NFL until the Baltimore Colts signed him late in the season. He got into one game and completed one of three passes for a grand total of one yard.

Hapes would be reinstated in 1954, but he never played again in the NFL.

24. Finally a Home of Their Own

The summer of 1950 turned out to be quite hectic for the Bert Bell family. For the first time in more than a dozen years they were going to own their own home again.

It wasn't necessarily by choice.

After his death in 1935, John C. Bell left his magnificent, 100-acre estate in Radnor to his two sons, John C. Jr. and Bert. "I remember it very slightly as a kid, Upton said. "It was really something. It had horses, homes, everything."

Unfortunately, just before World War II, Bert needed the money to keep the Eagles alive and persuaded his brother to sell the property. "I'm sure they sold it for under value, maybe $100,000, which was still a fortune in those days," Upton explained. "But it was a huge mistake, because the estate would be worth millions today.

"I can't tell you how many times we moved after that. For a couple of years, we even lived in the Ritz Carlton Hotel that my grandfather owned in Philadelphia. That's where I learned how to operate the escalators and run the elevators. I thought life couldn't be any better, moving to all these places. Little did I know that we were moving because he needed money to keep the Eagles afloat. It wasn't until much later that I found out that all these big mansions we lived in were all rented until we bought a house in Narberth. That's because he didn't have the cash to buy a house and he could rent a mansion for a helluva lot less."

Bert Bell's father had cut off all Bert's inheritance back in the 1930s before he married Frances Upton. From time to time, whenever she had some extra cash saved, she would give some to him. So did his grandfather, occasionally, but Bert was really on his own financially.

"My father never had a lot of money, which surprised a lot of people," Upton recalled. "We will never know how much money he went through in his lifetime. Or how much was owed to him. He really gave it away. He took care of his family. He took care of his friends. He took

care of every bum that wanted to borrow money. He was the most generous man I've ever met. To a fault. Money was not a driving force with
him. He didn't think money should be an important thing in life. That
was just his nature.

"My father was so anxious to move on as commissioner, he didn't get
the amount that he should have received for his 50% ownership in the
Steelers. He felt that he took a real financial beating on it."

"My father had great character," explained Bert Jr. "He was noble. He
wouldn't think of any kind of theft or doing anything underhanded. He
even turned down a basketball scholarship at La Salle College for Upton
because he said, 'We can afford it.' He didn't want another kid to fail to
make the team because he couldn't get the scholarship that Upton got."
Upton played at La Salle without an athletic grant.

After selling the estate in Radnor, Bert moved his family to the Ritz
Carlton Hotel in Center City for a while, then to a residence on Bryn
Mawr Avenue, a block off of City Line Avenue on the Philadelphia side. At
the beginning of World War II, the family began renting a property owned
by Presbyterian Hospital at 1073 Montgomery Avenue in Narberth.

"My dad was an air raid warden there during the war," Upton recalls.
"He loved going out and marching everybody around. It was a time of
rationing and victory gardens and all that stuff. The air raid sirens would
be blaring and here the chief executive of the Pittsburgh Steelers would be
strapping on a warden's helmet, going into the street like everybody else,
taking names and numbers. It was quite exciting."

In March 1950, Presbyterian Hospital officials decided to sell Bell's
home and initiated eviction proceedings. The family then purchased a large
Victorian corner house at 323 Haverford Avenue, in Narberth. That's
where Bert lived for the remaining years of his commissionership.

Dinners at the Bell household were never dull.

"There were always a lot of their friends dropping in because at that
time in their life my mother and father weren't going out that much." Upton recalled. "It was quite a scene. The patriarch of the family would be
sitting there with a forkful of steak in one hand, the phone in the other.
Whoever he was talking to, whether it was Marshall or Halas or some celebrity, it was just like a natural part of his day: 'What was the gate? Speak
up, will you George?'

"We didn't interrupt him and everybody else just continued on with
their conversation. It was just constant noise. My dad never finished a
meal. And my mother down at the other end of the table would be remind-
ing us of our manners—'Don't do that or I'll slap your hand . . . Use your
fork, Upton,' that kind of stuff. Other people would just drop in and be

invited to sit down. It was a very eclectic crowd—a lot of conversation about a lot of different things."

People didn't just drop by the Bell household for dinner. Sometimes they stayed for weeks or months at a time, even longer. "It seems that the more we moved from one house to the other, the more people we collected," Upton explained. "People would drop in and drop out."

At one point, about 30 football players from the Eagles or Steagles were living at the Bell residence on Montgomery Avenue as part of their pay package. Some of them, like John (Bull) Lipski, the big center from Temple, occasionally earned an extra $5 for babysitting the two Bell boys.

"What I remember most is a lot of large bodies sleeping on every available sofa and rug," Upton explained. "You had to step around them or climb over them to get to the bathroom. I also remember my dad practicing with them out on the lawn. I understood later that my parents' genteel neighbors weren't pleased. On the Main Line, you could keep as many horses as you wanted, but quartering professional football players just wasn't done."

Hugh L. (Shorty) Ray, whom Bell inherited as the league's technical advisor and supervisor of officials, lived with the Bells for a while. So did Harry Standish and his family. Harry was married to Frances Upton's sister, Hazel.

"They showed up one day from the Bronx with their daughter, Frances, and two dogs and they got a wing of the house," Upton recalled. Standish was one of Bell's first hires in the NFL office, working as the league's director of personnel. "Uncle Harry was a fun guy. He drove everybody everywhere."

The most intriguing household guest was a character named Mack MacGinnis, who appeared at the front door one day in a Navy uniform.

"My father said, 'Mack will be around here for a while,' Upton explained. "I thought he meant he would be here for dinner or something. I can't be sure because I was young, but it seemed to me that Mack ended up staying with us for three or four years. No background, no nothing. He'd tell a lot of jokes and do a lot of pantomimes. He was great for us, the kids. He would do odd jobs. He claimed that he was deaf, but I'm never really sure if he was. He once said it happened because of all the guns on the boat. He might not have even gone to war. It could have been a rented suit, who knows? He was a mystery man and all of a sudden he disappeared. And I said to my father, 'Where's Mack?' He just said, 'He's gone'!"

Each spring around Easter-time, Frances vacationed in Florida for a couple of months with the Standishes. The Bell children joined her after the school year ended. Meanwhile, Bert and the boys lived at his apartment in the Racquet Club in downtown Philadelphia.

"We would get up early in the morning, go across the street to this ham-and-eggs place that my father loved instead of eating in the Racquet Club," Upton explained. "Then a cab would take us out the Main Line to school at Waldron Academy. Afterward, we'd come home and have dinner. Whatever homework we couldn't finish, Shorty Ray finished for us. Then it was off to a baseball or basketball game, sitting on the bench beforehand at Shibe Park with Connie Mack, of the A's, or with Eddie Gottlieb, of the Warriors, at the Arena or Convention Hall.

"I mean, what a life."

25. The Dream Game Turns into a Shocker

By Labor Day 1950, anticipation for the upcoming Dream Game between the Cleveland Browns and the Philadelphia Eagles had reached sizzling proportions. Coach Greasy Neale's Eagles were coming off back-to-back NFL championships. The Browns had won all four AAFC titles but were still smarting from the remark made by Washington Redskins owner George Preston Marshall, who insulted their former league by saying, "The worst team in our league could beat the best team in theirs."

Realizing the incredible demand for tickets, Bert Bell moved the contest from the smaller Shibe Park to the 100,000-capacity Municipal Stadium and changed the kickoff from Sunday afternoon to Saturday night, September 16. It was a smart move. The Eagles drew 71,237 fans, the largest crowd in their history, for the contest.

The commissioner made another decision before the game, a decision that went unnoticed in some circles but one that set the stage for many significant developments in the future. He granted permission to the little-known DuMont television network to carry the game as far as the coaxial cable reached. Thus, thousands of fans as far west as Omaha, Nebraska, got their first taste of professional football. DuMont had been established in 1949 as the nation's "fourth network," with most of its popularity riding on the success of young, upcoming comedians Jackie Gleason and Art Carney.

Before the charged-up Browns took the field that night, Paul Brown called a meeting in Cleveland's locker room. Facing the squad with his steely, piercing eyes, according to the *Cleveland Plain Dealer,* the coach quietly said, "Today you boys will have a chance to touch the great Steve Van Buren."

They never got the chance. Van Buren and Philadelphia's other top running back, Bosh Pritchard, were sidelined with injuries. But with Bell and the Eagles' fans sitting in shocked disbelief, the Browns thoroughly dismantled the defending NFL champs, 35–10. After the game, the visibly subdued commissioner congratulated Brown and called Cleveland the most intense and best-prepared team he had ever seen.

"We had whetted our appetites to play that game for about three years," Brown told the *Plain Dealer.*

"When we played the Eagles in that first game," Browns quarterback Otto Graham later explained to Lonnie Wheeler of *Ohio Magazine,* "I would say that there was never another team in the history of sports, anywhere in the world, that was as prepared, physically and emotionally, to play a ball game. We would have played the Eagles for a keg of beer or a milkshake."

After the Browns edged the Los Angeles Rams, 30–28, for the NFL championship on December 24, Bell was once again his ecstatic self.

"It's the greatest football game I've ever seen," he said. "In Los Angeles, we probably have the finest personnel any club ever boasted. But in the Cleveland Browns, we probably have the most intensively coached club in history. The Browns overlook no detail in coaching or preparation for a game. They are ready for anything and they have that extra something of which champions are made."

There was another reason for Bell's elation. The hatchet finally appeared buried with his longtime adversary, Paul Brown.

"I just don't feel like trying to lord it over the National League," Brown told Edward Prell of the *Chicago Tribune* after the game. "Bert Bell is a smart and fine guy. He's a wonderful commissioner. He knows all the heartaches that go with this sport. He calls the shots as he sees them. Before the game when he talked to me about the officials, I said I would leave it up to him. I've learned to have confidence in Bert. During all our years of difficulties with the National League, he always was a gentleman."

The night before the game, relaxing in a cotton sweatshirt in his hotel suite, Bell had explained to sportswriters his feelings about Brown and his team.

"I don't know of a finer organization in football than the Browns," Bert said. "The players bring their lunch to practice and that's a fact. Their owner, Mickey McBride, is unlike most millionaires who go into sports. Mickey stays in the background and lets his team take the bows. I wish we had more like him in the league."

The commissioner also announced that radio and television receipts from the game totaled more than $45,000, which was about $15,000 more than the NFL ever realized from a championship contest. League-wide, professional football showed a profit for the first time in five years and average attendance jumped 10.4 percent higher than in 1949.

Steve Snyder of the United Press credited Bell with orchestrating the league's exciting climax to the 1950 season. "Bert eventually drew up a schedule that virtually was a masterpiece," Snyder wrote. "Like a handicapper for a horse race, Bell matched the teams so there'd be a showdown for a division lead almost every week. 'I hope we have ties in both divisions,' he said at the time. 'We can play all winter if we have to.' So there were ties in both divisions, forcing playoffs from which the Cleveland Browns emerged victorious on Christmas Eve."

Lost in the shuffle of the exciting divisional races was Baltimore's dismal performance as the league's swing team. The Colts lost 11 of 12 games (beating only Green Bay, 41–21). They drew 29,000 people for their home opener against the Redskins but averaged only 13,500 fans for the rest of the season.

Radio and television star Arthur Godfrey had considered purchasing the team but came to the conclusion that it would be a "Grade Z investment."

Godfrey was absolutely correct—at the time.

26. Problems with the Federal Government

On January 18, 1951, Baltimore's flamboyant owner, Abraham (Shorty) Watner, turned the franchise back to the league at the annual owners' meeting in Chicago. Watner had made millions operating a trucking firm, a railroad, and a cemetery but was financially in way over his head from the beginning—especially after agreeing to pay George Preston Marshall $150,000 for "invading" Washington's territory.

The end came when Marshall urged other club owners to decline Watner's request for financial assistance. The Associated Press reported that the Colts had dropped $760,000 in four years of operation in both professional leagues. Watner said that he had personally lost $106,000 in 1950 alone.

It wasn't the first time Watner had lost cash in spectacular style. Years earlier he made national headlines when he almost fell out of the eighth floor of an office building. It seems that a breeze had blown $10,000 in greenbacks off his desk and out of an open window into the clutching hands of astonished onlookers in the street below. Only about $200 was ever returned.

"I asked that every other team in the league give me one player," explained Watner, who was philosophical about his withdrawal. "I didn't ask for stars like Otto Graham or Bob Waterfield, just for one veteran player on each team which could make the club."

Bert Bell said that the other club owners turned Watner down because not knowing their own status due to the Korean War, they were unable to give him any players. Although the NFL owners declined Watner's request to "freeze" the franchise for a year, the commissioner announced that they had agreed to let him reestablish the Baltimore franchise if he desired at any time during the next three years.

The following day, the owners adopted a resolution to immediately establish a reserve fund in the amount of $10,000 annually in order to pay Commissioner Bell a pension of $10,000 per year in the event of (a) the completion of his present contract with the NFL, (b) his physical incapacity to continue to perform his duties as commissioner, or (c) his death, at which time his wife or estate would receive $10,000 annually until the reserve was exhausted.

Later, the club owners handed Bell a $10,000 yearly increase, making his annual salary $40,000 for the remainder of his eight-year term. In doubling Bell's salary from the time he was first appointed in 1946, the moguls also sent a sharp message of support in marked contrast to their counterparts in major league baseball, who had just recently refused to renew the $65,000 annual contract of Commissioner A. B. (Happy) Chandler.

By mid-January, Bell's name was being mentioned as a possible successor to Chandler. "I have heard from several sources close to those who are big in baseball that the diamond moguls really were toying with the idea of kidnapping football's czar for their very own," wrote *Philadelphia Daily News* sports editor Lance McCurley.

"I'd like to see them [the big league club owners] elect Bert Bell," said L. Wister Randolph, a Phillies vice president, to *Philadelphia Bulletin* sports editor Ed Pollock. "Bell has done a magnificent job in football, and in the broader baseball field he would do even better. If they're looking for someone nobody can run, he's their man."

Meanwhile, reeling from stormy discussions that lasted for seven days— the longest NFL meeting on record—Bell left the Windy City for his home in Narberth, sporting stubble of white whiskers. After failing to resolve a 36-hour deadlock over divisional reallocation, he was charged with reshuffling the league's two divisions and devising an appropriate schedule.

The stalemated meetings had dragged on for two extra days with many owners again displaying their "me first attitude," according to *Baltimore Sun* sports editor Paul Menton. Philadelphia Eagles secretary Paul C. Lewis finally made the motion to let the commissioner handle everything.

"It was okay with me," Bell explained. "What do you want us to do?— sit all year? They were all for themselves, not one for another. A checkmate was inevitable under these circumstances."

Before adjourning, the commissioner did settle one thorny issue temporarily with a surprising ruling. Despite the fact that the Los Angeles Rams suffered a 46 percent loss in attendance when they televised all of their home games in 1950, Bell convinced the owners to accept a motion allowing the televising of games in a team's home territory if the visiting and home clubs both agreed.

In addition, Bell announced, the visiting club may televise the game anywhere as long as it does not enter the territory of another team playing a game at that time or the territory of another team playing a road game which is being televised or broadcast to a home audience.

"In my opinion, there will be 75 per cent more televising of NFL games under the rule next year," Bell said, adding that he would confer with the Department of Justice on the new clause. "It would look on it with favor," he predicted. The motion, which carried by an 11–1 vote, eliminated the commissioner from the parties required to approve television. Television had been permitted in 1950 only if both clubs were involved *and* the commissioner approved.

Not surprisingly, the Rams refused to go along with the commissioner's recommendation for the 1951 season. The defending Western Conference champs became the second NFL team to black out all of their home games. The Philadelphia Eagles had done the same in 1949 after 40 percent of their season ticket holders said in a survey that they were going to stay home and watch the games on television.

An exasperated Bert Bell invited the owners back to Philadelphia on February 7 to review what he called "400 hours of moving dominoes." Before going into the meeting room, the commissioner made it clear that he had no intention of forcing his ideas on the owners, although he considered three of his proposed schedules to be workable and fair.

"I've figured out 30 schedules by moving the dominoes," he explained to reporters. "But 17 of them I wouldn't show to anybody, and I don't think one of them is fair and just to everybody. If they don't like any that I've worked out, I'll turn the dominoes over to them and say, 'Go to work!' "

As expected, the owners failed to agree on any of the proposed schedules. With approval by 11 owners needed, Bell's "four-year" proposal was endorsed by seven clubs, accepted with reservations by three others. Two owners voted "no."

The commissioner, as empowered, then took matters into his own hands. Bell's plan called for the two conferences to remain the same as previously outlined with every team in the American Conference traveling to the West Coast an equal number of times. Each team would play every other club at least once during the four years.

"Since the owners cannot agree on conference structure and a schedule, I am, at their direction, placing in effect a 'fair and equitable' setup," the commissioner announced. "The basis for the schedule is now set and all I have to do is make up the actual schedule with dates."

It was a blistering, humid July afternoon, a perfect day for Bell to get an early start to his seashore home in Margate. The commissioner was literally halfway out the door when the phone rang. Hugh Brown of the *Philadelphia Bulletin* was on the line.

"I have some good news for you, Bert," the veteran sportswriter said. Bell's eyes widened as he listened attentively. Brown was one of his most trusted sources for breaking news in the world of pro football. Hughie also enjoyed an unparalleled exalted status among NFL beat reporters. Each Sunday, after the other sportswriters gathered en masse to grill the head coach of the Philadelphia Eagles, Brown would sit down privately with the coach in his office, dissecting that afternoon's game. No other pro football writer in the league enjoyed such exclusive personal access with a coach.

Brown had some historic news for the commissioner. A circuit court judge in West Virginia's Kanawha County had issued a restraining order prohibiting the Los Angeles Rams' veteran tackle Dick Huffman from jumping to the Winnipeg Blue Bombers of the Canadian Football League. Huffman had played both offense and defense for four seasons in Los Angeles before signing to play in Canada. This decision preserved the legality of the NFL's option clause.

Like the NFL, the two Canadian professional leagues had experienced growing economic prosperity since the end of World War II. Composed of the Big Four (Toronto, Montreal, Hamilton, and Ottawa) and the Western Inter-Provincial (Winnipeg, Saskatchewan, Calgary, and Edmonton) loops, each Canadian club was limited to eight American players. Therefore, their owners could pay the Americans considerably more money than they paid the home-grown talent.

The option clause, also known as the reserve clause, was included in every NFL player's contract. When a player signed a pact for a specific year, he agreed to a fixed salary and approved a clause that gave his club the rights to his services for the following year at the same salary providing he was notified in writing before a certain determined date. Bell told reporters that Huffman's contract specified that the Rams had until the previous May to exercise their option for his services for 1951. That option was exercised, he said.

Bell was not surprised by the ruling but expressed some amazement when he learned that Judge Julian F. Bouchelle had threatened jail time for Huffman if the talented lineman ever returned to his hometown of Charleston, West Virginia, after violating the order.

The commissioner chuckled as Brown explained that Judge Bouchelle had based his opinion on an English court case from 1852. Then, a gifted young female soprano was ordered to desist once and for all from singing for anyone other than the master to whom she had given her written word.

Bell said that he was "highly gratified" by the decision. "The thing that pleased me was the fact that every clause in our standard player contract held up in court," he added.

Huffman had the last laugh, however. Winnipeg eventually won his rights when Chief Justice E. K. Williams of the Canadian Court of Kings ruled on September 11 that Huffman was the property of the Blue Bombers and not the Rams. The future Canadian Football League Hall-of-Famer went on to play for seven seasons for Winnipeg and the Calgary Stampeders.

On October 9, 1951, the first salvo was fired in what would become a decades-long tug-of-war when the federal government filed an antitrust suit against the NFL in an attempt to break up restrictions on the televising and broadcasting of its games.

A government spokesman said that the action was a forerunner of a campaign to end selective control of transmission of all sports events—professional and amateur—to outside audiences. The suit accused the 12 members of the NFL of violating the Sherman Anti-Trust Law by boycotting certain stations and blacking out telecasts and broadcasts of their games in certain areas.

"We feel that the American people are entitled to have free of monopoly the right to see or hear what they want," said Assistant Attorney General H. Graham Morison, speaking at the U.S. district court in Philadelphia. Calling the suit a test case, Morison added that the action resulted from protests by the public. This led to a Department of Justice inquiry brought to clarify the position of telecasting and broadcasting in their relation to the sports world.

Attorney General J. Howard McGrath indicated that the suit was aimed primarily at the NFL's "territorial rights" provision under which telecasts of league games were not carried in cities in which a league team was playing a home game.

Commissioner Bell, who was not named in the complaint, told the *New York Times* that the league "has no discriminatory policy whatsoever and certainly no trust. All we do is protect our home territories on the day of the game. I feel that our policies are more liberal than any other radio and television policy in sports."

Morison, who said that Bell has absolute control over the broadcasts and telecasts of league games, quoted what he said was a league by-law (Article X), which read:

No club shall cause or permit a game in which it is engaged to be telecast or broadcast into any area included within the home territory of any other club without the consent of such other club on the day that such other club is:

a. Engaged *in playing a game at home.*
b. *Engaged in playing a game away from home and causing or permitting telecast or broadcast of that game within its home territory.*
c. *No club shall telecast in territory in which said game is played without the consent of the home club, the visiting club and the commissioner, National Football League.*

Pledging that the league would fight the suit "with all our resources," Bell later told the *Philadelphia Inquirer* that the NFL had cooperated fully with the government investigation. "We have nothing to hide," he added. "We conferred with the Anti-Trust Division of the Department of Justice last November before drawing up our plans and we have their recommendations in writing."

During the federal probe, an agent from the FBI appeared at NFL headquarters, announcing that he was there to look over some records.

"My father had no secrets and said, 'Come in and do whatever you want,'" Bert Jr. recalled.

The commissioner was quite impressed with the agent asking the questions, who happened to be a neighbor whom he had never formally met.

The following year, in 1952, Bell would hire that agent, Austin Gunsel, to be the league's watchdog. The two men had much in common and became lifelong friends. Gunsel was a freshman in the University of Pennsylvania's Wharton School in Bell's last season as the Quakers' backfield coach. He joined the FBI in 1939 and served in the bureau's offices in Chicago, Detroit, and New York before becoming J. Edgar Hoover's administrative assistant for three years.

Gunsel actually declined Bell's first job offer that came shortly after he completed his investigation. "I can't go to work for you, Bert," he explained. "I might have to testify against the league."

"That's right," Bell replied. "I wouldn't want you to compromise yourself or do anything wrong."

Among his other duties when he joined the league, Gunsel coordinated a team of former FBI agents—at least one in each NFL city, as Bell told W. C. Heintz of *The Saturday Evening Post*—not only to watch the gamblers but also to check on the sale of any team stocks, new owners, new officials, or new broadcasters.

"The agents do not tail players, or otherwise show any distrust in them on our part," Bell later explained to Chester L. Smith of the *Pittsburgh Press*. "They do keep tab on local plungers and shady joints and if illogical betting moves develop, they investigate and report and a country-wide check can then be set up very rapidly. I want to know all I can about unsavory characters in order to protect players and game officials from the risk of making associations and frequenting places which might lead to embarrassing consequences, or worse."

The television issue was gradually consuming more and more of the commissioner's time.

Chicago Bears owner George Halas had convinced his counterpart from the Cardinals, Walter Wolfner, to join him in setting up their own TV network for the 1951 season. Eight home games of the Bears and Cardinals were televised to nine cities in Illinois, Indiana, Kentucky, Minnesota, Nebraska, Ohio, and Tennessee.

The venture lost $1,750, according to author Jeff Davis, but Bell was becoming more intrigued about the vast financial potential of television—especially since AT&T's $40 million coaxial cable relay system was now completed from coast to coast and national exposure was suddenly a reality.

Although he was still unable to convince NBC and CBS about the growing popularity of the professional game, Bell continued to do business with the DuMont Network. In addition to paying the NFL $75,000 for televising the 1951 NFL championship game *coast-to-coast for the first time*—the Los Angeles Rams upset the Cleveland Browns, 24–17—DuMont carried five regular-season games that year, paying the NFL an unheard-of sum of $1.1 million for the exclusive rights for the entire package.

Bell negotiated the lucrative contract with DuMont's managing director, Ted Bergmann. The two men immediately hit it off when they first got together early that summer at the Racquet Club in Philadelphia.

"I remember Bert as being very genial, affable, and completely candid about his problems with the league," Bergmann recalled. "He had a big blackboard in his cubbyhole—it was probably six feet long and four feet high—and it had the schedule of every team listed. He kept changing his entries on the blackboard to accommodate the owners of the various clubs. The fellow in Chicago, George Halas, was a real problem to him. Bert was very open with us about his problems, mostly in scheduling the home games versus the away games."

Bergmann lined up Westinghouse Electric Corporation as the national sponsor that year, although many of the individual teams had their own local sponsors.

"Bert was very accommodating, juggling the schedule around so that we could get maximum exposure for the national sponsor," the DuMont executive said. "We picked up several games to feed to different parts of the network simultaneously. That had never been done before."

[By 1954, DuMont was carrying 11 regular-season NFL games in addition to the league championship. Working at the network for a time was a young program assistant, Roone Pinckney Arledge, who would later become one of the most powerful men in television as president of ABC Sports.]

Later in 1951, Bell resolved another issue concerning the gradually escalating disturbance with the Canadian Football League. This time, the commissioner announced that he was returning quarterback George Ratterman to the good graces of the NFL. Ratterman had quit the New York Yanks earlier in the summer to play with the Montreal Alouettes but had little success north of the border.

Bell fined Ratterman $2,000 "for action detrimental to professional football" before reinstating the veteran quarterback prior the Yanks' game with San Francisco on November 11. The commissioner said that the former Notre Dame star had the right to terminate his contract with Montreal at the end of the 1951 season.

"There was no option clause," Bell explained. "Ratterman has no legal ties binding him to Canadian football or we would have refused to take him back. As far as we were concerned, Ratterman had a binding contract with the Yanks and I told him so before he jumped to Canada."

A few days later, Bell made the most radical suggestion ever proposed during his time as commissioner.

"Let's eliminate the point after touchdown and score each TD as seven points," he suggested.

Claiming that the extra point was "almost automatic" and a "waste of time," Bell said that this scoring change would reduce gambling by 60 percent. By eliminating it, "we will do away with the one-point spread in which gamblers are so much interested."

Opposition mounted quickly to Bell's proposed rules change. The most vociferous resistance came from the Cleveland Browns, who had one of pro football's best place kickers in Lou (The Toe) Groza. "We feel that the extra point isn't automatic at all and shouldn't be cut out of football," Cleveland's publicity manager Russ Gestner said. "And we don't feel that way just because we have Groza."

Bell's proposal wouldn't come up for discussion until the NFL's winter meetings, but most league observers were predicting that the commissioner was about to suffer one of his rare setbacks.

27. "Listen, Sonny, Just Sign the Contract!"

As Bert Bell prepared for the NFL's 1952 winter meetings, reports started circulating throughout the league about the state of his health.

Milwaukee Journal sports editor R. G. Lynch wrote in a column on January 8 that veteran coach E. L. (Curly) Lambeau was being groomed to succeed Bell as commissioner, a report that Bell immediately denied.

Bell told the Associated Press, "It's news to me," after hearing about Lynch's article that said Lambeau "is reported headed for the office as assistant to Commissioner Bert Bell to be groomed as an eventual successor. Bell has been a good commissioner and the post is his as long as he can fill it, but Bert's health is poor and last season he was not able to get around the league as he should. He needs an assistant to take some of the work off his hands."

Lambeau had retired after coaching in the NFL for 33 years, 31 with the Green Bay Packers and two with the Chicago Cardinals. Lynch said that the two "strong men" of the league, George Halas of the Chicago Bears and George Preston Marshall of the Washington Redskins, were said to be backing him.

When the league's Rules Committee convened at the Hotel Statler in New York City on January 16, it wasted no time rejecting Bell's proposal to eliminate the point after touchdown. With a 10–2 margin necessary for passage, Bell was able to muster only seven votes. Los Angeles, Detroit, Cleveland, Pittsburgh, and the New York Giants voted against.

The most stunning development came on January 20, the final day of the meeting, when Bell announced that Ted Collins of the New York Yanks was throwing in the towel, enabling the league to put a franchise in Dallas, thus expanding for the first time to the Deep South.

The commissioner initially declined to name the new owner—"Let's call him Mr. X," he said—but others soon identified the head of the Texas syndicate as Giles Miller, a wealthy textile entrepreneur.

"I have been informed that this Texas group is willing to assume any and all obligations the Yanks may have, pay off everyone and then set up business in Dallas," Bell said.

Collins lost an estimated $1.5 million in five years in Boston and three years in New York, including $90,000 in 1951 when his Yanks attracted only 31,879 fans for four home games at Yankee Stadium.

As one of the conditions imposed by the Mara family allowing him to move his franchise from New England, Collins was not permitted to schedule his home games until after the Giants had selected their dates at the Polo Grounds. Moreover, he was forced to play two home games on the road because of the World Series. After initially balking at the deal, he reluctantly agreed to sell the franchise back to the league for $100,000.

As Upton Bell recalls, his dad was not surprised to see Collins bailing out of the NFL.

"Kate Smith was America's songbird and everyone loved her," he explained. "But she made a huge mistake to let Collins run that franchise. It was always in a state of flux and he was taking money out of her entertainment revenue to pay the players. I remember my dad's upbeat expression would sag so he looked like a bulldog in mourning whenever he talked to Kate on the telephone while he sat with us at the dining room table:

How we doing up there in Boston, Kate. Your singing tour's going fine? That's great. Tell me, Kate, did you make the payroll this week? No? We gotta get the goddamned payroll paid, Kate! I don't care where you're singing. Tell Ted that you've got to make the payroll! If this gets in the papers, we're all in trouble.

"Then he would turn to us, shaking his head, and say, 'Christ, I gotta get on a train to Boston again.'

"'Oh, Bert,' my mother would say. 'I just love Boston. I opened all my shows in Boston.' Then my father would reply, 'Christ, Frances, you opened all your shows there. I gotta go up and close this show!' "

Bell later confirmed that the Dallas syndicate paid the NFL $300,000 for the Yanks' franchise, of which $200,000 would go in expenditures spread over eight years to Dan Topping to settle the remaining lease payments for Yankee Stadium negotiated by Collins.

"We are not seeking a profit," Bell explained. "We are interested only in the right group and the right site for our franchise and Dallas appears to qualify on both scores."

For a while earlier in the meetings, according to Louis Effrat of the *New York Times*, it appeared that Baltimore might be awarded a franchise again when it was revealed that Collins had received an offer of $250,000 to move there and still maintain control. The idea was discarded for a number of reasons including the territorial rights held by Marshall and the Redskins.

In other business, the owners approved Bell's proposal to number players for the first time according to their positions. Centers would wear numbers in the 50s, guards in the 60s, tackles in the 70s, ends in the 80s, halfbacks in the 20s and 40s, fullbacks in the 30s, and quarterbacks from 11 to 19. The commissioner explained that established stars like Sammy Baugh (No. 33), Bob Waterfield (7), and Otto Graham (60) and others could continue to wear their traditional numbers.

Finally, it was back to the dominoes for the commissioner when league owners again dropped the scheduling headache in his lap, this time with a decidedly southwestern flavor.

As the 1952 season unfolded, Bell found himself frequently discussing three topics with reporters that aroused his passion—officiating, the tendency of players to fake injuries, and the state of the league.

Commenting on a recent game between the Eagles and Redskins, Bell praised the officiating crew for being inconspicuous.

"They never put themselves unnecessarily out in front so that everyone could see them," he explained to *Philadelphia Bulletin* sports editor Ed Pollock. "Some officials appear to be too aggressive. As an example, some throw the flag in an antagonistic manner when they see a violation. That's irritating both to players and spectators."

At the beginning of the season, in an effort to rid the league of "militaristic, antagonistic" types, Bell hired eight new officials, all former football players and all under the age of 40. One of them, Stan Jaworowski, a football coach at Malvern Prep in the Philadelphia suburbs, had never officiated at a college game. Three of the newcomers—Davey O'Brien, Don Looney, and Joe Carter—hailed from Texas and had played for the Eagles. Jaworowski later became known as Stan "Javie."

Bell was particularly incensed when fans at a game between the Eagles and Steelers cheered when an official was injured after colliding with Philadelphia defensive halfback Joe Restic.

"Why should these fine, upstanding citizens be subject to such abuse and ridicule?" he complained to sportswriter Hugh Brown.

Adding that the league was spending $80,000 annually for officiating, Bell said, "Here they are, torn from the breasts of their family each Sunday to do their duty often hundreds of miles away from their homes. The money they get [between $900 and $1,500 a season] is not enough to pay them for the exactness of their work. These men officiate only because they love the game of football."

Disturbed over the tendency of some players who fake injuries solely to kill the clock in the final minutes of a game, the commissioner threatened to introduce a new rule at the next league meeting discouraging such practices.

"I'm tired of seeing three or four men go down and claim an injury just to stop the clock," Bell said. "A play runs, time is running out, and they begin dropping like flies all over the field without anyone near them. The referee can't ignore them. A boy might actually be hurt. But we're after the fakers just trying to beat the rules."

Under the existing rules, time is out while an injured player is helped to the sidelines and his team has an opportunity to huddle and plan a play. Under Bell's proposed new rule, after an injured player left the field the referee would start the clock and run it for 15 seconds. No play would be permitted before the 15 seconds elapsed.

"I'll watch the players this season," Bell promised. "If the coaches go along and clean out the fake injuries themselves, I won't introduce the rule. If it clears up, swell. If it continues, I'll ask in January for the rule."

At the halfway mark of the 1952 season, Bell admitted to Stan Baumgartner of the *Sporting News* that only four of the 12 teams in the league were breaking even financially. Although Bell declined to name the clubs, Baumgartner surmised the successful franchises as the New York Giants, Chicago Bears, Washington Redskins, and Cleveland Browns.

"Don't let anyone get the idea that owning a National Football League football franchise is a bowl of cherries," Bell said. "It's a rugged business. It's no longer a sport. A man doesn't get any fun out of it anymore. It's sweat and tears. If you get into this business and don't work at it, you can lose $150,000 or $200,000 a year, not just $25,000.

"We have given out 43 franchises in this league. Thirty-one have been broke, forfeited, and discontinued."

Explaining that NFL players got paid between $75 and $150 a game in the early days, Bell said that good players requested $4,000 to $5,000 a year with the stars earning considerably more, putting them almost on par with major league baseball players. "The cost of running a professional football team has gone up 400 to 500 per cent in the last ten years."

Bell criticized the management in Dallas for having "the only really unsatisfactory showing in attendance" so far. Only 17,500 fans showed up for the Texans' home opening 24–6 loss to the New York Giants. Tim Mara's visitors lost $18,000 in payroll and traveling expenses to make the trip.

"They didn't go about things in the right manner," Bell explained. "They thought it would be a club just for Dallas and Dallas would support the team. We have learned, just as they learned in baseball, that a team must draw from the surrounding area to be successful. The Philadelphia Eagles, for example, draw 60 per cent of their clientele from outside Philadelphia. The Dallas owners must get out their spurs and go to work in the surrounding towns of Fort Worth, Austin, Waco. Gosh, those Texans don't think anything of driving 500 miles to see a football game."

Bell soon found himself facing a more serious problem than Dallas. It involved that new professional football league north of the border and one of the NFL's top young players.

Harold (Bud) Grant, Philadelphia's number-one draft choice (12th overall) in 1951, was in his second year with the Eagles. An outstanding two-sport athlete at the University of Minnesota, he also played professional basketball in the NBA for two seasons with the hometown Lakers.

Since most observers considered him "the best offensive or defensive end in the Big Nine," Grant realized that his future was in pro football. He soon decided to take the Eagles' offer of $7,500. By the time he got to Philadelphia, however, the offer had been reduced to $7,000.

"I thought I had some leverage, but I didn't," Grant recalled. "I had no leverage at all. Then, when I looked at my contract, it had something in there called an 'Option.' I didn't understand it necessarily—it was my first experience with contracts, but my first child had been born and I needed a little more security."

Although signed as a wide receiver, Grant ended up playing well as a defensive end in his rookie season after the Eagles' starter went down with an injury in the opening game at the Chicago Cardinals. When his contract arrived prior to the 1952 season, Grant told the Eagles that he wanted assurances that he could return to the offensive side and declined to sign his contract when he reported to training camp.

"I ended up second in the league in receiving and being selected for the Pro Bowl," Grant recalled. "I was having a pretty good season and every week, the general manager Vince McNally would say, 'Well Harry, come down here. We want you to sign a contract.' 'I have a contract,' I would reply. 'I know, but that's just a formality. Why don't you sign a real contract?'"

Grant refused, and the next thing he knew the young player was sitting in Bert Bell's office, a couple of blocks away from the Eagles' headquarters in Center City Philadelphia.

Still reeling from the losses of Dick Huffman and later his Eagles team-mate Neill Armstrong to Canada in 1951, the commissioner was in no mood to see any athlete from the NFL play out his option, especially one from Philadelphia.

The NFL had abolished the reserve clause, similar to major league baseball, in 1948 and adopted the procedure of signing players to one-year contracts with the option of maintaining their services for another year in 1949.

"Bell talked to me like he was talking to some lawyer, or something," Grant said. "He was kind of pompous, I thought. He was looking down at a player that was taking up his time. At first, he gave me very fatherly advice: 'Sign the contract. It's best for you. It's best for us. It's best for the league. We don't want to get this started, you know, playing out an option. That's just a formality and maybe even shouldn't be in there.'"

Grant refused. Two weeks later, he got called again to the Commissioner's Office. The litany was the same: "You've got to sign this contract! You're the only one in the league who hasn't signed a contract." "But I have a contract," Grant insisted. "It says right here. You picked up my option. Here's my option letter. That's all I know about it. If I can read it that way, am I right?" "Well, technically, yes you are."

"Well then," Grant said, "I don't want to sign a contract. You didn't give me a raise, so there's no incentive. Give me a raise."

Grant was trying to use his situation as leverage to get a better contract. "If they gave me $500 more, that would have made a little difference," he recalled. "Then I got a little stubborn because they tried to say, 'Well, you've got to sign or we just can't have you play under this option the whole year.'

"I said, 'Where does it say that?' Things were tough for the Eagles. I remember Vince saying, 'Well, we can't pay you more than Pete Pihos [the Eagles top receiver].'

"So Bert got kind of testy and said, 'Listen, son, let me tell you something. Let me give you some good fatherly advice: SIGN THE CONTRACT!'"

Again Grant refused. "I don't remember how many trips I made—it was at least four. Vince would say, 'Hey, Mr. Bell wants to see you. Run across the street to his office.' So I'd run over there and again he'd give me a different spiel every time, but it didn't really work."

Before Philadelphia's season finale in Washington, team officials gave Grant a letter notifying him that he had been selected to play in the Pro Bowl. "But they said, 'You can't go to the Pro Bowl and won't get paid $500 unless you have a contract.' 'Where does it say that? I replied. 'Well, that's just league policy . . . the season's over . . . the contract's over . . . if you get hurt.'"

Grant went home that night and called the coach of the Winnipeg Blue Bombers. He was soon offered $10,000 for the following year. He led the league in receiving, played for three seasons, made the All-Star team, and saw his salary jump to $12,000. Then after coaching the Blue Bombers, he returned to the NFL and led the Minnesota Vikings to four Super Bowls. He is the only person to be named Coach of the Year and be elected to the Pro Football Halls of Fame in both Canada and the NFL.

Bud Grant never saw Bert Bell again. "I was only this lowly player and here's this commissioner," he remembers. "I had a lot of respect for him until he told me, 'Listen, sonny, SIGN THE CONTRACT!' That's when he lost me. I was the first player in the National Football League to play out his option."

Bell admitted at the time that Grant was within his legal rights in joining a team outside the NFL.

As hard as he tried, the commissioner couldn't get the antitrust business out of his mind. He constantly talked up the NFL's side and confidently predicted victory whenever the opportunity arose—to club owners, players, writers, fans, his family—just about to anyone who would listen. In October, he made his annual appearance at the weekly New York Football Writers luncheon at Toots Shor's Restaurant.

"We aren't in favor of socialized medicine and we don't believe in socialized TV," he thundered. "No one can make us televise against our home gate. TV will help us but only as long as we keep it out of the city where the game is being played. I don't think we are unreasonable and I don't think we will lose the suit."

Then pledging to fight the suit right up to the U.S. Supreme Court, he said, "We're not gonna lose."

On November 14, the commissioner paced back and forth in his office, glancing at his watch, peeking out the door. For a half an hour he waited. He finally realized that he was being stood up. When it became obvious that representatives of the Dallas Texans were not going to show up for a hearing that would determine the franchise's future, he angrily picked up the telephone.

"Put Giles Miller on the line," he bellowed. Then he read the following statement to the team president and reporters standing across from his desk:

I have determined that the Dallas Texans Football Club, Inc., is guilty of acts detrimental to the National Football League, namely a refusal to continue to operate the club and field a team throughout the balance of the 1952 season. The franchise is hereby cancelled and forfeited and the player contracts, including the reserve-player list, are hereby taken over by the National Football League on behalf of the remaining clubs in the league.

Bell added that the league would continue to field the team, allowing it to play all road games under the name of the Dallas Texans, for the balance of the 1952 season. The club would be headquartered in Hershey, Pennsylvania, the site of the training camp of the Philadelphia Eagles.

After finishing his prepared statement, the commissioner mellowed.

"I think you were a wonderful sport," he told Miller, the Dallas president. "I want you to know that I will never forget that you and your brother [Connell] and Harlan Ray [another stockholder] dug into your own pockets to pay the Los Angeles Rams their $20,000 guarantee."

Bell hung up the phone and then explained to reporters that the Millers and Ray had paid the Rams their guarantee when the gate turned out to be too small to meet their obligation. The money was paid the day before the Texans decided that they could not finance the team for the rest of the season and turned the franchise back to the NFL.

"Even the eyes of Texans popped a little at the size of the deficit," marveled *Time* magazine at the fact that Dallas dropped almost $250,000 after the first two months of the season.

The Texans only needed crowds of 24,000 to break even, but attendance dropped off to 12,000 a game as they lost seven straight contests. Playing the rest of the season on the road, the team didn't do much better. In fact, they drew only 3,000 fans in Akron, Ohio, for a game against the Chicago Bears on Thanksgiving Day.

The commissioner declined to speculate on the future of the Dallas franchise. He mentioned Baltimore and Buffalo as possibilities for 1953 and later denied a request by one of the 16 stockholders of the Texans to repurchase the club.

The trustee, John J. Coyle, said that his group was willing to raise $500,000 to guarantee operation of the team for the next three years but refused to pay the $200,000 debt it assumed for the financial obligations of the New York Yanks.

"I told Coyle that they bought the club under that obligation, knew what they were buying, and should abide by it," the commissioner told the United Press.

At the end of the 1952 regular season, according to Doc Greene of the *Detroit News,* Pete Pihos stormed into Bell's office in downtown Philadelphia. "They're cutting my salary and I won't stand for it," he told the commissioner. "I insist on being traded or released or something."

"If I owned the club, Pete, I'd cut you more," answered Bell. "You caught 12 passes last year and an end like you ought to have caught three times that many. You earn your salary on the field. Go back and do it!"

Pihos led the league in receptions the next three seasons and played in six consecutive Pro Bowl games.

The 1952 NFL championship, won by the Detroit Lions over the Browns, 17–7, before 50,934 fans in Cleveland on December 28, should have been the cause of jubilation for the league's owners. Instead it was quite the opposite.

Despite attracting the NFL's highest total attendance in history, only six teams finished in the black, and one of them reported a profit of only about $2,500. The mood was so gloomy that Bell reportedly offered to take a pay cut of $12,000 a year.

"Bert knows that even if he volunteered to take a cut," wrote *Philadelphia Inquirer* executive sports editor Leo Riordan, "this savings of $1,000 per club would solve nothing. What he is trying to create is a climate of thrift on one hand and a step-up in promotional operations on the other."

Expressing concern about "extravagant expenditures," the commissioner said that he would advocate a reduction in team rosters from 33 to 30 players when league owners convened in January 1953.

"That alone would cut payrolls by at least $15,000," he explained, adding that he opposed cutting players' salaries. "We've finally attained a standard that seems fair to the athlete. He's the one putting on a show each Sunday afternoon. He deserves to be paid a living wage."

Asked if he was concerned about the financial status of the league, Bell replied emphatically, raising his voice with each word, "If I didn't worry, who would? We have four clubs in this league that can go by way of Dallas if they don't watch their Ps and Qs financially. Do you think I want that to happen? Certainly not! How can a five or six team league operate? That would mean no league.

"No league means no job for Commissioner Bertram Bell. No sir! We don't want that to happen ever."

Bell explained that the league lost $65,000 operating the Dallas franchise for its final four games, even though the Texans received the usual $20,000 guarantee for each of the two games it played on the road.

"Part of that loss was the result of pampering players," he said. "A private plane cost $4,500 to transport the squad from Dallas to Detroit and that's $9,000 both ways. And, at a first class spot in Hershey, Pa., some of the Texans turned up their noses at the thought of eating in a cafeteria. Let's not spoil the boys."

According to published reports, the Chicago Bears, Cleveland, Detroit, Los Angeles, San Francisco, and New York reported profits in 1952. Washington and Pittsburgh finished slightly in the red. Moreover, each NFL team made a record $70,000 from local and national telecasts, but Bell was beginning to sense that the league had to step a little more carefully into the world of television.

Bell told sportswriter Stan Baumgartner that it would take crowds of between 24,000 and 26,000 fans per game to keep teams profitable. Otherwise, he told his owners, "they will have to gear their expenses to an average attendance of 16,000 to 18,000."

Many factors had altered the overall sports picture within the past few years, the commissioner warned:

"First and foremost has been television. The movies took the public out of the homes and put them on the streets; got them out of slippers and robes, made them toss away their pipes and put aside their knitting, gave them a mental urge to go places.

"Television has taken them back off the streets and put them in the home, in easy chairs, and has given them a different mental approach. It is much easier to sit at home and watch the best actors, the best singers, and see the finest plays than it is to go out.

"People are naturally lazy. American people are essentially hero worshippers. When teams lose these super stars, they lose their hold on the public. The '20s was the roaring age of sports because of Bobby Jones, Bill Tilden, Babe Ruth, Jack Dempsey—all super stars. Today we have to find and build up new super stars, make them colorful. Let them be individuals, reach a sensible, appealing balance between showmanship and discipline.

"No magnate, regardless of wealth, can balance an elephant on a toothpick indefinitely. Sooner or later he will be crushed and the costs of sports today—as run by our owners—is an elephant which they are trying to balance on a toothpick of attendance."

An elephant was about to return to Baltimore. But this time the toothpick wouldn't break.

28. Baltimore Rises from the Ashes

As 1952 drew to a close, Bert Bell pondered one of the most complex dilemmas he faced since becoming commissioner. The problem had been tormenting him for more than a year—ever since Abraham Watner turned the Baltimore Colts back to the league in January 1951.

It turns out, according to Mike Devitt of the *Indianapolis Star-News*, that the Colts' board of directors had known nothing of Watner's plans to dissolve the team before it was too late and filed a lawsuit against him and the NFL. In an effort to head off litigation, Bell admitted that the league was wrong in allowing Watner to abandon the franchise and offered to return the team to Baltimore if its debt could be cleared.

Devitt recalled that Bell's promise wasn't good enough for the city's attorney, William D. MacMillan.

"Instead of sitting on their hands, MacMillan proceeded with the lawsuit, which accused Watner and the league of, among other things, violating the Sherman Antitrust Act and restraining trade. Faced with the very real chance of losing such litigation (several preliminary rulings had gone in the city's favor; the case would have been tried in Baltimore; and the judge expected to rule on the case was a devoted Colts fan), in December of 1952 Bell issued a challenge to the city: sell 15,000 season tickets in six weeks, and the league would reward Baltimore with another football team."

Bell's action came after he again had sought legal advice from his brother, John C., who had recently been elected to a 21-year term as a Pennsylvania Supreme Court justice.

Traveling to Baltimore to make the announcement, Bell told a crowded news conference on December 3 that he would happily find an owner if fans would buy $250,000 worth of season tickets by January 22, which coincides with the annual league meeting.

"I don't have an owner now, but I guarantee you will have one," Bell said, adding that he had two or three names in mind. "The reason I don't have one is I'm not going to make any agreement with an owner who is not going to operate the franchise as a business 365 days a year."

MacMillan, who also served as the Colts' attorney, attended the news conference with Bell. He said that he had already received more than 1,000 requests for season tickets. The team had never sold more than 6,500 season tickets in the past but exceeded its 15,000 goal by 775 tickets in a little more than four weeks.

MacMillan had served as one of Whittaker Chambers's attorneys in the famous Alger Hiss perjury trial in 1950. He and Bell soon became close friends. "He's a guy my father loved," Bert's son Upton said. "He knew everybody in Washington."

On January 12, 1953, Bell reached back into his familiar Ivy League roots to announce the new majority owner of the Colts. He was Carroll Rosenbloom, a local textile manufacturer, who played halfback at the University of Pennsylvania in 1928–1929.

Bell was his backfield coach the first season and the two ex-Quakers stayed in touch while Rosenbloom worked as a consultant at the Philadelphia Quartermaster Depot and added to his considerable fortune by making uniforms and parachutes during World War II. It took some doing, but Bell finally persuaded his good friend to buy 51 percent of the franchise for $250,000 during a conversation in the living room of the commissioner's home in Margate.

"He twisted my arm," Rosenbloom told friends, according to William Henry Paul, author of *The Gray-Flannel Pigskin: Movers and Shakers of Pro Football*. "He told me it was my civic responsibility, that I was Baltimore's last hope. He made it so that if I didn't take the club, I was one son of a bitch."

"I think Carroll wanted to be the owner all along," recalled Bert Bell Jr., who later worked for Rosenbloom and the Colts. "He just wanted to be persuaded. He wanted to be convinced."

"It's a good thing he's in the shirt business, because he's going to lose his," Bell later confided to his associates, according to Rich Roberts of the *Los Angeles Times*.

Rosenbloom eventually bought out his four co-owners to assume sole control of the Colts. He also became one of Bell's closest confidants in the league and helped make Baltimore one of the NFL's most successful franchises.

At the same time, Bell named another former Quaker, Don Kellett, as the Colts' president and general manager. A 1934 Penn graduate who later coached basketball at his alma mater and Ursinus College, Kellett was working as director of operations at Philadelphia's WFIL Radio and TV.

Later he would become the architect of Baltimore's NFL championship teams by signing coach Weeb Ewbank and quarterback Johnny Unitas, both future Pro Football Hall-of-Famers.

The commissioner was in a jubilant mood when he opened the 1953 owners' meeting on the evening of January 21 at the Bellevue Stratford Hotel in Philadelphia.

Declaring that the 1952 season was the "best in league history in both attendance and financially," Bell said that 2,149,633 fans attended 72 regular-season and playoff games—a 1.6 percent increase over the 1950 season, the biggest previous year, and 8.3 percent better than in 1951. The league also lost $69,200 operating the now-defunct Dallas club in 1952.

While not disclosing official receipts—"I don't know who made money and who didn't. I didn't see the books"—Bell suddenly turned serious as he urged owners to cut expenses because the bottom five or six teams "took too great" a financial gamble.

"It's time for clubs to operate on a budget, run like a business project," he explained. "I don't believe in cutting salaries, but there are many other ways expenses can be knocked down."

Possible cost-cutting moves could be to reduce team rosters from 33 to 30 players and slice guarantees of visiting teams down to $15,000. "Cutting three players would shave expenses by $20,000 or $25,000," Bell declared.

"Would you take a cut?" the commissioner was asked, according to Stan Baumgartner of the *Philadelphia Inquirer.* "Yes, I am willing to take a cut if it fits into the economy program," Bell replied.

When the club owners wearily reconvened two days later, after the annual player draft had dragged on for 15 hours into the previous night, their first order of business was to again reject Bell's proposal to eliminate the extra point.

"It merely wastes time, it's practically automatic," the commissioner repeated time and time again before the measure was defeated by the same 7–5 margin (in favor, but not enough to carry) they had voted in 1952.

Then the owners made a number of rule changes, decided to retain the 33-player roster limit and $20,000 guarantee, and agreed that no player could be forced to take more than a 10 percent salary cut—even though major league baseball could slash salaries up to 25 percent. They also reaffirmed their policy of "reasonable restraint" in televising league games—a policy soon to be challenged by the federal government.

Finally, early Sunday morning, after deliberating for almost 12 hours, the owners agreed by an 11–1 vote (with Philadelphia, surprisingly, dissenting) on a new, permanent scheduling pattern. It called for each team to play every other team in its division twice each season home and away. Moreover, each club would play home and away games against two teams from the opposite division each year during the 12-game season.

The names of the league's two divisions were changed, with the American Conference becoming the Eastern Division and the National, the Western Division. Baltimore was placed in the west after George Preston Marshall was given assurances that the home-and-home rivalry between his Redskins and Colts would be preserved along with the traditional matchup between the Chicago Bears and Cardinals.

As Joseph H. Sheehan reported in the *New York Times,* the owners again authorized Commissioner Bell "to work out the details of the new schedule under the solid directive that he demanded as one of the two alternative conditions for again tackling the job of satisfying the diverse interests of the every-man-for-himself professional football fraternity."

Bell was elated that the owners had hurdled a major stumbling block to recent league harmony, simplifying his scheduling responsibilities considerably by merely requiring him to assign dates. "It's the greatest thing that has ever happened to our system of scheduling," he said, calling the system "foolproof."

The commissioner explained that he was impressed by the spirit of the club owners, especially Marshall, in making important concessions that gave all clubs an equal share of choice playing dates, ending the squabbling for the league's top money-making attractions. "They were all cooperative, and Marshall could not have been more fair," Bell said. "No man ever did more for club harmony."

On February 25, the commissioner was called to the stand in the U.S. district court in Philadelphia to testify in the federal government's case against the NFL in which the government contended that the league's policy limiting the telecasting and broadcasting of its games was a violation of the Sherman Anti-Trust Act.

It was a very tense time for the Bell family. Bert Bell Jr., who had just celebrated his 17th birthday the previous week, walked into the family dining room the night before the trial and heard a conversation between his dad and his uncle, John C. Bell, the family's trusted legal advisor.

"My dad was one of the first people to really understand the potential of television if it was handled correctly," Bert Jr. recalled. "My dad felt: 'Gee, we're getting free advertising from televising our games. General Motors can't afford to pay for that advertising and we're getting it for nothing.' It really upset him when my uncle told my father, 'Bert, there's no way that you can win that case.'

"My dad replied, 'If they win, they will put us out of business.'"

And that's one of the first things the commissioner said when he began testifying. Unrestricted television of NFL games would "positively sound the death knell of professional football," he told Judge Allan K. Grim, who was hearing the case without a jury.

Bell, who spent most of the day on the stand, explained that all 12 club presidents agreed after lengthy discussion to implement the section of the league bylaws prohibiting telecasts in cities where the home team is playing.

"I can say this because anyone who can see the game at home on television for free will wait until the day of the game or the last minute to see what the weather is like," he added. "If the weather is bad or threatening, they will stay home."

Returning to the witness stand the following day, Bell was cross-examined by W. Perry Epes, the chief government trial attorney, who was assisted by six other trial lawyers. Much of the commissioner's testimony centered on the league's contention that it is not violating the Sherman Act because it is not a business under the interpretation of the act.

Citing statistics that 34 of the 46 franchises issued since the NFL started operating went broke, Bell pointed out that most surviving clubs just about broke even and only about four teams consistently made a profit.

"This is certainly not a business," Bell contended. "The fellows operating these clubs are philanthropists interested in keeping the sport going." Soon, the operators would have to "stop operating with the heart and start operating with the head."

Judge Grim asked Bell why professional football showed an increase in attendance in 1952 while major league baseball attendance had been steadily decreasing.

"We don't televise our home games and baseball does," the commissioner replied. "I really think—and it is only my opinion—that baseball is coming to no television of home games."

Epes reminded Bell that at one time baseball inserted a clause in its bylaws restricting broadcast and telecasts but later struck it out.

"Has its elimination sounded the death knell to baseball?" Epes asked.

"No," Bell replied. "But it will."

Bell went on to claim that 50 percent of the minor league baseball teams had folded in the last several years and added that several major league teams were in financial trouble.

"Have you heard that more Philadelphia big league games are going to be on television this year than last?" Epes asked.

"I read something about that," Bell replied.

Judge Grim then asked Bell if he ever heard claims that eventually big sporting events would be held in empty stadiums, parks, or studios solely for television audiences.

"Mike Jacobs predicted five years ago that some day, championship fights would be seen by live audiences of less than 1,000," the commissioner responded. "But people must understand that there is a certain electricity in watching a football game in a packed stadium. Without the thrill of the crowd, professional football would deteriorate."

Bell predicted that television would probably help all sports in the future but that right now sports and television must learn to live together.

"After all," he added, "set makers advertise that people should buy a set and get a seat on the 50-yard line. How can we compete with that?"

The trial would go on for a total of 19 days. It ended with Judge Grim announcing that he would make his decision at a later date. Austin Gunsel was never called to testify against the NFL.

Despite his public pronouncements urging caution with the relatively unknown medium, Bell spent much of the spring discussing the pros and cons of television with his closest friends and advisors. Soon he made two important decisions that helped to propel the National Football League closer to the national spotlight.

The first deal came early in May when Bell and DuMont's Ted Bergmann met for the third and final time and came up with the idea for a Saturday afternoon, Saturday night, and Sunday television package for the 1953 and 1954 seasons.

Not only was it the richest professional football television agreement ever consummated—a deal that guaranteed each NFL club a minimum of $50,000—it marked the first time that league games would be carried live, coast to coast, in prime time for the entire season.

This arrangement predated ABC's much-heralded Monday Night Football by 17 years. Most of the regular-season games originated in New York, Pittsburgh, and Washington, where DuMont owned and operated stations, but the additional exposure given to the league was significant.

Bell made the announcement at a heavily attended press conference at the Bellevue Stratford Hotel in Philadelphia on May 13. He was joined by executives of the Westinghouse Electric Corporation, who announced that they would expend more than $1.3 million to sponsor the 19 telecasts to at least 65 cities throughout the nation.

In a comment obviously aimed at federal antitrust investigators, Bell stressed that "the agreement is with each individual club and that the league does not enter into the agreement whatsoever."

Then on September 15, the commissioner announced that ABC would televise 12 home games and one preseason contest of the Chicago Cardinals and Chicago Bears into 58 cities from coast to coast.

"In covering the complete home schedules of both the Cardinals and Bears, ABC will present a nationwide audience with games involving every one of our teams," Bell said in a statement. He added that Harold (Red) Grange would handle the play-by-play with Bill Stern acting as master of ceremonies.

Midway through the summer of 1953, Bell invited United Press sportswriter Jack Cuddy to his Center City Philadelphia headquarters on Walnut Street to discuss the league's "comparatively new security policy," a program that he unabashedly credited for the NFL's record-breaking popularity.

"The fans turned out in record numbers last year because we gave them the roughest, toughest, and cleanest football ever played," the commissioner explained cheerfully while tapping a pencil on his large wooden desk. "Our security policy paid off in that brand of football."

Calling the policy "a modern two-lane approach to the sport," Bell said that the league was trying to assure the ultimate financial security of the player while at the same time attempting to protect professional football "from even a rumor" of dishonesty.

Before the league began experimenting with this new policy in 1947, Bell continued, professional football players were generally regarded as merely representatives of the city for which they played—not actually members of the community. Now, the 12 NFL teams were campaigning vigorously to have as many players as possible get off-season jobs and become permanent residents in the cities where they perform.

"If a player knows he's going to live in his club's city and that his future is tied up in that city, it increases his all-important desire to win," Bell explained. "I say *all-important* because no player can be great in football without a burning desire to win. It's a rough, tough game that demands the ultimate in alertness and condition."

In addition, the commissioner emphasized, the people of a city become much more enthused about their team if most of the players are fellow townsmen. Then the fans are rooting for real "home boys." At least 20 Eagles players were now working at off-season jobs in Philadelphia, and "somewhat similar" numbers of players were becoming members of their team's communities in other cities.

Concerning the league's protection against "even rumors of dishonest play," Bell said that his office now requested that players mingle only with "known and reliable" members of their own communities at home and that they "beware of strangers" on the road.

"A stranger can ask a player to have dinner with him," Bell explained. "It might be an innocent invitation. But it might also be from a city's leading bookmaker or from some big-time gambler. We don't want it and won't have it!"

While still awaiting Judge Grim's decision on October 2, the commissioner became visibly disturbed when a regional telecast of a Friday night 21–21 tie game between the Eagles and the Redskins at Philadelphia's Connie Mack Stadium was suddenly canceled—and it had nothing to do with any federal legislation.

"They call us into court and keep us there for two months, telling us how vital televising of football games is to the public, then they pull this on us," Bell fumed after being informed that the telecast of the game by ABC to 12 cities running through the south from Baltimore, Washington, and Atlanta was scuttled when the coaxial cables failed to arrive in time.

Bell's blood pressure soared after he learned that ABC had confirmed to the Redskins months earlier that the cables were available. But hours before kickoff, the American Oil Company, the telecast's sponsor, was notified that the cables could not be delivered.

"I want to know if television is a one-way street," Bell demanded, hinting at a conspiracy. "This game was canceled without warning after it had been confirmed!"

A few weeks later, Bell attempted to sooth the nerves of some of his owners who were becoming increasingly agitated over the perceived aggressiveness of their counterparts in Canada, who had attracted about 85 American players north of the border since 1951.

Many of the players were marginal at best, but Canada had also signed big-name stars like 1952 Heisman Trophy winner Billy Vessels of Oklahoma and quarterback Eddie LeBaron, who would later return to excel for more than a decade in the NFL. The Canadian League was providing another profitable economic alternative, especially after the AAFC folded.

John Steadman was working as the Baltimore Colts' assistant general manager and publicity director at the time. He recalled sitting in the stands in Hershey, watching the Colts and Philadelphia Eagles square off in their annual preseason game. Bert Bell was sitting nearby with his pals from Narberth, and Steadman described their conversation years later in an interview with NFL Films.

"I said, 'What about the threat, Bert? What do you think about the Canadian Football League? They're taking a lot of players.' He said, 'John, old boy, all I know about Canadian football is that they have a thing called a rouge. The only thing I know about rouge is it's something that dames used to put on their face when they were in vaudeville shows.'

"Now that was Bert. He could reduce it to the greatest words of simplicity."

Emphasizing that "we are not going to enter into any agreement with the Canadians," Bell surprised many people a few days after his conversation with Steadman when he told Stan Baumgartner of *The Sporting News,* "Canadian football is a good thing."

With both professional leagues bidding for college players, it was a very healthy situation, providing they recognize the rights of contract, he explained. However, "we do not wish to do anything that would make us vulnerable to a charge by our government that we are running a monopoly in restraint of the players."

Bell conceded that in some cases, the Canadians undoubtedly offered more money than the NFL offered to American players.

"But we feel that it would be a poor morale builder for a club in our league to offer a raw rookie the same amount that an established star is making. We do not want to lose outstanding players, but if they outbid us we have to complain. The National Football League has reached the position where the team is generally more important than the player. Our salaries have increased 400 per cent in the past ten years due to the balanced power of our clubs."

Bell later told James Ellis of the *Baltimore Evening Sun* that the rivalry with Canada "makes me happy" and revealed that he even advised San Francisco 49ers' defensive halfback Jim Cason to play out his option.

"Cason told me that he could make $9,500 in Canada and that his top salary in our league would be $8,000," the commissioner explained. "I told him if he thought he'd be better off up there to go ahead."

Reiterating that he never expected to reach an agreement with his counterparts north of the border, Bell said, "Competition with them is a healthy thing for us. It proves we are not operating a monopoly."

Finally, on November 12, Judge Grim handed down his long-awaited decision. It was a 20-page opinion that was essentially favorable to professional football. While upholding the league's blackout rule as it applied to restricting telecasts within a 75-mile radius of a team's home territory where a home game was being played, Grim partially granted the government's request for an injunction by ruling that the NFL could not prevent any team from telecasting its games in another team's home territory on days where there was no home game.

According to numerous published reports, Grim was persuaded by the NFL's claim that allowing telecasts of home games in home territories "has an adverse effect" on home attendance and that this factor "clearly indicates by implication that the telecast of an outside game, particularly a head-on game, also adversely affects attendance at a home game."

Concluding that NFL television restrictions were "pro-competitive under the Sherman Act," Grim explained that "the league is truly a unique business enterprise, which is entitled to protect its very existence by agreeing to reasonable restrictions on its member clubs. The first type of restriction imposed by Article X is a reasonable one and a legal restraint of trade."

Bell looked visibly relieved as he spoke with reporters at the NFL headquarters after hearing of the verdict. Professional football "has won the most important part of its case," he said. The court had understood the vital need of professional football at that time, namely, "the protection of our home gate if we are to continue our existence."

The commissioner conceded that the court's decision would become "a victory only when we prove to the public that we are conducting our sport in a manner which serves their best interest."

"The blackout of home games proved to be a remarkably shrewd decision," wrote John Devaney in the *American Legion Magazine*.

Fans watched telecasts of their team's road games and, for the first time, had a close-up look at this savagery on Sunday. On the TV screen they got to know the players, not only the backfield stars, but those big rough men in the line. TV explained the game, and soon you weren't "in" if you didn't know a linebacker from a safetyman, a flanker from a tight end. When the teams came off the road, excited fans—knowing they couldn't see the home games on TV—lined up to buy tickets.

The ruling by Grim, a former Democratic Party official who was appointed to the bench by President Truman in 1950, did not end the federal government's crusade against the television policies of Bert Bell and the NFL.

It wasn't a complete victory for the commissioner, either, because Grim decreed that Bell could no longer completely control radio broadcasts. Nor could a team ban television in its home territory while that club was on the road. But Grim's far-reaching decision certainly helped the league live for another day.

By December 1953, as an estimated 2.2 million fans poured through turnstiles to set a new NFL attendance record—and each team earned $125,000 from television and radio revenue, according to *Time* magazine—Bell again gloated about "the greatest season in our history."

The million-dollar coast-to-coast television project that he arranged with the DuMont network "created thousands of new fans," the commissioner claimed. It was a far cry from the not-too-distant days before television when the entire league earned only $14,000 from radio rights.

"I think TV is terrific," Bell told the Associated Press. "The more we have, the more I like it!"

29. More Warfare and the Sermon on the Mount

Shortly after New Year's Day 1954, the Canadian situation resurfaced. This time, however, Bert Bell reacted quite differently and surprised everyone by changing his tune.

"The war is on," the commissioner bellowed after learning that the New York Giants' Arnie Weinmeister, one of the NFL's top tackles, had played out his option and jumped to the new British Columbia Lions franchise in Vancouver. "The Canadian League has again breached our contracts. They had better start counting their players."

As Bell stepped into Philadelphia's Bellevue-Stratford Hotel to open the annual league meetings he disclosed a new approach, emphasizing that the NFL was prepared to counteract the Canadians' encroachment by bidding for their top native players.

"We have a list of all the Canadian players, some of whom could make our league," he explained. "I repeat. If they want a player war, they're going to get one."

Orville Burke, the vice president of the Calgary Stampeders, quickly responded by declaring that an all-out war over players was in the offing. Furthermore, he accused the NFL of hiring a "propagandist" to slander the Canadian game and persuade college players to stay home in the United States.

"If he means we are telling the American players the truth about Canadian football, then we're hiring a propagandist," Bell replied, identifying the new league consultant as Bob Snyder, a former Canadian coach, who frequently told the players that conditions in Canada aren't always as bright as they appear.

Jim McCaffrey, president of the Ottawa Rough Riders, accused Bell of "popping off" and charged that the NFL had recently held a secret draft meeting to get a jump on their professional counterparts north of the border.

"Mr. McCaffrey has a wonderful imagination," Bell responded. The commissioner then invited the Canadian official to "stand outside the Bellevue-Stratford to see for himself" the annual NFL player draft in progress.

Otherwise, the four-day confab was the "shortest and most harmonious winter meeting in the history of the NFL," according to various written accounts. Explaining why the meetings were held "without one bitter argument," Bell pointed out that only one team, the Chicago Cardinals, failed to make a profit in 1953. In addition, three other teams avoided red ink because of television revenue.

Despite some agitation for it from the players, the commissioner said that the owners never considered implementing a pension plan similar to that of major league baseball.

"Our players average only three or four years," he explained. "They don't stay with us long enough to warrant such a plan. We have discussed the possibility of life insurance for the players."

The owners unanimously agreed not to appeal Judge Grim's antitrust ruling and rewrote Article X to conform to his decision. They agreed to play all games on Sundays whenever possible—Eagles officials explained that three night games in 1953 cut heavily into their upstate attendance—and defeated a proposal to increase rosters from 33 to 35 players.

They also slapped Bell gently on the wrist by again rejecting his perennial plea for the elimination of the extra point. "Just say my defeat was humiliating," the commissioner joked.

Bell could afford to be magnanimous, especially after George Halas announced that the owners had unanimously agreed to extend his contract for 12 years until 1965. Entering his ninth year as commissioner—he previously had three-, five-, and ten-year contracts—Bell later told reporters that he declined an increase in pay because too many clubs were still near the "money-losing" line.

"We spent over $200,000 over the past two years in league business, including [fighting the U.S. government] anti-trust case, the Yankee Stadium lease, the [Dallas] Texas loss, the Baltimore settlement, and so forth," he explained.

In May, the pro football "war" shifted to television when NBC announced that it would be carrying 13 Canadian Football games in the United States during the 1954 season. The *Toronto Globe and Mail* estimated that the network would receive $320,000 for the games, which included all playoff contests.

Bell told the Associated Press that he had no problem with the deal. "I heartily approve of all the free advertising football can get, whether it be from the newspapers, the radio or television," he said. "As a matter of fact, the Canadian games will not be competing with the NFL, but even if they were, I'd still be for it."

In July, the commissioner began his traditional pilgrimages to the league's training camps. Known as his "Sermon on the Mount," Bell's customary ritual had long become a tradition of mirth, seriousness, and bewilderment among the players. He hated flying, so all of his trips were made by train or automobile. That precluded traveling to the West Coast every year, but there were other factors that sometimes curbed his enthusiasm for traveling west of the Mississippi.

For various reasons, some people felt that Bell just wasn't as warmly received on the Pacific Coast as he was in the Midwest or on the Eastern Seaboard. Some of it perhaps had to do with a published report back in 1950 that the two California club owners angled to have him ousted as commissioner.

There was also an incident in August 1949 when he was reprimanded by the Southern California chapter of the National Football Writers Association for banning ex-football star Tommy Harmon from telecasting a game between the Rams and Washington Redskins. Harmon charged that Bell kept him off the telecast because he had broadcast a game for the Los Angeles Dons of the rival AAFC. And then, there was the ongoing litigation in the case of Bill Radovich, who claimed that he was blacklisted by the NFL after playing with the Dons for two years.

For whatever reason, Bert sometimes just didn't feel as comfortable near the Pacific Ocean as he did elsewhere, even when such writers as John B. Old of the *Los Angeles Herald Express* would occasionally sing his praises.

"Of course we have no way of knowing what the final decision will be," Old wrote one time when Bell did make the trip to the coast. "But when the last chapter of professional sports is written and the man upstairs gets around to grading the commissioners, Bert Bell of the National Football League doubtless will be given the top-drawer rating."

For Bell's children—Bert Jr., Upton, and Janie—it was quite a different story. They absolutely loved traveling to the West Coast when they were young. The commissioner would always make time to take his daughter to the glitzy shows and meet stars like Sophie Tucker and to make sure that the kids saw all the sights.

"You'd go to Chicago, then over the Rocky Mountains to Los Angeles and San Francisco by train," Upton explained. "It was a whole different way of life. Celebrities would be with you on the train for three days. We'd stop in Albuquerque and Indians would get up and dance on the train.

"The Rams in the late 40s and early 50s were really Hollywood. The stars would come out to practices and there would be parties. Of course, Jane Russell was married to Bob Waterfield. Bob Hope owned a piece of the Rams. Bing Crosby owned part of the Pittsburgh Pirates. I mean it was like a whole other world."

During one of his trips, Bell went out of his way to heap praise on the Pacific Coast in an interview with Paul Zimmerman of the *Los Angeles Times*.

"It made firm the financial structure of the league when the Los Angeles Rams and San Francisco 49ers became members," he said. "I can remember when members of our league complained when the schedule called for them to come out to the coast in those early days. Now the same gentlemen are squawking if they don't get the games scheduled out here because of your fine attendance."

Bell's summer excursion usually began in Hershey, Pennsylvania, where he would speak to players from the Philadelphia Eagles and Baltimore Colts before their annual exhibition game. If he couldn't make it to a particular training facility, he talked over a telephone and locker room amplifying system, usually opening by saying, "Now remember, boys, I want football to be the number one game in America."

"He talked to us like a father," recalled former Eagles Hall of Famer Chuck Bednarik. "He was strict but fair."

"This game of pro football is the roughest game of the world," Bell shouted one year in his foghorn voice to members of the Eagles, who were listening attentively at their training facility. "The other guy will hit you hard, and in return you are expected to hit him hard. Or maybe even harder!"

Sportswriter Hugh Brown recalled the scene in Hershey. "Bertie added something to the effect that even if a player has just had an ear torn from his head, or a leg wrenched loose from a socket, he should always strive to be civil to paying patrons calling him names and newspapermen asking him silly questions."

"It was mostly about the integrity of the game," said Don Shula, who was playing for the Colts at the time. "Bert always stressed playing within the rules and doing it the right way. He always talked about the safety measures. I spent a lot of years on the Competition Committee and our whole thrust was player safety and making the game as excitable as we could make it and I think those were the beliefs that I got from him. That's what I believed in as a young coach."

"Everybody knew Bert Bell," former Giants and Redskins linebacking great Sam Huff once told sportswriter Ray Didinger. "He would always say, "Gentlemen, let me tell you something. There's three ways to get you out of this league—drinking, gambling, and women. And let me tell you something. When you put them all together, you're history! Okay? But if you have any problems, call me. Call me collect." He was a great old guy. He was part of the foundation that made football in those days."

Gambling was a particular concern to the commissioner. "Each year he made the same speech to the players," wrote *Pittsburgh Post-Gazette* sports editor Phil Musick:

> Gamblers bet millions on our games. You boys go around knocking the officials and people will get dirty ideas. Watch out for the wise guys . . . the winkers. They're not gamblers or bookies or even fans. They are winkers. They come up to you in a restaurant and say, "You're Jimmy Smith, let me buy you dinner." Then they go back to the bar and say, "Bet such-and-such real big. You just saw me talking to Smith, didn't you?" Watch out for winkers.

"I also tell them to play clean," Bell told sportswriter Jack Orr. "There's no need for fighting or playing dirty. By playing clean, too, they keep their prestige with the local businessmen who can help them in their business affairs. We cannot have dirty stuff in football. We are trying to sell the game to women and children. Dirty playing doesn't belong in the game of football."

After speaking on a variety of topics including how to dress—"Be sure to wear a coat and tie on the road"—and how to act in public, the commissioner would emphasize the importance of preparing for the future, "your life after football," he would say.

> It's a means to an end, gentlemen. With all the publicity you receive, work to become well known in the community in which you play. That's where you should establish your home. And fellas, I always want you to be good to your families. Remember that paycheck belongs to the little lady at home. Then he would end every session by shouting: "Don't forget boys, if you've got a problem call me collect any time night or day—MOHAWK 4-4400."

Many players did just that. One of them was defensive back Johnny Sample, who lived in the Philadelphia area.

"The first house I ever bought in my life, I went to make a closing and they upped the price on me like $4,000," explained Sample in an interview with NFL Films. "I didn't have the money. I just didn't have it. And I called the Commissioner's Office. I told Bert Bell about my problem. He said,

'Well, it's no problem. Just come over here and get it.' I got right in my car. Rode over to City Line Avenue. Went in his office. He handed me the check. It was great. I tell you, I admire the man. I think without him, the NFL would not be where it is today."

Another player taking advantage of Bell's invitation was Herb Rich, who was traded by the Los Angeles Rams to the New York Giants prior to Week 2 of the 1954 season.

According to David Maraniss in his book *When Pride Still Mattered: The Life of Vince Lombardi*, Rich was concerned that neither team would pay him for his first game. He called the commissioner. "Bell answered the phone, listened to Rich's concern and resolved it immediately, ordering the Rams to pay the salary. That is how simple life was in the league then—a defensive back picking up the phone and talking directly to the commissioner: no agents, lawyers, unions, league bureaucrats in the way."

Bell also displayed a great sense of humor to the players. "After we heard the same speech in Hershey for maybe four or five years, Bert was due to come in again," recalled Baltimore's John Steadman in an interview with NFL Films.

"The players are all assembled and our center, Buzz Nutter, got up. He went into his imitation about Bert Bell, about what they were going to hear, because he had heard it so many times. Well, unbeknownst to Buzz Nutter, as he was giving his talk and his imitation of Bert Bell, Bert walked in behind him. And he stood there with his arms folded and just enjoyed the performance more than any of us that were looking at Buzz head-on."

"To see him go into a locker room filled with all these big beefy guys and control that room was quite a sight," recalled Bell's son Upton. "He was just so overpowering, but he always let the players kid and say things like, 'Yo, Bert!' There usually was a lot of give and take. He would wait outside the room before being introduced and usually each team had a guy who would mimic him. Then he'd walk in the room and somebody would say, 'Oh my God he's here . . .' and everybody would laugh like hell. It was serious but it was hilarious. Times were different then. Most of the guys came out of the war—either World War II or Korea—so he was a man talking to men. So they showed that real respect for him."

"Bell had a rapport with the players like no other sports commissioner ever has had," Steadman once wrote in *The Sporting News*. "Bert indeed had the down home approach. He would warn the players about staying away from gamblers, going into bad saloons, and tell them to be especially nice to sportswriters who covered the league's activity. 'I don't want to hear of any of you guys charging for interviews or getting into arguments with Joe King or Ed Prell or Hughie Brown or Harold Weissman. Those guys and the rest of the writers give you a million dollars worth of free publicity.' That was always his message."

DuMont was now carrying 11 regular-season games and had nine of the 12 NFL teams under contract. Only the two Chicago teams and Washington were still operating under their own television agreements. Network officials were initially ecstatic after an internal memorandum revealed that Nielsen ratings for professional football were 26 percent higher than in 1953. Meanwhile, NCAA football viewership had dropped 15 percent.

But rumors started circulating that DuMont was having serious financial problems and NBC officials began to take another look at the NFL.

The rumors were true. Actually, DuMont's problems had been festering for a while—ever since Westinghouse suddenly dropped its sponsorship a month before the beginning of the 1954 season and a promising deal with General Motors fell through.

"We gave the games to our affiliate stations for co-op sponsorships," recalled Ted Bergmann, DuMont's managing director. "We ended up having to eat a great deal of our rights, facilities, and cable costs—a loss amounting to an ill-affordable $2 million. Bert Bell wasn't involved. He just sat back and collected the money. We had a commitment to him that was in the contract. He didn't care how we paid it off, whether we had sponsors or not."

Despite DuMont's impending demise, the combined television and radio revenue for NFL games in 1954 approached a record $1.8 million, according to Bell's calculations. A total of 51 contests were televised over 160 stations stretching from Massachusetts to Seattle.

Some 32 million people watched the games on television throughout the season, according to Arthur Daley of the *New York Times,* and the NFL earned approximately $8 million from attendance and electronic revenue sources. DuMont officials estimated that 400 million viewers saw the games and that 8.5 million homes were tuned in to NFL action each weekend.

The regular season was relatively uneventful except for opening week, when a 48–0 win by the Los Angeles Rams over the Baltimore Colts was highlighted by a controversial 80-yard touchdown pass on the first play of the game. Los Angeles halfback Skeets Quinlan lined up next to his bench virtually obscured in a sea of yellow Rams jerseys, far from his teammates, who took their stances in a conventional fashion on the 20 yard-line.

None of the Baltimore players and few of the 36,215 fans noticed Quinlan streaking down the sideline when the ball was snapped. Norman Van Brocklin hit him with an easy 45-yard touchdown pass. The cornerback victimized on the play? Don Shula, the future Hall of Fame coach of the Colts.

Bell reacted—or overreacted—immediately. He labeled the sleeper pass play "unsportsmanlike" and instructed all referees and coaches that any similar incident in the future should be penalized. After watching films of the play, however, Los Angeles executive Tex Schramm denied that the Rams players on the sideline had formed an illegal backdrop and said that the club resented Bell's implication.

Maxwell Stiles, of the *Los Angeles Mirror-News*, also viewed the film and demanded a public apology from Bell after determining that none of Quinlan's teammates were within 11 yards of the halfback.

"The sleeper play is one of the oldest plays in football," Stiles wrote, adding that the Rams used it at least 90 percent of the game, primarily to compensate for players who were unable to block effectively.

Bell quickly relented. "I put out the directive after hearing from the Baltimore papers and Baltimore fans that Quinlan couldn't be seen very well on the way," the commissioner explained. "If the movies show differently, then that settles it."

The sleeper play was outlawed by the NFL Rules Committee the following January.

Concerns about Bell's health surfaced again when he was forced to miss the NFL championship game in Cleveland, won by the Browns, 56–10, over the Detroit Lions. Joe Labrum, the league spokesman, said that the commissioner was suffering from "fatigue" because he was "overworked" and had been ordered to bed by his physician, Dr. Harrison Flippin.

It was no secret that Bell was suffering from high blood pressure. Despite pleas to slow down, he persisted in working 15-hour days. Then he'd go home and spend most of the night either on the telephone or moving dominoes around. The final straw for Dr. Flippin came when Bert collapsed one day at the Racquet Club about a week before the title game.

As it turned out, scheduling wouldn't be Bell's only concern as 1954 came winding down. Violence among players in the league would soon vie for his attention, especially after a *Time* magazine article late in the year praised his "benevolent paternalism" on one hand but raised red flags on the other about how the pros "practice a high and violent art" on Sundays.

"We play rough and we teach rough," Detroit Lions coach Buddy Parker told *Time*. "And when I say rough, I don't mean poking a guy in the eye. I mean gang tackling—right close to piling on."

"When the 49ers fullback Hardy Brown was carried out of his first game with the Lions this year, his groin ripped open by a set of slashing cleats, a reporter in the press box had the last word," the magazine said. "'Pro football is getting like atomic war. There are no winners, only survivors.'"

As *Time* editorialized, "Commissioner Bell runs the league with a firm hand and has prevented warfare between the teams except on the field."

The warfare—at least a battle of words—would soon spread to the Commissioner's Office.

30. Flare-Ups, Pile-Ups, and a Move to Oust the Commissioner

When the bells tolled for New Year's Day 1955, it was pretty much the same old story for Bert Bell. The familiar Canadian situation just wouldn't go away—only this time it took more twists and turns than one of Crazy Legs Hirsch's touchdown runs.

On January 22, after hosting representatives from Canada's Big Four at the Racquet Club in Philadelphia, the commissioner announced that they had "laid the groundwork for a permanent peace" that would end the bodysnatching of professional football players on both sides of the border. Bell was optimistic because the Big Four consisted of the Canadian League's prestigious eastern franchises—Hamilton, Montreal, Ottawa, and Toronto—the clubs that would probably be most influential with their counterparts.

"The problem requires a little more study and we will try to work out a solution," Bell explained. "Neither the Canadian representatives or myself clearly know how many players are involved."

Bell also disclosed that he had met with representatives of the Hamilton Tiger-Cats the previous July and had been led to understand that at least six of the nine Canadian teams were in a peaceful mood.

On January 24, though, a Canadian Western Conference official called peace plans with the NFL "just good propaganda." Another Canadian official said, "Toronto Argonauts already have them on the run, so let's strike while the iron is hot."

Brian Cooper, the president of the Big Four, immediately threatened to have the Argonauts' operators replaced because he said that three-fourths of the league were in favor of making peace. Toronto had persistently refused to surrender any of its players who were under contract to NFL teams.

The following day, Bell confirmed that he had made a verbal agreement with the Edmonton Eskimos, the only Canadian team that had never taken a football player under contract to an NFL club.

"I agreed that pending the results of our peace negotiations with the remaining Canadian football teams that no NFL members would make overtures to players already under contract to Edmonton," the commissioner explained.

As the annual owners' meetings unfolded at the Hotel Warwick in New York City, it was obvious that Bell was not pleased with the progress of a possible truce. He reiterated that the Canadians would find a friendly reception if they wanted to discuss the issue but stressed that the NFL owners were prepared to meet any challenge to protect their own interests, if necessary.

On February 1, Bell held a four-hour meeting with representatives of the rebel Toronto Argonauts. He advised them to settle their own Canadian football problems before attempting to reach a peace agreement with the NFL and urged them to work toward the appointment of a commissioner with powers to speak for *all* Canadian football.

On February 25, the Philadelphia Eagles and Washington Redskins signed "no raiding agreements" with three Canadian teams, a move hailed by Bell as "a step in the right direction." The Eagles signed pacts with Edmonton and Winnipeg, while the Redskins ended their feud with Calgary. It was expected that future peace settlements would be made with similar club-by-club arrangements.

Then it all came apart on March 17, when Bell issued a statement that said, in part, "If Canadian pro footballers want warfare, they're going to get it."

Bell was outraged to learn that Toronto had recently signed two NFL players under contract to the Detroit Lions and that the Ottawa Rough Riders had done the same with a player under option to the Cleveland Browns.

"I have tried everything within reason to bring about peace between Canada and the United States but it is obvious that Canadians cannot control their own teams," the commissioner lamented.

Bell also disclosed that he had just had a heated telephone exchange with Ottawa's J. P. McCaffrey during which he told the Rough Riders' manager that he was "out of line" in signing Cleveland's lineman Tom King.

"King was only under option," McCaffrey replied.

"You know that's wrong," said Bell.

"Well, Toronto has four U.S. players and we have to keep up with them," McCaffrey answered.

On March 28, the club owners met in an executive session at the Hotel Warwick in New York to discuss and approve Bell's "squeeze play" against Canadian clubs. The meeting actually was requested by Detroit after Bell refused to recognize the Lions' signing of University of Miami halfback Gordon Malloy because he was under contract to the Montreal Alouettes. The commissioner changed his mind, however, after the raids by Toronto and Ottawa.

"It's up to the Canadian members now," Bell said after the nine-hour meeting ended. "They have no constitution, no central office, and nobody who has the authority to make an agreement. They'll have to control their own situation and their own clubs."

Bell told the owners that he felt that separate, workable agreements would pressure the renegade owners into line to respect valid NFL contracts as they became outnumbered. Then, hopefully, he would be able to negotiate a permanent armistice.

The commissioner emphasized that he had the power to act accordingly.

"I still have the authority to make an agreement," he explained, "if they're willing to be fair, to respect our contracts and options and to respect the college eligibility rules by not signing players before the completion of their four years of eligibility."

By a roll-call vote, at Bell's request to substantiate his position, the owners unanimously reaffirmed the commissioner's authority to approve or disapprove all player's contracts. Furthermore, the motion stated, "If he rules that a player or anyone connected with the National Football League has committed any action which the commissioner considers detrimental to the welfare of the National Football League or of professional football, after notice and hearing, his decision shall be final, conclusive, and unappealable."

Although it attracted very little publicity at the time, Bell arranged for an old friend, Joseph A. (Jiggs) Donoghue, the executive vice president of the Philadelphia Eagles, to be elected to a part-time, but influential, position of assistant treasurer of the NFL.

Donoghue, who turned out to be a very significant member of Bell's administration in his later years, was conceivably the commissioner's most trusted advisor and confidant. The two men met in France during World War I. Donoghue had been rejected for military service because of his 5-foot-4-inch height but convinced the Army to let him enlist as an entertainer. He was in Europe entertaining troops as an actor and, as he said later, "living it up" when he met Bell, who was serving with a hospital unit. The two became inseparable friends.

For years, Donoghue and Bell kept up a witty running banter, exchanging insults and entertaining guests at the weekly Maxwell Club luncheons in Philadelphia. Some observers billed their repartee as the city's longest-running vaudeville act. It was frequently said, in fact, that Donoghue was the only person who could get away with calling the NFL commissioner a "bum" to his face.

As the 1955 regular season got under way, the NFL's television picture got bleaker for the first time in years. DuMont continued to suffer financially. It was now carrying virtually no programming except for sports, but network officials assured Bell that it wasn't about to fold. DuMont even picked up a 10th NFL team, the Washington Redskins, and now only the two Chicago clubs were handling television independently.

Late in September, Bell announced that the league's Saturday night program was being curtailed because of what he called "excessive charges" for cables by AT&T. The commissioner explained that regional telecasts of some away games back to home cities would continue but that coast-to-coast and other long-distance regional telecasts appeared doomed because of the prohibitive price of cable. Sunday games would not be affected. The loss of the Saturday night television package would probably cost the participating teams between $250,000 and $300,000 in revenue.

"We want to televise regionally and nationally and we have plenty of sponsors willing to go along with us," Bell said. "However, when it comes to buying cable we're in trouble. We can't get the networks to take our Saturday games since they have programs such as Jackie Gleason and Perry Como on during the hours we want to telecast. We don't blame the networks. That's only good business."

Bell explained that it cost the NFL four times as much to buy cables for telecasts ($1 a mile per hour) as it did the networks (between 13 and 40 cents) because the networks bought it in great volume. The preceding year, DuMont had been able to buy cable at network prices but no longer qualified for this discount. Therefore, the overall package of televising long distances was now too high for most sponsors to absorb.

"AT&T really clobbered all of us," said Ted Bergmann, DuMont's managing director. "Regardless of whether you were dropping off programs in any city, you still had to pay your full cable cost on a monthly rental basis across the country. It cost a lot of money and the only way you could amortize it was to have stations along the way carry your programs. And if they didn't, you were paying through the nose just to run past the cities. It got very prohibitive. I think our cable bill was $2.5 million a year."

Bell finally convinced one of the major networks to hop aboard the pro football bandwagon on a national basis for the first time when NBC agreed to carry the NFL championship game for a one-year $100,000 fee.

The regular season itself caused considerably more grief to the commissioner than he usually was forced to endure. It was particularly painful after Bell found it necessary to fine his old friend Walter Kiesling, the coach of the Pittsburgh Steelers, $500 for an altercation with officials following a last-second, 27–26 loss to the Rams in Los Angeles in Week 2.

Kiesling had the reputation for being soft-spoken and easygoing. But he had to be restrained when he charged toward referee Joe Gonzales and made gestures after the Rams won the game with a field goal following a personal foul penalty against the Steelers. Earlier in the game, he had grabbed head linesman James Underhill by the arm.

"I had to take into consideration his long and fine record with the league over a long period of years," said Bell, who could have suspended Kiesling for life and fined him $2,000. "His record is very clean in every way. It was one of faithfulness."

Then the October 24, 1955, issue of *Life* magazine hit the newsstands with an exposé entitled "Savagery on Sunday." The article criticized the "epidemic" of dirty play in professional football and included a number of incriminating photographs. It focused primarily on two members of the Philadelphia Eagles, Frank (Bucko) Kilroy, a middle guard, and Wayne Robinson, a linebacker.

The commissioner later encouraged the two Eagles players to initiate a $250,000 libel suit against Time, Inc., the magazine's publisher. The four-page complaint was filed in U.S. district court in Philadelphia on October 28.

The case would not come to trial for another two years—not until April 1958. Then, after eight days of testimony from scores of players and league officials including Commissioner Bell, the jury awarded Kilroy and Robinson $5,000 each for damage to their reputations and an additional $6,600 each for punitive damages.

Bell was quite familiar with Kilroy, who played his football at Philadelphia's Northeast Catholic High School and Temple University before joining the NFL as a member of the Steagles in 1943. The commissioner had once fined Kilroy $250 following an incident in a preseason game when Kilroy kicked Ray Bray of the Chicago Bears in the groin.

"My wife gave him hell," Kilroy later said in Stuart Leuthner's book *Iron Men*. "She told him that he had cost her a new coat, so Bert said if I behaved myself and didn't get thrown out of any more games he'd give me the money back. I didn't get into any real trouble the rest of the season, and after the last game, Bert gave me a check and made me endorse it over to my wife. The joke was that Bert made a mistake and the check was for $500. When she called Bert and told him about it, he said, 'Boy am I lucky. If Bucko had gotten his hands on that money, I would have never seen the other $250.'"

The smoke had just begun to settle after the *Life* magazine article when Cleveland Browns quarterback Otto Graham again put Bell on the defensive by charging that professional football is "rough, tough, and dirty."

Alleging that game officials were allowing players to get away with too much rough stuff, Graham then took a swipe at the commissioner by saying that Bell and the club owners "could do something about it, if they wanted to. Things haven't got out of hand yet, but unless something is done, they will."

Reached at his Narberth home, Bell told *Philadelphia Bulletin* sportswriter Frank Yeutter that the "game is not the way Graham describes it." He pointed out that some of the flare-ups in the game resulted from the continuance of the present rule, which allowed a ball carrier to continue going forward until he was actually downed. Being "actually downed," Bell explained, is when "the ball carrier goes to the ground with anything but hands and feet touching the ground and when he is detained by a defensive player."

The commissioner added that it is difficult for a ball carrier to know when he is being held. It is equally confusing to the defensive player to know when the ball carrier is actually down. Hence, when the ball carrier hits the ground, the pile-ups occur. The defensive players want to make certain the ball carrier isn't going to spring to his feet and take off again.

"I introduced a rule that provided when a defensive man makes contact with the ball carrier and the ball carrier goes down, the ball is dead at that point," Bell said. "We needed ten votes to pass my proposed rule. We got eight." (Bell finally got the rule changed after the 1955 season.)

The commissioner couldn't understand why the bigger, stronger players of today should complain that the game is so rough and tough. "I played football long before these guys did. I wasn't as big as a lot of them. I had my nose broken three times. I got a broken collarbone, several cracked ribs, and a badly injured knee. I didn't consider the game dirty. Pro football today is a highly aggressive game. The teams are so evenly balanced and so closely bunched that competition is bound to be aggressive. Under the present rule that I oppose, flare-ups and pile-ups are bound to occur. But I've had no reports from officials or club owners that the game is dirty."

Bell was particularly incensed by Graham's scathing criticism. Just a few months earlier he had helped make the Browns' quarterback the highest-paid player in the league. Graham once described how it happened to his teammate, Mike McCormack, the Hall-of-Famer who later coached the Philadelphia Eagles, Baltimore Colts, and Seattle Seahawks.

"Graham had announced his retirement after the 1954 season, but coach Paul Brown wanted him to come back and play in 1955," McCormack later said in an interview with NFL Films.

"Otto tells the story that he went into Paul's office and said, 'Paul, if I come back for the '55 season, I want to be the highest paid player in the league.' So Paul got Bert Bell on the phone and he explained the situation and Bert told him, 'Well, Doak Walker is making $24,000 and I know if you'd accept $25,000 for the '55 season, you'd be the highest paid player in the league.' So Otto did."

Early in December, Bell teamed up with his longtime buddy, John B. Kelly, the former Olympic rowing hero, to lobby for a new stadium in Philadelphia to replace the city's outdated facilities. Kelly was the construction magnate whom Bell had unsuccessfully touted for NFL commissioner more than a dozen years previously.

Testifying before the City Council, both men called for a double-decked multipurpose facility with ample parking and complete access to public transportation. It was desperately needed, they said, to replace the dirty, antiquated Connie Mack Stadium, the crumbling eyesore of a home field for both the Phillies and Eagles. The city had recently lost its American League baseball franchise when the Athletics moved to Kansas City in 1954.

"What a place," former Eagles tackle Marion Campbell once exclaimed about the stadium formerly known as Shibe Park. "I don't think the groundskeepers ever showed up except to collect their pay. The field was so bad, you could've played hockey and basketball on it and not hurt it. Late in the season, you couldn't put a hole in that field with a jackhammer. Our locker room? I don't think we had one."

"People are disgusted with traffic and parking conditions and I don't want to fight it either," Bell said.

Estimating that from 60 to 70 percent of the fans attending six Eagles home games came from out of town, the former Birds owner observed, "I could have gotten the Eagles a better deal than they now have if they had wanted to move to another city."

Kelly recommended doing away with the musty, 100,000-capacity Municipal Stadium and then shocked city officials by adding, "I would tear down [University of Pennsylvania's historic] Franklin Field. And if we soon don't do something, we may lose both the Phillies and the Eagles."

After hearing more testimony, Bell walked out of the City Council chambers, hopped down the steps to the first floor, and said goodbye to his friend Jack Kelly in the City Hall courtyard. As usual, a number of passersby stopped to shake hands with the commissioner, who was in his familiar jovial mood despite being told again by municipal authorities that a new stadium was a long way off.

Bell had just settled back in his Center City office when Joe Labrum came bursting through the door with a copy of a copyrighted story written by Vincent X. Flaherty in the *Los Angeles Examiner*'s December 13 edition.

"The grenade that was touched off in the front office of the Los Angeles Rams when Daniel F. Reeves, president of the club, was put on notice exploded in the office of Bert Bell, the pro football commissioner, late last week," the story began.

Flaherty explained that a secret telephone vote had recently been taken among the 12 National League owners in an effort to fire the commissioner and that the voted ended in a 6–6 deadlock, which was far short of the 10 votes needed to remove him. Bell would have been offered five years' salary in settlement for his contract and another vote would be taken at the upcoming owners' meeting.

Los Angeles, San Francisco, Green Bay, Detroit, Cleveland, and the Chicago Cardinals voted to fire Bell, according to Flaherty. New York, Philadelphia, Washington, Baltimore, Pittsburgh, and the Chicago Bears voted to retain the commissioner.

"Several National League owners have had differences with the commissioner," the article continued. "His latest run-in with a club representative came on Monday, November 28, when a draft meeting was held at the Bellevue Stratford Hotel in Philadelphia. Ed Pauley, Jr., representing his father, complained bitterly to Bell about the officiating the day before when the Rams were almost knocked out of the championship by severe penalties in the last moments of the fray. Bell became angered by the younger Pauley's protest and [used] explosive language. 'Tell your father he can sell his stock,' Bell was heard to say."

The argument between Pauley and Bell centered on three straight penalties called against the Rams in the last two minutes of the game, which helped the Philadelphia Eagles take a temporary 21–20 lead.

"The weird officiating caused some of the Rams to feel they were being jobbed," Flaherty wrote. "Motion pictures showed there was technical justification for the penalties, but Tom Fears, the great Los Angeles end, complained: 'An official could call the same kind of penalties on every play. But this man called three in a row that just about knocked us out of the game. None of the fouls were flagrant enough to warrant that kind of damage.' Sid Gillman, the Rams' coach, also was bitter about the unusual action, but he calmed down when Los Angeles won out in the last seven seconds of play, 23–21, on Les Richter's 26-yard field goal."

The flare-up between Bell and the owners of the Rams began when Reeves was ousted as the team's operational head by his partners that included, in addition to Pauley, Fred Levy, Hal Seley, and entertainer Bob Hope. The commissioner was known to strongly support Reeves in his campaign to remain in charge of the club.

"Meanwhile, Reeves has been mustering strength among the owners with whom he has been associated many years," Flaherty's article continued. "According to the league's constitution and by-laws, Reeves has the power to call for a dissolution of the partnership, in which case the club can be put up for sale by auction to the highest bidder. However, before a new owner can take possession, he must be approved by 10 of the 12 owners. Reeves believes he can get the necessary 10 votes in the event he repurchases the club by auction."

Most, but not all, of the NFL owners quickly jumped to Bell's defense—as they had back in 1950 when rumors surfaced that the two California clubs had been angling for his removal. Published reports this time indicated that only two clubs were not in the commissioner's corner—Los Angeles for the reasons mentioned above, and the Chicago Cardinals because Bell reportedly wanted the franchise to move to Buffalo.

Edwin J. Anderson, president of the Lions, and Verne C. Lewellen, general manager of the Green Bay Packers, vigorously denied Flaherty's allegations that their clubs voted to oust the commissioner.

"The report that Bell's job is in jeopardy is strictly the bunk as far as I'm concerned," said Anderson. "I'm certain no such meeting ever was held," added Lewellen, who called the story "completely false."

"Nothing to it," fumed George Preston Marshall, the owner of the Redskins. "The only thing we're concerned about is Bell's health. We want him there for 40 more years."

"Never heard of such a thing," said Paul Brown, the coach and general manager of the Cleveland Browns.

"Most ridiculous story I ever heard," sniffed Tim Mara of the New York Giants.

Bell later told *Philadelphia Bulletin* sports editor Ed Pollock that Pauley's complaints were made not at the league meeting but at the commissioner's suite in the Bellevue Stratford. Concerning his use of "explosive language," Bert said, "I don't know what kind of language you want to call it, but it wasn't soft. It's against league by-laws for anyone connected with the league or a club to publicly criticize officials, and anyone doing so can be cited for conduct detrimental to football. Anyone who does can't expect to get a soft answer from me."

Meanwhile, NFL attendance for the 1955 season reached new highs for the fifth straight year as more than 2,520,000 fans attended 72 regular-season games, a 14 percent increase over 1954.

A record NFL championship game crowd of 85,693 filled the Los Angeles Coliseum and watched Otto Graham wind up his career by leading Cleveland to a 38–14 win over the Rams on December 26. Graham passed for two touchdowns and ran for two others and the Browns intercepted Norman Van Brocklin six times as the league provided a perfect showcase for NBC's first national telecast.

Two days later, the phone rang in Ralph Bernstein's home in northwest Philadelphia. It was 3:00 A.M. The Associated Press sportswriter groggily picked it up and heard a gruff voice on the other end. "Hey kid, what are you doing?" asked Bert Bell. "I'm sleeping, just like normal people do at this time," Bernstein answered rather testily.

Bell then proceeded to tip Ralph off that his chief competitor, the United Press, had just learned that the Mara family had been offered $1 million to sell the New York Giants. "I want to make sure that you don't miss out on this story," said Bell. "I just want to keep you covered."

Bernstein quickly dressed, rushed into the Associated Press office in Center City, made a few phone calls, and soon had the story on the national wire, a story with major ramifications for the Giants and the entire NFL.

The Giants had indeed been offered a cool million for the franchise, but the Mara family turned it down. Ernie Accorsi, who would later become the club's general manager, recalled hearing the details behind the incredible offer a number of years later. The account came from Wellington Mara, one of the two sons of Tim Mara, the team's owner.

"Wellington was 38. Jack, the other son, was 42 or 43," Accorsi explained,

> "Mr. Mara came into their office and said, 'I just got a call from the commissioner. He wants to come up and talk to me. It's very important.' Bert soon arrived and said, 'Look Tim. I just got an offer. I can't tell you who it's from but he's a very wealthy Texan and he wants to offer you a million dollars for your ball club. I don't know how you can possibly turn it down.'
>
> "Bert went on telling Tim how important he and his team were to the league, and all that. The Giants weren't making any money at the time, plus the younger Maras never had any outside interests. The old man did. He owned a piece of Gene Tunney and had been a racetrack cowboy. Once the team got off the ground—by that time it was way off the ground—he didn't do any of that stuff.
>
> "Wellington told me that his dad was only a $2 bettor. They weren't poor, but they didn't have a lot of money. 'There's only one condition to this sale,' Bell told Tim. 'It's on the condition that this

new prospective owner gets a lease to play in Yankee Stadium. He thinks it's important to upgrade this prestigious franchise.'

"Wellington told me that he had long suspected that the Texan was Clint Murchison, Jr., but he was pretty sure it was not. The timing—it was in 1955 and Murchison ends up buying the Cowboys in '59—would have made sense, but Wellington said 'I could never prove it and we never knew who it was. My dad didn't say anything and Jack and I were just stunned and thought *Oh No!*' This was because Jack ran the business and Wellington ran the personnel side.

"Wellington hung out with some of the older players. He and Chuck Conerly were about the same age and were really close friends. There was like a dead silence and Wellington said, 'Pop, what are you going to do?' He replied, 'What we are going to do, we're going to Yankee Stadium and get a lease to play there. If this is worth a million dollars for somebody to move to Yankee Stadium, then we'll move to Yankee Stadium. We better move over there quickly.'

"Wellington explained, 'Jack and I were in the room later when my dad called Bert Bell back and he said, 'We're not going to sell. We're going to keep it.' I don't know what Bert said on the other end, but I remember my father saying, 'I can't do it to the boys.' Tim pretty much turned the team over to Jack and Wellington at that point. Moving to Yankee Stadium was a huge step up for them because they won the championship in '56 and playing in that regal tabernacle added so much prestige to the National Football League."

Bell later told Bernstein that the bid for the Giants was the largest offer for a franchise in the history of pro football. It would have given the Maras 400 times their original investment. "After acting as emissary in this million dollar offer, I felt depressed for a week," the commissioner said. "I bought the Philadelphia Eagles many years ago for $2,500 and sold them for $160,000."

Ironically, the Giants were one of only three NFL teams to suffer a drop in attendance in 1955. They drew 163,847 fans for six games for their 30th and final season at the Polo Grounds, ranking ninth out of the league's 12 teams.

At the end of the year, in an article exclusively written for the United Press, Bell again tried to make the case that professional football isn't a dirty game.

"The teams are so evenly matched in manpower and ability, and so close to each other in their respective conferences through most of the season, that the competition is bound to produce a game in which aggressiveness, individually and collectively, is paramount to success," the commissioner wrote.

"We have what we believe to be the most competent officials in football. They are men of considerable experience not only in football but in other walks of life. They know the rules and how to enforce them. They would not stand for dirty football any more than I would stand for it. If they should see any indication of it, they would quickly respond."

Claiming that the officials "called very few disqualifications and none of these were for dirty football," Bell added, "If the game is dirty, as some carping critics allege, isn't it natural to expect that the number of players sent off the field for conduct detrimental to the game would be much greater?"

Privately, the commissioner was telling friends that he was beginning to hear more criticism about violence and dirty play in professional football. With the advent of television, more fans were taking notice and expressing misgivings about the rough behavior of some players. Also, it wasn't the first time that Graham popped off. The quarterback had recently written an article for *Sports Illustrated* claiming that "football is getting too vicious."

Surely, Bell had occasionally moved in to curb the violence on the field. Back in 1947, for example, he had suspended Jack Matheson, the outstanding Chicago Bears end, for one game for fighting and had been pleasantly relieved when George Halas backed him up by saying that it was "entirely within the province of Mr. Bell" to take such action.

Maybe it was time, the commissioner thought, to tone down the action—both on the field and in the perception of the fans, who could now see the game for themselves on television.

31. The Commissioner's Working Style

Although he was frequently compared favorably with major league baseball's legendary commissioner Judge Kenesaw Mountain Landis—"Bell was the second and last of the czars," Lyall Smith wrote in the *Detroit Free Press*—Bert disdained the term *czar*.

"I do not wish to behave like a czar," he would say when he periodically stormed out of owners' meetings totally frustrated by their unwillingness to accept his direction. "But unless you permit me to save the game by running it my own way, I will give it back to you."

"Actually I think he got my uncle John to write that into the NFL Constitution that he was the sole arbiter of everything," Bell's son Upton explained. "A lot of the league's bylaws were written by John C. Bell. I remember club owners often telling me, 'The great thing about Bert is we don't have to think anymore. He thinks for us.'"

Bell didn't mind doing the thinking for the owners, but he disdained the squabbling that went on at the league meeting, especially when news of the quarreling got out to the press.

"When they bicker, they tend to imply that he—czar Bell—is the stooge of one rival owner or the other," John Lardner once wrote in *Newsweek*. "Practically every week, de Benneville said, the public gets the impression that he makes his home in the hip pocket of one of his employers. In bad weeks he is accused of belonging body and soul to as many as three magnates, and to spend all his time representing their interests against the rights and interests of the others.

"'Let us all hang together, or we will hang separately,' said de Benneville Bell, in effect. He never spoke a truer word."

The commissioner preferred conducting league meetings in his hometown. First of all, he hated to fly and didn't like to travel unless it was absolutely necessary. And, as Upton recalls, he also wanted the sessions to be short as possible.

"My father would say, 'We're going to have them in Philadelphia because we're not coming here for everybody to be screwing around. Get the meetings done and you go home or go out with your girlfriends or do what you want.'"

Ed Kiely remembers that Bell would frequently entertain the league's 10 or 12 beat writers in his hotel suite. "He'd have a bar and a couple of bottles of whiskey, some beer and maybe a few sandwiches," explained the former Pittsburgh Steelers public relations director, who recalls Bell's assistant Joe Labrum counting the bottles of liquor to make sure the full containers didn't slip out the door.

"The writers would come in and ask a lot of questions and everything. Then he'd get tired and he'd go in and sleep for a couple of hours. Then he'd come back out again and start talking to them. It was the funniest thing you ever saw in your life. My old friend Joe King, of the *New York World Telegram*, one time didn't like the sandwiches and went out and got a roasted chicken from a butcher shop. He brought it in and had his own party."

"League meetings were always a scream," said Baltimore sportswriter John Steadman in an interview with NFL Films. "Bert would be going through the halls, the pressroom area, and the executive area where the leagues were going to meet. He'd say, 'Who wants chicken sandwiches? Who wants chocolate ice cream? Order what you want, boys,' meaning the press. 'It's all on the Eagles. They made all the money this year.'"

"The league loved Bert Bell for that," explained Jim Gallagher of the Philadelphia Eagles. There were only a half-dozen writers waiting outside— guys from the AP, UP, and the Philly and New York papers, maybe. Bert would always stop the meeting and go outside to chat with them. He knew their deadlines. He never hid anything and sometimes would go *off-the-record* to make sure that they were informed. He was always very honest with the media, always anxious to fill the boys in."

"The sportswriters always had a poker game going at the league meetings," recalled Art Daley of the *Green Bay Press Gazette*. "During breaks, Bert would come out and kibitz with us. He'd walk around the poker table, look at our playing hands and say, 'Let me take a look. I can do better than that.' He loved to play poker but said that it wouldn't look right for him to join us. He was always a lot of fun."

David Eisenberg of the *New York Journal American* once wrote that to newspapermen, the commissioner has always remained one of the boys. "The secret of Bell's success is that he has always remained his natural self. He understands the owners, having been one of them. He fights without hesitation, which several other league heads fail to do. He remained personally friendly with virtually every newspaperman covering the pro football beat."

Dick Hackenberg of the *Chicago Sun-Times* remembered that Bell had "a wrinkled face that appeared unreasonably stern until you saw the twinkle in the wrinkle. Then he was the kindest of friends, the most jovial of interviewees, and the funniest story-teller ever."

"Once I phoned Bell at his Philadelphia office," explained sportswriter John Devaney. "I never met him and he didn't know me. But I called him from New York because I was doing an article on Johnny Unitas and a Colt official had told me I couldn't visit their camp to talk to Unitas.

"I told this to Bell. In his gruff voice he said he'd call me back. Fifteen minutes later he called me. He'd just finished talking to the Colt official. 'You go down to the Colt camp,' he said. 'And if anybody tries to stop you from interviewing Unitas, call me.' Nobody tried to stop me. Bert Bell had spoken."

Not all of the league owners appreciated Bell's candor with sportswriters. "Sometimes I get irritated at the way he runs meetings—running out all the time to talk to newspapermen," one of them told sportswriter Jack Orr. "I think that's a sloppy way to do business. But I know where his heart is—whatever's good for our league."

"Why shouldn't I be available to press, radio, and television?" Bell once said to sportswriter Ralph Bernstein. "They provide us with millions of dollars' worth of free publicity a year. We couldn't exist without them."

"Bell has been good copy, a great story teller, a newspaperman's delight since he was in college," Stan Baumgartner wrote in *The Sporting News*. One year, writers were having difficulty digging up interesting angles about an upcoming *Philadelphia Inquirer* Charities football game between the Eagles and the College All-Stars.

"One afternoon, Bell casually made the remark, 'If those collegians beat my professionals, I'll jump off the Delaware River Bridge.' It was a statement too good to keep and went into the paper. For the next ten days all Bell heard was, 'Hey Bert, when are you gonna jump off the bridge?'"

"Bell had his shortcomings, but he was a good commissioner," recalled Ed Kiely. "He helped to keep the thing afloat. The league wasn't as complicated then as it is now. He and Art Rooney were very close. When Bert needed somebody to get him a couple of votes on a league matter for an amendment, he'd see Art and Art would help him out."

"My father would talk to Bert every single night on the phone," explained Art Rooney's son, Dan, the current chairman of the Pittsburgh Steelers. "He really liked Bert and had a lot of confidence in him. He thought he was a very good commissioner, especially getting TV involved.

Bert was a very gracious guy. He could talk to everybody—owners, players, fans, members of Congress. He was a consensus builder."

"We used to gather in Bert's room and we'd talk far into the night," Art Rooney reminisced in a 1975 issue of an NFL game program. "Bert was a very persuasive man, a politician at heart. The battles between owners were classics, but Bert would just sit there, usually in his shorts, and interrupt only if it was needed to keep peace.

"Bert wasn't the kind of fellow who could stay up all night. When he got tired, he'd just get up and go into the other room and go to bed. Then when he got up in the morning, he'd come back to where we were, and a lot of times we'd still be going at it from the night before. Bert would quietly get back into his chair and resume his role, as though he'd never left."

Bell also had the flair for the dramatic. "When tempers got really strained at league meetings, he'd actually look like he was crying sometimes," recalled his son Upton. "When he wasn't getting his way, he would dab at his eyes with his handkerchief and say, 'Oh my God, you fellas got me so tired, my teeth hurt.' Then he'd take out his false teeth and put them in his water glass in front of him.

"Even though people would be screaming at the top of their lungs, they would quiet down when they saw Bert's teeth sitting in the middle of the table. Invariably some of the owners would start yelling at Halas or Marshall, or someone, telling them to shut up and sit down. 'Look how you're making Bert feel,' they'd say. 'He's crying. He's so tired, he's got his teeth on the table. Let's just pass the damn thing!' "

Stanley Woodward of the *New York Herald Tribune* remembers the old days when he spoke at owners' meetings to promote an All-Star game. "The shouting and name calling was deafening," he explained. "Bell produced order in the house, probably because he was a louder shouter and had a quality in his voice like the sound of a buzz-saw going through a pine knot. When shouting was out of order, he persuaded and in no time he had the factions exorcised and the brothers actually considering each other's interests."

New York Giants owner Wellington Mara once explained Bell's success with the club owners to *Pittsburgh Post-Gazette* columnist Phil Musick: "He'd have delegates staked out in advance; he always knew how many votes he needed to pass something, and where to get them. He could persuade you. Politics is the art of the possible and Bert knew what could be attempted. He passed important pieces of league legislation in four-day meetings by holding them until the last two hours because he knew we all wanted to go home. There wouldn't be big league football today without him."

"To deal with strong-willed people like George Halas in Chicago and George Preston Marshall in Washington took a diplomat of the order of Disraeli," former *Philadelphia Daily News* sports editor Larry Merchant said in an interview with NFL Films.

"How is it that this robust firebrand, who looks like an overage Mickey Rooney, can take strong stands while his counterparts in other sports stand timorously in the wings?" asked Jack Orr in his 1958 profile, "The Commissioner Who Commissions." "How is it he can convince the owners when necessary? Why do they stand for the type of commissioner who tells them off?"

Joe Donoghue, Bell's close friend and assistant league treasurer, had a logical explanation. "He knows more than they do, that's why," Donoghue told Orr. "He has been in the game for a long time and he knows every angle. The owners know he knows what he's doing and, whatever it is, must be good for football. I have seen the respect for Bert grow gradually over the years. They know he is square. He will fight and argue, but he doesn't hold a grudge. No matter how friendly you are with him, if he thinks you are wrong, he'll tell you. They know there wouldn't be big-league football without him."

No one knew Bert Bell better than "Jiggs" Donoghue. They were like the Odd Couple—the blue-collar city guy from a hardscrabble neighborhood in North Philadelphia, and Bell, a classic blue blood from the uppity Main Line. Even though they grew up under totally different circumstances, they were virtually inseparable ever since first meeting in France during World War I. Donoghue joined the Eagles as their ticket manager in 1949.

"Mr. Donoghue was a character," said Jim Gallagher, the Philadelphia Eagles executive who married Donoghue's daughter, Betty, in 1958. "He was a short, friendly guy with a great personality. They'd be on the phone all the time. Their offices were a little more than a block away. Mr. Donoghue would say to Bert: 'Don't use your phone. Just open your window and I can hear you clearly.'"

Jack Orr once asked Bell what he thought about the owners and the way they let him operate as commissioner.

"They're just great guys," he replied while puffing on a cigarette and walking around his office. "They are terrific fellows because most of them have been through the hard times this league has seen. They are not in it primarily for money."

Asked if the owners ever get out of line or if he ever had to slap them down, Bell said, "I do it only occasionally. You never read about it because it never gets to a point where I issue a proclamation or anything like that.

"I'm in touch with them all the time by this telephone here, and if they are doing something I don't think is in the best interest of the game, I ask them to stop. It says so in this book, the league constitution. That's what I go by. It says that anything the commissioner thinks is detrimental to the game, he can throw out. For instance, I want football clubs in this league, corporations exclusively for football. I don't want holding companies or corporations with other interests or tax gimmicks. Just football."

"Mr. B. was a very interesting man," recalled Elaine Emerson Blair, who worked as Bert Bell's secretary from 1950 to 1957. "He was a man very dedicated to his work. He loved football beyond words. At times he was very demanding. He required everything to be done perfectly. Often, he would want two things done at once. I would have to say, 'Mr. B., the type-writer can only do one thing at a time.' But at other times he was a very happy-go-lucky type of person. They were fun days. I enjoyed every minute of it. I never had a dull moment."

Blair had been working for H. Jamison Swartz, Penn's athletic director, when Joe Labrum invited her to join the commissioner's staff. Besides handling Bell's telephone calls, she took care of all player's contracts, press credentials, and league statistics—typing up the latter early on Monday mornings and having 13 carbon copies available for the Western Union delivery man before 10:00 A.M.

The NFL headquarters on Walnut Street had two secretaries at the time who shared separate offices with their bosses. Ruth McClellan, a high school classmate of Blair's, worked for Labrum. Dennis Shea, Austin Gunsel, and Harry Standish squeezed into the other office. There was no air conditioning. "We frequently had to turn the fan on my desk off because it would blow papers all over," recalled Blair, whose husband, Jack, still bowls every week with Gino Marchetti, the former Baltimore Colts defensive star, near their home outside West Chester, Pennsylvania.

The commissioner frequently clashed behind closed doors with the owners, but most of the time everything would be forgotten a few days later. His battles with Cleveland owner and coach Paul Brown lasted longer. They dated back to the days when the Browns dominated the league, and they led many people to believe that the two strong-willed men simply did not like each other.

"Not so," said Bell's son Bert Jr. "My dad once made the Browns change their uniforms at night because he knew that Paul Brown was a sharp guy, always looking for an edge. Paul Brown liked to use white uniforms for night games, making it tougher for the opposing team to pick up his players clearly under the lights.

"Paul thought my dad didn't like him because of the uniform situation, the headsets, things like that. I asked my dad one time if something happened to you, who would you want to be commissioner? I was curious to know what a guy would think about his possible successor. He said Paul Brown.

"I got a chance to tell Paul Brown that one time when we were sitting next to each other at a banquet in Philadelphia. He told me that he always thought that the commissioner was after him because he was from the other league—the old All-America Football Conference."

There had been some tension between the two men back in 1949 when reports of a merger between the NFL and AAFC first leaked out. Brown initially hinted that he might not go along with the merger. "I am disappointed in the entire settlement of the situation," he said at the time. "This is not to be the distinct two-league setup that I and others had hoped for." Bell said that he didn't anticipate any difficulty with Brown and he was right.

In the 1950s, Bell hired Jim Gallagher, the Philadelphia Eagles executive, to sit at his side and take notes at the league meetings.

"They were held in typical smoke-filled rooms because nearly everyone was smoking," Gallagher explained. "Many of them smoked cigars like Art Rooney and Joe Donoghue. Bert Bell just kept puffing away on those long Chesterfield cigarettes. He had a little microphone in front of him but most of the time he didn't even need it."

Gallagher remembers how Bell murdered the King's English at the annual player draft meetings. "God bless Bert," Gallagher explained in an interview with NFL Films. "We used to laugh at him. He used to call San Jose San *Josie*. Juniata College in Western Pennsylvania was *Juanita*.

"My mother always told my father that for an aristocrat he used bad grammar," said Upton. "He would answer her back by saying, 'Frances, it ain't nothing I can do about it.' His voice sounded like an untuned chain saw. He had this way of speaking—slow, with an exaggerated 'R,' like a truck in second gear."

John Steadman once wrote in the *Baltimore Sun* that Bell's voice sounded like "gravel rolling inside a tin can." His voice sounded like "scraping sandpaper over an empty orange crate," some of his other friends said.

The commissioner didn't make much of a fashion statement, either. "Fancy clothes he just didn't like," explained Upton, who remembers his dad owning two double-breasted suits at a time—a brown gabardine and a blue serge, plus a camel hair top coat that he would often wear until June 1.

"My father also had this terrible-looking old hat," Upton recalled. "He must have been wearing it since Garfield was president. Maybe even before then. One time his buddies that he hung around with bought him a new hat for his birthday and made a big production of presenting it to him.

"Naturally, he was overwhelmed and thanked them profusely. They told him that being the commissioner he should make a better-looking appearance. They took off his old hat, threw it on the ground, and jumped on top of it. But my father leaned down, picked it up, and put it back on his head. He took the new gift hat home but never wore it."

Notorious as a chain-smoking chocoholic who napped every afternoon, Bell never took a vacation or a day off. He was fond of working 18-hour days, eating, drinking, and talking football. He had no time left for hobbies. At home he spent countless hours working three or four telephones deep into the night. His long-distance phone calls cost upward of $10,000 a year.

Ed Pollock, the sports editor of the *Philadelphia Bulletin,* once tried telephoning Bell at the Philadelphia Racquet Club at 11:30 P.M. There was no response. The phone rang again and again.

"I'm afraid he's asleep," the operator said. "I'll have to send a boy to wake him up."

"There's no need to do that," Pollock replied. "Oh, no," the operator insisted. "Mr. Bell left orders. We're to wake him up for every telephone call."

A few minutes later, a drowsy voice said hello. "What's the idea of putting yourself on call 24 hours a day?" Pollock asked. "Even a football commissioner is supposed to sleep."

"Not at 30 grand a year, he isn't," Bell replied. "Anyhow, I was only dozing."

"I live by the phone," the commissioner once told columnist Jimmy Breslin. "I made a rule about phone calls years ago and my wife didn't like it for a while. That was to take any call that came, no matter what time of the day. When you're in this business you got to remember the other fellow is making a living."

"I often said that his heart was shaped like a football," quipped Baltimore's John Steadman.

"He was forever on a diet, but somehow the diet never seemed to work," recalled Pittsburgh's Ed Kiely, who often watched Bert order black coffee, saccharin, and two extra-large scoops of chocolate ice cream at meals.

The commissioner was a huge baseball fan. During the summer, he would sit until 2:00 or 3:00 in the morning rehashing that night's Phillies or A's game with major league umpires like Charlie Berry and Cal Hubbard at Lew Tendler's restaurant, often with his two sons at his side, sipping sodas in a booth while he drank cup after cup of coffee.

Tendler's was Philadelphia's version of Toots Shor's Restaurant in New York, and Bell counted both restaurateurs among his best friends. Others who were close to him included sports writing legend Grantland Rice, George Halas, Bing Miller, Eddie Gottlieb, Herman Taylor the boxing promoter, and, of course, Art Rooney, the founder of the Pittsburgh Steelers.

Bell preferred to write out everything himself, in longhand. He even wrote terms of the NFL's agreement with the AAFC on a legal-sized pad. But he insisted that all correspondence be kept as short as possible. He would become terribly annoyed if colleagues got too verbose. Legalese absolutely drove him up the wall, as Bill Campbell, the Philadelphia Eagles' play-by-play man, learned the hard way.

"When I was at WCAU, if there was anything involving the signing of a contract that concerned the league, Bert was involved in it somehow," Campbell explained. "The general manager of 'CAU didn't know Bert from Adam, but he knew that I did. He used to send me up to Bert's office on City Line Avenue with these documents.

"Sometimes it would be three or four pages or more and Bert would always say the same thing: 'Why does this have to be three and four and five pages? Boil it all down to one page and bring it back.' He said he wanted things very simple. The guy who was our general manager didn't like that. So I used to say to him, 'Well you call Bert. I'm just a messenger boy here.' So he did one day. And Bert told him: 'Look, you boil all of this stuff down to one page and give it to Willie. And Willie will bring it up here and I'll sign the damn thing and that will be the end of it.'

"Now the station is sold by the *Philadelphia Bulletin* to CBS, so all our orders are coming from New York. Now we're told to run everything by CBS Legal. So I go up to Bert's office one day and said, 'Bert, the way we've been doing this is going to change. We're now owned by this big corporate thing in New York and I've been told to tell you that every document must be signed and run by the CBS Legal Department.'

And Bert said: 'I'll tell you what to tell them. You tell them that my father was the attorney general of Pennsylvania and my brother is the chief justice of the Pennsylvania Supreme Court. After living with those two guys all my life, I don't sign anything except "Happy Birthday!"'

"I said, 'You expect me to tell them that?' He said, 'You bet and you can quote me!' I called the Legal official at CBS and told him this. I thought the guy would die on the phone. But that was the end of it. We never heard another word. The general manager would dictate the stuff and I took it to

Bert. It was usually one page even though it had clauses in there like ASCAP music and all that legalese."

John Steadman recalled the time that the NFL records were being subpoenaed by some congressional committee. Sheriffs came into Bell's office. They said they were going to confiscate the league's records and would be back the following morning with an eighteen-wheeled truck to pick them up.

"Bert said, 'No, you can take them all now. Just pull open that top drawer of that file cabinet.' The league's records dating back to 1920, you could carry them in one hand. They were in five or six Manila envelopes.

"That's the way Bert [initially] ran the league. Most of it was out of his head. And he knew that the worst thing you could do was put a promise down in a letter, or make a statement on the letter that could come back, and you'd have to eat that or be liable for it in a court of law. So Bert didn't believe in writing letters."

That's the way the commissioner liked it—short and simple. "Why write it when you can say it?" he frequently exclaimed.

32. At Home in Narberth

Bert Bell's daily ritual at home in Narberth rarely changed. An early riser, he dressed quickly, went downstairs, and fried himself some eggs.

"I always dreaded what came next," his son Upton explained.

'GET UP, GET UP . . . THE SUN IS UP . . . THE BIRDS ARE IN THE ROOM . . .'

"Then he would follow with:

'OH, HOW I HATE TO GET UP IN THE MORNING. . . . OH HOW I HATE TO GET UP IN THE DAY . . .'

"You could hear him all over the house. But he loved to sing. His words were always kind of keyed in with something he wanted you to do."

The Saturday before Bell passed away, he was at home dressed in a sweatshirt, talking on the phone. As usual, he had the Penn football game on television.

"Barney Berlinger catches a pass and they beat Princeton or somebody," Upton recalled. "And in the middle of the telephone conversation, he breaks out singing:

'FIGHT ON, PENNSYLVANIA . . . BRING THE BALL RIGHT DOWN THAT FIELD . . .'

"He's screaming it all over the house, he was so thrilled by Penn. And then he would call another friend and start singing again: 'RED AND BLUE WE'RE WITH YOU . . .'"

Next to his family and his NFL cohorts like Joe Donoghue and Art Rooney, Bell got his greatest enjoyment hanging out with friends from the neighborhood at The Tavern, at 261 Montgomery Avenue in Bala Cynwyd in Lower Merion Township, and at Davis General Store, at 224 Haverford Avenue, in Narberth. He hardly ever missed a day at either place, stopping for newspapers and coffee in the morning at The Tavern or for a soda after dinner at Davis.

Every summer, Bell took the whole gang to Hershey for a few days—"Everything's on me, guys!"—where they sat in the upper deck of the old Memorial Stadium watching their beloved Eagles. Then they often partied into the wee hours of the morning.

Bert's cronies at the Narberth Sunrise Society, as he called it, included people like Ed Dixon, the neighborhood landscaper, Ox the Roofer, Clyde the Soda Jerk, and Jakes (Jiggs) Torchiano, the local gas station owner.

There were others who occasionally stopped by like Bing Miller, who played in two World Series for the Philadelphia Athletics; Willie Draper, a local basketball standout who was one of the few African Americans who lived in the town; and Bill Campbell, who would drop by after his morning radio show on WCAU.

"The days I didn't show up, he'd get on me," Campbell recalled. "He'd say, 'Willie, where were you yesterday?' "

"They were a great bunch of characters," Upton Bell explained. "It was hilarious for me as a kid watching my dad playing Liar's Poker with them. If he had a really sticky problem going on in the National Football League, or a new innovation he was considering, he would come down to the corner and discuss it with them. That's where he got his best advice unless he needed technical advice from an expert. They were all smart guys, town characters, who had their own businesses."

"After dinner, my father would change his clothes, walk down and get my mother a soda," Bert Jr. recalled. "Often, he'd have a milk shake that he wasn't supposed to have. Then, if it wasn't too hot, they'd all go outside, lean on the parking meters, and talk sports. He was never too much of a big shot that he couldn't be around them."

"Everybody knew Bert in Narberth," said Bell's colleague Austin Gunsel in an interview for *The Sporting News*. Gunsel was a neighbor who never formally met the commissioner until he called on him at his NFL office during the Department of Justice antitrust investigation in 1950–1951.

"We weren't close neighbors, but we used to see him on the street, in Davis' store, places like that," Gunsel remembered.

Bell felt especially close to Howard E. Davis, the owner of the general store—now known as Mapes 5 & 10—because his grandson, Eugene H. Davis Jr., had served as captain of the University of Pennsylvania football team in 1941. But the old man didn't always feel the same way toward the commissioner.

Victoria Donohoe, the longtime art critic of the *Philadelphia Inquirer,* and a neighbor of the Bell's, remembered why. "The Davis Store had a long marble soda fountain," she said. "Bert would be sitting there for a long time talking with his friends and old Mr. Davis would come out and tell him,

'You're taking up valuable space. I need this table for my customers.' And Bert would just order another coke."

Bob Paul, the University of Pennsylvania sports publicist who later became public relations director of the U.S. Olympic Committee, remembers frequently stopping at the store to buy an early edition of the *Philadelphia Inquirer.*

"One evening I said, Bert, I want to bring something to your attention. I don't believe that any of your fans have ever seen a game of yours on television. He said, 'What does that have to do with it?' I said television is black and white. It doesn't distinguish between the colors. I said I might be the only one who knows which team is the Eagles because of their helmets. So he said, 'What are you driving at?'

"I said, next fall, in 1956, the Ivy League is going to dress each team in its home colors and the visiting team is going to wear white and I suggest you do that for the pro's.

"And he bought it.

"That was accomplished over a Coca-Cola with ice."

33. The NFL Welcomes
Bubble Gum Cards and CBS-TV

In January 1956, the NFL owners commemorated the first Pro Bowl game by holding the annual league meetings and player draft at the Ambassador Hotel in Los Angeles.

The commissioner, of course, insisted on traveling by train. He was joined on the three-night cross-country ride by the league's new treasurer, Austin Gunsel, and Jim Gallagher, who had recently been appointed scouting director of the Philadelphia Eagles.

Glenn Davis, the former Army star who was working for the *Los Angeles Times,* met the train. "I was just a kid and didn't get a chance to meet him, Gallagher recalled. "But I remember that he made a big fuss over Bert Bell."

Gallagher was one of Bell's most trusted aides, even though he did not work full-time for the commissioner.

After the Eagles' home games on Sundays, Jim would rush from Connie Mack Stadium to Bell's office in Center City, answer the telephone, and type up the league statistics. Then he would head to the Post Office and mail copies to the Philadelphia and New York papers and the wire services.

For this work he received an extra $10 a week. Now the commissioner was paying him $100 for taking notes of the league meetings in shorthand and typing them up immediately after the proceedings. It was a tough job, but the money was good.

"The owners would be discussing some rule change and there'd be a lot of chatter going back and forth, a lot of confusion," Gallagher explained. "Bert would say, 'Get that vote down, Jimmy! Keep the meeting moving!' Teams voted in alphabetical order and it was difficult keeping up with the roll call. I probably got a couple of rules changed that didn't belong to be changed."

During the player draft, Gallagher sat at the head of a U-shaped table with Bell—trying to juggle his stenographic skills for the owners while processing player information for the Eagles.

"I was betwixt and between. I was taking shorthand, putting up names on the board, and calling out 'You're up next!' on one hand, while trying to coordinate information for our coaches," he recalled.

Meanwhile, the commissioner sat there, puffing on his Chesterfield cigarettes. He was thoroughly enjoying the proceedings. At one point he raved about the wonderful publicity the league was receiving. He told the owners that he had stopped to purchase newspapers in various cities and said that there was always something in the papers regarding the member clubs.

On the second day of the meetings in California, Bell announced the appointment of longtime referee Samuel (Mike) Wilson as the league's technical advisor on rules and supervisor of officials.

But his most newsworthy announcement had come the previous day when he described details of the NFL's first bubble gum card deal he had negotiated with the Bowman Card Company, an outfit that was soon purchased by Topps.

The NFL received about $17,000 for the first year for the cards, which were distributed to more than 70 million children. Bell predicted that the league "could do $10 million worth of business in five to ten years."

Sy Berger, who was Topps's sports and licensing vice president, negotiated the agreement with Bell. Berger was already well known as one of the shrewdest marketing executives in professional sports.

In 1952, he had designed and written the copy for the first modern set of major league baseball cards ever produced, and now Topps wanted to get into the football business. Berger was assigned to travel down from the company's headquarters in New York City to introduce himself to Bell.

Unbeknownst to the commissioner, it would not be their first meeting.

Back in October 1938, Berger, then a 15-year-old high school student, went to the Polo Grounds to watch the New York Giants defeat the Philadelphia Eagles, 17–7. The Birds happened to be coached by Bert Bell. After the game, Sy ran out onto the field, joining hundreds of other fans in a victory celebration.

"I saw a guy jump over the bleachers and run towards the crowd near Bert Bell," Berger recalled. "He had an accent. Suddenly he starts shouting, 'You dirty son of a bitch. . . . You killed that boy.' He was referring to Dave Smukler, the Eagles quarterback who had done everything that day. He ran, he kicked, he scored the touchdown, he kicked the extra point. After the game, Smukler was bleeding, and this guy pulled his arm back and belted Bert Bell right on the chin. He knocked him down on the ground, then walked away.

"And who was standing behind him? Me! I helped pick him up.

"When I introduced myself to Bert, I politely said, 'You should know me because I know you.' He replied, 'How should I know you?' And I told him about the day when he was killing his quarterback and this guy belted him. I said, 'I helped pick you up.' And he looked at me and said, 'Yeh, I remember—fat little kid.'

"So already we had a bonding. Then I looked at the wall and said, 'Wow, that's a beautiful picture. Boy, does your wife know that you have a picture like that hanging in your office?' He says, 'That *IS* my wife!' "

During their discussion, Bell emphasized that he was not primarily concerned about the financial aspects of the deal.

"I don't need money," he explained. "I need publicity! I have to show my owners that these cards are doing right for our league."

Berger mentioned a figure. "It really was a very slight payment," he recalled. Then reacting to Bell's "I've got plenty of money" statement—and being unsure if player's contracts stipulated any rights fees to sell the players' likenesses—Berger suggested that the lump-sum proceeds go into a fund for the players. Bell quickly agreed.

"We'll have a thing just like the baseball people have," the commissioner replied.

Berger took his boss, Joe Shorin, to Bell's summer home in Margate, to sign the contract.

"We talked a little, signed the contract and then Bert said, 'You know what? I'm going to take you guys to lunch. I'm going to take you to the Savoy.' And I'm thinking I spent some time at the Savoy in London during World War II and it was quite a ritzy place. My boss raised his eyes—the *Savoy?* We got into Bert's car, and we pull up and I'm thinking about a fancy restaurant. It was a kosher delicatessen.

"And that," said Berger, "was the start of the Bert Bell Benefit Fund." It was also the beginning of a lifelong friendship.

"Bert took to me like I was his son," Sy explained. "I came down to visit him three or four times a year and got to know his family and his boys. I loved him like a daddy. He was such a wonderful man. Just sitting at his desk in his small office, I learned so much. I felt that he was a great part of my life."

Later, on a number of occasions the commissioner told Sy that he would be awarded the next NFL franchise.

"I don't know if he was kidding me or not, but he seemed very sincere," Berger said. "He told me the story how Rosenbloom got the Baltimore deal and he said, 'The next expansion team in this league, you're going to get.' I said, 'Bert. I'm just a working stiff. I haven't got that kind of money.' And he said to me, 'Sy, they'll run after you with barrels full of cash.' "

Berger, who was known as the "Father of the Modern Baseball Card," worked for The Topps Company, Inc., for 50 years and has been a long-time advisor to baseball Hall-of-Famer Willie Mays, his best friend.

Elated over a 15.1 percent increase in attendance in 1955—only the New York Giants and Pittsburgh Steelers failed to show higher numbers at home—the owners closed the 1956 league meetings by awarding the commissioner a $10,000 bonus. "We voted Mr. Bell the money for all he did to make our success possible and as additional proof of the confidence the member clubs have in his leadership," they said in a statement.

When Bell returned to Philadelphia, he called a news conference on February 1 to announce for the first time that the NFL was seriously considering expanding, possibly into Miami and Buffalo.

"There is nothing immediate about this thing," the commissioner explained while emphasizing that no team in the league was for sale or contemplating moving. "We have to be ready for the future and expanding our league to 14 teams is a definite part of that future. I think Miami and Buffalo would be ideal for pro football, but we have to be sure."

Bell said that he had assigned Walter Wolfner of the Chicago Cardinals to investigate the possibility of putting a new team in Miami. Asked when the league would likely expand, the commissioner replied that it could happen when the bottom teams in each of the league's two conferences each win at least four games. "It's not too far away, either," he said.

Among the qualifications needed for a city to be considered, Bell mentioned a stadium with excellent parking facilities, public transportation, and multiple traffic arteries; a long lease and first call on playing dates; a fair and equitable rental deal; and the ability of the club to own and operate its own program magazine.

The commissioner's call for expansion came at the time when he was being pressured by a number of owners of clubs in the larger cities to do something about the Green Bay Packers—either straighten them out or throw them out of the league.

In addition to representing the smallest city in professional sports, the team played its home games in an old, dilapidated stadium that would be an embarrassment to many high school teams, not to mention NFL players. Moreover, the Packers hadn't had a winning season since 1947 when they went 6–5–1. Five of their teams in between won no more than three games.

"The team had become pro football's provincial joke," author David Maraniss wrote. "College stars dreaded being drafted by the Packers. When veteran John Sandusky was traded from Cleveland to Green Bay during training camp in 1956, Bob Skoronski, the rookie tackle from Indiana University, greeted him with the words, 'John, welcome to the end of the earth.' Misbehaving players on the other eleven NFL teams were threatened with trades to 'the salt mines of Siberia,' as Green Bay was known around the league."

After a vigorous campaign sponsored by a group called the "Citizen's Committee for the Stadium"—and featuring a public telegram by the commissioner urging passage—voters in Green Bay approved a $980,000 bond issue authorizing the construction of the new facility by an 11–4 margin on April 3.

"This is the greatest thing I've heard in sports," Bell exclaimed to Art Daley of the *Green Bay Press Gazette*. "Can you imagine it? A little town of 65,000 getting together and building a stadium for a big league football team. That should open the eyes of a lot of big metropolitan cities. Green Bay is the greatest sports town in the world and will always have a place in the National Football League."

Daley recalled that the commissioner had tears in his eyes when he walked out on the field with a group of dignitaries, including Vice President Richard Nixon, to dedicate the new stadium on September 29, 1957.

"I got to know Bert Bell pretty well, but that was the last time I saw him," Daley said. "I will always remember the statement that he made to me several years before he died: 'There will always be a Green Bay in the National Football League.' Bert Bell loved Green Bay!"

The commissioner spent the next few months settling disputes and crossing swords with various club owners, including his nemeses on the West Coast.

In June, he invoked Article I, section 14, paragraph (b) of the league constitution to dissuade owners of the Detroit Lions from entering major league baseball and purchasing the Detroit Tigers to settle the estate of the late Walter O. Briggs. Supported by 10 other NFL club owners—the Los Angeles Rams declined to vote—he told Lions president Edwin J. Anderson that such a purchase would be detrimental to the league.

Bell expressed concern about the deal because when football and baseball ownerships were combined in the past, football invariably came out second best.

"It's time pro football should stand on its own feet," he said, pointing to the Brooklyn Dodgers and New York Yankees as examples of owners unable to handle both sports successfully at the same time.

"We feel it is in the best interest of professional football to continue to maintain separate and distinct status from any other sport or business," the commissioner said, adding that the league "of course" would have no objection if "any or all of the Lion stockholders form a separate corporation and buy the Tigers."

Detroit Lions officials decided not to risk a fight with their NFL counterparts.

In August, Bell successfully intervened in another dispute involving the Los Angeles Rams when the defending Western Division champions threatened to boycott their second exhibition game, against the Cleveland Browns, unless they were paid beforehand. The players had demanded $75 a week for veterans and $50 weekly for rookies during the exhibition season.

The commissioner called the Rams players' representatives at their training camp in California and asked them to delay any boycott until he had a chance to speak to the club owners. Fully aware that some owners had advanced players as much as $40,000 if they desperately needed cash, Bell strongly reminded the reps that the salary in their contract included training camp and preseason games. The players agreed to forgo any boycott.

Afterward, Los Angeles' general manager Tex Schramm promised to arbitrate the salary matter at the end of the season, a decision that was delayed because he had to go back and forth to get the approval of the Rams' embattled owners—Dan Reeves, Ed Pauley, Fred Levy, and Hal Seley.

As the 1956 season got under way, various electronic devices started popping up during games throughout the league. Officials from the Cleveland Browns and Chicago Cardinals were the first to claim credit for originating radio dispatchers and receivers to relay offensive and defensive orders from the bench to the playing field.

The Browns even petitioned the Federal Communications Commission for a specific wavelength so quarterback George Ratterman could use a radio receiver in his helmet. The innovation seemed to have little effect when Detroit won an exhibition game, 31–14. It backfired later during the regular season when the New York Giants said that they intercepted orders from Cleveland coach Paul Brown and used the information to pull off a 21–9 upset victory.

The Cardinals buried wires to carry power along the sidelines and behind the goalposts at Comiskey Park. Two assistant coaches radioed instructions from the press box to head coach Ray Richards on the sidelines. He then relayed the information to quarterback Lamar McHan, who had a tiny receiver in the top of his helmet.

The Detroit Lions installed wiring under Briggs Stadium for their game with Los Angeles. After losing the contest, 24–21, Rams officials complained to Bell that their team was refused use of the same facilities.

"The Rams said they were told certain equipment was denied them, that they weren't cut into the wire," Bell explained. "If the Lions wire the field, I think everyone is entitled to the use of that wire."

The Pittsburgh Steelers planned to use a bench-to-quarterback system in their game against Philadelphia, but static developed in quarterback Ted Marchibroda's helmet before the kickoff and coach Walt Kiesling was unable to use his microphone. The Eagles were approached about a hookup by representatives from Philco but declined, primarily because of the unlimited possibilities for jamming the wavelength.

Finally, after admitting that "squawks and howls reminiscent of the old crystal sets were ringing in his ears," Bell took action on October 18, banning the use of all electronic devices.

By unanimous consent of the 13 NFL clubs, the commissioner said, "All electronic devices, including walkie-talkies to the sidelines, hearing aids of any description used to receive messages, radio-equipped helmets or any other devices of this nature, must be eliminated for the remainder of the season. This does not pertain to telephone lines to the bench or a telephone line with extra footage used by a coach on the sidelines."

George Halas of the Chicago Bears echoed the feelings of most of the league's officials, saying that the quarterback is in a better position to call the plays than anyone on the sidelines. "The coach doesn't have to call the plays," Papa Bear explained. "He's called them before the team goes on the field."

Even Paul Brown agreed with Bell's decision. "He called me this morning on another matter and the subject of electronic devices came up," the commissioner explained. "He was willing to go along with the others."

Bell's truce with the Cleveland Browns coach didn't last long. Neither did his peaceful coexistence with Tony Morabito, the co-owner of the San Francisco 49ers.

It all exploded after the visiting Chicago Bears trimmed the 49ers 38–21 on October 28 at Kezar Stadium. In a bitter locker room tirade, Morabito blasted the "incompetent" officiating, called the commissioner a "dictator," and threatened to "get his job."

Speaking from Cleveland, where his Browns dropped their fourth game in five starts, 24–16, to the Pittsburgh Steelers, Paul Brown seconded Morabito's criticism of the officials. "There is a general feeling around the league that the officiating has to be improved," he said.

NFL game officials were "no more competent than the commissioner who appoints them—and that is very incompetent. The quintessence of nothing," Morabito said. Bell was a "dictator" whose high-handed methods were responsible for "90 percent of the poor officiating."

Morabito, who referred to the officials as "Bell's beauties," was still steaming a day later. "I'm going to try to get Bert Bell's job," he repeated to Bruce Lee of the *San Francisco Chronicle*. "I don't know how far I'll get, but there are other directors, I'm sure, who feel the same way I do, although I fully realize I can't speak for them. But I know this—I'm going to bring it up at the league meeting next January."

"He has a perfect right to bring up anything he wishes, but the only way in the book to fire me is for moral turpitude," Bell told Lee from his office in Philadelphia. "And it would cost approximately $400,000 to buy up my contract. I feel that I have done the best I can, a conscientious job. I have nothing against Morabito and will treat him like anyone else at the league's next meeting."

As expected, Bell defended the league's officials and emphasized to the writers that he didn't resent Morabito's accusations. "In fact, I like him, the commissioner told the United Press. "The officials are very competent and they have the toughest job in the world. I'll always stand up for them."

Other NFL executives quickly rallied behind Bell and his referees. Don Kellett, the general manager of the Baltimore Colts and one of the commissioner's closest friends, was the most vociferous—especially in firing back at Paul Brown.

"He's on the other side of the fence now and learning how the rest of us have been living," Kellett told the Associated Press. "Now that quarterback Otto Graham is gone, the officials are no good. We know that the officials aren't absolute, that they can make mistakes. But they are doing their human best."

Calling Bell "a very good man," Chicago Bears owner George Halas said that his colleagues were solidly behind their leader. "If Morabito is out to get the commissioner, no one else is," Halas told Prescott Sullivan of the *San Francisco Examiner.* "Even he may think better of the idea when he cools off."

Los Angeles Rams general manager Tex Schramm and coach Sid Gillman sided with Morabito and Brown, at least about the officiating.

"We feel there should be a continuing program to survey the work of the officials with an eye to improving the officiating and keeping it abreast of the game as played in the NFL," they said in a statement.

Bell became entangled in more turmoil in successive weeks in December. Both incidents involved the Chicago Bears and their fierce defensive end, Ed Meadows.

First, the Bears' bitter cross-town rivals, the Cardinals, accused the commissioner of "unfair tactics and censorship" and again for being overly protective of his officials. Then, Detroit Lions coach Buddy Parker was so outraged by a blindside hit on his quarterback Bobby Layne that he threatened to quit.

Following his team's 10–3 loss to the Bears on December 9, Cardinals managing director Walter Wolfner announced plans to run films on television pointing out "23 rules infractions by the Bears" that he contended were not called by officials. Some of the plays involved Meadows tackling Cardinals quarterback Lamar McHan.

After viewing the film at his home with Chuck Drulis, a Cardinals assistant coach, the commissioner telephoned Wolfner and told him that he could "run the films all day and all night," so long as no one connected with the team stopped the film and commented to the detriment of the officials. Claiming that the 23 cases were "judgment plays," Bell said that the Cardinals would be subject to a fine and suspension if they used the film in any way to criticize the officials.

Wolfner reluctantly agreed to cancel the television showing. "We were penalized nine times during the course of the game," he said, "two resulting in calling back touchdown runs of 65 and 83 yards by Ollie Matson. We have positive proof from the pictures that we are 100 per cent correct in our claim that the 23 rules infractions by the Bears not called are not judgment plays but rules violations."

Wolfner was further infuriated when the Bears were permitted to show *their* films of the game with still shots and comments. "Why the commissioner has one set of rules for one club and not for another club, we don't know, but we intend to find out and make the same public," he said.

Bell replied that the Bears were allowed to comment on the film because they had nothing but praise for the officials.

The following week, Parker exploded after Layne suffered a concussion when he was hammered by Meadows during Detroit's 38–21 loss to the Bears in the Western Conference championship game. Meadows was not penalized on the play but was later ejected from the game for unsportsmanlike conduct after punching Lions tackle Lou Creekmur.

Lashing out at what he called "a disastrous trend that is making pro football a slugging match," Parker said the game "has gotten far out of line because of deliberate and flagrant infractions." Furthermore, he charged that the game was being "run" by Halas and George Preston Marshall, the owner of the Washington Redskins.

"If that's so, how come neither of them has won a championship in ten years," Bell replied. "Halas is a pillar of this league."

"It's gotten so there's nothing at all wholesome about pro football," Parker said. "Halas is the only person I know of who sells standing room on the field—just so he can rake in that extra dollar or two. The fans are too close to the players and that brings on more trouble."

The Detroit coach was joined by Lions owner Edwin J. Anderson and some of his players in accusing Meadows of deliberately setting out to *get* Layne on instructions of Halas. Anderson immediately sent a three-page letter to Bell demanding that he ban Meadows from pro football for life.

The following day, the commissioner said that he had not seen the films or received Anderson's letter but had talked to officials after the game. They reported that they had not seen Meadows do anything illegal. He also labeled as "outrageous" the charge that Halas ordered the hit on Layne.

"The Lions ought to look at motion pictures of the game and get any other evidence they think they have before accusing that boy of deliberately injuring another player," Bell added. "The Lions have no right to crucify this kid. This is still America and a man still is innocent until he is proven guilty."

Later, after a brief investigation, Bell declared that Meadows and Halas were innocent of any conspiracy to get Layne. According to *The Pro Football Chronicle,* however, footage of the actual play is missing in the game film in the archives of the Pro Football Hall of Fame in Canton, Ohio.

The 1956 season turned out to be the turning point for the NFL and national television. By August, the DuMont Television Network was out of business. Ted Bergmann, its managing director, continued on a 60-year career in the industry, most recently as president of T.T.C. Productions, Inc., coproducer of the television series *Three's Company.*

Sensing DuMont's impending demise, Bell was determined to enhance pro football's national profile. Working the phones endlessly from his office in Bala Cynwyd and from his home a few miles away in Narberth, the commissioner struck a $1 million deal with the Columbia Broadcasting System (CBS) and convinced the 12 NFL owners to go along. Only Cleveland balked initially, but the Browns soon fell in line.

The only professional football games that CBS televised nationally were the Thanksgiving Day contest won by Green Bay over Detroit and a pair of Saturday games from the West Coast.

Although no one probably realized it at the time, the coast-to-coast telecasts involving California teams provided a watershed moment. Major league baseball was still considered the national pastime, but for the first time the NFL was able to showcase its product from an area where big league baseball didn't exist.

Pro football was closing the gap in the national consciousness.

Sig Mickelson, who would later become the first president of CBS News, described in his book *The Decade That Shaped Television News: CBS in the*

1950s how Tex Schramm, then the publicity director of the Los Angeles Rams, suggested that Sig get together with Bert Bell to work out that deal with the NFL.

Mickelson hired Bill MacPhail, the young general manager of the Colorado Springs Blue Sox, a farm team of the Chicago White Sox, as the network's sports director to handle negotiations with the NFL commissioner. Then, they both had to convince William S. Paley, CBS's chairman of the board, to sign off on the unprecedented deal.

Until then, CBS had been focusing primarily on carrying public service programming on Sunday afternoons. But regional telecasts of NFL games on competing stations had recently sliced CBS's rating so dramatically that the network's most popular show, *Face the Nation,* appeared on only 23 of some 200 CBS affiliates once the pro football season started.

As Mickelson remembered, "It was a disaster."

Paley said that he needed time to digest details of the deal, especially when it was pointed out to him that CBS could lose approximately $5 million if the NFL package of 72 games failed to generate revenue.

Fortunately for Bell and the NFL, one of Paley's classmates at the University of Pennsylvania was Carroll Rosenbloom, the new owner of the Baltimore Colts. Somehow, wrote Mickelson, Rosenbloom convinced his Ivy League buddy "that the risk was minimal and the rewards might be enormous. Reluctantly, Paley gave his approval."

One hurdle remained in the negotiations, of which the commissioner was a key participant.

"Green Bay was such an unattractive prospect that McPhail told Bell we would bypass it," Mickelson recalled. "Bell's reply, 'No Green Bay, no deal!' McPhail settled for a $50,000 fee for the Packers' season. It paid off handsomely" later when, under Vince Lombardi, they began to win championships.

Once the deal was finalized, said Mickelson, "the most complex problem involved building a schedule that would meet Bell's mandate that all away from home games be" televised back to the home market. When that problem was resolved, "CBS for the first time since the beginning of television a decade earlier had moved into a position to become a serious factor in the race for broadcast sports supremacy.

"Professional football not only proved to be a triumph for CBS News, it was a phenomenon that would revolutionize behavior patterns during fall weekends. It not only raised Sunday afternoon ratings to new highs and drew substantial advertising revenues, but also filled football stadiums and increased gate receipts. It elevated the income of star players to levels previously paid only to Hollywood stars."

The television contracts that Bell negotiated were "more visionary than anybody could understand at the time," said former *Philadelphia Daily News* sports editor Larry Merchant years later in an interview with NFL Films. "Television meant that New York was not the center of the universe anymore. You didn't have to be near Madison Avenue to become a star. You could play in Green Bay or anywhere else, and become a national figure, a star, a personality, a celebrity."

Creating a league that shared national television revenues equitably also helped to level the playing field competitively.

Bell also negotiated a five-year, $1 million deal with NBC to be the exclusive carrier of the NFL championship game. The first game under this contract, on December 30, 1956, was won by the New York Giants over the Chicago Bears, 47–7, before 56,836 fans at Yankee Stadium. It was blacked out in New York.

"My father was a genius as far as TV was concerned," Upton Bell said. "He brought television into the modern era of the NFL. He knew that TV, not the live gate, was the long-term answer. I remember that Tex Schramm and Bill McPhail would call up from CBS and say, 'Bert, we've got the regular season. We have to have the championship game.' Then, Tom Gallery, of NBC, would be on the phone saying, 'Bert, we have the championship game. What about the regular season?'

"My father would tell the owners, 'You never know when another professional football league is going to come along. We have both networks tied up.' ABC was not a major player at the time—this was before Roone Arledge—and he felt that as long as he protected the rights of the NFL with CBS and NBC, the new league would have nowhere to go."

Bert Bell "was a brilliant pioneer who spanned the ages of the game," wrote William O. Johnson Jr. in his book *Super Spectator and the Electric Lilliputians*. Praising the commissioner for having "successfully shepherded his sport through some of the toughest years," Johnson continued, "he had eased it cautiously past the perils that nearly ruined other sports.

"Commissioner Bell perceived a quintessential truth about TV and sports" with his blackout policy. "Thus he avoided the catastrophic brush with box office disaster that nearly wrecked baseball in those same early years. While the National Pastime was being drained of its ball park spectators, attendance in the NFL climbed and climbed and climbed.

"To put that in its proper perspective, you must realize that professional football was a meek and feeble sport, struggling even to get space in local sports pages during most of the Twentieth Century. In the first thirty-four seasons of its existence, no less than forty franchises appeared, knocked about briefly, and expired.

"Had Bert Bell not ruled as he did, all of pro football could well have slipped away to extinction along with them."

Although no one realized it at the time, a far more significant event occurred a few miles away from Yankee Stadium where all eyes had been focused on the NFL championship game. It happened at the Waldorf-Astoria Hotel in midtown Manhattan.

Here, representatives of 10 teams announced at a press conference the creation of the National Football League Players Association—the first players' union in the history of professional football. The Chicago Bears were the only team not yet on board, and the Pittsburgh Steelers' representative was unable to attend.

Creighton Miller, a Cleveland attorney, introduced himself as the players' counsel. Miller had been the nation's leading rusher as a halfback on Notre Dame's national championship team in 1943 and was well respected in football circles. Norm Van Brocklin of the Los Angeles Rams and Kyle Rote of the New York Giants were chosen by the others to meet with Commissioner Bell.

Reading a carefully worded typewritten statement, Miller listed four subjects that he hoped to discuss with Bell—recognition of the organization, training camp expenses, a player's contract that would provide for compensation for injuries, and a pension plan.

"The players obviously want a continuous improvement in their economic condition with some control over their own destiny," Miller told Michael Strauss of the *New York Times*. "The football man, when dissatisfied, thinks not of revolt, but of negotiation."

Frank Gifford, the halfback of the New York Giants, had attended a secret meeting about the association in the Southern Cal locker room before the Pro Bowl in Los Angeles in 1953.

"Kyle Rote and I represented the Giants," Gifford explained. "Abe Gibron, from the Cleveland Browns, really did as much as anyone to get the Association going. He worked on the docks in the off-season. He had been in union battles before. He was a real rabble-rouser and a helluva football player.

"I think the first thing we complained about, we wanted laundry money. Also, we wanted to get paid for preseason games. We were all staying at a hotel on Wilshire Boulevard and we kind of swore that we wouldn't discuss it publicly. Then we went back and talked to our own teams."

Baltimore Colts captain Gino Marchetti also was involved from the beginning. "At first we had to meet in closets," he recalled. "It was kind of sneaky. I remember Carroll Rosenbloom calling me into his office. He had heard what was going on and I didn't deny it. He just said, 'Well, Gino, what ever you guys do, organize it well enough to try to take care of yourself when you retire.' That was probably the last time management ever talked to me about it."

Contacted at his hotel after the 1956 NFL title game, Bell claimed that he was always ready to meet with players and said that he had already held informal discussions about the topic with Miller.

"I think and hope it can be handled amicably," he added. "First, I have to know from the players what they want to meet about. I hope that nothing ever breaks down the club-player relationship in connection with jobs, loans, bonuses, and business help."

Several members of the Philadelphia Eagles who joined the organization told *Philadelphia Inquirer* sportswriter Herb Good that the commissioner had tried at length to dissuade them not to do so in a locker room talk to the team shortly after the group began to form.

The relationship between players and club owners in the NFL was about to change forever.

34. "You Can't Quit Now, Pete Rozelle"

Bert Bell spent much of his time in the early days of January 1957 working the phones, discussing the ramifications of the new Players Association with club owners and some of the players who had been selected to represent their teams.

One of his conversations was with Norm Van Brocklin. He agreed to meet "informally" with the Rams quarterback along with Kyle Rote of the New York Giants and attorney Creighton Miller in Philadelphia before the league's annual meeting.

Bell emphasized to Van Brocklin, however, that he did not "have the right to represent the teams" because the club owners "must represent themselves."

After hearing details of the commissioner's conversation with Van Brocklin, Miller, the players' legal counsel, reiterated that the association was not a union and that its main objective was "to improve the relationship between the players and owners peacefully without disrupting the game or creating animosities."

Meanwhile, on January 19, Bell received some good news. After learning that a Canadian court had upheld an NFL player's contract for the first time, the commissioner declared, in effect, the end to nearly six years of legal skirmishing that he and league owners had waged with the Canadian professional football teams.

Bell was obviously relieved when he learned that the Ontario Court of Appeals in Toronto ruled in favor of the Detroit Lions, who had brought a breach-of-contract action against quarterback Tom Dublinski. The Lions were awarded $6,950 in damages. Dublinski, a backup to Bobby Layne, had joined the Toronto Argonauts in 1955.

"I don't want it to appear that I'm gloating over the decision," Bell told reporters. "It's a great thing for Canadian football, too. This raiding business has by no means been one-sided. Our clubs have done it, too. The last year has been an amicable one between us. There has been no raiding and everything seems peaceful now."

As promised, the commissioner met with Rote, Van Brocklin, and Miller on January 30 to discuss the proposed new Players Association. Afterward, the participants appeared together at a press conference.

Bell, who earlier appeared rather cool to the Players Association, said that he would send a list of "proposals" to the club owners when their annual meeting opened the following day at the Bellevue Stratford Hotel in Philadelphia. They included recognition of the players' group by the owners and a minimum annual salary of $5,000.

Bell pledged to request a decision by the owners before the end of the meeting. The group then presented a formal statement adding that "in the event the owners take no immediate action on these proposals, Commissioner Bell assured the players' group of a meeting with the owners within the next few weeks."

Although Bell felt confident that the owners would accept the Players Association, the proposal never had a chance. A poll by sportswriter Russ Green taken before the meeting showed six owners in favor with only George Preston Marshall of the Washington Redskins outwardly opposed.

But when George Halas of the Chicago Bears—the only team without representation on the association—turned against the proposal during discussions, he was reportedly joined by Green Bay and San Francisco.

John Steadman, who was working for the Baltimore Colts at the time, recalls that the owners went into executive session to discuss the issue. They met from 9:00 A.M. to 5:00 P.M. without resolving anything.

"I can remember vividly that Arthur Rooney, Carroll Rosenbloom, and Edwin Anderson were strong proponents," Steadman said years later in an interview with NFL Films. "They said, 'We'll be better off with it.' Rooney said, 'I'm from a union town and it'll work fine.' Others had apprehension. They were antiunion.

"Finally, Joe Labrum said, 'Bert, the newspaper guys have early deadlines tonight. You are going to have to go down the hall and talk to them.' Bell replied, 'Well, what do you want me to tell them? There hasn't been anything happening.' So the owners took a recess, Bert put his teeth back in, and went down the hall."

Steadman then had another chance to witness the commissioner at his always accessible but double-talking best.

"He had a little bit of Casey Stengel in him," Steadman explained. "There were two real tough wire service reporters in Philadelphia—Russ Green with United Press, and Ralph Bernstein with Associated Press. Both were real good newspapermen, honorable men who knew how to work a story. They zeroed in: 'Now Bert, what about the union?'

"Well, he deviated and gave them a lot of double-talk. Finally, Ralph took him on and said, 'Bert, you're evading the issue.' And then Bert said to sidetrack him, 'Ralph, old boy. If your wife calls you down at the AP office and wants you to stop at the grocery store on the way home to get a loaf of bread. I know that woman and I know you, Ralph. You're going to stop and get that loaf of bread.' Now what that had to do with the union, I don't know. But that was the answer he gave him. Bert could kind of diffuse that kind of controversy before it even got under way."

According to the minutes of the owners' meeting of February 2, the following resolution denying formal recognition of the Players Association was passed unanimously:

> Under the Constitution and By-Laws of the National Football League any player or players have the right to meet with the Commissioner at any time for the purpose of discussing any problem. Accordingly the Commissioner did meet and in the future will continue to meet with either a single player or group of players at any time such a meeting is requested. The League believes, however, that the circumstances and conditions affecting each club are different and distinct. Hence, it is submitted that if any problems now exist or hereafter arise, the player or players on each club should meet with their individual owners for the purpose of discussing and resolving their particular grievances. If such meeting between the player or players and the owners of the affected club proves unsuccessful, Commissioner Bell is authorized under the Constitution and By-Laws to meet with the player or players and the decision of the Commissioner is final.

After announcing that the NFL "will not recognize anybody as a bargaining agent," Bell said that the owners also turned down the players' request for a minimum salary of $5,000 and rejected their demand for an injury clause guaranteeing a full season's salary.

The commissioner explained that the minimum salary demand was rejected because "there is no player in the National Football League who does not receive over this minimum. If there is one, and he tells me about it, I'll see that it's corrected."

As for the injury clause, Bell said: "There never has been a ballplayer who has been injured and brought it to our attention who has not been compensated in full. It is the policy of the league."

The owners did approve some of the players' requests including standardized fringe benefits like paying training camp transportation expenses, providing all players with game equipment for league games, and advancing players $12 a day for meals and lodging when they were unable to meet as a group. Players were also given the option of drawing an advance of $50 against their salary for each preseason game.

The owners were merely putting in writing "what they have been doing, anyway, over a period of years," Bell said.

Before adjourning the three-day meeting, the owners rejected a motion to expand to 14 teams in 1958 by an 8–3 margin with the Chicago Cardinals abstaining. Philadelphia, Pittsburgh, and Baltimore voted in favor after listening to proposals for franchises from seven cities.

Bell, who had indicated earlier that he thought the owners might vote to add two teams, told the Associated Press that they offered no reasons for their decision. "I guess they just feel we're not ready for it yet," he said.

Reaction from the Players Association came swiftly. Miller, Rote, and Van Brocklin issued a joint statement in Cleveland saying that the owners' refusal to recognize it probably would force them to affiliate with an industrial-type union. They announced that an official for such a union had already contacted them and they planned to meet with him.

"I don't know anything about the union and I can't comment on that," Bell responded. "What they do is their own business. I don't mean that in a sarcastic manner. I mean they have the right to discuss what they believe is better for them."

Bell added that he wasn't surprised that the players had already been contacted by a union official. "A fellow came to the front door of the Racquet Club and asked for them while we were meeting," the commissioner explained, referring to their dinner on January 30. "They went out and talked to him."

A report from Cleveland later identified the "fellow" who broached the formalized union idea to Van Brocklin, Rote, and Miller as a Washington union official.

Later, shortly after returning to Los Angeles, Van Brocklin said, "Bell had us stay at his private club and he picked up the tab—and then he gave us the guillotine. Either Bell doesn't carry much weight with the franchise owners or he has sold us down the river."

The Rams' signal-caller then calmly pointed out the league's shortcomings: "They haven't done anything for us. We requested inclusion of an injury clause in our contracts, which they haven't given us. We requested training camp expenses, which they haven't given us. We requested minimum pay, which they haven't given us.

"Bell has promised us another hearing. If nothing is done, we'll have to get together and find our own solution."

In Philadelphia, an unnamed member of the Eagles said that he wouldn't be surprised if his teammates voted to stay away from training camp. Quarterback Adrian Burke, the Eagles' representative, telephoned Bell and told the commissioner, "As a player in the NFL, I do not think that mature wisdom and sound judgment was exhibited in refusing recognition to the Players Association and those proposals submitted by their representatives."

On February 5, Miller produced a list containing 301 signatures of players who had joined the Players Association and promised 100 percent support from the Pittsburgh Steelers and Los Angeles Rams, who belatedly agreed to join the group. The Chicago Bears were the only NFL team not to express support.

"These lists show our strength," said Miller, who was responding to several owners who had indicated that they had to be shown that such an organization actually existed.

Two days later, Bell hinted to the *Chicago American* that he was not opposed to a players' union. "It is my firm belief, ambition, and hope that the current squabble over recognition by National Football League owners and the player organization will be ironed out amicably to the best interest of all concerned," he said.

Emphasizing that his was his personal opinion, Bell predicted that such an agreement "probably will be reached in the immediate future." Calling it "a matter of clarification," he added, "I know of no NFL owner who has been unwilling to discuss the matter or is dead set against the player organization."

On February 25—Bert Bell's 64th birthday—the U.S. Supreme Court handed the NFL a stinging defeat, ruling by a 6–3 margin that professional football is subject to federal antitrust laws. Moreover, the highest court in the land permitted professional baseball to enjoy the same immunity from antitrust legislation that it had affirmed as recently as 1953.

The Supreme Court's decision came in the case of Bill Radovich, the former Detroit Lions guard who had sued the NFL back in 1949, claiming that he had been blacklisted and prevented from earning a living in his profession. The high court did not award monetary damages in its decision. Radovich could have been entitled to $105,000 plus costs and attorney's fees. Instead, it sent the case back to the federal court of appeals in San Francisco.

Bell was devastated. It was the NFL's darkest hour.

The entire structure of the game was threatened—most notably the option clause and the player draft system.

Calling the decision "most astonishing" and a "tough thing to swallow," the commissioner said that "a lawyer, not retained by Radovich made an indirect contact to us saying that he could settle the case for $50,000."

"We refused to settle," Bell explained. "We wanted to display the moral courage of finding out just where we stood. And, incidentally, I have never turned down any player who wanted to return to the National Football League. We went into court with the belief that, under the Constitution, all people, and sports, too, were created equal. Unlike baseball, professional football does not bind a player for life, or until he is traded."

Bell added that, in his opinion, the main effect of the Supreme Court decision "would be to open us up to law suits, with the object of blackjacking us into out-of-court settlements."

Ironically, Radovich wanted to go to trial but finally agreed to a $42,500 out-of-court settlement with the league after his attorney, Maxwell Keith, urged him to drop the suit. Shortly afterward, according to William C. Rhoden of the *New York Times,* Radovich said that he had learned that Keith had been coaxed by the NFL to drop the suit. "My lawyer double crossed me," he said.

The commissioner told *Philadelphia Inquirer* sports editor Leo Riordan that he would enthusiastically welcome the chance to appear before any congressional or Senate committee investigating pro sports. "Boy do I want to testify," he exclaimed.

"People snort when we claim that pro football or baseball isn't business," Bell continued. "They say we make money so it's a business. But the banks don't think so. They know that our league has had 42 franchise failures. The Maras lost over $300,000 in one four-year span with the New York Giants. 1956 was our top year, but if you averaged out the profits, they wouldn't come to $60,000 a club.

"Green Bay went bankrupt and would have disappeared if the fans out there hadn't raised $118,000. Those fans know pro football isn't a very lucrative business. And most fans must realize that ball clubs can survive only with TV. Baseball has concessions. We have to lean on pre-season games."

The commissioner got his chance to appear before Congress again in March. Before traveling to Washington, he responded to a scathing letter from Republican Representative William E. Miller, the future vice-presidential candidate from New York, who criticized, among other items, the NFL's player draft and reserve clause. Speaking at a press conference in his office, Bell declared that NFL players have the best contract in sports history.

"Our players are in a great bargaining position," he said. "We have to pay at least 33 per cent of the drafted college players a bonus to sign." About the reserve clause, he added, "We could not exist without it. Without the reserve clause and draft selection system, the rich clubs would get richer and the others would go out of business."

Bell described how he and the NFL club owners went to great lengths to help promote the welfare of the players. He told the lawmakers how he once advised Pete Pihos, of the Philadelphia Eagles, to tell club officials that he was going to play out his option after they threatened to cut his pay. They didn't.

"Pro football is a means to an end," he said. "I've never talked to a new-comer without telling him not to play pro football unless he has a job to go with it. As proof of that, look at the pro players who have become successful businessmen and others who went on to study medicine, law, and dentistry. The Eagles loaned one player $15,000 to go into a business the player was advised not to touch. He lost the $15,000 and the Eagles are still paying off the notes. Art Rooney at Pittsburgh loaned $22,000 in one year. George Halas of the Chicago Bears loaned another player $10,000, and another owner loaned a total of $60,000 in one year to players who wanted to get started in business."

When Bell arrived on Capitol Hill to plead pro football's case against government regulation, he received a mixed reception. He was warmly greeted by House Republican leader Joseph Martin of Massachusetts but evidently made no headway with Democratic Representative Emanuel Celler of New York, the powerful chairman of the Judiciary Committee, who insisted that major league baseball and football are big business.

"I don't see how you can operate without some sort of reserve clause," Martin told Bell. But Celler accused the commissioner of harboring "absolute" labor theories after he tried to explain the league's position on recognizing a union-like players association.

"I'm not against the Players Association and I believe the players will find out that they can do better individually," Bell said, reading from a lengthy prepared statement while detailing his unsuccessful efforts to get the club owners to recognize such a group. "All the heads of corporations," replied Celler caustically, took the same position years ago when Congress framed present-day labor legislation.

Bell spent the remainder of his two-day trip visiting offices of such key congressional Democrats as Representative Oren Harris of Arkansas, Senator Estes Kefauver of Tennessee, and his hometown Senator Joseph S. Clark of Pennsylvania. In addition to pleading for the retention of the player draft and reserve clause, he asked that two other "essentials" of pro football operations be exempt from antitrust laws—the commissioner's powers to govern the game, and protecting territorial rights of teams.

The commissioner made it a point to confer at length with Representative Kenneth B. Keating of New York, who had dropped a bombshell during the hearings by charging that football and boxing had undergone infiltration by "gamblers and gangsters."

Bell jumped to his feet and said if Keating "knows anything then he should name names and he should already have reported it to the proper people. We have an ex-FBI agent in all cities where we can keep a check on things and we've had no trouble for a long time."

After chatting in Keating's office, the ranking Republican member of the Judiciary Committee told reporters waiting outside that Bell had agreed to help him draft a "Bill of Rights" for professional sports.

Keating explained that such a concept offered a middle ground between conflicting proposals to put baseball under the antitrust laws or exempt all professional sports from them. His proposal would exempt all sports from these laws but would set up a code of fair procedures between players and management.

Bell's son Bert Jr., who accompanied him to Washington, recalls that the trip took a huge physical toll on the commissioner.

"The punishment was unbelievable," he explained. "My father was carrying too much weight, but he didn't want anyone else doing the lobbying. It was hot and he went up and down those halls seeing every congressman and senator he could meet.

"I carried the suitcase while we went into all those offices. I remember Sam Rayburn, the Speaker of the House, wouldn't talk until he made sure I didn't have a recorder in the suitcase. Lyndon Johnson, the Senate Majority Leader, said I might be able to take out one of his daughters if I wanted to. 'We're going to have to get you two together. I'd think you'd be perfect for each other.' He had a picture of her right there on his desk."

After Bell returned home, he told *Philadelphia Bulletin* sportswriter Hugh Brown that he had talked with "40 or 50" senators and congressmen on the problems of professional football.

"I couldn't have been treated better," he said. "I am going back to Washington next week to talk to 40 or 50 more." Asked if any of them were aware of pro football's problems, Bell replied bluntly, "None of them knew anything about the game."

Bell described how a number of lawmakers asked if it was not inhuman to draft a college player and force him to play thousands of miles from his home.

"I cited them the case of Andy Robustelli, who was traded by the Los Angeles Rams to the New York Giants because he wanted to be near his three kids in Connecticut. And then there was Mike Jarmoluk, who was traded by the Chicago Bears to the Detroit Lions, but who wanted to play in Philadelphia. I told the Lions they would either have to trade Jarmoluk to the Eagles or ask waivers on him."

On the evening of March 29, the NFL headquarters were moved from 1518 Walnut Street in Center City Philadelphia to a modern suite of offices at 1 Bala Avenue in Bala Cynwyd, about a six-minute drive from Bell's home in Narberth.

Most of the old furniture was replaced except for Bert's large wooden desk, a veritable antique scarred on its edges with countless cigarette burns, stained with numerous coffee spills, and scratched from dozens of telephone numbers and other scribbling etched across its top.

"A beauty, isn't it?" Bell beamed to Hugh Brown. "I inherited it from (Elmer) Layden."

The desk has long been enshrined along with Bert Bell in the Pro Football Hall of Fame in Canton, Ohio. In the mid-1990s staffers were doing some work in the museum area when they made an incredible discovery. "We removed the drawers on the desk to make it lighter to move it from one area to another," recalled Saleem Choudhry, a researcher.

"We discovered that there were hidden compartments behind these drawers which contained several telegrams notifying Bell about trades that teams were making—nothing earthshaking, but just league correspondence. It's amazing because this desk has traveled and has been on display in so many places. People literally have been able to go up and touch it, even open the drawers if they were brave enough to do so."

One day in June, Bert Bell Jr. was home from college, hanging out in his father's apartment at the Racquet Club, when the phone rang. It was Pete Rozelle, the new general manager of the Los Angeles Rams. Bert Jr. could tell by the look in the commissioner's eyes that something serious was about to transpire.

"As the conversation went on, I heard my dad say, 'Listen, Pete, I know you're discouraged but you can't quit the Rams,'" the younger Bell recalled. "I knew exactly what he was talking about."

The infighting among the five partners who owned the Los Angeles Rams was now worse than ever. It reached such a fever pitch that Tex Schramm, the team's general manager for more than a decade, abruptly resigned to join CBS Sports. Bert Bell had long been an admirer of Rozelle, ever since his first stint as the Rams' public relations director from 1952 to 1955. Then after Rozelle was lured away to join a Los Angeles public relations firm headed by Ken Macker, Pete's professional reputation skyrocketed when he and Macker helped to salvage Australia's dwindling image when that nation was threatened with being stripped as host of the 1956 Olympics by the International Olympic Committee.

Bert Bell was determined to get Rozelle back with the Rams. He enlisted the help of a mutual friend, NFL coach Joe Kuharich, who had served in that capacity at the University of San Francisco when Rozelle was the school's publicity director. Following a relentless telephone campaign, Rozelle finally agreed to return to the Rams as general manager on April 8, 1957. As Pete recalled in a later interview with NFL Films, Bell finally convinced him when he said, "We checked around, and you are the first thing the Ram owners have agreed upon since Garfield was shot." But no sooner had Rozelle settled in at his new desk when he watched in disbelief as the office turmoil erupted around him.

"Pete was really frustrated that day," Bert Jr. explained. "The owners were fighting with each other now more than ever. Pete was getting barraged with all these different cross-currents of ideas—'Draft this player,' 'trade for that player,' 'sign this coach,' etc., etc.—and he couldn't take it anymore. He was going to quit and he just wanted to tell my dad that he just had had enough.

"My dad convinced him to stay. He assured Pete that he was *his* man in Los Angeles and whatever action he took, whatever decision he made, anything he did, just call each of the owners on the phone, and tell them what he was doing. If he could speak to them directly, fine; otherwise just leave a message. My dad kept emphasizing that Pete was directly responsible to him and only him in the league office. My dad kept assuring him that he would back him up completely.

"It was a conversation that probably lasted no more than five to seven minutes, but the words spoken over the transcontinental telephone lines that day, unknowingly to the participants, shaped the future of the National Football League less than three years later. Had my father not convinced Rozelle to remain in his post, the young GM would never have been in a position to succeed his mentor as commissioner in 1960."

After Rozelle had been elected to succeed his dad, Bert Bell Jr. continued working in the NFL offices in New York. He had joined the league staff right after Austin Gunsel became acting commissioner. One time, he recalls that Pete said to him, "I didn't know that you were in the room that day!"

"We were both amused by the fact of the irony of that telephone call, how my dad convinced him to stay with the Rams and he winds up with my dad's job. It's a *Runyanesque* quirk of fate."

Bert Bell's other son, Upton, wasn't in the room to hear the conversation with Rozelle that day, but he remembers his dad frequently talking about it.

"The Rams were always in the playoffs because they were the first ones to have a brilliant scouting system," Upton explained. "But the partners couldn't stop fighting. They wouldn't even talk to each other. Finally, my father had heard enough. He called Pete in 1957 and said, 'Look you're very diplomatic. You can get along with people better than anyone I know. I need you as general manager and I want you to report directly to me.' After Pete finally accepted, my father called the owners and told them what he had just done.

"Bert Bell actually ran the Rams for a while from the league office in Philadelphia. Pete was definitely going to quit that day because he had friends in the PR business. He could have gone back with Ken Macker. He could have gone to a lot of different places. My father talked him out of it. Told him it's not the time to quit. Told him the league will back him up if he needs his help.

"This was all about being in the right place at the right time in life. If Bert Bell hadn't called those owners out there and said: 'I'm appointing Pete Rozelle and I'm running your team from the league office.' Later, if he hadn't persuaded him not to quit, Rozelle never would have been commissioner."

35. The Players Finally Get a Union

With four bills already pending in the House of Representatives to eliminate football and other professional sports from antitrust laws, Bert Bell spent much of the spring of 1957 vigorously stepping up his campaign on behalf of the NFL.

First he officially registered as a lobbyist. Then he supervised the preparation of a 73-page brochure, *The Story of Professional Football In Summary*, outlining the "facts" of the league, which was mailed to every member of Congress.

Finally, after talking to an estimated 65 or 70 lawmakers, he called a press conference at his new headquarters in Bala Cynwyd on May 6, pleading for public hearings so that the issue could be brought before the public.

"I'm not trying to influence Congress," the commissioner said. "All I want is to get them to hear me, then they can decide if professional football is a business or a sport. I have nothing to hide; they can have all our records. Unless the league is permitted to retain its option clause, we cannot survive."

Bell again cited the difference between the two major professional sports.

"Baseball is a career," he explained, "whereas football is a means to an end for a player. The option clause does not hold a player prisoner to any one club, but is a bargaining point in a player's favor, instead. Our option and reserve clause is the greatest in the history of the world, including all sports, theatre, and television contracts. And I'm not saying that just because I wrote it. But if the courts hold that the clause is in restraint of trade, pro football will either have to go back to the early jungle days where 42 teams folded, or go out of business entirely."

Although the booklet primarily contained justification for Bell's well-publicized stances, it did provide some new information. For example:

- When Bell owned the Philadelphia Eagles in 1938, the team's annual payroll was less than $30,000. Now payrolls for the 12 teams average $300,000, not counting bonuses and coaches' salaries.

- Total sale value of all twelve clubs was $18 million. Total revenue from all sources in 1956 was $10.5 million. Total net profit was $600,000.
- The U.S. government collected $900,000 in amusement tax from admissions to all NFL games in 1956. That sum was $300,000 more than the teams' net profits.
- Twenty-six of the league's thirty-six preseason games were played for charity.
- Of the NFL's 396 active players, 30 percent held jobs in the cities with which their teams were affiliated. The Eagles recently ran advertisements in the Philadelphia newspapers urging employers to "take advantage of the varied skills" of their players.

Asked if he ever considered running for the U.S. Senate, Bell pounded his desk, held up a brochure, and replied, "I have never even thought of running for the Senate. I have every intention of living and dying with this."

The commissioner had another day in court on July 21. Serving as professional football's kickoff witness, Bell took the stand in Washington as a House Anti-Trust Subcommittee, headed by Representative Emanuel Celler, continued its lengthy investigation of professional sports. Representatives from major league baseball had testified previously.

Flanking Bell in front-row seats as he answered lawmakers' questions for nearly three hours were some of professional football's biggest names. Players like Red Grange, Sid Luckman, and Chuck Bednarik sat with Chicago Bears president George Halas, patiently waiting for their turn to testify.

Bell wasted no time in painting an opposite picture from the one portrayed by the baseball club owners. He declared in no uncertain terms that pro football wanted nothing to do with pay television or a farm system designed to groom young prospects. Conceding that revenue from commercial television had helped football over the financial hump, the commissioner said the NFL "doesn't think so much of money" that it would scrap free TV in favor of paid telecasts. "The kids of this country are entitled to see sports free on TV," he added.

Later he said that pro football chose "to go on our own" without minor league affiliations. When the questioning turned to gambling, Bell explained again how the NFL employed ex-FBI agents. "There isn't any such thing as a fix," he said. Claiming that the federal tax on gambling had reduced betting, Bell estimated that there were only about 10 to 15 "big bettors in the country now."

At one point, Celler questioned the legality of the NFL's bonus pick system—the long-standing policy of the league's allowing a different team each year to pick an extra player in advance of the regular draft.

"How do you decide which is the lucky team?" he asked. "We pull its name out of a hat," Bell replied. "That sounds like a lottery to me," Celler responded. "If you think it's a lottery, we'll eliminate it," the commissioner said.

Bell again emphasized that he personally did not object to efforts by players to organize for bargaining purposes with owners. "But I think the players will find out they do better individually, bargaining with their own clubs."

Celler then asked Bell whether he felt more loyal to the club owners or to the players. "I owe a greater loyalty to the players than [to] the owners, because they're younger and they don't know the different angles in the situations," he replied, adding that the players were "careless" because "80 percent of them don't even read their contracts outside of what they are getting paid."

A few days later, Creighton Miller, the attorney for the Players Association, took the stand and accused Bell of reneging on a promise to quit as NFL commissioner when the club owners refused to recognize the players' group. Miller testified that Bell made the promise to resign the previous January in Philadelphia before attending a meeting of 12 club owners.

Miller claimed that Bell told the players that if they issued a news release endorsing the player draft and the option clause, they would have no trouble being recognized. But the owners refused to recognize the association and Bell "got either $10,000 or $20,000 from the owners."

Miller then testified that after presenting the players' case to the owners, Bell seemed to be losing "confidence" the next day and the players told him they would delete the two items from the news release. He quoted Bell as warning that "if you don't leave that in the press release, I'm not going before the owners." The players agreed to keep the items in the release and Bell reassured them that the owners would bargain with them. "You're not going to have any trouble," Bell told them, according to Miller. "If they don't recognize you, I'll quit."

Bell responded that the reason the club owners refused to recognize the players' group was because "there was doubt that the association was truly representative of players in the league." Referring to a *Sports Review* magazine article written by Baltimore Colts owner Carroll Rosenbloom in September 1957, Bell said the owners resisted because players from the Chicago Bears had not joined the union.

The commissioner quoted Rosenbloom as saying in the article that the owners were told that members of another club voted to send a spokesman to the players' meeting but then "more than half the squad refused to ante up" $5 apiece to pay his expenses.

Warning that he might petition the National Labor Relations Board for an order directing the owners to deal with the players, Miller said that the players should have a vote in selecting the commissioner. "How can a commissioner selected by the owners and paid by the owners judge a dispute between the owners and the players?" he asked.

Facing what one observer called a "fourth down and 30-yards-to-go situation on his own five-yard line," Bell formally recognized the Players Association in a statement prepared for the House Subcommittee on August 1. He later told reporters that he was ready to open negotiations immediately on such issues as minimum pay and working conditions and said that he was acting under authority in the NFL Constitution to deal with matters "detrimental to the welfare" of pro football.

"Accordingly, in keeping with my assurances that we would do whatever you gentlemen consider to be in the best interest of the public on behalf of the National Football League, I hereby recognize the National Football League's Players Association and I am prepared to negotiate immediately with representatives of the association concerning any differences between the players and the clubs that may exist," Bell said, reading from his statement.

The commissioner's action was immediately challenged by George Preston Marshall. "Bert is supposed to carry out the wishes of the owners," the Washington Redskins owner said. "We never gave him the authority to change the contractual arrangements between the players and the clubs."

Bert Bell Jr. remembers having dinner with his dad and Marshall at the Mayflower Hotel the previous night. "My father told Marshall that he was going to recognize the players' union. 'You're going to get fired,' Marshall replied. 'What are you going to do? You can't get a job anywhere.' My dad said, 'If I get fired, I get fired,' or words to that effect."

George Halas, the owner of the Chicago Bears, finally expressed support to Bell with a "qualification" that each club is represented in the Players Association.

The Bears were the only team that did not belong to the group and would not join until 1962 when National Football League Players Association president Pete Retzlaff of the Philadelphia Eagles came in and gave "one hellacious presentation to the players," according to author Jeff Davis.

"I don't know what Bert Bell's authority is on this question," said Paul Brown, the coach and general manager of the Cleveland Browns. "I think it's a matter for legal interpretation."

All of the other club officials quickly rallied behind the commissioner. "There's no doubt that Bell has the right to negotiate any differences between the players and the owners," said Jack Mara, the president of the New York Giants.

"If Bell has made the announcement, I feel the league will undoubtedly abide by his recognition of the association," added Pete Rozelle, the general manager of the Los Angeles Rams.

Celler, an outspoken advocate of bringing all sports under antitrust laws, said afterward that he was "willing to modify my views" as the result of testimony heard to date. Bell's announcement, he added, "shows the committee is doing some good." Later, he commented that the NFL presented a better case in two days than organized baseball had in three weeks of hearings.

Miller said that he was "most gratified" by the NFL's formal recognition of the Players Association. The attorney and commissioner quickly sought each other out after the session adjourned, talked briefly, and agreed to meet in Chicago when they attended the College All-Star game.

Things were not quite as cordial when the two men got together on August 8 at the Blackstone Hotel in the Windy City. Miller, who was accompanied by players Kyle Rote and Norm Van Brocklin, presented a written acceptance agreement to Bell, then tersely told the commissioner that he had 10 days to sign it.

"I don't know why I have to sign an agreement," Bell replied. "I've testified before Congress that I recognize the Association. I'll consult with lawyers before I sign."

Instead of a signed agreement, Miller soon received a letter from Clinton Hester, the NFL's attorney, saying that he had advised Bell not to sign the pact because it was not necessary and that league owners needed more time to review the Players Association's proposals. On August 21, speaking from Cleveland, Miller accused Bell of "stalling" and said that he planned to file an action with the National Labor Relations Board.

"Let's make it clear that our attorney wrote Miller, August 19, suggesting he go to the NLRB," Bell said from his vacation home in New Jersey the following day. "It is our idea to go to the NLRB, not Miller's. I recognized the Players Association, but Miller knows it takes 10 of 12 club owners to sign an agreement. We can't execute the proposed recognition agreement of August 8 because it goes far beyond recognition of the association. Since the Supreme Court has held that pro football is a business engaged in interstate commerce, the Taft-Hartley Law is clearly applicable. We have already requested that Miller join us in asking the NLRB to assume jurisdiction over pro football."

On November 21, Miller announced intentions to file a $4.2 million lawsuit against the NFL owners on December 4 if they failed to grant formal recognition to the Players Association at a preliminary draft meeting to be held in Philadelphia on December 2.

"In the last two months Commissioner Bell and I have been discussing our difficulties," Miller explained from his office in Cleveland. "But we've made no progress in negotiations with the owners."

The commissioner was clearly annoyed by Miller's threat but said that his hands were tied. "I don't know how anyone could give the Players Association more recognition than I did," he thundered. "However, I do not have the right to make any agreement with anyone without the vote of 10 of the 12 clubs."

Admitting that the Cleveland Browns and Chicago Bears were still opposed, Bell explained that he had made recommendations to the owners on October 16 (urging them to give the players what they wanted) and added several more proposals on November 4, "long before Miller's decision to file suit. I did tell him that things were going along very well and that Rome wasn't built in a day."

Finally on December 2, at their meeting at the Warwick Hotel in Philadelphia, the owners formally recognized the Players Association and approved three of their major demands—a minimum salary of $5,000 for drafted players only, a minimum of $50 for preseason games, and a new contract clause protecting players in case of injury. After hours of haggling, Art Rooney of the Pittsburgh Steelers, assisted by Carroll Rosenbloom of the Baltimore Colts, finally forced the issue that carried by a 10–2 vote.

"George Marshall and George Halas didn't want to recognize the union," explained Art Rooney's son, Dan, the current chairman of the Pittsburgh Steelers, who attended the contentious meeting. "My father really was the guy who got up and said, 'You have to vote so the players could have a union.'

"Marshall and Halas were yelling at him and he said, 'Listen, Bert went before Congress and told them he was going to get that done. If you don't do this, his effectiveness as the commissioner is finished. We need him. He's capable and he's the best guy we could ever get.' The owners finally got it done. It was the right thing to do."

In making the announcement, Bell insisted that he himself had "formally recognized" the association in testimony before Congress and that the owners merely confirmed it. He said the vote to approve his recommendations was unanimous and that the league also took several steps to comply with suggestions made by the congressional committee. The most significant move was permitting a player to take a dispute between himself and a club directly to court rather than to Bell.

Later that evening, Miller announced that the Players Association had accepted the owners' recognition action and immediately dropped plans to file a $4.2 million antitrust suit.

The new Players Association didn't come to fruition without a cost to some of its early supporters.

"We suddenly started getting players cut from other teams because they were involved in setting up the union," recalled Tom Brookshier, who had rejoined the Philadelphia Eagles' defensive backfield in 1956. "We got Abe Gibron, who was Cleveland's starting guard, and we couldn't figure out why Paul Brown let him go. Kenny Gorgal, a safety, was one of Abe's friends and he ended up going to Green Bay. Guys that were instrumental in the union at first were probably treated pretty roughly."

Just before the Christmas holidays, Bell sat down at his office in Bala Cynwyd, picked up the telephone, and proclaimed to Louis Effrat of the *New York Times* that the 1957 NFL season was "the greatest ever."

You said the same thing last year and the year before, the commissioner was reminded.

"Yes and the year before that, too," he replied, referring to 2.8 million fans who created a new attendance record for the sixth straight season—an increase of almost 10 percent over 1956.

"Competition was keener," Bell explained. "Teams that were favored managed to win only about half the time, proving that on any given day any team was capable of winning. Home fields, which used to mean so much, meant little."

As if dealing with Congress wasn't difficult enough, the commissioner stuck to his guns again during the 1957 NFL championship playoffs. This time he even stood up to the vice president of the United States. The issue was Bell's television blackout policy. He refused to lift it in San Francisco when the Detroit Lions defeated the 49ers, 31–27, for the Western Division title, and again the following week in Detroit when the Cleveland Browns throttled the Lions, 59–14, for the NFL crown. Both games were sellouts.

"I do not believe in taking people's money under the impression that we're not going to televise and then televise after all, Bell explained to San Francisco Mayor George Christopher.

"No siree," he told Soapy Williams after the Michigan governor pleaded with him to lift the blackout. "That's my Christmas message. That's been our policy for 12 years and it will continue to be our policy, no matter if the game is a sellout, or if it's a playoff or championship game."

Fans in Detroit had endured a raging snowstorm for hours, waiting in line for tickets, knowing that this was their only way to see the game. "My father told the press that he wasn't going to go back on his word to these people," Upton Bell recalled. "Soapy Williams called him and said, 'Your action is highly unreasonable.' My father replied that he didn't think it was honest to sell tickets to thousands of people who didn't expect the game to be televised, and then give the game to TV when all the tickets were sold."

The *Detroit Free Press* editorialized, "Throw out your silly rule, you dictator." Two nights before the championship game, Williams stepped up the pressure and flew Vice President Richard Nixon into Detroit for a private dinner with Bell and some other luminaries. "My father told Nixon that if he gave in, the fans who bought tickets would lose faith in his word," Upton explained. "He told Nixon he's not budging."

There was no television within 75 miles of the game. It was seen only by 55,263 fans sitting in frigid Briggs Stadium.

36. The "Hands-On" Commissioner

ert Bell was sitting at his desk at his apartment at the Racquet Club in mid-January 1958 gathering his notes for the upcoming NFL owners' meeting. Suddenly an unexpected guest arrived. It was Frank McNamee, the president of the financially strapped Philadelphia Eagles.

"I've just worked out a deal to move our home games to Franklin Field," McNamee exclaimed, referring to the picturesque, 60,237-capacity home of the University of Pennsylvania football team. "Next to the Coliseum in Los Angeles, we now have the largest NFL stadium."

Bell was taken aback by the news. Several times in the past he had approached Penn president Gaylord Harnwell about the possibility, but discussions had never gotten anywhere. The National Collegiate Athletic Association was adamantly opposed to allowing professional football teams play in college stadiums, and many old grads from the Ivy League felt the same way.

Bell's reaction was understandable.

"'Aw, you're crazy'," McNamee recalled the commissioner saying. "So I took him out to see John L. Moore to prove it."

McNamee and Moore, a university vice president, were good friends who had worked together on the War Assets Administration during World War II. Penn had recently deemphasized football. No longer were the Quakers drawing crowds of 78,000 for games against the Notre Dames and Michigans. Like the Eagles, the school was struggling financially. Somehow, Moore and athletic director Jerry Ford persuaded Harnwell and the university trustees to open their stadium to the NFL.

When the announcement was made on January 20, Bell was ecstatic. "It's the only thing that could have saved pro football for Philadelphia," he said. "If things continued as they had, the Eagles would have been out of here by 1960."

Crowds at Connie Mack Stadium had been steadily dwindling for the Eagles, whose fans rarely filled its 39,000 seats. Primarily built for baseball, the decaying facility was plagued by poor parking and heavy traffic congestion. Two years earlier, McNamee had entertained, then declined a proposal from promoters interested in transferring the Eagles' franchise to Louisville, Kentucky.

The move to Franklin Field, one of the most beautiful stadiums in the country, was indeed the turning point for the NFL in Philadelphia.

"Franklin Field moved us uptown," Tom Brookshier, the great Eagles defensive back, said later. "We became socially acceptable. We began to feel like we really belonged. It was an incredible amphitheater. Plus, I never thought there was a bad seat in the house."

The four-day owners' meetings the following week at the Warwick Hotel, in Philadelphia, were relatively uneventful. Most of the conversation focused on the Eagles' recent announcement. The owners knew that only one other NFL franchise—the Detroit Lions—had ever played in a college stadium, and that was for only one season at the University of Detroit field. Later in 1958, the Pittsburgh Steelers would reach an agreement to use the University of Pittsburgh's stadium.

Even Bell was underwhelmed when the owners adjourned. "Most of what we did didn't amount to much," he quipped.

Actually there was some news. The league eliminated the bonus choice from the annual player draft, primarily to comply with congressional concerns that the out-of-the-hat draw bordered on a lottery. The idea for the extra pick was initiated by Bell in 1947. The Chicago Cardinals, the only club that had never participated, had completed the cycle a few weeks earlier by selecting Rice University quarterback King Hill. The owners also authorized Hall-of-Famer Bill Dudley, one of Bell's favorite players from his Pittsburgh Steelers days, to formulate a pension plan and report back to a joint committee of NFL owners and players.

In February, Bell traveled to New York to attend the funeral of Tim Mara, the founder of the New York Giants. By the time the commissioner returned to his home in Narberth, he had contracted a severe case of bronchitis. He was admitted to Lankenau Hospital and ordered to take a complete rest by Dr. Harrison Flippin, his physician.

After regaining his strength and returning to the office, Bell turned his attention to another dilemma—the struggling Philadelphia franchise. The Eagles had solved their stadium problem a few weeks earlier, but the team hadn't won a championship since the back-to-back titles in 1948–1949. The Birds were coming off three straight losing seasons. The first words out of Buck Shaw's mouth when he was announced as their new coach a few months earlier were, "I've got to have a veteran passing quarterback."

Bell was aware that Vince McNally, the Eagles' general manager, had been working since March in an effort to obtain Norm Van Brocklin, the 32-year-old passing and punting wizard who said he no longer wanted to play for the Los Angeles Rams. Three other NFL teams had the same idea, so the commissioner started working the phones. He knew that the NFL's third largest market needed a shot in the arm, especially with those 60,000 seats to fill.

"I do remember a conversation my father had with Pete Rozelle," recalled Upton Bell. "He essentially told the Rams GM: 'We have to do something for the Eagles. . . . They have a real problem here. . . . Getting Van Brocklin might help the league and the Eagles.'"

Bert Bell Jr. recalled hearing another telephone conversation at the Racquet Club—this time between the commissioner and Van Brocklin. "He didn't want to come to the Eagles," Bert's oldest son recalled. "My dad prevailed on him that he'd be starting here. It was a very short conversation. He finally convinced him to come."

On May 27, the deal was announced. In return for Van Brocklin, the Rams obtained veteran offensive tackle Buck Lansford and defensive back Jimmy Harris, who quarterbacked Oklahoma to a pair of national collegiate championships and was the Eagles' first pick in the 1959 player draft.

How much influence the commissioner had in bringing the Rams' quarterback to Philadelphia will never be known. Neither will it be known if Van Brocklin was really promised that he would be the next coach of the Philadelphia Eagles when he retired.

Upton Bell said that it was his recollection that Van Brocklin was promised the job. "The Eagles went back on their word," he claimed.

Bert Bell Jr. remembers from their telephone conversation that it definitely wasn't his father who made any such guarantee to Van Brocklin. "It was more like: 'You can go right into coaching after your career.' If you think about it, my dad wouldn't make any promise like that for somebody else's franchise."

Van Brocklin claimed that, as part of the enticement for him to leave the West Coast, Bell promised he would succeed Buck Shaw when he retired. "We had dinner together in a restaurant in Bala Cynwyd and Bert said to me, 'If you come here you'll be the next Eagles coach,'" the quarterback later told sportswriters. "We had a terrible season in 1958 and I was disgusted and ready to quit again because I never played with a worse football team. But again, Bert Bell persuaded me to stay, saying 'You're the next coach. Do you want it in writing?' I told Bert that I didn't want anything in writing, that his word was good enough for me."

Years later, Frank McNamee, who was then the Eagles' president, told sportswriter Hugh Brown that *he* was the one who informed Van Brocklin that he would not be getting the Eagles job after the quarterback turned down an offer to remain with the team as a player-coach following their exciting NFL title run in 1960.

Van Brocklin had wanted a free hand to name his own assistant coaches, something that the Eagles' management was reluctant to allow. Shaw's assistants, especially Nick Skorich, Jerry Williams, and Charlie Gauer, were all highly respected football men. Skorich was named head coach a few weeks later.

McNamee said that the Van Brocklin situation might have turned out differently had Jim Clark, the team's majority owner, not been ill in the hospital. Because club officials wanted to keep his illness a secret, Van Brocklin was not informed why Clark had failed to show up at an earlier meeting to discuss his future with the Eagles. Thinking that he had been given the runaround, the temperamental quarterback stormed out and headed for the Pro Bowl in Los Angeles.

Clark then called McNamee from his hospital bed and instructed him to offer Van Brocklin a $40,000 salary, a paid-up mortgage on his $40,000 home, and three shares of Eagles stock. "I want him," Clark said. "Call him up on the coast." But it was too late. The Dutchman had agreed to be the head coach of the new Minnesota Vikings.

Bell's intervention in the Van Brocklin situation wasn't the only time the commissioner got involved with a player or a team official. His hands-on exploits were legendary. They dated well back into the 1930s when he first purchased the Frankford Yellow Jackets and brought them into the NFL.

"Bert was the coach, the owner, the water boy; you name it, he did it," said Ralph Bernstein of the Associated Press. "One day he was down on the sidelines at the Baker Bowl and they were playing the Chicago Bears. They had a capacity crowd, standing room only, and he was helping to hold the ropes to keep the fans off the field. And the Bears were kicking the hell out of the Eagles, something like 40–0. One guy was standing right in back of Bell and said, 'This is awful. It's criminal to pay 85 cents to see this. I'm taking off.' Bell turned around and said to him, 'What are you kicking about? I have to stay!' "

"Even though he was the commissioner, Bert Bell always took care of the football players," recalled Bill Mackrides, who spent most of his career as a backup quarterback with the Eagles. "I had just been cut by the Giants in 1953 and he called me at home. He told me there was an opening with the Steelers. He arranged for me to go to their training camp." Mackrides ended up playing four more games in Pittsburgh.

Gino Marchetti, the great defensive end for the Baltimore Colts, may never have been elected to the Pro Football Hall of Fame had it not been for some gentle persuasion by the commissioner.

"One summer I wanted to retire and I drove up to Atlantic City to see [Colts owner] Carroll Rosenbloom," Marchetti explained. "I had no idea that Bert Bell was going to be at the meeting. I think it was in 1959, the year that he died. We sat around a table and talked a little bit and I can remember Bert saying: 'Gino, you don't want to retire. You've got too much left on your body, and once you quit, it's forever. You ought to really give it a lot of thought.'

"On the way back to Baltimore, I felt pretty proud about that—the commissioner asking me to stay. I gave it a lot of thought and I signed up for another couple of years."

Marchetti ended up making All-Pro seven times and playing in ten Pro Bowl games before retiring in 1966. Three years later, he was named the NFL's top defensive end for the league's first 50 years.

In 1956, during a stopover in Chicago on the way to the league meetings in Los Angeles, Bell hopped off the train to place a call to Hugh Devore, who was wrestling with the decision whether to stay at the University of Dayton or take the Eagles' coaching job. After briefly speaking to Devore and his wife—and emphasizing that the Eagles badly needed him to turn their fortunes around—Bert quickly had him convinced to come to Philadelphia.

"It was the advice of that genial gentleman in whom I have the utmost confidence," Devore said. "I've known Bert for a long time and I decided to ask his advice on the matter. He convinced me that it was a chance of a lifetime and that I had enough college experience to take on the assignment."

Unfortunately, Devore's "chance of a lifetime" didn't last long. He was fired after guiding the Birds to a 7–16–1 record in two years at the helm.

Shortly afterward, the Eagles' negotiations with Buck Shaw bogged down for a while. Bell then got involved in recruiting Vince Lombardi, the highly regarded assistant coach of the New York Giants, for the position, "calling him on a Saturday morning," according to author David Maraniss. "Lombardi told Bell that he would take the job. Within minutes, the Maras were on the line, pressing to keep him." Lombardi decided to stay with the Giants and the Eagles soon hired Shaw.

Early in 1959, still feeling pressure to straighten out the Green Bay situation once and for all, Bell realized that the Packers needed a strong presence to run their football operation. The perfect man obviously was Lombardi, but Bell knew that it would take some arm-twisting. For one thing, he wasn't sure that the Giants would agree to let their prized assistant go. And there was no guarantee that Lombardi would be willing to relocate to the frozen upper Midwest, especially to take over a downtrodden franchise.

First the commissioner called John Mara. Surprisingly, the Giants owner assured Bell that he would release Lombardi from his contract if he and the Packers reached an agreement. Then Bell told Green Bay's president Dominic Olejniczak in no uncertain terms that he wanted Lombardi to run the Packers.

Bert Bell Jr., who was working in his dad's office at the time, remembers what happened next. "He never shut his door and didn't care who listened when he was on the phone," the commissioner's son recalled. "I happened to overhear his conversation with Vince Lombardi. The gist of it was, 'We need a strong man out there. As a favor to me would you please go out there and be the coach and general manager.' Then I distinctly remember him saying, just as he had to Pete Rozelle a year or so earlier, 'You are the boss. The only one you're responsible for in that job is me.' "

After wrestling with the decision for quite a while, Lombardi finally agreed to go to Green Bay. Within two years, he had the Packers playing in the NFL championship game. Ironically it was in a losing cause against the Philadelphia Eagles—the only setback the Hall of Fame coach ever suffered before winning five NFL titles and two Super Bowl championships.

A few years later when Bert Bell Jr. was working for Pete Rozelle, he occasionally represented the NFL commissioner at funerals. "One time Lombardi picked me up at the airport. He told me, 'I'm so glad your dad did this for me so that I was able to come out here. This is a great town to raise your kids in.' "

Pittsburgh's Art Rooney once told sportswriter Dick Hackenberg that no other commissioner ever got as close to his players as Bert did. "He thought so much about their welfare there were times when we owners thought he was their agent," the longtime Steelers owner said. "He knew everybody's problems—the owners, the players, everyone. And he knew the book well, the league rules, the playing rules. His decisions were logical and firm."

Not as logical were Bell's occasional outbursts of temper. Tom Brookshier, who became a sportscaster on CBS-TV after his NFL career ended, recalls hearing about one explosion while the commissioner was on his way to a nice peaceful dinner with his wife and another couple at Philadelphia's Vesper Club.

"When they pulled up at the Vesper, Bert let Frances and the other couple out to go inside and get the table," Brookshier explained. "Then he went to park the car. When he reached the parking lot, some guy yelled across, 'The Eagles are bums! The Eagles are bums!' So Bert parks the car and goes inside and excuses himself. He says that he's going to the men's room. Instead, he goes outside and punches this guy who probably lost a $10 bet or something over the Eagles. His friends heard the ruckus. They go out and Bert Bell is rolling around in that little street fighting this guy. He's out there defending the Eagles. Who else would have a commissioner fighting for you like that?"

Upton Bell recalls another time that his dad lost his temper. It happened on one of the few occasions that Bert decided to sit in the commissioner's box at Franklin Field. ("He was the only commissioner in history who bought his own tickets," Upton said.) The Eagles were hammering the Chicago Cardinals en route to a 49–21 victory and Chicago's managing director Walt Wolfner was getting angrier by the minute.

"Late in the game there was a crucial call and you remember my father as far as officials are concerned," Upton explained. "He protected them like the Spanish Armada. Wolfner actually came out of his box in the stands and was walking down the cinder track that surrounds the football field. He was yelling, 'Bert, did you see that? Did you see that? What a terrible call! He blew it! We can never get a fair break! It's going to cost us the game!' Wolfner kept screaming, the crowd was watching, and finally my father had enough. He really went after him. He chewed his ass out right in front of everyone: 'Don't you ever talk to me about the officials! Go back to your seat and shut up. It's not your right to talk about the officials. They're calling the game. You don't know what you're talking about! Who the hell do you think you are.' I mean he told him off right in front of 30,000 people."

Ed Kiely, the veteran public relations director of the Pittsburgh Steelers, also experienced Bell's wrath. It happened early in his career, also in Philadelphia, shortly after Bert became commissioner.

"Something happened in the game and I was very upset with the officials," Kiely said. "I was mumbling and grousing in the press box and I didn't know that Bell was sitting at the other end. Somebody told him that I was debasing his officials and he came up to me and said, 'You're suspended for two weeks!' What could I say? The game ended. I think the Eagles won it. I went into the office the day after the game and went into Art Rooney and said, 'What am I supposed to do?' He said 'What do you mean? You're supposed to do like you always do.' I said, 'I can't because Bell suspended me. I was hollering about his officials.' He said 'Forget about it! Go to work!' Bell did talk to me later about it. He discussed it when he got me alone."

"Bert could be gruff but he had a good sense of humor and could really be warm at times," recalled Jim Gallagher, the Philadelphia Eagles executive who occasionally helped out at league meetings and shared a hotel suite with the commissioner. "He was an absolute joy to be around. He had a million funny stories. We'd be in the hotel room sometimes after midnight and writers would come knocking on the door. 'Let them in, Jimmy,' he would say."

"Bert Bell saved my job," said Les Keiter, the longtime play-by-play man for the New York Giants who later became one of the first sportscasters of the new American Football League. It happened in the mid-1950s. After being carried for six years on WINS, where Keiter also served as the station's sports director, the Giants games were switched to WCBS.

"I got a phone call from Jimmy Dolan, the main guy at WCBS," Keiter recalled. "Dolan said, 'Les, I hate to call you on this but we're not going to use your services this year as the voice of the Giants. We have the rights now and you are too well identified around New York as sports director of WINS.' I told him I understood, thanked him, and hung up."

About an hour later the phone rang. "'Les,' this gruff, loud voice said. 'Bert Bell, Philadelphia, calling. What's this crap I hear'—he didn't say *crap*; he said something stronger—'about you not doing the Giants next year? I don't care what station it's on. You're the voice of the National Football League in New York and I want you to know that you're going to continue. And nobody as long as I'm commissioner . . .'—and by now he's yelling at me. 'Who is this guy over at that other station?' I told him his name and Bell said, 'You'll hear from me later.' And he hung up. A couple of hours later, the phone rings again and it's Jimmy Dolan. 'Les, I'm so sorry about my previous phone call. We made a mistake. I want you to know that we are delighted to have you carry on as the play-by-play announcer for the Giants on WCBS. I want to have lunch with you tomorrow and work out a new contract.'

"I knew Bert Bell casually and I called him to express my appreciation for what he had done. He said, 'Les, you don't have to thank me. You don't owe me anything. You are the voice of the NFL in New York as long as I'm commissioner.' And with that he hung up. Two weeks later, he came by me at a cocktail party in Philadelphia before the Eagles-Giants game. He winked at me and he said, 'Well, kid I guess we certainly showed them, didn't we!'"

Bob Wolff, who broadcast two of the greatest sports events in the history of Yankee Stadium, recalled the commissioner as a small, domineering guy with a raspy voice who ran the league like a little dictator. "He kept a careful tab on everything that was going on," Wolff explained. "So much so that one day I was doing an exhibition game—the Baltimore Colts against the Chicago Bears or somebody—down in Texas, I believe. How he was able to hear it, I have no idea. About 3 o'clock in the morning I get this call in my hotel room. It's Bert Bell."

> WOLFF: Yes, commissioner, what is it?
> BELL: I watched your telecast tonight.
> WOLFF: Well, what did you think?
> BELL: You did a good job but I have a couple of suggestions for you: I never want to hear the words *exhibition game*. We don't play *exhibition* games. We play *preseason* games, so make sure you never do that again.

"Then he said, 'On one play you had a guy going through the line and you said he was *tripped up*. Our players don't go around tripping. We attack them and bring them down. We don't trip! Another thing you said: 'He was wrestled to the ground.' We don't wrestle in our sport, either.'

"I said, 'Anything else?' He said, 'No. Otherwise you're okay. Goodnight.'

"Nowadays in the Commissioner's Office, they have a vice president for marketing, a vice president for public relations, a vice president for media relations, on and on," Wolff explained. "I guarantee, nobody's getting memos from the commissioner or phone calls in the middle of the night about preseason games or on words to use. With Bert Bell, I knew that Big Brother was listening all the time, but I thought it was great that anybody would have that much interest in a broadcast."

Wolff, who was in the radio booth when Don Larsen of the New York Yankees pitched a perfect game in the 1956 World Series, was chosen by Bell to broadcast the famous NFL sudden-death championship game won by the Baltimore Colts over the New York Giants two years later.

One summer, the Eagles played an exhibition game against San Francisco in Texas. Near the end of the first half, just as 49ers quarterback Frankie Albert went back to pass, every light in the city of San Antonio went out. They had a total blackout while the ball was in the air. It lasted for about half an hour.

"Nobody could use a phone or do anything involving electricity," explained Bill Campbell, who was broadcasting the game back to Philadelphia. "Would you believe while I'm sitting there waiting for the lights to come back on, some press guy from the 49ers walks over to me and said,

'You're wanted on the phone.' I said, 'You can't call next door; how could I be wanted on the phone?' He said, 'You'd better answer it. It's the commissioner.'

"How the hell he got through I'll never tell you. I had to walk all the way down the length of the Press Box to pick up the phone. 'Willie, what the hell's going on out there?' I said, 'Bert, how did you get this call through?' He said, 'I'll ask all the questions here! What's going on down there?' I said, 'The lights went out. There's no power!' Bert got that call through. I don't know how the hell he did it.

"Bert had this big old Atwater Kent floor model radio in his home in Narberth. It had to be two or three feet high. At that time I don't think the West Coast teams were in the league, so Bert could get just about every game on this radio. He could pick up St. Louis, Chicago, Washington—he used to listen to everybody. And he knew everything that we said. When we screwed up, he knew about it immediately. One day he took me in his house and he said, 'Don't ever fool with me, pal, this is my magic box.' I remember screwing things up on the air and thinking to myself, 'Well, at least Bert won't hear this. He can't get this broadcast.' But somehow he got it. He was amazing. He really was on top of everything."

Image-wise, there wasn't an element of professional football that didn't come under close scrutiny of the commissioner. No one defended the league and its personnel more vigorously. He insisted on maintaining complete control over every facet of its operation—everything from the officiating to the way the players carried themselves on and off the field, how his hand-picked broadcasters described (and sometimes embellished) their performance during the game, and, as much as possible, how the press portrayed the NFL.

No one associated with the league escaped his scrutiny, neither the club owners nor the team executives. Even player nicknames needed his approval. He wasn't above telephoning a coach personally to warn him that a moniker like *Slasher* or *Hatchetman* was off-limits.

"Nothing happens anywhere in the National League or in football that he doesn't hear or learn about," wrote the *Bulletin*'s Ed Pollock. "That's why he's on the telephone through so many hours of the day and night. He gets all the information and thus is prepared to answer any complaints or to make any decision. No one in sports puts in more hours on the job."

At times, players and club owners accused the commissioner of favoring the other. Some players called him a "company man." Certain owners asked him whether he worked "for the players or us."

"I work for professional football which includes both players and owners," Bell frequently responded. "I'll battle for what's good for the game. The owners know it and the players should."

Most of them did. Take the case of Tank Younger, the huge Los Angeles Rams fullback who had a propensity for trouble.

"I called him into my office and fined him $150," Bell once told sportswriter Hugh Brown. "He didn't like it at all, said he was dead-broke, and needed that $150 bad. Could he get it back if he behaved? I said yes, and Tank did behave. He was so overjoyed at getting his money back that he said he would see that the rest of the Rams played clean. A little later, I got a letter from another Rams player asking if I would remit his $150 fine; that he was behaving, too. On the bottom of the letter, there was written: 'Approved by Tank Younger, Commissioner of Discipline for the Los Angeles Rams.'"

As for criticism that he was a domineering, self-opinioned czar who actually ran some of the teams in the league such as Baltimore and Philadelphia, Bell once said, "So what? They're making money, aren't they? And as commissioner, if I can help them, why not?"

Stan Javie, who officiated in the NFL for 30 years, remembered his first encounter with Norm Van Brocklin of the Los Angeles Rams when he was working as a back judge in 1951. Van Brocklin was playing against the New York Giants as a replacement for injured quarterback Bob Waterfield. Near the end of the game, Javie made a call determining that Los Angeles was short on a crucial fourth-down running play.

"The Rams were going off the field letting me have it, and the Dutchman had a vocabulary of four-letter words that you can't believe," Javie explained in *Iron Men*. "Now I was a rookie, and this was a crucial game, so I kept backing up and backing up, but finally I'd had enough. 'Knock it off,' I told them. With that, Van Brocklin started in again, so I flipped the flag. 'Van Brocklin, you're gone.' By now the whole Rams' bench was going goofy and Joe Stydahar, their coach, said, 'What the hell am I supposed to do now? I don't have another quarterback.'"

The Giants won the game. "We were playing at the old Polo Grounds and I was thinking to myself as I was running across the field: 'Wonder what Bert Bell is going to say about this rookie?' Sure enough, Bert called me the next day. 'What the hell happened, Stan?' I told him exactly what Van Brocklin said, and Bert told me, 'Way to go, kid!'"

Art McNally probably never would have been the NFL's supervisor of officials for 23 years if he hadn't been persuaded by the commissioner to join the league before the 1959 season. McNally was perfectly happy teaching at Philadelphia's Central High School and working as a college football and basketball official. He spent a year officiating in the National Basketball Association but had just decided to forgo pro basketball because of the heavy travel. Then Mike Wilson, the NFL's supervisor official, called with a job offer.

Still remembering the problems he encountered getting back home in time to teach school, McNally initially declined. The next thing he knew he was sitting in Bert Bell's house in Narberth. "I want to give the kid a chance to come into the NFL and he doesn't want to go," Wilson said, growing more exasperated with every word.

"Bert Bell just kept looking at me," McNally recalled. "Finally, he said, 'What do you want to do? Do you want to work the Army-Navy game?' I said, 'Yes, I want to work an Army-Navy game.' And Bell said, 'Every one of our games is equal to or probably is going to be bigger than the Army-Navy game.'"

McNally thought it over, talked to some friends, and finally signed a contract for $1,800 for the entire year. He officiated for nine seasons and served as an alternate referee for Super Bowl I. He's still working part time in the league today as assistant supervisor of officials. All because of a few words from Bert Bell!

"Bert was a *fan* as well as a commissioner," explained Bill Dudley, the Hall of Fame triple-threat who played in the 1940s and 1950s. "One time when I was with Detroit he called me into his office. We had quite a discussion about gambling because he was really sensitive about the league's image and concerned about gambling back then. He said, 'Bill I know that you go to certain bars in Detroit where the ballplayers hang out.' He named a bar that I frequented and asked me if I was approached by anybody or did I talk to people. I said, 'Commissioner, I don't recall noticing anything.' I said, as far as I'm concerned, I don't know of anybody gambling. I never heard of anybody betting on ballgames. I used to play football cards in college. He said, 'I know you're a high profile ballplayer and you're one of the people who are going to be asked what you think and you usually say what you think.' He said, 'Just be careful, that's all.'"

Toy Ledbetter, who played in the Philadelphia Eagles' backfield off and on between 1950 and 1955, was the only single player on the team for a while. "I used to go out a lot because I was bored," he recalled in *Iron Men*. Toy began hustling a good-looking woman only to find out that her boyfriend was a racketeer who was hiding out in Mexico. Soon Bert Bell called him into the league office. "He said to me, 'I want you to stay away from that broad.' I said, 'What broad?' He just shook his head. 'And I want you to stay out of the goddamn bars once in a while.' I didn't think they'd care if I went in those bars, but they did, and Bert laid down the law. Bert Bell was very shrewd and a fantastic guy. Without him, I doubt that professional football would be the game it is today."

W. C. Heintz described in the *Saturday Evening Post* how he once witnessed Bell lecturing a broadcaster about the league's officials. "Let them call it. That's what they're paid for," the commissioner said. "When a play doesn't go, don't knock a player. Give credit to the guy who stopped it. Another thing: brush off altercations. Just say: 'There's a little disturbance down there, but the officials have it well in hand.' Then talk about something else. Also, don't dwell on injuries. Say: 'So-and-So was shaken up on that play, but he'll be all right.' And one more thing: People say we pass too much in this league, so stress the running game. Any time a guy makes a good run, play it up."

One year, Washington general manager Dick McCann wrote an article in the Redskins' press guide blaming injuries and some bad calls by officials for the team's 3–9 record the previous season. The ink wasn't dry on the publication when McCann was summoned to Philadelphia by the commissioner, who had a reputation for fiercely protecting his officials.

"McCann had no idea," sportswriter John Steadman said in an interview with NFL Films. "He thought he was going to be de-franchised as GM. It was like he was walking into a courtroom with legal secretaries there to take dictation and attorneys. He said he was scared to death. Bert said to him, 'Now why would you make a statement like that?' He said, 'Well commissioner, you have to understand. You owned the Eagles, didn't you?' Bell said, 'That's right.' He said, 'They weren't a very good team.' Bell said, 'That's right.' He said, 'They weren't very good because you tried to coach them for a period of time.' Bell said, 'That's right.' He said, 'We're in the business of trying to sell season tickets. And if there's some way we can take that bad team and blame someone else for their errors on the field, it might be a way that we can pacify the public and sell those same season tickets again for next year.'

"And Bert dismissed the case. He told McCann to go on and be a good boy."

"Bert hated for you to ever talk about injuries at a football game when you were doing play-by-play," recalled Bill Campbell, the Eagles' broadcaster. "He would say, 'Where did you go to medical school? How can you do a diagnosis from up on top of the stadium? Wives and mothers all over are listening to these games and you're burying these guys because they're so hurt.'

"We had an exhibition game in Little Rock, Arkansas. Tobin Rote rolled out to throw a pass and Bucko Kilroy really hit him. Threw him up against the bench so hard that his helmet came off and his head hit the back of the bench and he sunk to the ground. Well, forgetting Bert's instructions, I really gave this a big dramatic treatment: 'Oh my God, he's passed out. They're bringing an ambulance on the field.' They placed him on a stretcher, put him in the back of the ambulance, and carted him away. I described every bit of it.

"The second half starts. I forget who replaced Rote at quarterback, but they took this guy out of the game after a few plays. By then we had a big lead. And a guy came into the game who wore no number. For a couple of series of plays we didn't know who the hell it was. Finally somebody told us it was Tobin Rote. Wherever they took him to the hospital, they checked him out and decided that his injury wasn't too serious. Tobin Rote had an unbelievable second half. I don't think he missed a pass. He was great and they beat us."

By the time Campbell arrived home to Broomall it was almost 4:00 the next morning. "My wife said to me, 'Call the commissioner. He sounds very excited. He said to call no matter what time you got in.' So I called him. He answered the phone and said, 'Willie, Tobin Rote did a helluva job throwing out of the ass end of that ambulance, didn't he?' He said, 'I'll tell you what to do. Why don't you come by the office around nine?' And I said to him, 'Bert, it's quarter to four now.' He said to me, 'I can tell time, Willie!'

"In those days, every play-by-play announcer in the league reported to the league office. You served at the pleasure of the commissioner. I had broken the rule about minimizing injuries. I just got carried away so he let me know about it. He told me that if I did it again, he would suspend me for a game. I didn't do it again."

Bell bristled whenever he was accused of censoring broadcasters, which, not surprisingly, happened frequently.

"There's not an element of censorship in it," he heatedly told Art Morrow of the *Philadelphia Inquirer* after the Rote incident. "In the first place, our rules do not apply to newspapers. The sports writer has to answer only to his paper, and he writes the game as he sees fit. But the broadcasters are different. You might say that they are being paid by their sponsors through the league—or even by the league through their sponsors—and that makes them salesmen for football. You never heard of a salesman saying that his product was no good, did you? Well, we don't want any of our broadcasters saying or even implying that about football. That's what our code is designed to protect."

Bell's concern about the problem of publicizing injuries was twofold. On one hand, he didn't want to alarm wives or mothers of players by showing them writhing in pain on the football field. On the other hand, knowing that the heaviest betting occurs during the two hours prior to game time, he insisted that teams release injury reports in a timely manner—48 hours before kickoff—to prevent any chance of gamblers obtaining and taking advantage of inside information.

That's why the commissioner compiled a list of all the big gamblers in the nation. His security chief Austin Gunsel constantly had former FBI agents monitoring point spreads in league cities. "Listening posts" were established to help determine if large amounts of money suddenly appeared in the betting of any one team or a particular game.

Each week, Bell received betting prices and point spreads on Monday, Wednesday, Thursday, and Friday nights, Saturday mornings, and Saturday nights from bookies like Footsie Stein, or Wingie, or Hockie, or Joe Frisco Legs. One time Bell's investigators watched as a heavily favored team's odds suddenly dropped to three points two days before a game. The reason? Five of its players suddenly came down with the Asian Flu.

On another occasion, Bell noticed a sudden drop in the odds on a Cleveland–Chicago Cardinals game. He immediately called a Browns official and was told that quarterback Otto Graham was injured. "Get it in the paper so the public will know about it," Bell ordered. "I can't do anything about people betting, but I'll make sure the public knows as much as the gamblers."

Harold Weissman of the *New York Mirror* was sitting with Bell in his hotel suite in Detroit the night before the 1957 NFL championship game between the Lions and the Cleveland Browns.

"Keep your guard up," Weissman cautioned. "I hear there are two guys around the country who have been getting down for $100,000 a pop." Bell's jowly countenance broke into a wide smile. "Yeah," he rasped. "I know. Their initials are R. R. and E. K. And they're betting $200,000, not $100,000, a game. But I'm not worried. I've got my finger on it every week. They've bet against each other every single time. If they ever go the same way, I'll step in."

W. C. Heintz described in *The Saturday Evening Post* an incident that occurred in 1948 when Bell received a phone call while attending an Eagles game at Philadelphia's Shibe Park. The caller informed him that a local gambler just out on parole was circulating a rumor about the point spread of a game being played on the West Coast. "Bell dashed from the ball park to Lew Tendler's Restaurant, where he got Harry Carlis, then Tendler's partner, to call in the man.

"Blazing now, Bell backed the gambler against the wall. 'But Bert, I didn't do it,' the gambler protested. 'I'll give ten thousand to any charity you name if you'll tell me who said this.'

"'I'm not that much of a sucker,' Bell shouted back. 'But I'll tell you this: If you do this again, I'll have you put back in the can where you belong.'"

Bell was one of the first people in professional football to recognize the potential of television as a marketing vehicle.

"When TV came of age in the 1950s, my dad saw a great opportunity for fans to see the players in a different light—without their helmets on, so to speak," Upton Bell recalled. "He realized that the players could be the league's most visible salesmen. He insisted that they be very friendly to the fans, sign autographs, and make themselves available whenever an opportunity came up to show themselves in front of the public.

"I remember when the *Ed Sullivan Show* came on, my dad would tell his PR guy Joe Labrum: 'I want to make sure that one of our players is on television every Sunday night. I want them on TV everywhere. I want them to wear a suit. I want them to look good!' And every Sunday, Sullivan would look out into the audience and ask Otto Graham, or Lou Groza, or Y. A. Tittle, or Alan Ameche, or Alex Webster to stand up and take a bow."

Television did something else for the game besides helping its popularity grow by leaps and bounds. It helped fans appreciate the good defensive performances that were not as evident on radio. Bell quickly recognized this. He saw that players like Chuck Bednarik and Sam Huff were turning fans on to aggressive, domineering defenses. Upton remembers him telling Chris Schenkel one time, "Chris, don't forget to introduce the defense. The fans are in love with defense, not with the damn offense."

Television also made Bell hypersensitive about players' altercations on the field.

"One day we were playing Cleveland at Connie Mack Stadium," recalled Philadelphia Eagles defensive back Tom Brookshier. "Chuck Noll had said early in the game to Chuck Bednarik, 'I'm going to come into your dressing room and whip your ass after this game's over!' And Chuck just said, 'Tough!'

"After the game, I go over to say hello to Galen Fiss, an old friend and captain of the Browns. Our players were pretty much gone, but the Browns players were still on the field making the long walk to the visitor's locker room. Bednarik went by me and said, 'Watch this!' I turn around with Galen Fiss as we were shaking hands and Chuck hits Chuck Noll a shot. Noll's helmet goes straight up in the air spinning, and he knocks him down. And then knocks him down a second time.

"Now I look around and all the Cleveland guys are running this way and I figure: 'Oh, this is not good—me and Chuck and all them.' They got about 10 feet away and Chuck turns around and says, 'That's it!' And they stop like there's an invisible fence. They walked back and forth and back and forth, yelling, 'You dirty . . . !'

"That night Chuck walks into his house and the phone was ringing and it was Bert Bell screaming, 'You big dumb . . . I'm trying to get this game accepted and respected and the closing credits on the game was you beating up Chuck Noll. And I'm trying to sell this game!' Bednarik said he chewed him out for 20 minutes. That was the commissioner. He went right to the individual."

37. "On Any Given Sunday . . ."

Bert Bell returned to the nation's capital in July 1958 to again plead his league's case for antitrust relief. The commissioner was accompanied by a new advisor—Clinton M. Hester, one of the most highly respected lobbyists in Washington, who knew most members of Congress personally.

Hester had been introduced to Bell by Detroit Lions president Edwin J. Anderson. He quickly earned the commissioner's trust. "Mr. Hester is one of the most competent, diligent, and honest men I have ever known," Bell had told the NFL club owners earlier in the year.

"We became very close," Hester later explained to Jack Walsh in an interview for *The Sporting News*, "but for some reason, never got on a first-name basis. I always called him Mr. Bell or Mr. Commissioner. In turn, he called me Mr. Hester. It got embarrassing to me. I asked him to please call me Clint. But he replied, 'As long as I live, you'll be Mr. Hester to me.' "

After pounding the marble halls of Congress with Hester for two days, Bell offered to compromise in professional football's fight for exemption from the antitrust laws. "Whatever you gentlemen do is all right with us," he said while being questioned by the Senate Antitrust Subcommittee.

Bell denied suggestions by witnesses from the Players Association that NFL owners blacklist players who exercise their rights under the reserve clause to become free agents after two years. He also defended the player draft and said that he believed that 98 percent of the players favored it. If the draft were scuttled, he added, "there won't be any more pro football."

Meanwhile, the players were again becoming frustrated because the owners still had not implemented the injury protection clause that had been promised. According to the *History of the National Football League Players Association*, some players still had not been paid $50 for each preseason game. Other proposals, including the pension plan, had been ignored.

When Billy Howton of the Green Bay Packers, the president of the National Football League Players Association, threatened to sue again for antitrust violations, the owners immediately responded with a benefit plan that included hospitalization, medical insurance, and life insurance with a plan for retirement benefits at age 65. Bell gave Howton his personal assurance that a pension plan would be developed.

On November 30, 1958, Pittsburgh upset the Chicago Bears, 24–10, for the Steelers' first win over the Bears in 14 games spanning more than 24 years. Afterward, a sportswriter asked Bell what he thought of the game. "It doesn't matter in the NFL how many games you win, what your score is, how well you do," he replied. "On any given Sunday, any team in the NFL can win."

"Commissioner Bert Bell had already coined a phrase that was soon to become a slogan: 'On any given Sunday, any team in the NFL can beat any other,' " Tom Callahan wrote in *Johnny: The Life and Times of John Unitas*.

"Both Upton and I heard my father say 'On any given Sunday . . .' many times," recalled Bert Jr., who obtained intellectual rights to the phrase a number of years ago.

But after the Steelers-Bears game that day in 1958, the commissioner's favorite saying received even more attention and was well on its way to becoming the defining axiom of the NFL.

The commissioner was not in a good mood during the executive session that followed the annual player draft at the Warwick Hotel on December 1, even though he was being congratulated by the owners for increasing their revenue during the season by permitting the regular use of television time-outs in all games, an innovation that he had introduced as an experiment in 1955.

First, he was again forced to urge the owners to convince their players to play in the Pro Bowl game if they were selected. The promoters are "doing a wonderful job," he insisted.

Then he said that coaches and owners' "popping off" and showing films to newspapermen after games about bad officiating must stop.

After that, Bell asked the owners to give serious consideration to the league's financial future. "Unless the rich clubs leave a little for the poor, four or five of our teams are going to be in serious trouble," he warned. "Operating expenses have risen so tremendously that with bad breaks in weather, a weak club could be forced to throw in the towel. It's up to you to see that this doesn't happen."

All the while, the commissioner was steaming over reports that some owners were spreading stories that he was a "stooge" for certain other owners. Dismissing such allegations as "ridiculous," Bell looked around the room and bellowed, "If you don't quit the squabbling among yourselves and make your coaches quit their squawking, you can have back my contract.

"Unless I am permitted to run this league as I have in the past 13 years—by persuasion rather than by the book—you can start running it yourselves. I don't want to be a czar, but I must run the league my own way with a free hand."

John Mara jumped to his feet and said that he and the New York Giants "were with the commissioner 100 per cent and that the commissioner had their vote of confidence."

Carroll Rosenbloom of the Baltimore Colts then got up and faced the other owners. "Everyone in the league feels that without the commissioner there would be no league," he said. "The way we feel about the commissioner is without question."

"A standing vote of confidence was given to Commissioner Bell by the members present," according to the minutes of the meeting.

Two weeks later, with his family gathered around their dining room table, Bell made a stunning announcement. "You all better go to church with me this week," he said. "I've decided to become a Catholic. I'm receiving my first Holy Communion."

For years, Frances had been urging her husband to convert to the Roman Catholic Church. Long ago, he had agreed to raise his children in the Catholic faith, and now her prayers were being answered. Undoubtedly Bert was influenced by her devotion to her faith.

"He never said a word beforehand to anybody," Bert's son Upton recalled. "Nobody even knew that he was taking instructions. Maybe he told my mother, we don't really know. He announced it to us very matter-of-factly, just like he would at a league meeting. I was really surprised because he had grown up in a WASP family amid the disdainful anti-Catholicism of the Main Line."

Bert made his first Confession on December 15 at Saint Margaret Church in Narberth. "He's in the confessional and you could hear him all over the place," Upton said. "'Bless me father for I have sinned,' and he has this litany going on all the way back to his days at Penn. Joe Donoghue, his godfather, yells out, 'Shut up, Bert. People can hear you all over the place. This is not a league meeting!' There he is in the confessional like he's speaking to the players."

The following day, dressed in a splendid new white suit, Bell was ready to be baptized and receive his first Holy Communion. As he walked up the steps of the church with his family and a few close friends, Joe Donoghue suddenly blurted out, "Bert, you don't have your teeth in!"

"What baby do you know who was christened had any teeth," Bell replied. "Babies don't have teeth. Why should I have mine?"

38. "Sudden Death" Finally Arrives

One day back in 1946, shortly after he was elected NFL commissioner, Bert Bell was relaxing with some of his friends from the Narberth Sunrise Society. "Hey Bert," one of them shouted, getting right up into his face, "What happens if there is a tie in a championship game? I'm a big pro football fan, but the thought of co-champions really turns me off!"

As Bell recounted that conversation many times over the years to his sons, Bert Jr. and Upton, he sat there for a few seconds pondering what he had just heard. "This guy's right," he thought. "If that happens and we have co-champions, who do we send to the College All-Star game?" "Give me some time, guys," he said." I'll think of something!"

Bert thought about the problem with tie games all the way home. "We can't send two teams to Chicago. What do we do, flip a coin? That'll never work." Then the light came on: "We'll play an extra period. . . . The first team to score wins the game . . . Sudden Death!"

When the owners got together the following January in Chicago, a few of them initially resisted the commissioner's proposal for sudden-death overtime. To some, the idea of "co-champions" was appealing. After listening to their arguments for a while, he finally stood up and said, "You realize of course that if you have co-champions, you'll have to send two teams to Chicago for the annual All-Star game. That means full pay for twice as many players."

That did it. As soon as the financial issue was raised with the cash-starved owners, they quickly fell into line. On January 24, 1947, the league's rules committee passed a motion that the sudden-death overtime method of deciding tie scores for divisional playoff and championship games *only* was to be included in the playing rules.

Over the next few years Bell tried unsuccessfully to have sudden-death overtime implemented into regular-season games.

In 1948, the rules committee rejected the idea before it came to a vote. In 1952, the owners again turned it down, this time by a 9–3 count. Bell tried to bring the measure up again at a later session that year but finally withdrew his proposal because the Green Bay Packers and Chicago Bears explained that they had no lighting facilities and overtime games could easily extend until after sundown. It was rejected again in 1954.

On August 25, 1955, Bell approved a pregame arrangement between the Los Angeles Rams and New York Giants for an experimental sudden-death overtime period if it was needed for their exhibition game in Portland, Oregon. As it turned out, the teams tied 17–17 in regulation before the Rams won the coin toss in the extra period. Quarterback Norm Van Brocklin then engineered a 70-yard drive in eight plays for the winning touchdown.

Over the next three years, Rule 14 covering sudden-death overtime was never needed. But the commissioner continued to entertain hopes. "If it ever happens, it will really call attention to pro football," he said in 1956.

Two years later, Bert Bell got his wish when the Baltimore Colts and New York Giants met for the NFL championship at Yankee Stadium on December 28, 1958.

After Steve Myhra of the Colts kicked a 20-yard field goal with seven seconds left in the fourth quarter to tie the score 17–17 and send the game into overtime for the first time in history, confusion reigned down on the field. Most, if not all, of the players were totally exhausted and thought the game was over.

"I mean I was damn tired," recalled Sam Huff of the New York Giants. "I played on all the special teams, kickoff teams, punting teams, punt return teams. All that plus regular middle linebacker."

"Personally my butt was worn out," added Baltimore's Raymond Berry, who set an NFL championship game record with 12 receptions that day. "We had been throwing the ball all afternoon and I wasn't looking forward to playing anymore."

"We were on the sidelines patting each other on the back," said Huff, who appeared on the cover of *Time* magazine as the NFL's first high-profile defensive player that year. "I was happy because I was thinking I would get half the [playoff] money."

Then referee Ronald Gibbs came over to the New York bench and said, "All right, it's going to be sudden death. In three minutes we're going to tee it up and kick it off, and the first team that scores wins the game."

"Wait a minute," Huff said. "The game's over!"

"No it's not, Sam," Gibbs replied. "It's a sudden-death overtime game."

"We didn't have a clue what overtime was, never heard of it," said Berry. "As I thought about it over the years, Ron Gibbs knew what the rule was. He knew exactly what to do and did it."

"No one knew quite how it worked," recalled Frank Gifford, who had caught a 15-yard touchdown pass from Charlie Conerly to put the Giants ahead 17–14 early in the fourth quarter. "I'm not sure if the officials really knew."

Gifford said that the confusion didn't last long, "maybe for two minutes. Then we tossed the coin."

Chuck Thompson, the Baltimore Colts announcer who shared the national television play-by-play duties that day with Chris Schenkel, his counterpart with the New York Giants, said that both sportscasters knew exactly what was going on.

"We had a meeting in the commissioner's office the day before the game and the possibility of overtime was discussed," Thompson later told sportswriter Dave Newhouse. "The fact that we were doing something historic didn't occur to me until afterward."

The Giants won the toss to begin the extra session but went three-and-out. Then quarterback Johnny Unitas drove the Colts 80 yards in 13 plays with Alan Ameche going over from the one-yard line to score the winning touchdown, eight minutes and 15 seconds into the first overtime game in NFL history.

Sitting with Bell in the commissioner's box high up in the stands as the game ended was his good friend Clinton Hester, the league's counsel. He turned to look at the commissioner. "Bell was so happy and proud that tears ran down his cheeks," Hester recalled.

Bert Bell was vindicated.

"Up in the grandstand, a man was crying tears of joy," Frank Graham wrote in the *New York Journal-American*. "It was Bert Bell. People told him he was smoking the wrong kind of cigarettes or else he had run one too many off-tackle plays in college when he came up with the idea of using 'sudden death.' He fought strong opposition to add the 'sudden death' feature. The National Football League has been Bert Bell's life. It doesn't take much for him to get sentimental over it."

Raymond Berry recalls standing in the street outside Yankee Stadium after everybody got dressed, getting ready to board the team buses. "As I was standing there, I saw Bert Bell," he explained. "I just remember it registered on me that he had tears in his eyes. It just is a memory that stuck with me. I'm not sure that I even processed it at the time. The memory stayed there.

"At some point, I got thinking: 'There's Bert Bell, and he's got tears in his eyes, and it's his game.' I started thinking about what thoughts he might have had there. Over the years, that dawned on me because, at that particular point, none of us as players had a clue what had taken place out there. We just loved to play the game and we were fortunate enough to win.

"I'm sure that Bert Bell later on, he of all people, understood the significance of what had just happened. And I think that—as I thought about it—he saw his baby get born. He knew it and it affected him. It was never going to be the same. That's all speculation, but there had to be some explanation why he was so emotional, and it made sense to me—that game was behind it.

"He was there from the beginning, I guess, and he of all people understood what had happened when none of the rest of us did."

Reflecting on the game later, Upton Bell thought that in many ways it was a bittersweet moment for his father. "I think that game took a lot out of him emotionally," Upton explained. "Seeing what was happening there, it was almost like his whole life was flashing in front of him. Physically he really wasn't getting better, and that game set in motion his desire to leave as commissioner. He probably felt that day that his job was finished. In a way, seeing the tears, I think he felt it was time to go."

Bell's old friend from Baltimore, John Steadman, bumped into the commissioner as he was walking with a crowd from the stadium with two of his children and Art Rooney, the owner of the Pittsburgh Steelers.

"Bell said it was the greatest game he had ever seen," Steadman recalled. "He said that we had just seen the greatest game in the history of professional football." And then he "added so cryptically, something I will always remember: 'John, old boy, I never thought I would live to see sudden death!'"

"This one game, more than any other thing you can point to, made the National Football League what it is today," Schenkel later told Newhouse. "This overtime game really stunned the nation. Everything was uphill from then on."

Don Maynard, who played in the game as a rookie wide receiver for the Giants, said that Bell deserves credit for another decision that he made that year. On at least one occasion previously, the NFL players had voted not to give playoff game monetary shares to their coaches.

"It kind of had to do with Cleveland and Paul Brown," Maynard explained, recalling that he had heard from other players that Bert Bell stepped in, changed the rule, and made sure that coaches were included.

The game drew the largest television audience in NFL history—some 45 million people, including President Dwight D. Eisenhower, who watched it with friends at his home in Gettysburg, Pennsylvania. As usual, fans living within a 75-mile radius of New York City didn't see it because of Bert Bell's blackout policy.

Local fans were also deprived of the usual pregame hype because of a 17-day newspaper strike that ended just before kickoff. That's probably why attendance for the game—64,185—was almost 7,000 fewer than the Yankee Stadium crowd that saw the Giants edge the Colts, 24–21, on November 9. But 49 percent of the radio sets in New York were tuned in.

Bell spent much of the day emphatically denying a rumor that originated at a Detroit radio station that he was resigning as commissioner. "That's just plain malarkey," he told writers as he walked out of Yankee Stadium. "These reports come up regularly, especially at this time of the year. It's probably just one of those drunken bums, who says the same thing every year about this time. Last year they said I had a heart attack and would retire at about the same time. I feel fine and have given no thought of resigning."

After returning home, Bell learned that the rumor had spread to Philadelphia's radio stations. He wasn't surprised. "Two years ago," he told *Philadelphia Inquirer* sportswriter John Dell, "I arrived for a playoff game and the hotel clerk said real surprised, 'Why, Mr. Bell. We cancelled your room. We got a call from your doctor saying you weren't coming.' "

A few days later, the commissioner had a change of heart about using sudden-death overtime during the regular season. The reason? Television.

"We can do it once or twice a year in playoffs, but not on a regular basis," he explained to the Associated Press. "We couldn't preempt the time necessary for sudden death. What sponsor is going to buy an incomplete game? And on the other side of the fence, what sponsor of a regular program is going to buy time which could be preempted by an overtime football game? It isn't feasible."

Another problem with sudden-death overtime, said the commissioner, is the lack of proper lighting in many stadiums. "If the home team was the Pittsburgh Steelers or Philadelphia Eagles, for example, and sudden death was necessary, we'd have to start before breakfast or continue the next day."

Although physically he wasn't feeling as strong as he would like, Bell was sitting on top of the world. Not only had he helped orchestrate the most dramatic championship game in the history of professional football, NFL attendance in 1958 went over 3 million fans for the first time—a 97 percent increase in ten years!

Bell chuckled when someone showed him the breakdown of the full playoff shares. Each member of the Colts received $4,718.77; every Giants player was awarded $3,111.33.

"In 1933 when I brought the Eagles into the league, each player on the Chicago Bears got $210.34 for beating the Giants," he quipped. "The losers received $140.22."

39. Anxiety over the AFC, the Pension Plan, and the Pro Bowl

Bert Bell spent his first day at work in the New Year 1959 chatting on the phone with well-wishers anxious to talk about the fabulous sudden-death game between the Colts and Giants. But later that afternoon, Joe Labrum, his public relations man, came rushing in with some disconcerting news.

"Bobby Layne and Ollie Matson didn't report for practice today," he told the commissioner. "They're passing up the Pro Bowl in Los Angeles. They're playing at the Hula Bowl in Hawaii instead, and *UPI* is on the phone looking for your reaction."

Bell was livid. Despite his frequent pleas to the owners to help him enforce the clause in the player's contract that required them to play in the Pro Bowl in Los Angeles if selected, the bigger stars—like Layne, the great Detroit quarterback, and Matson, the outstanding Chicago Cardinals halfback—often chose a trip to Hawaii.

The Hula Bowl had been around since 1946, but the game took on added luster early in the 1950s when NFL players were first invited to join the Hawaiian All-Star team to strengthen their chances against a national "college" squad.

The commissioner picked up the phone and told the United Press International reporter that he would recommend a "severe penalty" for recalcitrant players when he put the matter on the agenda at the annual league meeting in two weeks.

"A lot of ballplayers want to play in the Pro Bowl game because the money means a lot to them," he said. "But the rich players want to go to the Hula game. They can take their wives with them and it's like a vacation. Ballplayers expect the owners to live up to the contracts, so they should do the same."

Frank Gifford of the New York Giants was another player who chose the more exotic trip. He lived only about a half a mile from the Coliseum where he had played for USC. He was back in Los Angeles doing some film work, and appearing in another game in his hometown meant absolutely nothing.

"I remember talking to Wellington Mara about it," Gifford explained years later. "I said, 'Look, I've got a chance to go play in Hawaii. I can take my wife and I'm going to have a two week vacation.' And he kinda looked at me and said something to the effect of, 'Well I don't know what you're going to do, but I know what I would have done.' All I wanted was his blessing, but he couldn't go against the commissioner. He basically said, 'Go ahead and enjoy it.'"

The night before convening the three-day owners' meeting at the Warwick Hotel in Philadelphia, Bell sat down for a private dinner with the three leaders of the Players Association—Billy Howton of the Green Bay Packers, Kyle Rote of the New York Giants, and Bill Pellington of the Baltimore Colts.

The players told Bell that their counterparts from every NFL team except the Chicago Bears were planning to remain in the Quaker City for the duration of the owners' meetings to "clarify the pension issue."

The commissioner could see from the looks in the players' eyes that they were a fiercely determined group. Although he was still not convinced personally, he decided to take the high road. He quickly invited all of their representatives to attend the sessions when the owners discussed the situation with Bill Dudley, the former Pittsburgh Steelers triple-threat star who was now a successful life insurance entrepreneur branching out into group and benefit plans.

When the owners reconvened on January 22—following a long, tedious player draft that went long into the previous night—they heard what the commissioner had to say and immediately agreed to invite the players. In addition to Howton, Rote, and Pellington, Dick Alban of the Pittsburgh Steelers, Joseph Perry of the San Francisco 49ers, Bobby Walston of the Philadelphia Eagles, and Ron Waller of the Los Angeles Rams were welcomed into the meetings.

Dudley made a compelling presentation. It was so impressive that Bell reversed his position afterward and described himself as "open-minded" on the issue.

"After listening to Dudley, I am for one perfectly willing to study the plan, listen to some other insurance people, and investigate this thing thoroughly," he said. "There are many complications that must be considered, but maybe it is feasible."

The commissioner and the owners reportedly were pleased to learn that the players did not expect the clubs to contribute any cash to the plan. Dudley said that a satisfactory pension could be started by raising $213,000 through league sources and by players' contributions totaling $125,000 annually with each player kicking in $300.

Although George Halas of the Chicago Bears and George Preston Marshall of the Washington Redskins still voiced strong objections, Bell told Herb Good of the *Philadelphia Inquirer* that the owners were "serious and honest" in their study of the players' request for a minimum $100-a-month pension for five-year men at the age of 55.

"They [the owners] evidently mean business," said Dudley. "I don't think they would waste that much time on it if they didn't."

"Although nothing definite was decided, the fact that both morning and afternoon sessions were amicable made progress in pension negotiations certain," wrote Jack Sell in the *Pittsburgh Post-Gazette*.

"Bell said none of the owners heckled any of the Players Association delegates at any time. Only ripple on the surface of tranquility was the barring of Creighton Miller from the confabs. 'I just don't want him in there,' Bell said curtly and refused to give an explanation."

Later in the day, after announcing that he had received an offer of $650,000 for a franchise in Miami from a "very high-class, high-type man," Bell offered "a million thanks" to members of the Colts and Giants and called their 1958 title game "the greatest TV show ever carried."

Mentioning that the league publicity of all types increased by 25 percent, the commissioner added, "An Associated Press feature writer told me that his service plans to cover our training camps like they cover the baseball camps."

The commissioner explained that even though the league had "the greatest year financially that we have ever had in the history of pro football—an increase of 11.5 per cent," two NFL clubs finished in the red in 1958. Two other teams finished in the black only because of good road attendance in one case, and larger crowds in the last two games at home for the other. "Just because we had this kind of attendance and money, it still isn't any bed of roses," he warned. "Unless a team sells 25,000 season tickets, it can run into rough times."

Bell then brought up the Pro Bowl/Hula Bowl situation. "I will enforce it in 1959; I don't care who it is," he said after the owners discussed the player's contract. "We better have discipline or it is going to be rough." A motion that no player can play in a game not authorized by the NFL passed unanimously. "I will fix the penalty for violations before the next season begins," Bell said.

The commissioner urged the club owners to "build up" the NFL. "Don't argue among yourselves; it can only hurt us," he said. "I guess that I am getting a little old and sentimental and mellow, but I hate arguments between teams and between coaches. You have the greatest spectator sport in the world, and let us keep it that way. I have no desire to run the league like a czar. Pro football is my life. Please let me decide disputes without publicity and according to the book. As God is my judge, I will give a fair and honest decision. Try to let me run the league without arguments."

Then, glancing around the room, Bell told the owners that he was going to make a decision. "It is the toughest thing I have had to do since my entry into the league in 1933," he said. "I am making it as honestly and justly as I can. I was advised in this decision. I spent long hours discussing the case with my brother, who is a Pennsylvania Supreme Court Justice."

Bell slowly read his two-and-a-half-page decision that settled a long-simmering territorial dispute between the Chicago Bears and Chicago Cardinals. The feud began in 1931 when Charlie Bidwell, then the Cardinals' owner, conceded that everything north of Madison Avenue belonged to George Halas and the Bears.

Although the Cardinals claimed that there was never an official agreement, Bell supported Halas and ruled that the accord was still in effect despite the fact that the Cardinals had been a financial drain on the rest of the league because of their dwindling attendance. Both Chicago teams suffered from the NFL's television blackout policy. The Bears could not televise their road games when the Cardinals were at home and vice versa.

Halas asked the commissioner to act after the Cardinals filed a suit in Chicago's Superior Court to test the legality of the 1931 agreement. They had earlier announced intentions to move their games from Comiskey Park in the city's South Side into Dyche Stadium on the suburban campus of Northwestern University, which is located in the Bears' territory. Bell's ruling denied such a move.

Before adjourning "the most harmonious meeting in National Football League history," according to George Strickler of the *Chicago Tribune*, the owners surprisingly voted unanimously to reduce the size of the annual player draft from 30 to 20 rounds. They also called for a special meeting in Chicago on April 23 to consider the pension proposals of the Players Association.

"The player representatives left the meeting greatly encouraged by the friendly and cooperative reception accorded them," Strickler wrote of the historic occasion. It was the first time that the league owners as a group heard members of the Players Association speak at an official NFL meeting.

Howton, the president of the association, said that they had only one regret. "We wish Commissioner Bell would approve the Hula Bowl game," he explained. "We agree with the resolution in that we feel that it is the obligation of every National League player to appear in the Pro Bowl game if he is selected. But the Hula Bowl game gave less fortunate players an opportunity to pick up a little extra cash and get a vacation trip after the season."

When the Baltimore Colts held their victory banquet at the Emerson Hotel on March 9, Bell was unable to attend because of a two-week battle with bronchitis. Speaking by telephone through an amplifier from his bed at Lankenau Hospital, the commissioner admitted to the 800 dinner-guests one of the worst-kept secrets in sports—that he had been a Colts rooter for some time.

"The last few years, I've been just living to see the Colts win," Bell said. "And now I've made it."

The commissioner called the tremendous enthusiasm of Baltimore fans one of the "best things" that ever happened to professional football.

"I've seen Army-Navy games, Penn-Cornell games, traditional games in the Big Ten and all sorts of games where enthusiasm is supposed to reach its peak," Bell proclaimed in his raspy voice. "But I've never seen anything to top the support you people give the Colts."

Afterward, Gino Marchetti of the Colts presented a plaque from Mayor Tommy D'Alesandro and the Greater Baltimore Committee to the commissioner via telephone remote control. "Bell does a pretty good job of reading—for a *lineman*," toastmaster Morris Frank quipped after the presentation.

Sitting up in his hospital bed, the old Penn *quarterback* must have chuckled at that one.

The owners assembled for a special meeting in Philadelphia's Warwick Hotel on April 23–24 to hear the commissioner discuss his proposed pension plan for players.

Surprisingly, Bell had worked out the details with a Baltimore insurance executive who was a close friend of Colts owner Carroll Rosenbloom, and *not* with his friend, former Pittsburgh Steelers standout Bill Dudley, who had been expected to win the business.

"I have had Sig Hyman as my advisor," the commissioner told the owners. "I am simply telling you my plan which I think is feasible and the best plan."

Bell enthusiastically described details of the plan to the owners. "And the beauty of it all," he exclaimed at one point, "is that it doesn't cost the owners anything and the players don't have to contribute a nickel themselves!"

In addition to calling for an undetermined lifetime stipend from the age of 65 for players who have played four years and at least one game into the fifth season beginning with the 1959 season, all of the league's players would become eligible immediately for hospitalization benefits and $6,000 to $20,000 in life insurance.

Bell explained that the financing of the plan would come from "quite a few sources," including the league's championship games, increased television payments beginning in 1961, and a half-dozen other money-raising ventures to be decided in the future. One possibility he said was a postseason game between the second-place finishers in each division. It would be played in a warm climate. Winners would receive $800 with the losers earning $600.

"It is not a *Pension* Plan," Bell emphasized while asking the owners for permission to let him work out the fine details with Hyman. "It is a *National Football League Benefit Plan for Players*, and players will not be required to put any money into it. I think the greatest thing about this is its public relations value."

"The players told Sig Hyman they would like to take 20 per cent of the 70 per cent players' share of the championship game," Bell added during the closed-door session. "I said no!"

Both Hyman and Bell explained that it would be impossible at the present time to estimate a maximum or minimum figure that could be contributed to a plan that did not go into effect until the 1961 championship game. "We can't tell what the income is going to be," the commissioner explained. "If the game is played in New York, you have over 60,000 seats. In Washington, you have around 32,000 seats."

After a two-hour-and-15-minute discussion, Joseph A. Donoghue, the league's assistant treasurer, made a motion, seconded by Baltimore Colts owner Carroll Rosenbloom, that the NFL approve the framework of the benefit plan for players to be finalized and administered by the commissioner and two trustees to be appointed in the future. It passed unanimously.

The members of the Players Association had earlier discussed the details of the plan with Hyman, so their stamp of approval at the afternoon session was merely a formality and took less than a minute. "We are very happy with it," Howton told the owners. "We are very happy that the matter has come out the way it has. As far as I am concerned, it is settled."

Later, a highly elated Howton pointed out to reporters that the Players Association had been in existence only three years and in that short period of time had gotten virtually everything it had requested from the club owners. "The benefit plan is one of the finest things ever to happen in pro football," he said. Then, referring to Commissioner Bell and the owners, he added, "I'm sure they will do a good job on the plan."

Howton acknowledged that there was some grumbling from veterans around the age of thirty with eight or more years of experience who would still have to serve an additional four years (plus one game) to be eligible for payments. "There was no way we could get around it," he said.

Before adjourning, the owners approved a disaster plan, whereby each team would again pay $460 for insurance and contribute three players to any member franchise wiped out in an aerial accident. They also rejected a plea to sanction the Hula Bowl, even though its promoters changed the date of the game to avoid conflicting with the Pro Bowl.

Late in the spring, Bell received word that Lamar Hunt, the son of H. L. Hunt, the multimillionaire Texas oil tycoon, wanted to come to Philadelphia to sit down with him. The commissioner had never met Hunt but agreed to meet with him for lunch at The Tavern, in Merion, on June 3. Joining them were Bell's close friend Joe Donoghue, and Bell's son Bert Jr.

"Halfway through lunch, Hunt hadn't said a word," the younger Bell recalled. "He was almost like a kid sitting there very quietly. So my father finally said to him, 'Why are you here? Is there some reason why you wanted to come and see me?'"

Hunt, the 26-year-old son of one of the world's wealthiest men, finally spoke up. He said that he wanted an NFL franchise. Bell advised him to attempt to buy the Chicago Cardinals, knowing that he would probably transfer the franchise to Texas and solve one of the commissioner's major headaches.

"My father told him that the NFL wasn't ready to expand yet," Bert Jr. explained. "The league still had a few doormats and wasn't balanced enough. My dad said he needed three more teams in the black before the NFL could expand."

Hunt returned home, then had some conversations with the Walter Wolfner family, who owned the Cardinals. "I talked with them about moving the Cardinals to Dallas," he later told sportswriter Randy Harvey. "As it worked out, they ultimately agreed to sell 20%, but not move the team."

By mid-July, Hunt had tentative plans for a new professional football league comprising at least six teams. He sent an emissary, Davey O'Brien, the former Philadelphia Eagles quarterback, up to Margate to get the NFL commissioner's blessing. O'Brien had been one of Bell's favorite players when he owned the Eagles, and he was welcomed warmly. Without revealing Hunt's name, O'Brien asked Bell for his cooperation in getting the league started. Bell said that he would be happy to meet with the organizers of the new loop and added that he saw no reason why the new league wouldn't go over.

Bell knew that expansion in pro football was inevitable. He had appointed Chicago Bears owner George Halas to head a committee to study the situation in 1958. At first Bell favored Buffalo and Louisville, but the league eventually focused on the Southwest, particularly Houston and Dallas. By the time the owners met in January 1959, all of the NFL teams except the Washington Redskins favored expanding. But Halas told Bell not to bring the issue up, because George Preston Marshall would kill the idea. At the time, only one vote was needed to defeat such a proposal.

Bell was also well aware that the antitrust issue still hovered over the NFL like a black cloud. Congress was constantly looking over his shoulder just waiting to throw the dreaded *Monopoly* charge at the league. So it was back to Washington for the commissioner on July 25; only this time he had members of the House Anti-Trust Subcommittee in stitches by the time his first day of testimony was completed.

After being accused of "censorship" because he gave prior approval to sportscasters assigned to NFL games and then prohibited them from showing fights or injuries on the field, Bell said that he acted only to "protect the game." Then the commissioner cited entertainer Elvis Presley, "who wiggles while he warbles," as a precedent for regulating what is shown on telecasts of football games.

"Someone decided that Mr. Presley wasn't in the best interest of the public for kids looking in and they raised the camera on that, too," Bell testified, referring to a recent television show when cameras focused only on the upper part of Presley's torso.

Bell returned to the witness stand on July 28 and immediately stole the spotlight from the Senate subcommittee's business of the day—a discussion of a bill by its chairman, Senator Estes Kefauver, to apply antitrust restrictions to all pro sports.

The commissioner jolted the crowded chamber with the announcement that a second professional football loop would soon be formed. "We're in favor of the new league," he quickly declared. "Not one owner is opposed to it."

Within minutes, the historic room fell into a stunned silence. Then a ripple—a buzz—of shocked disbelief gradually worked its way throughout the area.

Speaking slowly, Bell provided more details:

The NFL welcomes the competition and will be glad to discuss a possible football world series with the newcomers. . . . I understand that the new league plans to begin operating next year, probably with six teams. . . . I expect to meet with some of the new league's founders in Philadelphia soon. . . . The backers are Texans and I know they don't need money. . . . They authorized me to make the announcement.

While declining to name the promoters—he said he knew one of them personally—Bell identified O'Brien as the "go-between" who brought the news of the new league to him. He emphasized that Davey had nothing to do with the new organization, financially or otherwise. "I told him to tell the new people that we definitely were in favor of the new league. The more teams and the more competition, the better."

The commissioner was asked if he would object to the new league locating teams in cities already represented in his league. "Certainly not," he replied. "The more the merrier. Competition is the life of sports. Even the great George Preston Marshall, of the Redskins, says that if it is a good league, it will help football. If not, the promoters will only hurt themselves."

It was a stroke of genius.

"Bert Bell, the pro football commissioner who is very smart, casually pulled one out of the hat to impress the Senate," wrote Shirley Povich in the *Washington Post* the following day. "He knew that would please the committee which deplores monopoly. They did not hug and embrace Mr. Bell, but their tone toward him softened because here, surely, was a fine man who stood for what the Senators stood for, pro football for everybody and not merely the little clique of cities lucky enough to be in the NFL. The Senators from New York, Colorado, and Tennessee had to be impressed."

"It follows that Bell has gotten away with the trickiest play in many a season," added Wayne Spoelstra of the *Detroit News*. "Senator Kefauver and his teammates on the Senate Anti-Trust and Monopoly Subcommittee are probably waking up today to the fact that Old Pro Bell whipped them handily at the scrimmage line."

Earlier, Bell had asked O'Brien, the intermediary, to request Hunt's permission for him to make the announcement. Hunt immediately said yes. "In truth," Joe McGuff, the sports editor of the *Kansas City Star*, wrote later, "Hunt had only four teams, but he covered up this little problem by telling Bell that the names of the cities and the owners were not to be announced until later. Hunt flew back to Washington for the hearing and sat in the back of the committee room listening to Bell's testimony."

The following day, Philadelphia sportscaster Bill Campbell bumped into the commissioner on the Atlantic City Boardwalk. "He told me where his place was in Margate [110 South Union Avenue on the beach] and invited my wife, Jo, and me to stop by that evening," Campbell recalled. "He said, 'Frances would love to see you.' So we did. We went there and Bert finally came to the door and barely let us in. He was not himself at all. He was very unfriendly and very inhospitable. It was obvious that something was going on inside and he didn't want me to know about it. I had no idea what it was. After a 10- minute conversation we left."

It was learned later that Bell's secret guests on the evening of July 29 were Hunt and O'Brien. Just about the time Bill Campbell and his wife arrived at the front door, Hunt was telling Bell that the new league desired to maintain a friendly relationship with the NFL. He proposed that Bell serve as a common commissioner of both the new league, which would be called the American Football League (AFL) and the NFL. He also suggested, that the two leagues hold a common player draft; and that arrangements be made to black out television during home games in both leagues. Bell rejected all of these offers but gave Hunt advice and information about television, drafting of players, and other details of operating a league.

Bell also advised Hunt and his partners to get started immediately if they expected to operate in 1960. "They've got a tremendous task ahead of them," the commissioner told reporters later. "They have to make television arrangements, draw up contracts, draft players, secure stadium rights, arrange publicity, get their franchises, and many other details. There will be absolutely no connection between our league and any other except to recognize and respect contracts, nor would there be any bonus battles for players similar to big-league baseball. None of our owners believe in such nonsense."

Bell explained that he "asked no questions, merely answered," during the four-and-a-half-hour meeting that was veiled in secrecy at the request of his guests. "The session was very affable. We got along fine. I answered all questions as frankly as possible. I told them anything they wanted to know. They took no notes." Although no future meetings were scheduled, Bell said, "I'm available any time they want to talk. They indicated that they'd be in touch with me later."

Upon arriving home at the Dallas airport, Hunt confirmed that he was the wealthy Texan mentioned as the financial backer of the new professional football league. He mentioned the likely members as Dallas, Houston, Denver, Minneapolis, Los Angeles, and New York. When Hunt was asked his reaction to observations circulating in some circles that Bell has no intention of allowing the new league to be formed, O'Brien spoke up: "I know Bert Bell and I trust him. When he says he is serious, he is."

Bell's annual visit to Hershey in August coincided with an exhibition game between the Philadelphia Eagles and New York Giants. After one of his "Sermon on the Mount" visits, the commissioner told the *Philadelphia Bulletin*'s Hugh Brown that he was worried about the increasing number of rookies—the average was now about 40—who desert NFL training camps each summer.

"A lot of these boys are strange and home sick," Bell explained. "It prevents them from giving their best efforts. They are afraid to slam into the veterans lest they be considered fresh upstarts. Many are cut just because they were slow to play up to their capacity."

Calling for more teams to arrange social programs and off-field recreation for the players, Bell said, "The Steelers have a good idea. They arrange vaudeville skits with rookies only participating. The Steelers have always had one of the lowest desertion rates."

The commissioner loved visiting Hershey because he never forgot a helping hand. "I've come back here every year since these kind people raised $5,000 for an exhibition in 1939 when we sometimes didn't make that much in a league game," he once told Joe King of the *New York World Telegram.*

Late in August, Bell sat down with nationally syndicated columnist Jimmy Breslin for an "As Told To" interview. The subject was gambling and the commissioner repeated many of his old stories about checking on betting odds frequently during the week, his relationship with bookmakers, and his obsession with keeping professional football aboveboard. Two new revelations came out, however, illustrating how difficult it is to protect the game's reputation.

"Take this fellow I spoke to the other day," Bell wrote. "He is a big bettor on professional football games. But he also happens to be a friend, a close one, too, of a man who is connected with one of the teams—as an owner. 'Look,' I told this fellow who bets, 'you've got to make up your mind. You can bet on anything. I don't care if you bet on English rugby on Sundays. But I don't want you betting on professional football because you are going to have people saying that your friend has a piece of the action. And I can't stand for that.' The guy stopped betting. I know because I heard through my bookmaking contacts that he refused to touch a couple of exhibition games."

"Gamblers," he continued, "have even come up with a trick I haven't heard of being used in years. They try and get an athlete to go in on a horse bet with them. 'If you don't have the money, I'll put it up for you,' they say. Naturally the bet loses. 'We'll make it back. I'll bet $20 for you to bet on the next one,' the chiseler says. Pretty soon he has the athlete stuck a grand or so and then he puts it to him. He wants to do business."

The "truce" with the proposed new AFL lasted less than a month.

On August 29, George Halas, the chairman of the NFL's expansion committee, recommended that Houston and Dallas—the new league's flagship cities—be added to the NFL. Halas said that two groups in Dallas and one in Houston would apply for franchises and be considered at the annual owners' meeting in January 1960.

Lamar Hunt was not happy.

"I'd say that Mr. Halas' action is probably unfortunate for the National League," he told the Associated Press. "I think that he must have been poorly advised in making this statement because the Senators or Congressmen from Colorado, the state of Washington, Minnesota, and Florida are not going to be happy about it at all, as you can imagine. They were aware that the National League has been trying to sabotage the formation of this league and I think their reaction is going to be very strong."

Informed of Hunt's remarks at his summer home in Margate, Bell replied that Dallas and Houston were "open" cities and that seven other cities had applied for NFL franchises.

"Any city in the country is fair game for either league," Bell told United Press International while stressing that he made no agreement with Hunt on any cities. "They're going into New York and Los Angeles. We have teams there, but we did not complain. Pro football is expanding to all parts of the country and there's room for everybody."

The commissioner later predicted that the NFL would expand to 14 teams in 1961 and possibly to 16 in 1963. "There is a great demand for pro football all over the country," he explained. "Our owners apparently agree with me or they wouldn't have voted for the increase of the player limit from 35 to 36 players." The increase, he said, was predicated on the proposition that each NFL club would contribute a minimum of two players—one to each new franchise—when expansion became a reality.

One day early in the 1959 season, CBS-TV executive Tex Schramm picked up the phone at his office in New York. The commissioner was on the other end.

"Bert told me he needed a favor from the network," Schramm later told Randy Galloway of the *Fort Worth Star-Telegram.* "CBS had been the first to recognize what the NFL could become, so that's why he was calling us. Bert asked if CBS could please donate $10,000 to the Green Bay Packers because it was a small market team with very little TV and radio income. And many of the big market teams were way ahead in revenue. Bert told me, 'They got nothing in Green Bay.' I cut the Packers a check for $15,000. I threw in more money, thinking it would be good for the network in the long run."

It was probably one of the last official telephone calls that Bert Bell ever made.

40. A Poetic Ending at Franklin Field

The end for Bert Bell came suddenly and without warning on October 12, 1959, about four months shy of his 67th birthday. He was stricken with a heart attack in the final two minutes of an Eagles-Steelers contest at Franklin Field in Philadelphia, watching the game he loved, between two teams he once owned, at the stadium where he began his football career as a Penn quarterback in 1914.

"It was like Caruso dying in the third act of *Pagliacci*," wrote Phil Musick in *PRO!* magazine.

Philadelphia's future Hall-of-Famer Tommy McDonald had just scored the go-ahead touchdown with a leaping catch of an 18-yard-pass from Norm Van Brocklin to cement a 28–24 Eagles victory. He was walking back along the sidelines and looked up toward the stands.

"Half of the stadium was cheering but the whole mob of people on the other side of the stadium were yelling and running the other way," he recalled. "Ten minutes later we learned that Mr. Bell had died. I'll never forget it."

McDonald had fond memories of Bert Bell.

"He kept me out of jail one time when I was a rookie," Tommy recalled. It happened in 1957 when he went into an airline office in Center City Philadelphia to confirm a return flight to Oklahoma where he had enjoyed an All-America career with the Sooners. Suddenly people started yelling, "There he is! There he is!" They mistakenly confused McDonald with the notorious "Kissing Bandit," who had been holding up ticket offices in the city and then planting kisses on cheeks of victims before escaping. Police arrived and threw Tommy up against the wall. "I'm an Eagle," he screamed. "If you don't believe me, call Mr. Bell!" They did, and the commissioner quickly straightened the situation out.

In his first start as a rookie, Tommy had caught touchdown passes of 61 and 25 yards from Sonny Jurgensen in a 21–12 win over the Washington

Redskins. "Bert Bell came up to me after the game and said, 'That 61-yarder was the greatest catch I've ever seen.'"

"After we kicked off, I was covering Jimmy Orr or somebody," recalled former Eagles defensive back Tom Brookshier. "And all of a sudden we all stopped and pointed to that section of the stands. Someone said, 'Hey, there's something going on over there.' And [linebacker] Bob Pellegrini said, 'Hey, the commissioner just passed away. He's over there in the stands.'"

At about 4:04 P.M. with about 90 seconds remaining in the game, Joe Labrum, Bell's classmate at Penn and the NFL's public relations director, was walking along the cinder track surrounding he football field. Suddenly he looked up into the stands and noticed that a lone figure had slumped and fallen. Labrum stiffened with shock and yelled, "It's Bert!"

[Full disclosure: The author was a young reporter working on the city desk of the *Philadelphia Bulletin* that afternoon. I took the phone call from Joe Labrum, who proceeded to give me the first details of the events surrounding Mr. Bell's death. I passed my notes on to Anthony Day, who followed up by gathering additional information and writing fresh stories for various editions of the next day's paper.]

"I wasn't sure what was going on," said Jim Gallagher, who was the Eagles' personnel director at the time. "You just saw some police and security people running into the stands."

Play was stopped while several stadium guards ran across the field to the Pittsburgh bench to summon Dr. Paul Schrode, a staff member at University Hospital, the physician who was regularly assigned to athletic events at Franklin Field. Dr. Schrode said Bell was "unconscious and pale white" when he reached his side. "We administered oxygen and adrenalin," Dr. Schrode explained. "It must have been a very massive thing to take his life so instantly."

Within minutes a cabulance stationed at the field was driven through the big iron gates at the southwest end of the stadium. Dr. Schrode said that Bell was "barely alive" during the ride to the nearby University of Pennsylvania hospital, where he was pronounced dead minutes later. At his side were his two sons, Upton and Bert Jr., and his daughter, Jane. The Rev. John Walsh of nearby St. James Church and the Rev. Joseph Marron of the Princeton, New Jersey, Seminary administered Last Rites of the Roman Catholic Church.

The commissioner, who appeared to be in good health at the beginning of the game, had spent the first half sitting on the north side of the stadium with his close friend Joe Donoghue, the executive vice president of the

Eagles and assistant NFL treasurer. As was his custom, during halftime Bert moved to the south side to avoid the sun. He also wanted to say hello to Pennsylvania Governor David L. Lawrence, who was sitting there with James P. Clark, the majority owner of the Eagles.

"It was the worst blow I've ever had in my life," Donoghue later told the New York Times. "This is the greatest loss professional football has ever had."

Upton Bell, who had seen his dad briefly before the game when he went into the Eagles' office to pick up his tickets, noticed a disturbance in the crowd behind Philadelphia's end zone.

"When I got my binoculars into focus, I could see that a fan wearing a brown suit had collapsed, someone was running up the stadium steps with an oxygen tank, and people were gathering around him," he recalled. "My father always wore either a brown suit or a blue one to games. That day, he was wearing brown.

"At first I didn't think it could be him. I knew that he had been sitting with Art Rooney and Governor Lawrence. Then I remembered that he often left his sideline seats to go sit with his Narberth pals in the end zone. I jumped down from my own 50-yard-line seat and raced across the field. When I got there, he was already gone. I rode with his body to the hospital. Everything was noise and confusion. Flashbulbs were popping and reporters were everywhere. A priest was talking quietly in Latin."

Bell's son Bert Jr. said that his father had suffered a mild heart attack the previous February but had complained of no serious ailments since then except a few head colds. However, a physician had told Bert sometime in 1958 that he should not attend football games. "I'd rather die watching football than in my bed with my boots off," he replied.

Bert Jr., who had driven with his father to the game, said that there was no indication that he was not feeling well. "We really didn't talk that much in the car except for some small talk about football," he recalled.

Art Rooney, who shared so many memories with Bell both on and off the field, was shocked. "People tell me that he was almost killed when he wandered into the path of a trolley car while hurrying over to the hospital," Upton Bell explained.

Rooney told Dick Hackenberg of the Chicago Sun-Times that he had talked with Bell before the game. "He was in excellent spirits," Rooney explained. "There was no sign at all of what was to happen. We talked and kidded just like we always do until almost game time. We talked about the rich guys in the league and the poor guys and the champions and the teams that were hustling."

Before the game, the commissioner appeared to be normal. He followed his usual ritual in the Eagles' office at Weightman Hall, drinking coffee, meeting people, checking ticket sales, and joking with Joe Donoghue. He swapped stories with John Lipski, one of his favorite Eagles players from the early days who had come in to borrow some money. Upton Bell could hear his dad's voice in the crowded anteroom: "Look, Bull, I know that things aren't going well. Take this and stop by the office next week."

Stan Sokolis, who played tackle on Bell's first Eagles team in 1933, was on security duty at Franklin Field that day. "We had been kidding each other just the day before about how much the present day pros earn," Sokolis later told sportswriter Jack McKinney. "He tried to rib me by saying if I got $60 a game I was overpaid. Actually I got $110 a game. The money wasn't always there on time but we could always go to Bert and he'd get it up out of his own pocket. We played before crowds of 3,000 in the old Phillies Ball Park those days, but I remember him always saying, 'Mark my words, boys. Someday, we'll outdraw college football.'"

Bill Campbell, the Eagles' play-by-play man, had seen Bell before the kickoff and asked him to do the postgame radio show. "He gave me a big song and dance, Campbell recalled. 'Well, Willie, I can't climb those steps at Franklin Field.' Finally he said he would try to go up to the mezzanine level with about five minutes to go in the game and if he wasn't too out of breath, then he would go the rest of the way. But if he found that to be a chore, that would be it.

"The game ended and I did the postgame show and the commercial. He never showed. I kind of half expected that because he wasn't very enthusiastic about doing it. I did not know anything happened to him. When I came down onto the field my wife, Jo, was at the game. I saw Gloria Van Brocklin and a bunch of women clustered around the entrance to the Eagles locker room. I said to my wife, 'What's going on?' She said, 'Haven't you heard? Bert Bell died in the stands.'"

Harold Weissman, of the *New York Mirror,* was among a group of sportswriters who chatted with Bell an hour before the game about one of the commissioner's favorite topics—gambling. "I have a contact with one of the biggest gamblers in the country," Bell told the reporters. "This party calls me a half-hour before the games and gives me the dope on the size of the biggest bets, where they were made, who they were made on, and by whom."

Ed Dixon, a neighbor of the Bell family in Narberth, was seven years old. "I remember that day like it was yesterday," he recalled. "Somebody called my father from Franklin Field and told him that Bert had passed away and could he run up to the house so they could make sure there was somebody there with Mrs. Bell. So my dad drove up to Bert's house and he stayed there. He told Mrs. Bell that he was doing something for Bert until one of the kids could come up from Franklin Field. They were afraid she might hear it on the radio."

Mrs. Bell was informed shortly afterward when her children called from the hospital.

Word of Bell's death quickly spread throughout the league. Les Keiter, whose job as the radio voice of the New York (football) Giants had been saved by Bell, was sitting on the Giants' charter plane taking the team back from Cleveland, where they had just defeated the Browns, 10–6. "I'll never forget it," Keiter said. "Jack Mara, who died shortly after that, was sitting with Wellington one seat behind me. He leaned over, tapped me on the shoulder and said, 'Did you hear about Bert Bell? He passed away about an hour ago at Franklin Field watching the Eagles and Steelers play.'"

Larry Merchant, the sports editor of the *Philadelphia Daily News,* epitomized the feelings of football experts throughout the country when he wrote a glowing tribute: "Thanks to Bell's leadership, the National Football League never had it so good. In a quarter century, it has achieved a condition of profit and a status of respect."

"Nobody typified America more than Bert Bell," wrote columnist Westbrook Pegler.

"As commissioner, he made the pro grid game a truly big-time sport," said *Newsweek.*

"He was the best commissioner any professional sport has had since the death of Kenesaw Mountain Landis," added *Sports Illustrated* under the headline "The Game's Grievous Loss."

"His death is a great loss," Green Bay Packers coach Vince Lombardi told the *New York Times.* "I don't know how we'll replace him in the league. I lost a great personal friend."

Calling him the "Benevolent Dictator," Arthur Daley of the *Times* wrote, "There is no such thing as an indispensable man. Yet Bert Bell came closer to it than most in his role as commissioner. Bert was many things to many people—owners, players, press, and public. They had confidence both in his integrity and in the integrity of the sport he administered so ably. He was more than a great man. He was a great guy."

"Bell has done more for professional football than any other man," added Edwin J. Anderson, president of the Detroit Lions.

"As we see it," John B. Old wrote in the *Los Angeles Herald Express,* "the National Football League as it is today is a living monument to the ideals, generalship, and courage of Commissioner Bert Bell. Because of his keen foresight and firm hand, the NFL has made its greatest advancement under his guidance."

"He was the greatest guy that ever lived," said Carroll Rosenbloom, the owner of the Baltimore Colts, who played for Bell when he was an assistant coach at the University of Pennsylvania. "I don't know what we're going to do about our loss."

An estimated 3,000 mourners paid their respects at Bell's viewing at the Bringhurst Funeral Home, at 20th and Walnut Streets in Philadelphia. John B. Kelly, Bell's World War I buddy and the father of Princess Grace of Monaco, was the first person through the line to view Bert's open casket. He was followed by Philadelphia Warriors owner Eddie Gottlieb, New York restaurateur Toots Shor, and, surprisingly, Philadelphia publisher Walter Annenberg, who hadn't spoken with Bert since their falling out late in 1948. Then came the former teammates and other football dignitaries and players, the politicians, the clergy, and the countless friends. They came from all walks of life—cronies from the Narberth Sunrise Society and distinguished government officials and diplomats.

Hundreds attended Bell's funeral Mass at St. Margaret Roman Catholic Church in his beloved hometown of Narberth, not far from the NFL offices in Bala Cynwyd. It was celebrated on October 14, 1959, a dreary, rainy day. Rt. Rev. Monsignor Cornelius P. Brennan, the church's rector, officiated at the Mass assisted by Rev. Francis V. Carr as deacon and Rev. John J. Goodfellow as subdeacon.

"It is not customary to deliver a eulogy and I know Bert would not have wanted one," Monsignor Brennan said after the Mass. "His life itself was a eulogy. He had faith in God, his country and his family. Bert also had a commodity that this world needs very much—integrity. He had integrity in abundance."

Honorary pall bearers were the owners of the twelve NFL clubs: Carroll D. Rosenbloom of the Baltimore Colts, George S. Halas of the Chicago Bears, Walter H. S. Wolfner of the Chicago Cardinals, David R. Jones of the Cleveland Browns, Edwin J. Anderson of the Detroit Lions, Dominic Olejniczak of the Green Bay Packers, Daniel F. Reeves of the Los Angeles Rams, John V. Mara of the New York Giants, Frank L. McNamee of the Philadelphia Eagles, Victor B. Morabito of the San Francisco 49ers, George P. Marshall of the Washington Redskins, and, of course, Arthur J. Rooney, his old buddy and partner from Pittsburgh.

The church was filled with other close friends and dignitaries like Anthony J. Drexel Biddle Jr., former U.S. ambassador to Poland; Ned Irish, the president of Madison Square Garden; Maurice Podoloff, president of the National Basketball Association; Ambrose (Bud) Dudley, founder of the

Liberty Bowl; Roy Mack, vice president of the Kansas City A's; coach Buck Shaw and the entire Eagles football team; the University of Pennsylvania football staff headed by coach Steve Sebo; and track luminaries Barney Berlinger, Jumbo Elliott, and Don Lippincott.

Burial was in Calvary Cemetery, in West Conshohocken near Valley Forge, Pennsylvania.

Among the 150 floral pieces displayed at the funeral was a large, colorful arrangement from the National Football League Players Association, the group that was first recognized by Bell after some contentious negotiations.

Epilogue

If Bert Bell had lived a few days longer, his children possibly could still own the Philadelphia Eagles today. Three days after his death—on Wednesday, October 14, 1959—Bert and James P. Clark, the club's majority owner, were scheduled to meet with officials of the Philadelphia National Bank to sign the papers enabling Bell to buy the Eagles for $950,000.

"My father was stepping down as commissioner and he was going to buy the Eagles back for his kids," Bert Jr. explained.

Upton Bell said that no one in the family knew about the impending sale until bank officials called the deal off within days of the funeral. "I remember that my jaw dropped when I heard about it," he recalled. "That moment remained with me for the rest of my life."

It wasn't the first time that Bert Bell had expressed a desire to buy an NFL franchise for his children. "I remember hearing my father telling Carroll Rosenbloom, the owner of the Colts, on the phone one time, 'Now, don't forget, Carroll, I want a piece of that team for my kids,'" Upton explained.

"I've also heard that my dad asked the owners for a franchise when he was commissioner. It was around the time when they were offering him another 10-year contract and they probably would have given him anything he wanted. He said that he really didn't care about the money, but he was interested in a franchise in Buffalo for his family. I'm not sure whether the league was going to grant him the rights to that territory or a team. And I don't know how that would have changed his life. But I do know he wanted to be an owner again."

When Bert Bell's will was filed in the Montgomery County Courthouse, at Norristown, Pennsylvania, a few weeks after his death, his estate was estimated for probate purposes at $80,000 in personal property and $15,000 in real estate.

Except for a $5,000 bequest to his brother and executor, Pennsylvania Supreme Court Justice John C. Bell, half of the estate went to Bell's wife, Frances Upton, for her lifetime. The remainder was placed in trust to be divided—along with anything left of her share—among Bell's children, or their descendants, 21 years after her death.

Although John C. Bell had picked up the tab when Bert dropped $50,000 in the stock market crash of 1929—and Bell later inherited some money when his dad died in 1935—Bert Bell was never a rich man.

"Most people thought my dad was rich with family money," said his son Upton. "But the fact was that his father left him very little. John C. considered professional football on the same level as burlesque."

On October 22, Billy Howton, the president of the National Football League Players Association, announced that a group insurance plan covering NFL players and their immediate families had been adopted. He added that negotiations were still in progress toward the formation of a pension plan.

Bullet Bill Dudley, the insurance executive who was one of Bert Bell's favorite players with the Pittsburgh Steelers, never got any of the business.

"I thought I had a pretty good shot to handle it, but just like everything else, I got shot down with some others," Dudley explained years later. "I was left out hanging. I had an appointment to go up and talk to Bert about it on the Monday after he died in the stands. But somebody in the league had more pull than I did."

Exactly three and a half months after Bell's death—on January 26, 1960—Pete Rozelle was elected commissioner of the NFL on the 23rd ballot after the 12 club owners deliberated for seven days.

"To say that filling the shoes of the late Bert Bell as commissioner would be a gross understatement," Rozelle told the *Los Angeles Times*. "No one will ever fill his shoes."

While the owners were wrestling with their decision, the names of two of Bell's colleagues briefly surfaced as candidates. They were Austin Gunsel, the league treasurer who had automatically assumed the role of acting commissioner upon Bell's death (as mandated by the league constitution), and Joseph A. Donoghue, Bell's close friend, who was executive vice president of the Eagles and assistant treasurer of the NFL.

Gunsel received four votes on the first ballot but never came closer to the three-fourths majority needed for election. Some of the owners then asked Donoghue to serve as interim commissioner, but he declined. "I'm 64 years old," he said. "And that's too old for this job." Later that year, when the motion to admit the new Dallas franchise into the NFL was made by Chicago Bears owner George Halas, the chairman of the league's expansion committee, it was seconded by Donoghue.

A few weeks later, Rozelle explained to *Philadelphia Bulletin* sportswriter Hugh Brown why he planned to move the NFL's headquarters to New York City. "Television is terribly important to the league and that's where the top offices are," he said. "Plus the ad agencies. I can't sit there in a suburb and do a job like Bert Bell did, even when he was ill. I'll be lucky to do half his job when I'm healthy."

Meanwhile, Frances Upton Bell continued to circulate socially in the Philadelphia area for a number of years, primarily appearing at various functions honoring her late husband.

Shortly after Bell's death, Tom Brookshier, the former Eagles defensive standout, suggested at a Board of Governors meeting of Philadelphia's Robert W. Maxwell Memorial Football Club that Frances be invited to sit at the head table at the prestigious group's annual dinner. Bell was the club's founder in 1937 and had served as its president for more than a dozen years.

"Three or four guys jumped up and said, 'A *woman* sitting at the head table, on the dais?' I said, 'Yeah, that's right—the widow of Bert Bell,' " Brookshier replied. "So we had a tremendous debate and finally the others agreed to invite her. And guess what! All the guys who were against it, we couldn't get them away from her. She came in and she was charming and she wore this big hat and she looked around and smiled the whole evening. She was so cute. And all these guys that were against having her were up there saying, 'Can I get you something? What can I do for you?' It was one of the great times of my life. It was the best Maxwell Dinner I ever saw."

Since Bell's death, the Maxwell Club has presented the Bert Bell Award for the Professional American Football Player of the Year. Baltimore Colts quarterback John Unitas was recipient of the first annual award in 1959.

The Playoff Bowl, officially known as the "Bert Bell Benefit Bowl," a postseason game for third place in the NFL, was played for ten years in the Orange Bowl, in Miami, from 1960 to 1969. It was discontinued when the merger between the NFL and AFL was completed in 1970.

On September 7, 1963, Bert Bell became the first of 17 charter members to be inducted into the new Pro Football of Fame, in Canton, Ohio. He was represented by his old friend, Art Rooney, the president of the Pittsburgh Steelers. His presenter was David J. McDonald, the president of the United Steelworkers of America.

After a two-week illness brought on by a heart condition, Frances Upton Bell died in Lankenau Hospital, outside Philadelphia, on November 27, 1975, at the age of 71. Honorary pallbearers at her funeral Mass at St. Margaret's Church included Tom Brookshier, Joe Donoghue, Mac Friedman, Louis Grasmick, George Halas, Wellington Mara, Ed Pollack, Art Rooney, Carroll Rosenbloom, Pete Rozelle, and John Steadman.

Bert Bell Jr., who had worked for his dad in the NFL Office for three years, continued as an assistant to Commissioner Pete Rozelle for about a year, primarily handling scheduling issues. He joined the Baltimore Colts' front office in 1961 and was eventually promoted to business manager before resigning in 1966. Afterward, he wrote a football column for the *Baltimore News American* and worked as a dealer at Resorts Atlantic City Casino Hotel, then as a floor person at Bally's Atlantic City Casino Hotel. Now retired, he lives in Ventnor, New Jersey.

Upton Bell joined the Baltimore Colts' sales and marketing department in 1961 and became the club's director of player personnel in 1966. During his five years in that position, the Colts went to the playoffs five times and reached the Super Bowl twice. After serving for two years as the general manager of the New England Patriots, he became part-owner of the New York Stars of the World Football League in 1974 and moved the franchise to Charlotte, North Carolina. He was the Hornets' president and general manager until the league folded in midseason 1975. Since then he has been a popular radio and television talk show host in Boston. He lives in Cambridge, Massachusetts.

Jane Upton Bell has been working primarily in the television industry since joining Philadelphia's WCAU-TV as an associate producer in 1967. In addition to writing such national television specials as *60 and Still Kicking,* commemorating the NFL's anniversary in 1981, she has worked as a producer or director for the Mike Douglas and Dinah Shore shows, among others, for various networks in Philadelphia, Boston, and Los Angeles. A member of the advisory board of the Los Angeles Rams from 1985 until the team moved to St. Louis in 1995, she lives in Los Angeles.

On November 22, 1997, the Bert Bell State Historical Marker, approved by the Pennsylvania Historical and Museum Commission, was dedicated. It is located outside Mapes 5 & 10, the current site of the famous Davis General Store and Ice Cream Parlor at 224–26 Haverford Avenue in Narberth, where Bert Bell, *The Football Man,* spent so many days discussing the sport he loved with the people he cherished as friends.

In 1999, more than 40 years after his death, *The Sporting News* named Bert Bell one of the Most Powerful People in Sports for the 20th Century.

Sources

The material in this book was compiled from multiple sources including personal interviews, the official minutes of NFL owners' meetings, documents in the Pro Football Hall of Fame in Canton, Ohio, including Bert Bell's personal scrapbooks of newspaper clippings, archives of NFL Films, New York Public Library for the Performing Arts, the Professional Football Researchers Association, the Associated Press, Hearst News Service, International News Service, United Press, United Press International, and the following publications: *Billboard, Baltimore Sun, Chicago Sun-Times, Chicago Tribune, Christian Science Monitor, Cleveland Plain Dealer, Detroit Free Press, Detroit News, Fort Worth Star-Telegram, Green Bay Press Gazette, Indianapolis Star-News, Kansas City Star, Los Angeles Daily News, Los Angeles Herald Express, Los Angeles Mirror-News, Los Angeles Times, Milwaukee Journal, New York Daily News, New York Herald Tribune, New York Journal American, New York Mirror, New York Morning Telegraph, New York Post, New York Times, New York World Telegram, Newsweek, Pennsylvania Gazette, Philadelphia Bulletin, Philadelphia Daily News, Philadelphia Inquirer, Philadelphia North American, Philadelphia Public Ledger, Philadelphia Record, Pittsburgh Post-Gazette, Pittsburgh Press, Pittsburgh Sun-Telegraph, San Francisco Chronicle, San Francisco Examiner, The Saturday Evening Post, Sport Magazine, The Sporting News, Sports Illustrated, Time, Toronto Globe and Mail,* and *Washington Post,* among others.

PERSONAL INTERVIEWS

NFL Executives, Coaches, and Players

Ernie Accorsi	Sam Huff
Chuck Bednarik	Harry Hulmes
Bert Bell Jr.	Ed Kiely
Upton Bell	Gino Marchetti
Raymond Berry	Don Maynard
Tom Brookshier	Tommy McDonald
Marion Campbell	Art McNally
Bill Dudley	Pete Retzlaff
Jim Gallagher	Daniel M. Rooney
Frank Gifford	Allie Sherman
Bud Grant	Don Shula
Ray Graves	Al Wistert

Writers and Broadcasters

Ralph Bernstein

Bill Campbell

Art Daley

Victoria Donohoe

Sandy Grady

Les Keiter

Larry Merchant

Bob Wolff

Others

Sy Berger

Ted Bergmann

Elaine Emerson Blair

Saleem Choudhry

Ed Dixon

Ambrose (Bud) Dudley

Ed Fabricius

Andrew Milner

Jean Wheeler Parsons

Bob Paul

BOOKS

Algeo, Matthew. *Last Team Standing: How The Steelers And The Eagles—"The Steagles"—Saved Pro Football During World War II*. Cambridge, MA: Da Capo Press, 2006.

Bell, Bert. *The Story of Professional Football In Summary*. Bala Cynwyd, PA: National Football League, 1957.

Callahan, Tom. *Johnny: The Life & Times of John Unitas*. New York: Crown Publishers, 2006.

Carroll, Bob, et al., eds. *Total Football: The Official Encyclopedia of the National Football League*. New York: HarperCollins, 1997.

Cohen, David. *Rugged and Enduring: The Eagles, the Browns, and 5 Years of Football*. Philadelphia: Xlibris Corporation, 2001.

Cope, Myron. *The Game That Was: The Early Days of Pro Football*. New York: World Publishing Company, 1970.

Daly, Dan, and Bob O'Donnell. *Pro Football Chronicle*. New York: Collier Books/Macmillan Publishing Company, 1990.

Davis, Jeffrey. *Papa Bear: The Life and Legacy of George Halas*. New York: McGraw-Hill, 2005.

Didinger, Ray. *Pittsburgh Steelers*. New York: Macmillan Publishing Company, 1974.

Didinger, Ray, and Robert S. Lyons. *The Eagles Encyclopedia*. Philadelphia: Temple University Press, 2002.

Fortunato, John A. *The Legacy of Pete Rozelle*. Lanham, MD: Taylor Trade Publishing, 2006.

Goldman, Herbert G. *Banjo Eyes: Eddie Cantor and the Birth of Modern Stardom*. New York: Oxford University Press, 1997.

Harris, David. *The League: The Rise and Decline of the NFL*. Toronto: Bantam Books, 1986.

Johnson, William O., Jr. *Super Spectator and the Electric Lilliputians*. Boston: Little, Brown and Company, 1971.

Klatell, David A., and Norman Marcus. *Inside Big-Time Sports: Television, Money & the Fans*. New York: MasterMedia Limited, 1996.

Kuklick, Bruce. *To Every Thing a Season: Shibe Park and Urban Philadelphia, 1909–1976*. Princeton, NJ: Princeton University Press, 1991.

Leuthner, Stuart. *Iron Men: Bucko, Crazylegs, and the Boys Recall the Golden Days of Professional Football.*. New York: Doubleday, 1988.

MacCambridge, Michael. *America's Game: The Epic Story of How Pro Football Captured a Nation*. New York: Random House, 2004.

Maraniss, David. *When Pride Still Mattered: The Life of Vince Lombardi*. New York: Simon & Schuster, 1999.

Mickelson, Sig. *The Decade That Shaped Television News: CBS in the 1950s*. Westport, CT: Praeger Publishers, 1998.

Miller, Marion Mills, ed. *Great Debates in American History*. New York: Current Literature Publishing Co., 1913.

O'Toole, Andrew. *Smiling Irish Eyes: Art Rooney and the Pittsburgh Steelers*. Haworth, NJ: St. Johann Press, 2004.

Paul, William Henry. *The Gray-Flannel Pigskin: Movers and Shakers of Pro Football*. Philadelphia: J. B. Lippincott Company, 1974.

Steadman, John. *From Colts to Ravens: A Behind-the-Scenes Look at Baltimore Professional Football*. Centreville, MD: Tidewater Publishers, 1997.

Wiebusch, John, and Brian Silverman, eds. *A Game of Passion: The NFL Literary Companion*. Atlanta: Turner Publishing, 1994.

Yost, Mark. *Tailgating, Sacks, and Salary Caps: How the NFL Became the Most Successful Sports League in History*. Chicago: Kaplan Publishing, 2006.

Ziemba, Joe. *When Football Was Football: The Chicago Cardinals and the Birth of the NFL*. Chicago: Triumph Books, 1999.

NEWSPAPER, MAGAZINE, AND ON-LINE ARTICLES

Bell, Upton, with Dick Chanoff. "Any Given Sunday." *Philadelphia*, September 2000.

Devaney, John. "From Rags to Riches: The Story of Professional Football." *American Legion Magazine*, October 1966.

Devitt, Mike. "Descendants of the Mayflower: The Story of the Baltimore/Indianapolis Colts." *Indianapolis Star-News Online*, March–April 1998.

Harvey, Randy. "Talking Football with . . . Lamar Hunt." *Football Digest*, February 1979.

Heinz, W. C. "Boss of the Behemoths." *Saturday Evening Post*, December 3, 1955.

Hirshberg, Al. "He Calls the Signals for Pro Football." *New York Times Magazine*, November 23, 1958.

Martin, Pete. "Do Gamblers Make a Sucker Out of You?" *Saturday Evening Post*, November 6, 1948.

Musick, Phil. "A Football Man." *PRO!*, July 31, 1976.

Newhouse, Dave. "Television and the Big Game." *NFL Game Program*, December 14, 1975.

Orr, Jack. "The Commissioner Who Commissions." *PRO, PRO, PRO*, 1958.

"The Pigskin and the Picture Tube: The National Football League's First Full Season on the CBS Television Network." *Journal of Broadcasting and Electronic Media*, September 2007.

Voluntary Trade Council. "Fumbling the Antitrust Football: The NFL Blackouts of 2004–2005." *Voluntary Trade Reports No. 6,* December 2005.

Wheeler, Lonnie. "Father Football." *Ohio,* September 1989.

OTHER DOCUMENTS / SOURCES

"Interview: Pete Rozelle," Academy of Achievement, Washington, DC. May 15, 1991.

"About Us: NFLPA History." National Football League Players Association Online. February 19, 2007.

Index